Pervasive Computing for Business:
Trends and Applications

Varuna Godara
Sydney College of Management, Australia

BUSINESS SCIENCE REFERENCE
Hershey · New York

Director of Editorial Content:	Kristin Klinger
Director of Book Publications:	Julia Mosemann
Acquisitions Editor:	Lindsay Johnston
Development Editor:	Christine Bufton
Publishing Assistant:	Sean Woznicki
Typesetter:	Deanna Zombro
Production Editor:	Jamie Snavely
Cover Design:	Lisa Tosheff
Printed at:	Yurchak Printing Inc.

Published in the United States of America by
Business Science Reference (an imprint of IGI Global)
701 E. Chocolate Avenue
Hershey PA 17033
Tel: 717-533-8845
Fax: 717-533-8661
E-mail: cust@igi-global.com
Web site: http://www.igi-global.com/reference

Library of Congress Cataloging-in-Publication Data

Pervasive computing for business : trends and applications / Varuna Godara, editor.
p. cm.

Includes bibliographical references and index.

ISBN 978-1-60566-996-0 (hardcover) -- ISBN 978-1-60566-997-7 (ebook) 1. Business--Data processing. 2. Ubiquitous computing. I. Godara, Varuna.
HF5548.2.P4734 2010
658'.05--dc22

2009047075

British Cataloguing in Publication Data
A Cataloguing in Publication record for this book is available from the British Library.

Dedication

Dedicated to my mum Chanderkala and dad Dr Nathuram Godara

Editorial Advisory Board

List of Reviewers

Table of Contents

Detailed Table of Contents

This chapter discusses the development of a Text to Speech Synthesis System for an Indian regional language. Beginning with the history of speech synthesis it explains the composition of Text-to-speech synthesis system which is a complex combination of language processing, signal processing and computer science. Then it covers various stages of the synthesis of text to speech such as Text normalization, Homograph disambiguation, Word to phoneme conversion, Prosody and Waveform synthesis. It gives detailed example of Bengali Text to Speech Synthesis system including its specific complexities, and various methods which may be used for speech synthesis. This chapter also discusses application of variations in the prosody of the speech that yields the emotional aspects (anger, happy, normal) in Text to Speech Synthesis System.

This chapter concentrates on investigating to what extent Small and Medium-Sized Organisations have understood and adopted lean manufacturing and the challenges they face in the implementation of lean manufacturing. This chapter looks at the role of latest technologies including pervasive computing technologies in improving the usage of lean manufacturing in SMEs. It also discusses the implementation of lean manufacturing in terms of its three important elements – buffer management, work practices and human resource management.

This chapter addresses the implications of markets with more and more customized products, with shorter life cycles that have in turn shifted mass production techniques in manufacturing systems to flexible automation techniques. For next generation, this chapter proposes increasing need of incorporating highly flexible and intelligent reconfigurable manufacturing systems. It discusses the concept of intelligent manufacturing systems that can maintain effective and efficient manufacturing operations with minimum downtime under conditions of uncertainty. This chapter presents some research issues related to the development of reconfigurable manufacturing systems with pervasive computing such as Structural design of reconfigurable machines, Manufacturing process and simulation Machines, Micro electro-mechanical devices for sensors, etc.

Section 3
Pervasive Computing in Quality Control

Chapter 6 discusses various applications of Pervasive computing in the Enterprise Context, such as in Automobile manufacturing. Due to increasing competition for products and services, and various suppliers of different raw materials and parts that becomes part of final products, quality assurance has become very crucial. To support the quality of final product the chapter proposes an adaptive quality assurance system that can be developed and implemented to integrate information from the various entities to facilitate decision making in a timely manner. This quality assurance system is responsive to the existing quality environment at the various sources that contribute to the manufacture of the product or delivery of the service. The chapter prepares a foundation for accomplishing such quality management objectives and proposes an approach to integrate decision making in the context of the entire supply chain.

Chapter 7 explains the Egyptian auditing scenario including the International Trage Agreement (ITA) and foreign auditing firms that has resulted in pressure to enhance audit effectiveness and quality of Egyptian auditing firm's performance. It looks at how Computer mediated communication (CMC) modes enhance the audit quality and effectiveness of FTF meetings. It identifies the most effective CMC mode and describes the effect of those communication modes on the participant's satisfaction. This chapter discusses how Computer-Mediated Communication (CMC) can enhance the auditor performance in auditing firms.

This chapter evaluates the web-based service quality and identifies six web-based service quality dimensions; information quality, responsiveness, web assistance, tangibles, empathy, and call-back. It is

This chapter highlights the importance of strategic human resource management and its effect on organisational performance. It discusses the changes occurring in the business environment and its implications for human resource functionaries and the changing role of human resource management. It gives historical background of strategic human resource management and emerging future trends which might become key issues for high performance in the organization of new era. It draws conclusion on what needs to be done on the part of the HR functionaries and the organization itself to enhance the strategic fit between the various HR practices and the overall organizational strategic plan.

Section 5
Pervasive Computing and Financial Systems

This chapter explains the lifecycle of design of an Automatic Trading System. It prepares the foundation by discussing the investment decision making process, Futures Market Environment including defining Future contracts and various trading states, various fundamental and technical indicators for price forecasting for decision making, Commissions and slippage barrier, etc. The chapter then discusses the ATS Principles, ATS lifecycle and various phases focusing on the proper environment selection, appropriate set of tools selection, and the automatic trading system creation which has to follow rules of money (risk) management and trading psychology. Finally it covers testing and optimization concepts.

Based on a study on manufacturing companies operating in Bahrain, this chapter provides evidence on the contextual features of firms adopting Activity-Based Costing (ABC) compared to those not adopting ABC. It looks at organisational and business environment variables which appear to have influenced the adoption of ABC including computing usage. The study hypothesised that firm size, the amount of overhead costs, the level of product variety, production complexity, the degree of competition, and the degree of computer usage are factors which encourage firms to adopt ABC. Significant relationships were found between the adoption of ABC and the variables selected for the study except production complexity and the degree of computer usage.

This chapter reviews one of the fundamental concerns financial institutions have, that is risk management. It discusses various financial innovations that triggered new ways in which financial institutions and Corporate cope with credit risk since the advent of credit derivatives. Financial institutions have many financial instruments, often complex products that offer significant advantages to market participants and its key players and in particular financial institutions. The chapter further explains how advanced computerization is by large the most important factor for the wide use of credit derivatives and its benefits to banks, such as more efficient loans portfolio management, further business expansion and confidentiality, etc. This chapter also describes various non financial firms benefit from credit derivatives such as financial systems' stability through increased liquidity, risk reallocation and credit risk pricing.

This chapter identifies the shift in the inflows of FDI to pervasive computing area in India. It explains the direct relationship between the flow of FDI and economic development and analyses the existence and nature of causalities, between FDI and economic growth in India since 1990, where growth of economic activities and FDI has been one of the most pronounced. Based on the research this chapter indicates that there is a strong correlation between FDI inflows and GDP in India and there is also unidirectional causal relation between FDI and GDP. Finally it suggests that there is no long run relationship between FDI and economic growth in India.

Based on a research this chapter shows a disparity between states in India and a shift from primary and secondary sectors to tertiary sectors and pervasive computing areas. It explains that during the last two decades, Foreign Direct Investment (FDI) has become most important source of finance and therefore increasingly important in the developing world and lots of developing countries including India are willing to attract substantial amounts of inward FDI. This chapter analyses the regional and sectoral disparities in Inflow of FDI in India since 1990.

Foreword

We are truly in a technological age where "technology determinism," "technology opportunism," "technology adoption," "technology innovation," "technology assimilation," "technology integration," "technology implementation," and many other similar terms or concepts have become commonly used phrases in not only professional arena bit also in general public arena. While all these terms may have specific academic meaning and can arguably be distinguished one from the other, yet these terms have become synonymous with efficient, effective, purposeful and intelligent business processes, the backbone of all forms of management systems used in different walks of human endeavors. Business processes themselves do not recognize products, services, organizations, cultures, social or economical or political boundaries, intellectual level of its users or the extent of perceptual sophistication. They are indeed indifferent to all these distinguishing features of the modern society. The only differing features of business processes that have any significance relate to the level of intelligence built into the processes, the extent of user-friendliness and adaptability to the ever changing human environment to remain ever efficient, effective and purposeful. Business Process Engineering subsumes all the technological, engineering, scientific, social science and human developments of the past century. It does not mean that the past innovations and developments, which are often classified under "hardware," "software" or "brain ware" have lost their individual significance. They attained popularity in the modern education and professional applications and are categorized as "mass production," "assembly lines," "lean manufacturing," "flexible systems," "transfer lines," "computer aided designs," "computer aided manufacturing," "computer integrated manufacturing," "automation," "management information systems," "total quality management," "organic systems," "e-business," "e-commerce," "e-governance," "real time systems," "artificial intelligence," "robotics', "neural networks," and numerous others. All these and many others have their relevance and use, and they add value to the processes. But essence of Business Process Engineering lies in its "holistic approach" which takes into account all available technologies, concepts and constructs and provides dynamic solutions incorporating whatever suits a particular application. Pervasive Computing and Business Process Engineering have an integral relationship.

Pervasiveness of computing has become inevitable in all walks of human life. It is witnessed whether one looks at human endeavors such as travelling millions of kilometers in space to various planets, and collecting and processing information and data and sending the same to the earth which enables looking back millions of years and predicting what lies in the future, or whether one looks at different strata (economically, educationally, socially or culturally) of the society in underdeveloped, developing or developed countries of the earth planet, or whether one looks at the functioning of various business and non-business entities including tiny, small, medium and large enterprises or even self-employed individuals such as hawkers, shopkeepers, house-hold workers, taxi drivers, delivery personnel, helpers and assistants, they all use computing technology in conjunction with the other technologies to produce gadgets and equipment of tiny or large sizes with amazing and often unimaginable capabilities. What was mere fiction or wishful thinking and pure imagination of creative writers has become a reality. Pervasive computing has only one limitation and that is the ability of the human mind to visualize and transcribe the same. If one expresses something, somebody somewhere produces it. Days are not far when the so-called "crystal balls" used by the Egyptian foretellers and various invisible gadgets used by sorcerers might become possible for the common human beings to use. Speed of light has become a practical concept, but it may be practically possible to reach the speed of human mind.

Dr. Varuna Godara made a pioneering attempt when she compiled and produced her first book entitled *Risk Assessment and Management in Pervasive Computing: Operational, Legal, Ethical and Financial Perspectives.* This book was released in 2008 and it gained immense popularity due not only to the innovativeness of the concept but also to the fact that various contributions (all focused on pervasive computing) came from different sectors of the economy and from various disciplines. The author proved the point that generality can also be bound within the scope of pervasive computing.

Dr. Varuna Godara's project on *Pervasive Computing for Business: Trends and Applications* is another attempt to drive the point home that Pervasive Computing is making a significant dent into numerous areas of business. The author in this book demonstrates the same by incorporating applications from various countries, from various socio-economic zones and from various well known disciplines. Areas explored in the book include business intelligence, advertising, text-to-speech synthesis systems, reconfigurable manufacturing systems, computer mediated communication systems for enhancing audit quality, automatic trading system, ambient intelligence development, seamless knowledge and virtual schools, activity based costing, human resource management, performance management, business excellence framework, technology adaptation in connection to organizational change, Web-Based Software System Service Quality, quality assurance systems and other conventional areas. All the applications included in the book come from the research and/or real life applications from learned academicians and practicing professionals. This is by no means a comprehensive treatise of Pervasive Computing Applications. But readers would gain a deep insight into a wide range of both conventional and unconventional applications of Pervasive Computing for Business. Serious reading of this book and contemplation will generate new ideas and new applications which, I hope, that readers would take on board for future development.

Rakesh K Agrawal
CEO/Principal Consultant
Business Continuity Innovation Centre

Rakesh K Agrawal *holds bachelor degree in Mechanical Engineering, Post Graduation in Industrial Engineering, Graduate Diploma in Adult Education and PhD in the area of Technology Management. He spent over 2 decades in business, industry and consulting before embarking upon educational career as a Professor of Industrial Engineering at NITIE India. He then worked in Kenya and moved to Australia and worked in several positions including a professorial appointment in the School of Management at the University of Western Sydney in Australia. Dr Agrawal had a glorified entrepreneurial career having set up his own businesses in manufacturing, trading, management consulting and education. He assisted many entrepreneurs for setting up educational, trading and manufacturing business projects. He currently heads the Business Continuity Innovation Centre at Sydney. His area of specialization includes Innovative Entrepreneurship, Technology Management, Performance Evaluation and Improvement, Business Continuity Management and Integrated Risk Management.*

Preface

Businesses come back to the basics irrespective of whatever innovative applications are developed, and whatever they promise. The bottom line is to calculate ROI or payback period before making any financial commitment toward the latest technology. Pervasive computing has also not been spared by financial business analysts. They are not looking for projects with merely positive ROI but with the prospect of highest ROI. Returns or gains can be maximized by developing stronger and better relationships with the customers, which in turn can be achieved by providing quality, timely, simple and omnipresent services and communication, providing value for their money, and managing supply chains and operations efficiently. Strategic deployment of Pervasive Computing applications promises these outputs as long as proper platform is chosen.

ROI is directly affected by business intelligence and the increased power of employees and customers in decision-making. Forget about fancy uses. Pervasive business intelligence is must to perform fundamental functions of management such as predictive analysis, planning, implementing, organizing, and controlling costs, and quality of processes, products and services. Pervasive devices are used in collecting and organizing data, and in various financial, analytical and forecasting tools that help businesses to improve their operational performance and profitability. We do not often realize that behind these simple helpful tools there are extremely sensitive devices collecting contextual information, using complex algorithms for processing data, and flexible systems. Chapter 1 of this book describes the concept of pervasive computing, introduces pervasive devices, technological factors and the impact of pervasive computing on decision making. It focuses on Business Intelligence and provides insights on real-time Business Intelligence and pervasive business intelligence and discusses related issues.

Flexible systems are useful not only in business intelligence but also in competitive manufacturing environment where thrust is on efficiency, collaborative activities, integrating processes, ever increasing flexibility of quantity, capability, personalization of operations. Pervasive manufacturing utilizes miniaturized robots, numerically controlled and sensor embedded instrumentation devices, susceptible inspection machines, real-time data oriented activities, representation on Semantic Web and inference engines. Capabilities of collecting real-time machining data, instrument messages, operation status, monitoring and real-time analysis using correlations, regressions, and trends make decision-making in manufacturing more informed and intelligent. Pervasive manufacturing not only increases efficiency but also helps in tackling issues of Six Sigma and achieving other standards.

An integrative approach has led Manufacturing to achieve a new paradigm by allowing all the participants sharing a common single fact sheet. The common fact sheet when extended to the full supply chain members gives them access to planning and optimizing resources, inventory control, committing orders, sourcing and purchasing, process and product tracking, inspecting, and scheduling. Pervasive devices such as RFIDs, WAP phones, and near frequency devices help in inventory control, buffer management, just-in-time manufacturing, lean manufacturing, flexible and reconfigurable manufacturing, etc. Chapter 4 in this book looks at the role of latest technologies including pervasive computing technologies in improving the usage of lean manufacturing in SMEs and discusses the implementation of lean manufacturing in terms of its three important elements–buffer management, work practices and human resource management. Chapter 5 of this book is concerned with production of highly customized products with shorter life cycles that need shift from mass production techniques in manufacturing systems to flexible automation techniques and intelligent reconfigurable manufacturing systems. All these are possible through pervasive devices, which introduce intelligent manufacturing systems that are capable of maintaining effective and efficient manufacturing operations with minimum downtime under conditions of uncertainty. They also help with tackling various research issues related to the development of reconfigurable manufacturing systems with pervasive computing such as structural design of reconfigurable machines, manufacturing process and simulation machines, micro electro-mechanical devices for sensors, etc.

Excited marketers who have been treated as being guilty of pushing their products without the need of the market are finding pervasive technology more effective and more rewarding. Humanoid robots are helping marketers in interactive advertising, providing uninterrupted services including entertainment to customers. Pervasive marketing is the integration of customer needs and supplier's capabilities to make progression towards real time interactive personalized product development, pricing, and distribution for achievement of satisfaction of customers and suppliers. Pervasive marketing not only helps advertisers to pervade into the eyes and ears of the people, but also helps people to convey their requirements anytime and anywhere without efforts and receiving timely services. Examples of Pervasive marketing would include sensing the need of interpretation and translation services when user a is in a meeting with somebody not speaking the same language (translation services anywhere and anytime using pervasive devices such as mobile phone), booking and payment services depending upon the location of the user (for movies, travel tickets, courses, restaurant seats, etc), personalized answers to missed telephone calls, categorizing and diverting telephone calls and messages based on the priorities, urgencies or any other criteria, personalized content, etc. Attracting attention has been traditionally the first and foremost step of advertising, which is possible with pervasive advertising. The next step is to engage people in the product and then selling the product. These two steps can easily be implemented with the help of interactive environment created by pervasive computing but not through traditional advertising. The level of attention gained by large visual advertisements is definitely different from the level of attention gained by the tiny pervasive devices. It is worth examining the effect of ever decreasing size and dissolving nature of pervasive media. As the characteristics of pervasive advertising are somewhat different from traditional advertising, the effect of using animation, emotion, repetition, etc. is also different. Chapter 2 looks at the impact of repetition and attention on the recognition of different types of online ads such as horizontal and vertical ads appearing in both animated and static forms.

Pervasive computing enables little and tiny devices and sensors to capture information, emotion and expectation of individuals to provide different services. It not only translates speech and expressions to text but it also synthesizes speech from text to provide services such as reading stories to children or reading novels to old people and entertaining them, reading emails to professionals while they are exercising, etc. This book includes a chapter on composition of Text-to-speech synthesis system which is a complex combination of language processing, signal processing and computer science. Expressions and emotions are integral part of our speech. These systems try to yield emotional speech that suits the context of the text. The third chapter of the book discusses application of variations in the prosody of the speech that yields the emotional aspects (anger, happy, normal) in Text to Speech Synthesis System.

There is an increased need for making manufacturing environments and products more energy efficient, safe and environment friendly. The use of Pervasive computing and humanoid robots in creating smart assembly and manufacturing environments allows safe quality control of processes and products even in hazardous and harmful manufacturing environments. Using sensor enabled robots in assembly and quality control is not only cost efficient but is also more productive and flexible. Cooperative robots are specialized intelligent robots dedicatedly inspecting the quality and continuously looking after the related production processes to detect any abnormalities. Chapter 6 of this book recognizes the need to integrate the real time information to help timely decision making and presents an adaptive quality assurance system to facilitate decision making in a timely manner in the context of the entire supply chain.

Broadband wireless access, Wi-Fi, Wi-Max, Wireless DOCSIS, 3G, 4G, 802.22, etc are the various wireless standards that increased the quality and effectiveness of Computer-Mediated Communication (CMC) that initially included emails, chat rooms, blogs, instant messages, bulletin-boards, list-servs, e-learning tools etc, and were concerned with the study of group dynamics and effects of interaction with computers on humans. With the use of sensor networks and pervasive devices, the scope of CMC increased. Now it also includes effects of interaction with pervasive devices on humans. Where CMC benefits users in different ways, it also brings with it cheating, frauds, lying behavior, and deception. Computer-Mediated Communication also helps in real-time auditing and accounts maintenance in business and non-business organizations. Chapter 7 draws attention on the Egyptian auditing scenario and discusses the use of CMC to enhance the audit quality and effectiveness of FTF meetings. It identifies the most effective CMC mode, its effect on the participant's satisfaction and explains how Computer-Mediated Communication can enhance the auditor performance in auditing firms.

We cannot forget the fact that Pervasive computing and devices are in their infancy. Many pervasive technology factors are still immature. Trustworthy security provisions, wireless and wired network integration, network topologies, wireless multimedia services, reliable physical layer transmission, radio technologies, and safe Near Frequency Technologies are required to provide quality services. Response time, interruptions, continuity of services, 24 hours help service, delays, errors, etc. are some of the important factors that determines the quality of experience and therefore determine the quality of service in Pervasive computing environment. Chapter 8 of this book is based on services provided by a Turkish firm. It evaluates Web-based service quality and identifies six Web-based service quality dimensions: information quality, responsiveness, Web assistance, tangibles, empathy, and call-back.

Pervasive computing supports typical human resource management processes such as recruiting, interviewing, giving remote self service access, employee e-training, etc. and enables the human resource department to be innovative in creating new functions and processes such as pervasive knowledge discovery and knowledge creation. Quality of human resource management processes determine the human resource administration effectiveness, employee motivation, professional development, morale of the employees, and overall culture and productivity of the organization. Chapter 9 of this book examines the implications of ISO 9000:2000 and EQA on HR issues in the context of Greek industrial organizations while improving quality. Chapter 10 focuses on the importance of planned organizational change when the technology is changing rapidly and so is the speed of technology adaptation. Based on a Croatian study, this chapter conceptualizes organizational change in terms of changes in technology, organizational structure, organizational culture, strategy, changes in employees' structure and changes in products and services. It also discusses various forms of organizational control: (1) control by one dominant shareholder; (2) control by coalition of several large block-holders and (3) managerial control and explains the influence of ownership concentration on the performance of a company. Chapter 11 of this book further looks at the importance of strategic human resource management and its effect on organizational performance. It explains the dynamic nature of business environment and its effects on human resource functionaries and the changing role of human resource management.

The movement of data from stand alone databases to integrated relational corporate database has opened the way to simplified and real-time accounting services and financial reporting for the organization, departments and cost centers. Indirect cost allocations and cost negotiations have become easier. Integration of sales and distribution, materials management, online payment, payroll, and other processes allow real-time data access and real time financial decisions, and allocation of resources. Various kinds of financial systems are being introduced to cater for different needs of different organizations. In this book, chapter 12 discusses the lifecycle design of an Automatic Trading System. It describes the investment decision making process, Futures Market Environment, various trading states, and various fundamental and technical indicators for price forecasting for decision making, commissions and slippage barrier. Chapter 13 of this book looks at providing examples of the contextual features of firms adopting Activity-Based Costing (ABC) compared to those not adopting ABC. In the context of Bahrain, it discusses the organizational and business environment variables which appear to have influenced the adoption of ABC including computing usage. Chapter 14 describes various innovative ways in which financial institutions and corporations cope with credit risk since the advent of credit derivatives. It also discusses advanced computerization as the most important factor for the wide use of credit derivatives and its benefits to banks, such as more efficient loans portfolio management, further business expansion and confidentiality, etc. Chapter 15 identifies the direct relationship between the flow of FDI and economic development and analyses the existence and nature of causalities, between FDI and economic growth in India since 1990. Based on the research, this chapter indicates that there is a strong correlation between FDI inflows and GDP in India and there is also unidirectional causal relation between FDI and GDP. Chapter 16 of this book further presents disparity between states in India and a shift from primary and secondary sectors to tertiary sectors and pervasive computing areas. It identifies that Foreign Direct Investment (FDI) is the most important source of finance in the last two decades and is, therefore, becoming increasingly important in the developing world.

Varuna Godara
CEO
Sydney College of Management, Australia
2 September 2009

Section 1
Pervasive Computing Applications in Intelligent Decision Making, Advertising and Emotions Expression

First section discusses various applications of Pervasive Computing in knowledge management, decision making, business intelligence, advertising and production of emotions while converting text to speech. It is comprised of three chapters. Chapter 1, "Pervasive Business Intelligence – Opportunities and Challenges", discusses various aspects of pervasive computing including pervasive computing environment, pervasive devices, and pervasive computing application in business intelligence including data analysis and triggering actions. Pervasive computing has beautifully made its own space in the world of advertising and marketing also. However, the fundamental issue to attracting the eyeballs and gaining attention remains the same. Chapter 2, "Attention and Pervasive Computing: A Case study of Online Advertising", describes attention as one of the most limited mental resources and discusses the impact of decreasing size of Pervasive devices and increasing rich media on the capacity of our visual attention. This chapter also describes the impact of repetition and attention on recognition for various types of advertisements. Chapter 3, "The Feature Extraction Algorithm for the Production of Emotions in Text-To-Speech (TTS) System for an Indian Regional Language", proposes the development of a Text to Speech Synthesis System for an Indian regional language and describes in detail various stages of the synthesis of text to speech such as Text normalization, Homograph disambiguation, Word to phoneme conversion, Prosody and Waveform synthesis. It discusses example of Bengali Text to Speech Synthesis system including its specific complexities, and various methods which may be used for speech synthesis. This chapter also discusses application of variations in the prosody of the speech that yields the emotional aspects (anger, happy, normal) in Text to Speech Synthesis System.

Chapter 1
Pervasive Business Intelligence: Opportunities and Challenges

Sujoy Pal
IIM, Ahmedabad, India

Rajanish Dass
IIM, Ahmedabad, India

ABSTRACT

Timeliness of information availability becomes very critical when it comes to decision making. Business organizations can gain high competitive advantage by reducing the time lag between the occurrence of a business event and action taken based on the available information. Though real-time business intelligence has helped reducing this time lag, this paper explains how the lag can be further reduced using pervasive business intelligence. In pervasive business intelligence, various devices will not only capture and transmit data, but would also analyze and take actions up to certain extent. The paper also mentions various opportunities and challenges in incorporating pervasive business intelligence.

INTRODUCTION

In recent years, Information Systems (IS) have evolved as a decision supporting tool for various business houses. Apart from the historical data, Business Intelligence/Analytics as it is popularly known considers various internal as well as external factors of the business organization in providing its expert support. Business intelligence software is already being used by thousands of companies to find new revenue opportunities, reduce costs, reallocate resources, and improve operational efficiency (MicroStrategy 2008).

The focus of BI is now shifting towards providing timely and accurate decision based on real-time data. In real-time information systems, all information generated at a point of creation (POC) is immediately made available to all points of action (POA) that leverage the information for better decision-making (Fleisch 2004). Even though using various real-time Business Intelligence methods achieves this target quite efficiently, still, there are limitations that force the system to take decisions based on high granular data. These limitations arise due to both technological and cost factors.

The advent and use of pervasive computing devices have opened the doors for exploring the

DOI: 10.4018/978-1-60566-996-0.ch001

opportunities for implementing pervasive-BI in various business sectors. As the pervasive computing devices have in-built capabilities of gathering, analyzing and transmitting data, these devices would be capable of making various types of decisions at different levels. The idea is to make the whole system capable of taking real-time decisions without much human intervention. This might pose some threats on the various aspects like privacy, environment, etc. In this paper we have tried to explore various opportunities and treats pertaining to the implementation of pervasive-BI across different business sectors.

BACKGROUND

Pervasive Computing

Computers have been used in various aspects of human life, but in most cases people have to adapt their behavior to each system. On the other hand ubiquitous computing as envisioned by (Weiser 2003) is a computing environment where computing systems weave themselves in the fabric of everyday life and become invisible. Invisibility is the most important aspect of Ubiquitous computing. The user is exposed to a few sets of services available to him/her and is oblivious to the complex system implementing those services (Satyanarayanan 2001). This takes the human-computer interaction into a whole different dimension, where the user is surrounded by a complete smart environment with devices/sensors communicating with each other and aggregating their functionalities to provide a set of consolidated services.

The terms Ubiquitous computing and Pervasive computing are used interchangeably (Saha and Mukherjee 2003), but they are conceptually different (Lyytinen and Yoo 2002). Ubiquitous computing uses the advances in Mobile computing and Pervasive computing to present a global computing environment. Mobile computing is about elevating computing services and making them available on mobile devices using the wireless infrastructure. The focus here is to reduce the size of the computing devices so that they can be carried anywhere or by providing access to computing capacity through high-speed networks. But Mobile computing has some limitations. The computing model does not change considerably as we move since the computing devices cannot acquire the context information and adjust accordingly. Pervasive computing, on the other hand, is about acquiring context from the environment and dynamically building computing models dependent on context. Pervasive computing is invisible to human users and yet provides useful computing services. Ubiquitous computing aims to provide Pervasive computing environments to a human user as s/he moves from one location to another.

A Ubiquitous computing environment can be built in two ways. The traditional approach is to achieve it by using Mobile computing and Pervasive computing together, in which the mobile devices remember the information about past environments they operated in and activate when we reenter into a known environment or proactively build up services as we walk into new environments (Lyytinen and Yoo 2002). (Singh, Puradkar et al. 2006) have presented an alternate approach and use Semantic Web technologies for Pervasive computing environments which allows context information to be stored on the Web and then shared across Pervasive computing environments via the Web to provide context-aware services.

Pervasive computing involves three converging areas of ICT: computing ('devices'), communications ('connectivity') and 'user interfaces'.

Devices

Pervasive Computing Systems (PCS) devices are likely to assume many different forms and sizes, from handheld units (similar to mobile phones) to near-invisible devices set into 'everyday' objects (like furniture and clothing). These will all be able to communicate with each other and act 'intelligently'. Such devices can be separated into three categories (viz. sensors, processors and actuators). Sensors are the input devices that detect environmental changes, user behaviors, human commands etc. Processors are the electronic systems that interpret and analyze input-data. While, actuators are output devices that respond to processed information by altering the environment via electronic or mechanical means. However the term actuator can also refer to devices which deliver information, rather than altering the environment physically.

Connectivity

Pervasive computing systems will rely on the interlinking of independent electronic devices into broader networks. This can be achieved via both wired (such as Broadband (ADSL) or Ethernet) and wireless networking technologies (such as WiFi or Bluetooth), with the devices themselves being capable of assessing the most effective form of connectivity in any given scenario. The effective development of pervasive computing systems depends on their degree of interoperability, as well as on the convergence of standards for wired and wireless technologies.

User Interfaces

User interfaces represent the point of contact between ICT and human users. For example with a personal computer, the mouse and keyboard are used to *input* information, while the monitor usually provides the *output.* With PCS, new user interfaces are being developed that will be capable of sensing and supplying more information about users, and the broader environment, to the computer for processing. With future user interfaces the input might be visual information – for example recognizing a person's face, or responding to gestures. It might also be based on sound, scent or touch recognition, or other sensory information like temperature. The output might also be in any of these formats. The technology could 'know' the user (for example through expressed preferences, attitudes, and behaviors) and tailor the physical environment to meet specific needs and demands. However, designing systems which can adapt to unforeseen situations presents considerable engineering challenges. There is debate over the degree of control users will have over future pervasive computing user interfaces as the technology develops (Pinkerton 2006).

TECHNOLOGICAL FACTORS

Deciding on the Granularity of Data

Data granularity can be described in four dimensions. The first dimension is dependent on the time scale. Time granularity is low when the data entry component of a business case only allows the occasional reality check. Time granularity is high, if a sensor technology's marginal costs enable a justification that favors ongoing checks with the physical environment (Figure 1). Information systems with such a high time granularity do not depend on the stochastic of the time scale—they are always operational. In principle, they can collect a complete history of a physical instance and detect real-world events in real time.

The next two granularity dimensions depend on the physical objects in order to be integrated. One dimension describes the type of object. With the advent of Pervasive Computing technologies, the objects that can be integrated with a positive business case tend to become smaller and less valuable. A justification now for tagging reusable transport containers very likely prevails. With the mandate of Wal-Mart, the U.S. Department of Defense, and Metro, the tagging of pallets and cartons is likely to reach a critical mass for writing a sound business case (RFID Journal 2003; Metro Group 2004; Department of Defense 2003). In some industries,

Figure 1. Pervasive computing increases time granularity (Fleisch 2004)

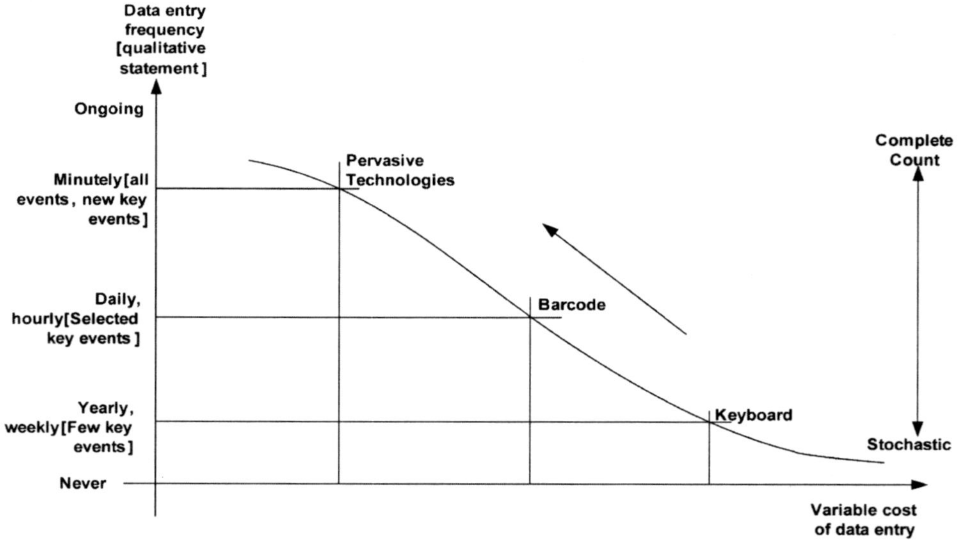

for example, in the textile industry, which deals with high-value and highly individual products, even item tagging starts to pay off.

The third granularity dimension describes how many physical objects of a class (*e.g.*, boxes) are integrated. As it becomes less expensive to integrate physical objects with the digital world, more objects (instances of boxes) within one object class (all boxes) will be equipped with Pervasive Computing technology. As a consequence, the number of objects per class granularity rises. For instance, if a mail order company equips 5% of its video camera boxes with RFID-Tags, the object granularity is rather low, compared to the maximum of 100%. However, in various situations, such as detecting where typical high-value shipments get delayed, lost, or stolen, a small object granularity might make sense.

The fourth dimension of data granularity likely to be increased by Pervasive Computing technology is the variety of data to be collected automatically. At minimum, the integration of physical objects requires a unique identifier of the object class or the object instance. Twenty-five years ago EAN/UCC started providing the retail business with a unique class identifier. In 2003, the Auto-ID Center proposed the electronic product code, a unique identifier at instance level. Advanced Pervasive Computing applications, for example, in the automotive and high-tech industry, already collect additional object-related data such as quality management data, the forthcoming production stages, customer name, or target configuration. Adding new sensors allows the integration of data from the immediate environment of the objects (Figure 2).

Pervasive Computing reduces the marginal cost of integrating the real with the virtual world. It thus enables information systems to collect more detailed data at the POC and eventually allows managers and machines at the POA to base and implement decisions on high granularity real-time information.

Reducing the Analysis Time

With pervasive computing devices capable of capturing data with high granularity at a relatively low cost, ultimately increases the availability of data for analysis. Hence, the pervasive computing devices capable of taking decisions on a real-time basis would need proper techniques to

Figure 2. Pervasive computing changing data granularity in business applications (Fleisch 2004)

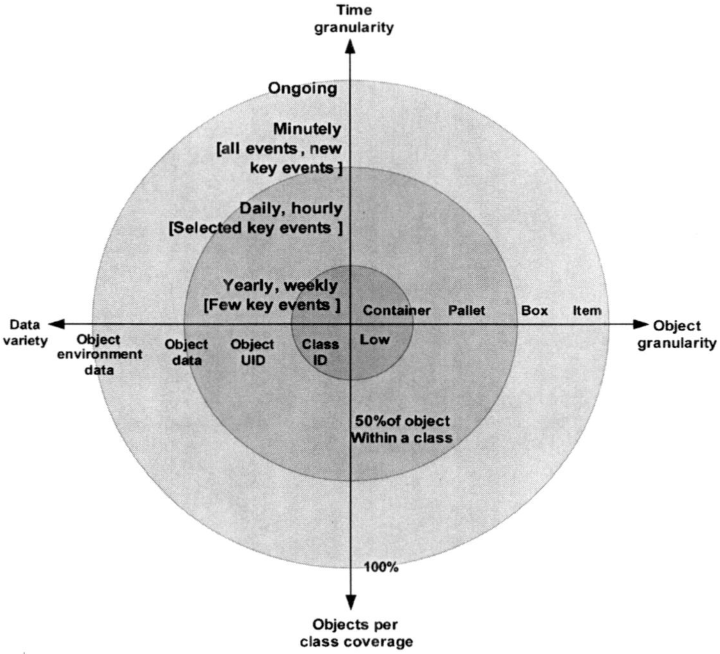

perform analysis on data streams. An emerging field of data-mining called stream mining deals with this issue.

In general, frequent pattern mining in data streams must be processed timely and should be completed through scanning data streams in a single pass, or a small number of passes while using less space of memory. One of the most crucial aspects is the fact that the mining process deals with a trade-off; response time and precise results, which are typically contradictory, and improving one usually incurs a decrease in the other. Recently, the algorithm research community has been fairly active in the area of data streams (Jiinlong, Conglfu et al. 2004).

Business Intelligence

The wish to be able to understand situations is a normal human response to having to make decisions when confronted with events. The challenge is to have the right information at the right time to be able to make the right decision. The inability to do this is not necessarily a factor of not having enough data, generally one of the issues is having too much data to be able to see exactly what is needed. Businesses have spent years and a great deal of money in capturing data, in the hope of turning this into ***'Knowledge'***, and perceive the problem as being their inability to make use of all of this data. The phrase ***'Knowledge has no value till it is used'*** expresses their frustration in trying to make valuable use of this asset (Mulholland and Gibbs 2004). Business Intelligence (BI) or Business Analytics helps in resolving this situation by providing decision support by using various data mining techniques on the existing historical data. In addition to the mining of historical data, BI also considers various other internal and external factors affecting the business while providing decision support. See Figure 3 for the structure of BI environment.

Way back in 1958, Hans Peter Luhn defined intelligence in a more general sense as "the ability to apprehend the interrelationships of presented facts in such a way as to guide action towards a

Figure 3. BI environment (Ranjan 2008)

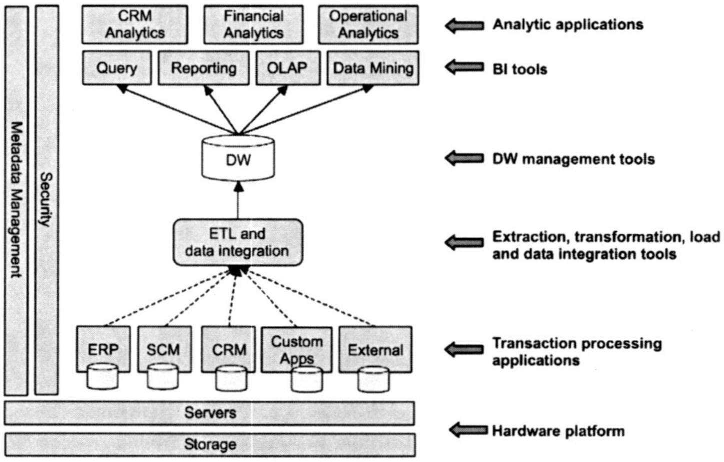

desired goal". In 1989 Howard Dresner, later a Gartner Group analyst, popularized BI as an umbrella term to describe "concepts and methods to improve business decision-making by using fact-based support systems". Over the years, different people have defined the term BI in various ways; some of them are as follows:

According to (Adelman, Moss et al. 2002), BI is a term that encompasses a broad range of analytical software and solutions for gathering, consolidating, analyzing and providing access to information in a way that is supposed to let an enterprise's users make better business decisions, (Malhotra 2000) describes BI that facilitates the connections in the new-form organization, bringing real-time information to centralized repositories and support analytics that can be exploited at every horizontal and vertical level within and outside the firm. (Gangadharan and Swamy 2004) define BI as an enterprise architecture for an integrated collection of operational as well as decision support applications and databases, which provides the business community easy access to their business data and allows them to make accurate business decisions.

Few more definitions of BI:

BI systems are those that provide directed background data and reporting tools to support and improve the decision-making process. (Inc. n.d.)

BI normally describes the result of in-depth analysis of detailed business data. It includes database and application technologies, as well as analysis practices. Sometimes used synonymously with "decision support," though business intelligence is technically much broader, potentially encompassing knowledge management, enterprise resource planning, and data mining, among other practices. (Chapter n.d.)

BI is a term used to refer to the process of business management. This technology consists of applications and technologies that allow users to gather, access, and analyze a company's data and information. Overall, it helps users to gain comprehensive knowledge of the factors that affect the company's overall performance. (CXOToday.com n.d.)

BI is the knowledge derived from analyzing an organization's information. (Cruz n.d.)

BI is actually an environment in which business users receive data that is reliable, consistent, understandable, easily manipulated and timely. With this data, business users are able to conduct analyses that yield overall understanding of where the business has been, where it is now and where it will be in the near future. Business intelligence serves two main purposes. It monitors the financial and operational health of the organization (reports, alerts, alarms, analysis tools, key performance indicators and dashboards). It also regulates the operation of the organization providing two- way integration with operational systems and information feedback analysis. (Markintell.com n.d.)

BI systems provide historical, current, and predictive views of business operations, most often using data that has been gathered into a data warehouse or a data mart and occasionally working from operational data. Software elements support reporting, interactive "slice-and-dice" pivot-table analyses, visualization, and statistical data mining. Applications tackle sales, production, financial, and many other sources of business data for purposes that include, notably, business performance management. (Netreturn.com.au n.d.)

Real-Time Business Intelligence

In recent years, business intelligence systems have played pivotal roles in helping organizations to fine-tune business goals such as improving customer retention, market penetration, profitability and efficiency. In most cases, these insights are driven by analyses of historic data. The next logical question in line will obviously be that if the historic data can help us make better decisions going forward, how real-time data can improve the decision making process (Dass and Mahanti 2005). ETL (extract, transform and load) is the process that enterprises use to build the consolidated data stores (e,g., data warehouses and data marts) required for effective BI. Traditionally, ETL processes have been run periodically, on a monthly or weekly basis, and use a bulk approach that moves and integrates the entire data set from the operational source systems to the target data warehouse. While this approach was acceptable for enterprises over the years, current business conditions require a new way of integrating data - in real time and in an efficient manner. Customer demand, competitive pressure and improved decisions require timely information. To make the most of BI in today's ever-accelerating business climate, managers should not be working with last week's or yesterday's data. Today, decision-makers need data that is updated a few times a day or even in real time (Ankorion 2005).

As shown in Figure 4, various types of latencies exist in BI based systems. The data latency is the time taken to transfer the data from the point of creation (POC) i.e. the business event to the data warehouse. Analysis latency is the time required for analyzing the data present in the data warehouse to provide appropriate information to the manager. The delay in taking appropriate action by the manager after receiving decision supporting information is termed as decision latency. Real-time information systems are capable of reducing the data latency by transmitting the data generated during the business event to the data warehouse in real-time.

MAIN FOCUS OF THE CHAPTER

Pervasive Business Intelligence

Real-time BI is devised to reduce the data latency i.e. the time taken to transfer the captured data about a business event to the data warehouse. But it can reduce the data latency only after the organization realizes that a business event has occurred. We found that even before the organization realizes (captures/registers) the occurrence of a business event, there is some amount of inertia present in most cases (Refer to Figure 5). We term this inertia as "realization latency". Realization latency can

Figure 4. Latencies in BI (Eckerson 2004)

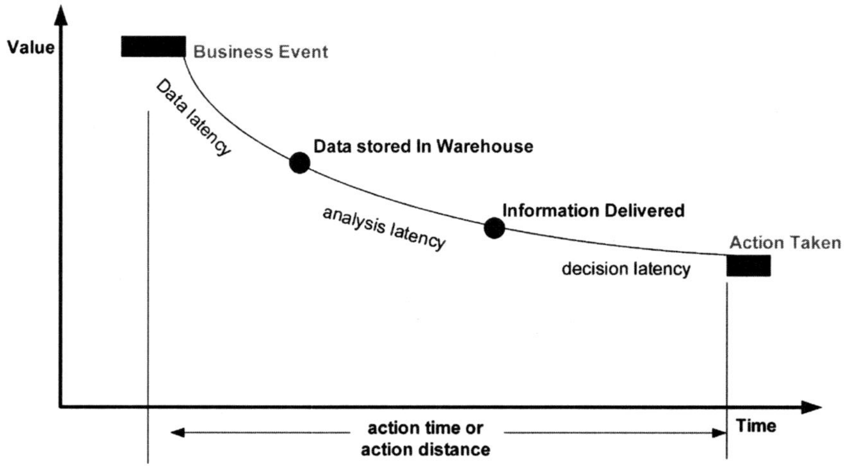

be defined as the time duration between the real occurrence of a business event and the moment when the organization records the event.

Even though real-time BI is capable of reducing the data latency, it is not able to make any difference to the realization latency. The realization latency can be dealt with only with the use of pervasive devices that are capable of capturing business events much ahead of the real-time systems. Pervasive BI can be defined as the form of BI that is capable of minimizing the action time to the greatest extent with the help of pervasive computing devices.

Data flows through various devices spread across different locations at various intervals of time. By making these devices intelligent enough to analyze data in real-time will ultimately transform the process of analysis and decision making from a batch processing model to a real-time model. But, this would also mean that the devices will take more time to allow the data to travel through them and hence making the process of data transfer slower. This indicates that the devices should not only be made smart to analyze the passing data, but should also be smart enough to decide which portion of the data to analyze and which not to analyze. If this aim can be achieved, then the time lag between the occurrence of an event and that of decision making based on the event will be reduced by a huge amount. Hence, the pervasive computing devices should not only be capable of capturing the business event, but, should also be able to analyze the captured data and even take action/provide actionable information to some extent.

Probable Business Impact

In a scenario of cut-throat competition, the organizations cannot afford to show the attitude of not keeping abreast with the latest changing demands and trends of their customers and get satisfied with periodical data. They have to act on the latest data that is available to them to react not only to the fierce global competition, but also market products keeping in mind the latest customer wishes. In such a scenario, the concept of a real-time enterprise has crept into the corporate board rooms of a number of organizations. Using up-to-date information, getting rid of delays, and using speed for competitive advantage is what the real-time enterprise is all about (Dass and Mahanti 2005). Pervasive BI being able to minimize the realization latency will provide a huge competitive advantage to the business organizations.

Figure 5. Realization latency in BI

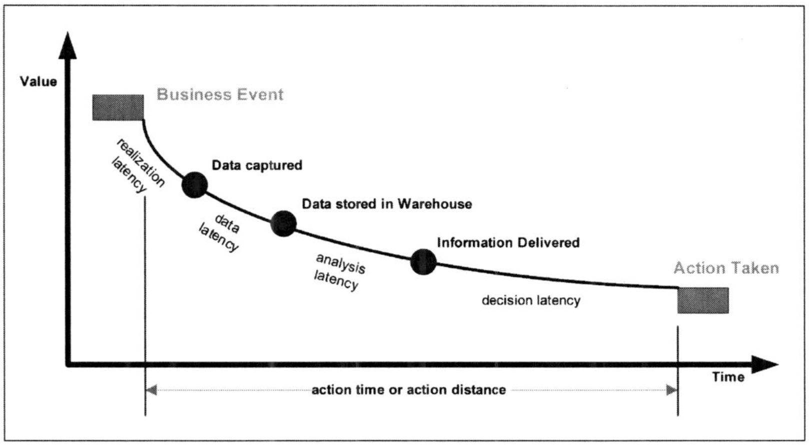

Embedded Services

Business organizations can earn huge benefits by providing services to the customers through pervasive computing devices embedded into their products like cars, mobile phones, air-conditioners, etc. Research has already revealed that product companies that also offer product-related services, on average earn more than companies that stick to product selling. The reasons for this trend are quite clear: On one hand, products are becoming commodities so that the profit margins decline. In addition, product companies provide an increasing number of free product-related services to the customer, which reduces the margin even more. On the other hand, the customer is willing to outsource many of the coordination tasks to services providers. The service business itself is quite appealing, because of its financial, marketing, and strategic opportunities. The substantial potential revenue, higher margins, and the fact that services are a more stable source of revenue, represent the financial benefit. Marketing opportunities can be understood in this context as the use of services to sell more products. Finally, there are strategic arguments such as competitive strategy based on services. By virtue of being more labor dependent, services are much more difficult to imitate than products. Services are thus becoming a sustainable source of competitive advantage. So many product companies are currently attempting to transform themselves into companies selling both products and product-related services.

Pervasive Computing clearly offers an opportunity for manufacturing companies to link products with ongoing high-margin services. A tagging or embedded system never creates value itself. It is always the service that generates value. Pervasive technology links objects with value-adding services (Fleisch 2004).

Implementation Scenarios

Pervasive BI can prove its worth in many different industrial sectors including aviation, telecommunication, health-care, insurance, retail and automobile. It is needless to say that the list is not exhaustive. Let us looks at some of these sectors and find out how pervasive BI can be beneficial.

Health-Care

The life-style of an individual makes a huge impact on his/her health. It is highly impossible for any general physician to monitor the life-style of any individual on a regular basis and suggest remedies to his/her health problems accordingly.

Devices like watches, mobile-phones, etc. can be made capable of monitoring the lifestyle of a person and provide health related suggestions whenever required or requested. Capturing such vital information of the patient on a regular basis would allow the general physician to take more accurate decisions.

The timeliness and accuracy of information becomes highly critical in cases of accidents. Taking prompt decisions on calling an ambulance and providing vital information like blood group, allergy, special condition (like pregnancy, hypertension, etc.) regarding the patient to the nearest health care center can increase the probability of saving human life to a large extent.

Retail

Consider a shopping cart capable of monitoring the actions of the customer and records all the products that have been kept into and out of the cart in real-time. Depending on these actions and the customer records, the cart itself should be able to suggest a product to the customer and even give dynamic discounts on various types of products. The cart can also be made capable of guiding the customers to find a specific product at the store and on the way can also suggest and offer discounts on other products as well. This will reduce (if not completely remove) the need of sales staff at the store and hence reduce the recurring (regularly increasing) expense of the store.

Automobile Industry

Maintenance

If various parts of an automobile are capable of sending out information regarding their usage, condition and wear-and-tear, then the car itself can decide about the services it requires including need for replacement of spare parts. This information can then be transmitted to the car manufacturing company and/or the service station to make sure that the required parts are available. This will also keep the manufacturing company and the service station informed about the possible replacements much ahead of its schedule and hence will allow them to manage their inventory in a better way.

Traffic Avoidance and Refueling

Imagine on your way back home from office, your car suggests you to take a different route well in advance after detecting traffic congestion in your regular route. This can save much of your valuable time and energy. In a different scenario, where in the midst of your long tour, the car after considering the existing amount of fuel and location of refueling stations, is able to suggest you the exact location from where you should refuel the car.

COST FACTORS

Data Entry Cost

Changing business requirements demand that IT organizations deliver real-time business intelligence based on timely data while, at the same time, reducing the cost of data integration (Ankorion 2005). Using pervasive computing, the cost of data entry reduces by a large extent (Refer Figure 6).

Power Consumption

Even though the cost of data entry decreases with the use of pervasive technology, the total power consumption would increase due to the fact that pervasive computing devices need to be continuously switched on. By increasing the use of renewable sources of energy to provide power to these devices, the cost of power consumption can be reduced.

Figure 6. Pervasive computing reduces cost of integrating the physical world (Fleisch 2004)

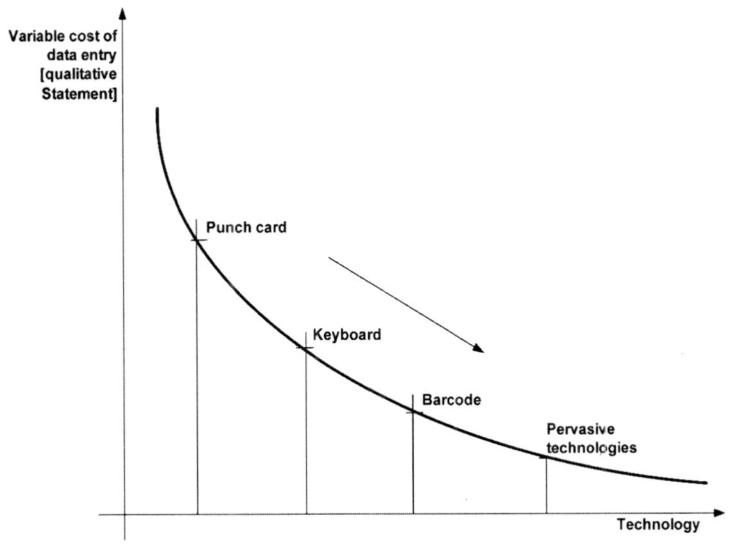

Data Storage

The pervasive computing devices are capable of capturing high granular data. The logging of highly granular data can reveal many minute details and can improve accountability. Storing high granular data would also lead to an increase in storage space requirement. Hence, the cost of data storage would also increase by a considerable amount. This issue can be managed to some extent by intelligently selecting the data that needs to be logged.

PERVASIVE BI PERTINENT ISSUES

Compatibility Issues

The promise of ubiquitous computing is viable only if service operators create a satisfactory experience for each set of adopters, who will in turn encourage those that follow. This will demand a new approach to the design and implementation of the out-of-the-box experience (OoBE). This article establishes the need to expand our perspective of OoBE beyond initial use, to encompass the selection and acquisition process during which users form expectations, and after initial use, during which the scope of use expands to fulfill emergent needs. It proposes an expanded model to capture activities throughout the product life cycle by all actors that shape the OoBE, and not only the user. It also makes a case for further research to redefine segmentation, based on the user context and skill set, and the development of OoBE designs that are suitable for each user segment. Analysis of IMARC and other OoBE research highlighted by the proposed model strongly suggests use of an interdisciplinary and user-centered approach to design. (Gilbert, Sangwan et al. 2005)

Privacy and Security Issues

Trust is an important aspect of decision making for pervasive applications and it is important to choose and use services efficiently in pervasive computing environments. Trust force is presented to specify trust relationships among interactive entities in a pervasive computing environment by using experience and knowledge in a social network and the coulomb¢s law in real word. Based on trust force, a Trust Management and Service Selection model are presented, named TMSS.

TMSS was tested and the experimental results show that our method for selecting service is not only more efficient than traditional and heuristic methods, but also can identify good services from bad ones. (GUAN, Xiao-sheDONG et al. 2008)

Due to the significance of service selection in pervasive computing environments, we present a service selection model, namely TMSS, based on trust force. The experimental results show that our method for selecting service is not only more efficient than traditional and heuristic methods, but also can identify good services from bad ones. In the future, we will implement and examine TMSS in the framework of the Constellation Model. (GUAN, Xiao-sheDONG et al. 2008)

Pervasive computing also gives rise to debate over safety. Integrated transport systems could involve road vehicles having actuating devices that intervene in the driving process, possibly responding to hazards more quickly than humans. For example the new Mercedes S-Class features an active braking system that can detect rapidly slowing vehicles in front, activating the brakes without driver intervention. While this may help avoid accidents, there are also potential risks, for example if the security of the vehicle's controlling software is breached. Similar concerns exist over prospective pervasive computing systems applications in domiciliary care. Breaches of security could expose vulnerable individuals to malicious acts within their own homes – for example the withholding or over-prescribing of medications.

Technological Measures

It is argued that privacy, safety and security can be better protected if appropriate procedures and protocols are integrated into pervasive computing systems at the design level rather than implemented retrospectively. Three measures are frequently cited as vital in establishing robust security measures:

- The volume of transmitted data should be kept to a minimum;
- Data that require transmission should be encrypted and sent anonymously (without reference to the owner);
- Security should be treated as an ongoing and integral element of pervasive computing systems.

These principles are accepted by many centres of pervasive computing systems research and development. However, some consumer groups say that developers need to give more consideration to privacy issues (Pinkerton 2006).

SOCIAL ISSUES

Digital Divide

There is a risk of technological and social isolation for those who do not use the technology (whether it be through choice, lack of income or skills). For instance, banking, education and retail services are likely to be delivered through PCS embedded within smart homes; this could lead to some consumers being deprived of access and freedom of choice. Pervasive computing could improve the lives of those with illnesses and disabilities, and the elderly (Pinkerton 2006).

ENVIRONMENTAL & HEALTH RELATED ISSUES

Environment

While Pervasive Computing is not expected to cause totally new types of impacts on the environment, it is likely to add to the well-known environmental impacts of today's ICT. Consumption of scarce raw materials for the production of electronics and the energy consumption of stationary infrastructure may increase. Furthermore,

Pervasive Computing will change electronic waste streams in their amount and quality. If no adequate solution is found for the end-of-life treatment of the electronic waste generated by millions of very small components, precious raw materials will be lost and pollutants will be emitted to the environment. In OECD countries the expected amounts of microelectronics in residual waste are controllable in terms of environmental and health risk. Greater challenges may arise, however, in countries without well-developed systems of waste treatment and recycling. An increasing concentration of electronic waste in household waste streams will aggravate waste-related impacts on environment and health, for example, in the case of illegal landfill or open burning.

On the other hand the intensified use of ICT in the era of Pervasive Computing might result in certain advantages to the environment. Intensified use of information services instead of physical goods can contribute to higher ecological efficiency in economics and consumption. Although Pervasive Computing could bring a potential for dematerialization, it has to be expected that energy and resource savings will not be realizable in every case due to a growth in demand that will overcompensate for the savings (rebound effects). There is a need for policies that exploit the environmental opportunities of pervasive computing while avoiding the risks at an early stage of technological and market development. (K¨ohler and Erdmann 2004)

Health

Non-ionizing radiation is a by-product of the wireless signals that are likely to be used to connect pervasive computing devices into broader networks. As these devices may be carried close to the body (more so than current ICT) and remain constantly activated, there may be increased risk from exposure of body tissues to the potentially damaging effects of such radiation (Pinkerton 2006).

With the number of electromagnetic field sources in human environments increasing, it appears appropriate to discuss the future levels of radio frequency (RF) exposure. The controversy about the adverse health effects of electromagnetic fields has been going on for years. The issue is discussed both in the general public ("electromagnetic pollution") and in scientific contexts. As of today the risk of health hazards below the thermal threshold remains essentially unresolved. The trend toward Pervasive Computing will strongly increase the number of EMF (electromagnetic field) sources in human environments. An intensified discussion in the context of the Precautionary Principle is needed (Behrendt 2004).

FUTURE TRENDS

There are many visions for the future development of pervasive computing devices. Several research groups are endeavoring to produce networks of devices that could be small as a grain of sand. The idea is that each one would function independently, with its own power supply, and could also communicate wirelessly with the others. These could be distributed throughout the environment to form dense, but almost invisible, pervasive computing networks, thus eliminating the need for overt devices.

At the other extreme, augmented reality would involve overlaying the real world with digital information. This approach emphasizes the use of mobile technologies, geographical positioning systems and internet-linked databases to distribute information via personal digital companions. Such devices could come in many forms: children might have them integrated into school bags, whereas adults might use devices more closely resembling personal digital assistants (PDAs).

Ultimately a spectrum of devices may become available. These will range from miniaturized (potentially embedded in surrounding objects) to a variety of mobile (including handheld and wearable) devices. While these could exist as standalone systems, it is likely that many will be interlinked to form more comprehensive systems. (Pinkerton 2006) With all these different types of pervasive devices in place, we would be talking more about pervasive environment rather than just pervasive computing or pervasive device. Hence, in such an environment, pervasive business intelligence would rather become an implicit term while talking about business intelligence. Through increased diffusion of pervasive technologies, business firms would be rather forced to adopt pervasive business intelligence techniques to remain sustainable in the competitive market.

CONCLUSION

There are huge opportunities for various business sectors in adopting pervasive business intelligence. By enabling products to take (or suggest) time critical decisions, the quality of service and level of customer satisfaction can be improved in order to gain competitive advantage. The products embedded with pervasive computing devices being capable of analyzing data in real-time, would reduce the total time lag between occurrence of a business event and action taken. This will allow managers to act upon information that is based on latest data and trend. Reducing the amount of human intervention in taking critical decisions on one hand will allow sectors like retailing to lower the cost and increase sales by providing better customer satisfaction, while on the other hand, will allow sectors like health-care to service mankind and save more lives.

As every coin has two sides, so does the use of pervasive business intelligence. Along with huge amount of benefits, extensive use of pervasive computing devices brings some inherent threats. The issue of threat on privacy and security of the users of such devices is considered to be most critical. This can develop mistrust and discomfort among the users of products embedded with pervasive computing devices. The threats of increase in digital divide among the society, threat to the environment and effect of radiation produced by such devices on human health are the other major concerns.

It is strongly believed that, with the advancement of technology and human awareness, the threats related to pervasive business intelligence will overcome. Looking at the enormous capability of pervasive BI in taking timely decisions, it seems that its use in almost every business sector would become inevitable for gaining competitive advantage and live-up to the expectations of the customers of the modern era.

REFERENCES

Adelman, S., Moss, L., & Barbusinski, L. (2002). I found several definitions of BI. *DM Review*.

Ankorion, I. (2005, January). Change Data Capture Efficient ETL for Real-Time BI. *DM Review*. Chapter, D. P. M. (n.d.). Data Warehouse Glossary. Retrieved November 19, 2008, from www.dama-pdx.org/Glossary28.doc.

Bridgefield Group, Inc. (n.d.). Bridgefield Group ERP/Supply chain Glossary. Retrieved November 19, 2008, from http://www.bridgefieldgroup.com/bridgefieldgroup/glos1.htm.

Cruz, U. S. (n.d.). Data Warehouse Glossary. Retrieved November 19, 2008, from http://planning.ucsc.edu/irps/dwh/DWHGLOSS.HTM.

CXOToday.com. (n.d.). Tech Terms. Retrieved November 19, 2008, from http://www.cxotoday.com/cxo/jsp/home.jsp?cat=1003.

Dass, R., & Mahanti, A. (2005). *An Efficient Brute-Force Technique for Frequent Pattern Mining in Real-Time Business Applications*. Paper presented at the Hawaii International Conference on System Sciences.

Eckerson, W. (2004, August). The "Soft Side" of Real-Time BI. *DM Review*.

Fleisch, E. (2004). *Business Impact of Pervasive Technologies: Opportunities and Risks*.

Gangadharan, G. R., & Swamy, S. N. (2004). *Business intelligence systems: design and implementation strategies.* Paper presented at the 26th International Conference on Information Technology Interfaces, Cavtat, Croatia.

Gilberg, L., Sangwan, S., & Ian, M. (2005). Beyond usability: the OoBE dynamics of mobile data services markets. *Personal and Ubiquitous Computing, 9*, 198–208. doi:10.1007/s00779-004-0321-8

Guan, S., Dong, X., Mei, Y., Zhu, Z., & Wu, W. (2008). Trust force-based service selection in pervasive computing environments. *Journal of Communication and Computer*, *5*(6), 27–31.

Kohler, A., & Erdmann, L. (2004). Expected Environmental Impacts of Pervasive Computing. *Human and Ecological Risk Assessment, 10*(5), 831–852. doi:10.1080/10807030490513856

Lyytinen, K., & Yoo, Y. (2002). Issues and challenges in Ubiquitous computing. *Communications of the ACM, 45*(12), 62–65. doi:10.1145/585597.585616

Malhotra, Y. (2000). Information management to knowledge management: beyond 'hi-tech hidebound' systems. *Knowledge Management for the Information Professional.* Markintell.com. (n.d.). Market Intelligence & Marketing Glossary. Retrieved November 19, 2008, from http://www.markintell.com/market-intelligence-glossary-a.

MicroStrategy. (2008). Application of Industrial-Strength Business Intelligence. Retrieved October 11, 2008 from http://www.microstrategy.com/Solutions/AppsBook.asp

Mulholland, A., & Gibbs, J. (2004). *A Point of View on Business Intelligence and Service Architecture*.

Netreturn.com.au. (n.d.). Netsuite Glossary. November 19, 2008, from http://www.netreturn.com.au/about-us/Faq-s/netsuite-glossary.html.

Pinkerton, A. (2006). Pervasive Computing. *postnote, 263*(May 2006).

Ranjan, J. (2008). Business justification with business intelligence. *VINE: The journal of information and knowledge management systems, 38*(4), 461-475.

Saha, D., & Mukherjee, A. (2003). Pervasive computing: A paradigm for the 21st century. *IEEE Comput, 36*, 25–31.

Satyanarayanan, M. (2001). Pervasive computing: vision and challenges. *IEEE Personal Commun, 8*, 10–17. doi:10.1109/98.943998

Singh, S., Puradkar, S., & Lee, Y. (2006). Ubiquitous computing: connecting Pervasive computing through Semantic Web. *Information Systems & e-Business Management, 4*(4), 421-439.

Wang, J., Xu, C., Chen, W., & Pan, Y. (2004). *Survey of the Study on Frequent Pattern Mining in Data Streams*. Paper presented at the International Conference on Systems, Man and Cybernetics.

Weiser, M. (2003). The computer for the 21st century. *Scientific American*, 94–104.

Würtenberger, F., & Behrendt, S. (2004). Electromagnetic Field Exposure from Pervasive Computing. *Human and Ecological Risk Assessment, 10*(5), 801–815. doi:10.1080/10807030490513829

ADDITIONAL READING

Back, T. (2002). Adaptive Business Intelligence Based on Evolution Strategies: Some Application Examples of Self-adaptive Software. *Information Sciences*, *148*, 113–121. doi:10.1016/S0020-0255(02)00283-9

Bhote, K. R. (1996). Beyond Customer Satisfaction to Customer Loyalty. In *Proceedings of the American Management Association*. New York, NY.

Bohn, J., Coroama, V., Langheinrich, M., Mattern, F., & Rohs, M. (2004). Living in a World of Smart Everyday Objects—Social, Economic, and Ethical Implications. *Human and Ecological Risk Assessment*, *10*(5), 763–785. doi:10.1080/10807030490513793

Cuff, D. (2003). Immanent Domain Pervasive Computing and the Public Realm. *Journal of Architectural Education*, 43-49.

Gonzales, M. L. (2004). Unearth BI in Real-time. *Teradata*.

Hilty, L., Som, C., & Köhler, A. (2004). Assessing the Human, Social, and Environmental Risks of Pervasive Computing. *Human and Ecological Risk Assessment*, *10*(5), 853–874. doi:10.1080/10807030490513874

Howard, S., Kjeldskov, J., & Skov, M. B. (2007). Pervasive computing in the domestic space. *Personal and Ubiquitous Computing*, 329–333. doi:10.1007/s00779-006-0081-8

Kara, D. (2000). Pervasive Computing Era - Get ready to integrate intelligent devices into the enterprise. *Softwaremag.commentary*, 18-22.

Kohavi, R., & Provost, F. (2001). Applications of Data Mining to Electronic Commerce. *Journal of Data Mining and Knowledge Discovery*, *5*, 5–10. doi:10.1023/A:1009840925866

Kung, H.-Y., Hsub, C.-Y., & Lin, M.-H. (2007). Sensor-based Pervasive Healthcare System: Design and implementation. *Journal of High Speed Networks*, 35-49.

Lawrence, R., & Almasi, G. (2001). Personalization of Supermarket Product Recommendations. *Journal of Data Mining and Knowledge Discovery*, *5*, 11–32. doi:10.1023/A:1009835726774

Mark, W. (1999). Turning Pervasive into Mediated Spaces. *IBM Systems Journal*, *38*(4), 677–692.

Montgomery, D. B., & Weinberg, C. E. (1981). Toward Strategic Intelligence Systems. *The McKinsey Quarterly*, Spring, 82-102.

Orlando, S., Palmerini, P., et al. (2002). Adaptive and Resource-Aware Mining of Frequent Sets. In V. Kumar, S. Tsumoto, P. S. Yu, & N. Zhong (Eds.), *Proceedings of the 2002 IEEE International Conference on Data Mining* (pp. 338-345). IEEE Computer Society.

Resnick, P., & Varian, H. (1997). Recommender Systems. *Communications of the ACM*, *40*(3), 56–58. doi:10.1145/245108.245121

Riggs, B. & P. McDougal (1999, October 18). Real-Time Analysis of Buying Habits. *Information week*, pp. 117.

Schafer, J., Konstan, J., et al. (1999). Recommender Systems in e-Commerce. In *Proceedings of the ACM E-Commerce.*

Schiefer, J., List, B. et al. (2003). *Process Data Store: A Real-Time Data Store for Monitoring Business Processes* (LNCS 2736, pp. 760-770).

Shenoy, P., Haritsa, J. R., et al. (2000). Turbo-Charging Vertical Mining of Large Databases. In W. Chen, J. F. Naughton & P. A. Bernstein (Eds.), *Proceedings of the 2000 ACM SIGMOD International Conference on Management of Data, 29*(2), 22-33.

Thyfault, M. E., & Stuart, J. J. (1998). The Service Imperative. *Information Week.*, *5*(October), 46.

KEY TERMS AND DEFINITIONS

Analysis Latency: Time required for analyzing the data present in the data warehouse to provide appropriate information to the manager.

Business Intelligence: Business intelligence is an enterprise architecture for an integrated collection of operational as well as decision support applications and databases, which provides the business community easy access to their business data and allows them to make accurate business decisions.

Data Latency: Time taken to transfer the data from the point of creation (i.e. the business event) to the data warehouse.

Decision Latency: The time lag between the action taken and information received by the decision maker.

Pervasive Business Intelligence: Pervasive BI can be defined as the form of BI that is capable of minimizing the action time to the greatest extent with the help of pervasive computing devices.

Real Time Business Intelligence: Real time BI can be defined as a form of BI that uses real time systems to reduce the data latency to the greatest extent.

Realization Latency: The time lag between the occurrence of an event and actually being realized by the business organization.

Chapter 2
Attention and Pervasive Computing:
A Case Study of Online Advertising

Jarmo Kuisma
Helsinki School of Economics HSE, Finland

Jaana Simola
Helsinki School of Economics HSE, Finland

Anssi Öörni
Helsinki School of Economics HSE, Finland

ABSTRACT

Attention is one of the most limited mental resources. The capacity of our visual attention is challenged by the increasingly rich media content and decreasing size of user interfaces embedded in many everyday appliances. Observations in fields such as advertising, with lengthy traditions in investigating the effects of visual attention and recognition may offer insights into effective interface design for pervasive computing applications. This study examines the impact of repetition and attention on recognition for four types of online ads: horizontal and vertical ads appearing in both animated and static forms. The authors observed that repetition enhanced recognition of ads, and that animated ads were generally better recognized while the effect of ad format was less significant. This chapter measured attention by eye fixations and fixation durations and found a strong relationship between attention and ad recognition.

INTRODUCTION

Emerging pervasive computing technologies and tools require more from our visual resources in both daily business and at home. Although pervasive computing devices are sometimes nearly invisible, like embedded intelligence in cars or smart homes, an interface is needed to access these applications. Typically, these interfaces are built around displays that may vary from standard computer screens to immersed miniaturized displays and even displays that we can wear.

The desirable quality of increasing intelligence of products and services is the higher potential for control it offers to consumers. Seizing this potential, however, depends crucially on our ability to acquire information to act on. To embed intelligence in

DOI: 10.4018/978-1-60566-996-0.ch002

ever-smaller objects, user interfaces also have to decrease in size or multiple devices must share an interface. This results in increasing load on our perceptual mechanism. Ravaja, Kallinen, Saari and Keltikangas-Järvinen (2004) studied cognitive responses when viewing video messages and postulated that message content is likely to elicit less attention, is perceived to be less creditable, and is remembered less effectively when presented on a small screen instead of a large screen. Visual attention, memory and learning by repeated exposures become critical for example when driving at night in a strange city and looking at small displays like speedometers and navigators while also observing the mirrors and traffic signs.

Like traffic, the Internet sites represent cluttered environments demanding attention for visual search and learning spatial locations of objects to navigate through various pages that often contain distracters such as animated ads and pop-ups before the user reaches the intended target information.

In the following we discuss the effectiveness of online advertising, a subject that has been debated among academics and practitioners since the commercialization of the Internet. As a consequence, advertisers have developed various types of advertising techniques and formats such as static and animated banners, skyscrapers, and pop-ups to attract consumers' attention. Despite the growing number of online advertising techniques, banner advertising still forms an important revenue stream and total Internet advertising revenues have increased annually by over 20% from 2002 to 2007 in the United States (PriceWaterhouseCoopers, 2008).

Previous research has offered contradictory results concerning the effectiveness of online ads. Some researchers have reported that consumers learn to avoid looking at banner ads (Benway & Lane, 1998; Bernard, 2001; Cho & Cheon, 2004; Stenfors, Morén, & Balkenius, 2003), that ad type or animation do not improve ad recognition, and that ads tend to distract information search (Burke, Hornof, Nielsen, & Gorman, 2005; Dréze & Hussherr, 2003; Hong, Thong, & Tam, 2004). Contrary findings have suggested that advertising type affects consumers' memory and brand recall, and that animation attracts attention and enhances recognition (Burns & Lutz, 2006; Yoo & Kim, 2006).

While banner advertising and the effects of animation on recognition have been widely examined, there has been relatively little research on the effects of repetition and attention on memory in the web environment. In conventional media such as TV or newspapers, the effectiveness of the message is supposed first to increase at low levels of repetition and then decrease relatively as message repetition increases above the optimal level (Berlyne, 1970; Cacioppo & Petty, 1979). In broadcast media, the frequency and duration of exposure is internally controlled and repetition may increase consumers' capability to remember advertisements. However, on the cluttered Internet sites, the opportunity to see ads and the duration of exposure also depends on consumers' navigational behaviour and information searching goals.

In this study, we explored how repetition, ad types and attention affect recognition memory in a controlled experiment using typical real-world web pages as stimuli. The background theory, hypothesis, research methodology, findings and conclusions are discussed in the following and general remarks and recommendations for pervasive computing applications are elaborated.

BACKGROUND

Repetition and Recognition

In general, effective advertising is remembered and believed and it is rationally and/or emotionally appealing and persuasive. Repetition of advertising is frequently used to improve message effectiveness. Both consumer researchers and marketers have attempted to understand the relationship between repetition and consumers' receptions to advertising messages (Campbell & Keller, 2003). Advertising budgets are commonly based on analyses of how many advertising exposures per sales cycle might be required per consumer (Aaker, Batra, & Myers, 1992). The amount of repetition varies depending on competition, the target audience and their brand awareness, and also on the product attributes. A prevailing view in off-line advertising practice suggests that on average at least three exposures are needed per sales cycle (Krugman, 1972).

Berlyne's (1970) two factor theory states that in the first ("wear-in") phase, repetition is needed because consumers may feel uncertainty when processing a new message. Increasing the frequency of exposures increases favorableness towards the message, and thus improves its effectiveness. In the second ("wear-out") phase, continued repetition leads to boredom and tediousness (Campbell & Keller, 2003). Cacioppo and Petty (1979) showed that consumers' positive arguments first increased and then decreased with message repetition while counterarguments showed an opposite pattern. Increasing exposures from low to moderate level provides a greater opportunity to elaborate the message and store the message content in memory (Malaviya, 2007).

Although the effects of repetition on learning and message elaboration have generated a considerable body of knowledge, studies examining the relationship between repetition and recall or recognition of online ads are limited and ambiguous as it is difficult to control the frequency of exposure per viewer. Researchers have reported high recall and recognition percentages for printed advertisements (e.g. Pieters & Wedel, 2004; Radach. Lemmer, Vorstius, Heller, & Radach, 2003; Wedel & Pieters, 2000). In the study by Rayner, Rotello, Stewart, Keir and Duffy (2001) participants recognized magazine ads correctly approximately 96% of the cases, whereas online ads have been poorly recognized with hit rates varying in the region of 20% (Bayles, 2002; Burke et al., 2005). Larger ad size has been shown to enhance both recall and recognition rates of printed advertisements (e.g. Lohse, 1997; Stapel, 1998). However, on cluttered web pages, ads are typically small and they compete with other ads for consumers' attention. Narayan, Obregon, Uppal and Sundar (1998) compared printed newspaper ads to the same online ad content, and showed that participants exposed to printed ads remembered significantly more ad material than participants exposed to the matching online version.

Other factors, such as frequency and duration of ad exposure, level of involvement, delay interval and the level of consumer expertise may also affect how well ads are memorized (Alba, Hutchinson, & Lynch, 1991). In addition, the advertisements are often irrelevant to consumers' information search or other tasks at hand. Pagendarm and Shaumburg (2001) proposed that casual browsers remembered banner ads better than goal-oriented searchers. Moreover, consumers' goal orientation (Cho & Cheon, 2004) and Internet expertise in information searching (Ylikoski, 2005) have been shown to affect perception, recognition and avoidance of ads. Based on mere exposure effect (Zajonc, 1968) and the two factor theory (Berlyne, 1970), Chatterjee (2004) hypothesized that recall and recognition of banners might be higher when consumers are not goal oriented compared with the situation when they are performing a specific task. His results suggested that repetition significantly improved memorizing of ads when participants were on a browsing orientation compared with goal orientation, and that the gains of repetition are higher when consumers are goal-oriented.

Fang, Singh and Ahluwalia (2007) suggested that regardless of low click-through rates, banner ads can still create favourable attitudes towards the ads due to repeated exposure. According to them, common wear-out effects were not apparent even after twenty exposures. Lee and Sundar (2002) observed a significant impact of banner advertising repetition on ad recall but not on ad recognition, and that ad clutter had a negative impact on ad recognition. Also, Dréze and Hussherr (2003) noticed that memory for online advertising increased with the frequency of exposures, and Yaveroglu and Donthu (2008) recently proposed that repetition leads to greater brand recall and intention to click banners. In sum, the previous research results on repetition in print and on the web, along with the findings considering consumers' goal orientation support the following hypothesis:

H1: Higher exposure frequency of online ads during a task performance improves ad recognition.

Ad Types and Recognition

This study examines the impact of two ad types, namely horizontal banners and vertical skyscrapers in both static and animated forms. By banners we refer to horizontal rectangular-shaped graphical elements at the top of web pages while skyscrapers are of similar form but vertically situated along the side of a Web page (see Burns & Lutz, 2006). The banners are embedded in the HTML documents as they are rendered on screen in a browser window. They often take the form of a banner occupying the top area of the screen but technically they may appear anywhere in the document. Supporting Benway and Lane's (1998) findings, Bernard (2001) suggests that consumers normally expect online advertisements to be centred at the top of a web page, and thus ignore them more often than banners located lower down on a page.

The term skyscraper describes an ad format whose height exceeds the width. These ads may also take the form of a floating picture layered on the primary page content. The contents of banners and skyscrapers are almost invariably graphics with or without animation, accompanied by a hyperlink to a website controlled by the advertiser. Although there is little research considering the effects of different ad types on recognition, Dréze and Hussherr (2003) reported a weak advantage for the vertical (skyscraper type) ads over the horizontal ones in the recognition scores. In our experiment, the vertical ads were located closer to the text area, and were therefore not as easily avoided as banners on the upper part of the page where ads are usually expected to be placed (see Benway & Lane, 1998; Bernard, 2001). Accordingly we postulate that:

H2: Vertical ad format (skyscraper) is recognized more accurately than horizontal (banner)

Animation has proven to be an especially divisive ad characteristic. Positive, neutral and even negative effects of animation have been reported. Bayles (2002) suggested that animation may have a slight positive impact on recognition of banners. Yoo and Kim (2006) proposed that a moderate amount of animation attracted attention and enhanced the recognition of banners significantly, but animation did not affect recall. Sundar and Kalayanaraman (2004) tested the effects of slow and fast banner animations on participants' arousal by measuring their skin conductance levels. Fast animations generated higher arousal levels than slow animations, but the higher rate of animation did not improve memory results, indicating that excessive animation may deteriorate recognition accuracy.

Other studies have suggested that animation does not increase visual attention capture when participants perform instructed search tasks (Burke et al., 2005; Diaper & Waeland, 2000; Dréze & Hussherr, 2003; Hong & al., 2004). Drèze and Hussherr (2003) did not find animated ads more effective than static ads. Burke et al. (2005) reported poor overall recognition of banners (with a hit rate of 20%). Rather surprisingly, in their study, the static banners were remembered more accurately than the animated banners. In sum, previous studies have provided contradictory results about the influence of animation on ad recognition. In addition, the results of recognition tests have typically been close to chance level. As discussed further in the following chapter, it is widely acknowledged that motion attracts consumers' gaze in visual search. Peripheral motion detection as an early warning system captures our attention and motion may disturb the task at hand (e.g. Duchowski, 2007; Nielsen, 2000). This distraction may also affect recognition accuracy and thus according to the findings by Bayles (2002) and Yoo and Kim (2006), we propose that:

H3: Animation enhances recognition accuracy of ads

Attention and Recognition

Traditional advertising hierarchy models, such as AIDA (Aaker et al., 1992), presume that attention is an antecedent of interest and information processing. Thus, attention is necessary before a detailed elaboration and memory encoding of an online ad is possible. Burke et al. (2005) proposed, however, that attention measured by eye fixations does not support this explanation. In their experiment, 94% of the correctly recognized banners were not looked at directly during the search tasks. It is possible that participants have deciphered ads by their peripheral vision and restored them in memory and it is logical to assume that ads receiving additional attention are easier to recognize. We examined the relationship between attention and recognition by using two different types of ads, both types appeared randomly in static or in animated forms on real-world Web pages. Our hypothesis proposes that:

H4: Attention in the form of higher number and longer duration of eye fixations enhances the recognition accuracy of ads.

METHODS

Variables and Their Measurement

In this study, we explored how repetition, ad type and attention to ads affect recognition of the ads in two controlled experiments where typical real-world web pages were used as stimuli. Figure 1 illustrates these variables and their relations to the hypotheses. The effect of repetition was measured by how well participants could recognize the ads after varying the number of ad exposures. The effect of ad type was studied by presenting the same content in four different formats: as horizontal and vertical formats that both appeared in animated and static forms. Moreover, we studied whether attention to ads affects the recognition accuracy of ads. Attention was measured by recording the frequency and duration of the participants' eye fixations to the ads.

Data Collection

The effects of repetition, ad format and attention were tested in two experiments in which the participants' task was to read on-line text passages. In the first, high-exposure experiment, each ad appeared four times during the reading tasks. During the second, low-exposure experiment, each ad was presented two times. In both experiments, the participants' eye movements were recorded and the participants were instructed to read 32 texts in order to be able to answer a multiple-choice question about the text content after reading each text. The website layout was adopted from the former home page of the teleoperator TeliaSonera's consumer portal (Figure 2). The participants were told that the experiment concerned reading texts on websites and nothing was mentioned about the ads. After participants had finished reading the texts we administered a recognition memory tests for the ads.

The recognition memory test was identical in the two experiments and comprised 16 ads that were presented during the reading tasks and 16

Figure 1. The independent and dependent variables and their operationalization along with the research hypotheses

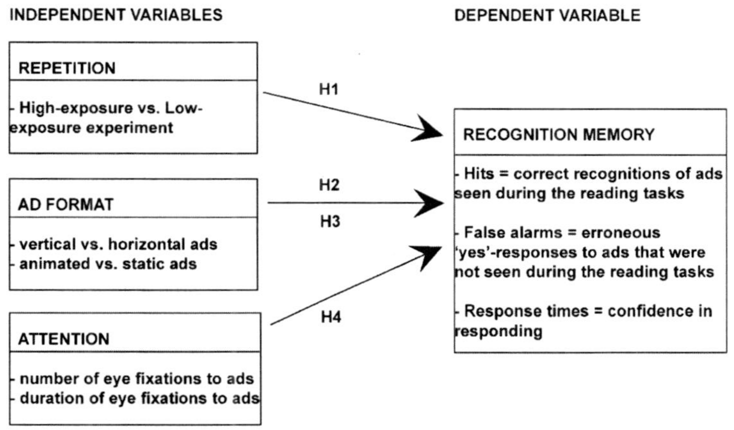

ads that were new to participants. The ads were presented one at a time in randomized order and participants answered "yes" or "no" depending on whether they had seen the ad earlier during the experiment.

To provide qualitative control for the influence of ad contents, we asked participants to recall ads after completing the reading tasks. They were asked to write down the names of advertised products and/or any visual components or other characteristics of the ads they could recall.

Apparatus

The presentation of web pages and ads in the recognition memory test was controlled with a Java servlet developed specifically for this project. The web pages were presented on a 17-inch TFT display located at the eye level of the participants at a distance of 60 cm. In both experiments, the participants' eye movements were recorded by a Tobii 1750 remote eye-tracking system with a spatial accuracy of 0.5 degrees and a sampling rate of 50 Hz. The system was calibrated individually for each participant before the experiment, and the screen coordinates of both eyes of the participants were recorded. In data preprocessing, the fixations and saccadic eye movements were extracted from the raw eye coordinates by an algorithm provided with the Tobii software. Samples landing on a fixation window of 40 pixels within 100 ms were classified as fixations. The stimulus pages were divided into three regions of interest (ROIs), comprising the areas of the horizontal ad, the vertical ad and the text (Figure 2). The eye fixations landing on the ad areas were further analyzed in relation to their frequency and duration.

High-Exposure Experiment

Participants

A convenience sample of thirty volunteers with a normal or corrected to normal vision was selected in the first experiment. The sample was balanced by gender and represented the average educated adult population in Finland within the age range of 19 to 49 years. Subjects received a lunch ticket as a reward for their participation.

Stimulus Material and Experimental Design

The stimuli consisted of 32 texts (each approximately 100 words) and of 16 various online ad topics, each presented four times during the ex-

Figure 2. An example of a web page used in both experiments. The text area is in the middle surrounded by vertical and horizontal menus and ads. The vertical (skyscraper) ad was presented on the right side of the text and the horizontal (banner) ad was located at the top of the page

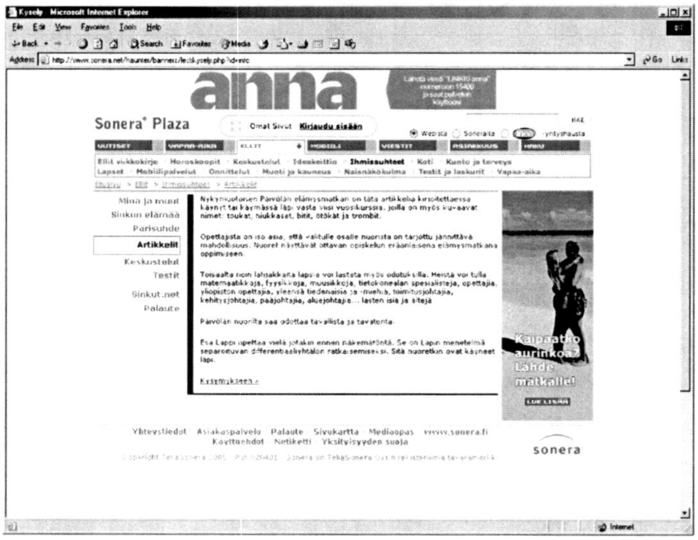

periment. The ads had previously been used on TeliaSonera's website. To control the effect of various ad contents, four versions of each ad were professionally designed in horizontal and vertical formats in both static and animated forms.

In the first experiment, both horizontal and vertical ads were simultaneously presented on the stimulus websites (Figure 2). The horizontal ad was located on top of the web page and a vertical ad was placed on the right side of the page beside the text area. To measure the effects of ad format (the effects of animation and horizontal or vertical format), the experimental design comprised four conditions that appeared in random order including randomly selected combinations of texts and ads. The following conditions were used:

1) Both ads were static
2) The horizontal ad was static and the vertical ad was animated
3) The horizontal ad was animated and the vertical ad was static
4) Both ads were animated

For statistical analyses, the fixations to ads were collapsed so that the fixations to the vertical ads in conditions 1 and 3 (where the vertical ad was static) were averaged together, and the fixations to the vertical ads in conditions 2 and 4 (where the vertical ad was animated) were averaged together. The same procedure was also applied to fixations to horizontal ads.

Low-Exposure Experiment

Participants

Thirty-two new volunteers, who were not aware of the purpose of the study, were selected for the second experiment. They also had normal or corrected to normal vision. The sample was within the age range of 18 to 53 years, balanced by gender and representing the average Finnish population. Participants in both experiments gave their informed consents before the experiments started and were rewarded with a lunch ticket.

Stimulus Material and Experimental Design

The same ads and text stimuli used in the first experiment were also utilized in the second experiment. In order to test the effect of repetition, we reduced the number of ad exposures by half (2 exposures per ad) compared with the first experiment. A condition in which no ads were presented was added to obtain the reduced number of ads and to keep the test duration comparable to the first experiment. The condition 2 from the first experiment was kept unchanged, but from the two remaining conditions the ads were removed so that only one animated horizontal and one animated vertical ad was presented at a time. Therefore, the vertical ad did not appear in static form in the second experiment.

Data Analysis

We began the data analyses by examining the participants' performance in the recognition memory tests between the high- and low-exposure experiments. Participants responded "yes" or "no" to each ad presented in the recognition memory tests. "Yes" responses to ads that were presented during the reading task were scored as "hits", whereas "false alarms" were erroneous "yes" responses to new ads that were not presented during the reading task. Hit and false alarm scores were analyzed with a 2 (Repetition: recognition of ads after high-exposure vs. low-exposure experiments) x 2 (Format: horizontal vs. vertical) x 2 (Animation: animated vs. static) mixed ANOVA, with repetition as a between subjects variable. In order to test participants' confidence in their responses, we analyzed the response times in the recognition memory test.

In order to analyze the relation between attention and recognition of ads, we calculated bivariate correlations between the recognition memory results and number of fixations along with their durations.

RESULTS

The Recognition Memory Scores

The recognition memory results across the experiments and ad formats are shown in Table 1. The analysis showed that ads were recognized better after the high-exposure than the low-exposure experiment, as indicated by a significant main effect of Repetition [$F(1,60) = 5.32$, $p = .025$, $\eta_p^2 = .081$] on hit scores. Thus increased number of exposures improved recognition as proposed in H1.

There was no effect of ad format on hit scores, and the assumption in H2 that vertical ads would be better recognized was not supported. Instead, the results showed that animated ads were recognized more accurately than the static ones [$F(1,60) = 4.48$, $p = .038$, $\eta_p^2 = .069$], and therefore the H3 proposing that animation enhances recognition accuracy of ads was supported.

The observed main effects of repetition and animation were mediated by an animation x repetition interaction [$F(1,60) = 5.76$, $p = .020$, $\eta_p^2 = .088$]. To investigate this interaction further, independent samples t-tests were performed for animated and static ads between the High-and Low-exposure experiments. The results suggested that repetition also significantly improved the recognition for static ads [$t(60) = 3.34$, $p = .002$, $d = 0.86$], giving further support for H1.

There was no effect of repetition or format on the false alarm rates. However, the false alarms showed a significant main effect of animation [$F(1,60) = 9.64$, $p = .003$, $\eta_p^2 = .138$], indicating less false alarms for animated than for static ads, supporting H3.

The Response Times in Recognition Memory Test

In addition, we analyzed the response times in recognition memory tests. We assumed that shorter response times would reflect more confidence,

Table 1. Mean ± SD hit and false alarm rates and mean response times for each ad type across the experiments

Ad type	Horizontal		Vertical	
	Animated	Static	Animated	Static
High-exposure experiment				
Hit rate (%)	50.00 ± 34.74	45.00 ± 31.76	40.83 ± 35.04	47.50 ± 33.70
False alarm rate (%)	9.17 ± 16.72	11.67 ± 19.40	10.00 ± 15.54	20.83 ± 19.79
Response time (ms)	6714.38 ± 2691.53	6412.57 ± 2510.58	6213.70 ± 2912.49	5662.80 ± 2014.45
Low-exposure experiment				
Hit rate (%)	34.38 ± 27.50	22.66 ± 23.21	42.19 ± 32.60	27.34 ± 24.06
False alarm rate (%)	5.47 ± 10.50	8.59 ± 18.64	7.03 ± 13.07	10.94 ± 16.72
Response time (ms)	7025.24 ± 2293.23	6834.08 ± 2510.58	6553.42 ± 2151.66	6420.36 ± 2474.81

whereas longer response times would reflect uncertainty about the responses. Repetition or animation of ads did not affect the response times. However, the participants were more confident about their responses to vertical than to horizontal ads [$F(1,60) = 10.55$, $p = .002$, $\eta_p^2 = .150$].

The Effect of Attention on Recognition of the Ads

The results indicated a strong positive correlation between attention and recognition memory. The number of fixations to ads correlated with the hit scores ($r = .48$, $p = .000$) and also the fixation durations were positively correlated with the hits ($r = .52$, $p = .000$). Thus, the assumption in H4 about the relationship between attention and recognition was supported. Separate analyses for ad formats were subsequently conducted and the results are summarized in Table 2. Overall, the effect of attention on recognition did not seem to vary much between ad formats. Instead, attention was correlated with recognition in all except vertical static ad format.

Qualitative Free Recall Results

The results of spontaneous recall also indicated a positive effect of repetition on memory. After the high-exposure experiment, participants could recall around 3 ad contents, whereas after the low-exposure experiment they recalled only 1.7 ad contents on average. Moreover, the accuracy of the participants in describing ad contents or product attributes decreased in a similar manner from the high-exposure experiment to the low-exposure experiment.

FUTURE TRENDS

The goal of pervasive computing is to enable access to services anytime, anywhere, and on any device (Wei-Tsung, Yau-Hwang, & Steinmetz, R. 2008). This goal can be reached through increased adaptation to the relevant consumption context. Conventionally, adaptation has been defined as awareness of the time, place, and device of access. There is, however, more to adaptation to consumption context than identifying the spatial and temporal whereabouts of the user. More re-

Table 2. Bivariate correlation coefficients (Pearson's r) between the number of fixations and fixation durations for hit rates in each ad format across the experiments (N = 60)

Hit rate	Horizontal		Vertical	
	Animated	Static	Animated	Static
Number of fixations	0.36 (p = .005)**	0.30 (p = .020)*	0.46 (p = .000)***	0.19 (p = .344)
Fixation durations	0.36 (p = .005)**	0.32 (p = .012)*	0.49 (p = .000)***	0.40 (p = .037)*

fined sensing often requires communication with the user at some level. This need for communication is typically time constrained and requires that the attention of the user is captured to some extent. Technologies based on urban sensing and data commons, for example, promise to leverage social interaction such as citizen participation in politics, civics, aesthetics, and science. These promising avenues almost invariably call for embedded decision support systems (Burstein and Holsapple, 2008), which are difficult to fathom to work without extensive user interaction. The better we get at sensing the whereabouts of pervasive computing, the more attention we can afford to spend on investigating the mental scenery of such consumption. We have only scratched the surface when it comes to understanding the human sensorial and perception mechanisms and memory in the context of a variety of pervasive computing applications and environments.

The smaller the devices and displays become, the more attentional resources and new techniques are required to speed information search and to decrease cognitive load. The omnidirectional attention funnel, which directs users' attention with strong bottom-up spatial attention cues to a target object, is an example of using augmented reality techniques for navigation in real environments (Biocca, Owen, Tang, & Bohil, 2007). The authors compared the attention funnel to highlighting and audio cueing techniques and noticed that search speed increased by 50% with this technique and perceived cognitive load decreased by 18%.

Eye tracking is still technically complicated in 3D environments but our results may contribute urther study on applications, such as, mobile computing, electronic books and virtual agents. Although agents can find and filter information and help users to complete various tasks on their behalf, they are not as widely used by consumers as one might expect. Perhaps the agents are not considered emotionally attractive or intelligent enough to aid the online consumer on cluttered web sites or mobile devices. Measuring attention by eye tracking can augment and explain the usability issues of agents as well as that of interfaces in general.

In this study we utilized eye-tracking methodology to measure the level and quality of attention to online ads. Interactive eye tracking or eye-based interaction provides innovative opportunities for pervasive computing applications that also handicapped people can use. These include eye typing, eye drawing, attentive user interfaces, and usability. Eye trackers can be installed in computers, mobiles, videoconference cameras and related devices (Duchowski, 2007). As interfaces can trace and learn from users' eye movements, the usability and intelligence of pervasive computing applications may more effortlessly benefit both handicapped and normal users.

Emerging trend in computer science and advertising research is to utilize other psychophysical methods and measures, such as, functional MRI, EEG, facial expressions and skin conduct levels simultaneously with eye movements recording. This assists to measure not only attention but also emotional responses to physical stimuli perceived.

Moreover, natural events and objects are usually multisensory and effective pervasive computing applications may benefit from multisensory processing as it shortens reaction time and signal detectability (Mather, G., 2009).

CONCLUSION

The purpose of this study was to examine the impacts of repetition, online ad type and attention on recognition of ads in a real-world web environment. We studied the impacts of repetition on recognition memory with two experiments by varying the number of ad exposures. Our results show that recognition of ads was significantly higher when the frequency of exposure of each ad was doubled from two up to four exposures. Both animated and static ads were more accurately recognized when the number of exposures was higher. In the high-exposure experiment the overall hit rate was 45.83% being 31.65% in the low-exposure experiment. The spontaneous recall results showed a similar trend with recognition. On average, the participants recalled 3 ads after the higher-exposure experiment and respectively only 1.7 after the lower-exposure experiment. Our results were contrary to Lee and Sundar (2002) who found no effects of ad repetition on recognition. Moreover, the average hit rates in our study were higher than reported in earlier studies (Bayles, 2002; Burke et al., 2005) probably due to the number of exposures to ads and the different type of task that the participants were instructed to accomplish.

Earlier findings about the effect of animation on memory are divisive, and some studies have suggested that animation has no effect on memory (Burke et al., 2005; Dréze & Husshern, 2003). In contrast, we found that both horizontal and vertical animated ads were more accurately recognized than static forms of the same ads, supporting the findings of Yoo and Kim (2006) and Burns and Lutz (2006). However, the effect of animation interacted with repetition, suggesting that static ads were more accurately recognized after Higher-exposure experiment than after the low-exposure experiment. Although, we did not observe any difference in recognition between horizontal and vertical ads, we found that the response times for vertical ads were significantly shorter than for horizontal ads. This may indicate that the participants felt more confident when responding to vertical ads than to horizontal ads. Repetition had no significant effect on response times.

To measure the participants' attention to ads we recorded their eye movements during the reading tasks and analyzed the number and duration of their eye fixations to ads. The effect of attention on memory for ads was studied by correlating the number and duration of fixations with recognition memory scores. Contrary to the results by Burke et al. (2005) we found a positive correlation between eye fixations and recognition, suggesting that increased attention to ads enhanced the recognition accuracy of ads. This result is in line with the standard hierarchy of effects models.

The results support the prevailing assumption that repetition is an important factor for advertising effectiveness also in online environment. However, advertisers may have to increase the frequency of exposure in online media more than in conventional media, such as TV and print to receive desired effectiveness. More repetition is required because the number of competing stimuli is higher and the ad sizes are typically smaller on the web. Moreover, browsers probably are exposed less frequently to the same ads on the web compared with conventional media. Drèze and Hussher (2003) have reported that a browser's probability of seeing a banner ad on a website is approximately 50% while in TV and print, the respective probabilities are over 90% (Lohse, 1997; Siddarth, 2002). Also the wear-out effect of ads may be prolonged online. Fang et al. (2007) found no wear-out effects after 22 exposures of online ads. This may indicate that online audiences do not get bored quickly with ads or that it is difficult to attract attention with only a few exposures. Still, there is a risk that repetition of irrelevant ads may cause boredom or even irritation among consumers especially when they are completing a task. Previous studies have suggested that the nature of the participants' task affects the frequency of correctly recognize ads, and that goal-oriented participants could recognize less ads that those who were only surfing on Web pages (Chatterjee, 2004; Pagendarm & Schaumburg, 2001). In our study, the repetition effects were examined when the participants were reading texts. In free browsing situation probably fewer repetitions can yield similar recognition results as higher repetition frequency in task-oriented viewing situations.

Several studies indicate that ads attract little attention, and that consumers are banner blind (Benway & Lane, 1998; Pagendarm & Schaumburg, 2001; Bernard, 2001), avoid ads (Cho & Cheon, 2004; Stenfors et al., 2003) and experience online ads as intrusive (McCoy, Everard, Polak, & Galletta, 2007). According to our findings when attention is paid to ads, it affects their recognition. It is obvious that advertisers also try to attract consumer's attention with salient ad contents and formats.

Although animation and repetition seem to increase advertising effectiveness to a certain extent, excessive repetition and animation may even have negative effects if consumers become bored or even irritated by online ads. Our study did not find differences between horizontal and vertical ads in recognition, but for the advertisers it may still be worthwhile to vary ad types in order to restrain boredom and other negative effects of excessive repetition. The optimal frequency of the exposure and recognition accuracy of ads depends also on the amount of clutter on a Web page (Lee & Sundar, 2002). Hence, visually strongly salient ad types, such as pop-ups, which by compulsion attract attention, need to be studied further.

Our study stems from online advertising and two obvious limitations have to be considered before generalizing the results to other pervasive computing situations. First, online ads are seldom target objects but rather irrelevant distracters when the users' intention is to search for a specific piece of information or a service. Second, the Internet sites employed were two dimensional and only visual and textual stimuli without voice or video impulse were utilized. Thus, our results on the effects of animation, repetition, ad type and attention on recognition memory should be tested in 3D virtual and augmented reality environments in order to study how visual and spatial perception processes evolve and are applied by users.

REFERENCES

Aaker, D. A., Batra, R., & Myers, J. G. (1992). *Advertising management*. Englewood Cliffs, NJ: Prentice Hall.

Alba, J. W., Hutchinson, J. W., & Lynch, J. G. (1991). Memory and decision making. In T. Robertson & H. Kassarjian (Eds.), *Handbook of consumer behavior* (pp. 1-50). Engelwood Cliffs, NJ: Prentice-Hall.

Bayles, M. E. (2002). *Designing online banner advertisements: Should we animate?* Paper presented at the CHI 2002 Conference, Minneapolis, Minnesota, USA.

Benway, J. P., & Lane, D. M. (1998) Banner Blindness: Web Searches Often Miss "Obvious" Links.

Berlyne, D. (1970). Novelty, complexity and hedonic value. *Perception & Psychophysics*, *8*, 279–286.

Bernard, M. L. (2001). *Developing schemas for the location of common web objects.* Paper presented at the Human Factors and Ergonomics Society 45th Annual Meeting, Minneapolis, Minnesota.

Biocca, F., Owen, C., Tang, A., & Bohil, C. (2007). Attention issues in spatial information systems: Directing mobile user's visual attention using augmented reality. *Journal of Management Information Systems, 23*(4), 163–184. doi:10.2753/MIS0742-1222230408

Burke, M., Hornof, A., Nilsen, E., & Gorman, N. (2005). High-cost banner blindness: Ads increase perceived workload, hinder visual search, and are forgotten. *Transactions on Computer-Human Interaction, 12*(4), 423–445. doi:10.1145/1121112.1121116

Burns, K. S., & Lutz, R. J. (2006). The function of format consumer responses to six on-line advertising formats. *Journal of Advertising, 35*(1), 53–63. doi:10.2753/JOA0091-3367350104

Burstein, F. and C. W. Holsapple (2008). New horizons at the core of information systems: decision support system advances. *Information Systems and eBusiness Management, 6*(2), 109.

Cacioppo, J. T., & Petty, R. E. (1979). Effects of message repetition and position on cognitive responses, recall, and persuasion. *Journal of Personality and Social Psychology, 37*, 97–109. doi:10.1037/0022-3514.37.1.97

Campbell, M. C., & Keller, K. L. (2003). Brand familiarity and advertising repetition effects. *The Journal of Consumer Research, 30*, 292–304. doi:10.1086/376800

Chatterjee, P. (2004, October). *Changing Banner Ad Executions on the Web: Impact on Click-throughs and Communication Outcomes*. Paper presented at Association for Consumer

Cho, C.-H., & Cheon, J. H. (2004). Why do people avoid advertising on the internet? *Journal of Advertising, 33*(4), 89–97.

Diaper, D., & Waeland, P. (2000). World wide web working whilst ignoring graphics: Good new for web page designer. *Interacting with Computers, 13*, 163–181. doi:10.1016/S0953-5438(00)00036-9

Dréze, X., & Hussherr, F.-X. (2003). Internet advertising: Is anybody watching? *Journal of Interactive Marketing, 17*(4), 8–23. doi:10.1002/dir.10063

Duchowski, A. T. (2007) *Eye Tracking Methodology: Theory and Practise,* London: Springer Verlag

Fang, X., Singh, S., & Ahluwalia, R. (2007). An examination of different explanations for the mere exposure effect. *The Journal of Consumer Research, 34*(1), 97–103. doi:10.1086/513050

Hong, W., Thong, J. Y. L., & Tam, K. Y. (2004). Does animation attract online users' attention? The effects of flash on information search performance and perceptions. *Information Systems Research, 15*(1), 60–86. doi:10.1287/isre.1040.0017

Internetworking (December1998: 1.3), ITG Newsletter. Retrieved March 27, 2009 from http://www.intertg.org/newsletter/dec98/banner blindness.html

Krugman, H. E. (1972). Why three exposures may be enough. *Journal of Advertising Research, 12*(6), 11–14.

Lee, S. Y., & Sundar, S. S. (2002). *Psychological effects of frequency and clutter in web advertising.* Paper presented at the 52nd annual conference of the International Communication Association (ICA), Seoul, South Korea.

Lohse, G. L. (1997). Consumer eye movement patterns on yellow pages advertising. *Journal of Advertising, 26*(1), 61–73.

Malaviya, P. (2007). The moderating influence of advertising context on ad repetition effects: The role of amount and type of elaboration. *The Journal of Consumer Research, 34*(1), 32–40. doi:10.1086/513044

Mather, G. (2009). *Foundations of Sensation and Perception.* New York: Taylor & Francis Group

McCoy, S., Everard, A., Polak, P., & Galletta, D. F. (2007). The effects of online advertising. *Communications of the ACM, 50*(3), 84–88. doi:10.1145/1226736.1226740

Narayan, S., Obregon, R., Uppal, C., & Sundar, S. S. (1998). Does web advertising work? Memory for print vs. Online media. *Journalism & Mass Communication Quarterly, 75*(4), 822–835.

Nielsen, J. (2000). *Designing Web Usability.* New Riders Publishing

Pagendarm, M., & Schaumburg, H. (2001). Why are users banner-blind? The impact of navigation style on perception of web banners. *Journal of Digital Information, 2*(1). Retrieved March 30, 2009 from http//jodi.tamu.edu/Articles/v02/01/Pagendarm/

Pieters, F. G. M., & Wedel, M. (2004). Attention capture and transfer by elements of advertisements. *Journal of Marketing, 68*(2), 36–50. doi:10.1509/jmkg.68.2.36.27794

PriceWaterhouseCoopers. (2008). *Internet advertising revenues 2007.* Retrieved May 6, 2008 from http://www.workboxers.com/2008/02/27/record-internet-advertising-revenues-in-2007/

Radach, R., Lemmer, S., Vorstius, C., Heller, D., & Radach, K. (2003). Eye movements in the processing of print advertisements. In J. Hyönä, R. Radach & H. Deubel (Eds.), *The mind's eye: Cognitive and applied aspects of eye movement research* (pp. 609-632). Amsterdam, The Netherlands: Elsevier.

Ravaja, N., Kallinen, K., Saari, T., & Keltikangas-Järvinen, L. (2004). Suboptimal exposure to facial expressions when viewing video messages from a small screen: Effects on emotion, attention and memory. *Journal of Experimental Psychology. Applied, 10*(2), 120–131. doi:10.1037/1076-898X.10.2.120

Rayner, K., Rotello, C. M., Stewart, A. J., Keir, J., & Duffy, S. A. (2001). Integrating text and pictorial information: Eye movements when looking at print advertisements. *Journal of Experimental Psychology. Applied, 7*(3), 219–226. doi:10.1037/1076-898X.7.3.219

Research 2004 Conference, Portland, Oregon.

Siddarth, S. (2002). *Describing the dynamics of attention to TV commercials: A proportional hazards model of the time to zap and ad.* Los Angeles: CA: University of Southern California.

Stapel, J. (1998). Recall and recognition: A very close relationship. *Journal of Advertising Research, 38*(4), 41–45.

Stenfors, I., Morén, J., & Balkenius, C. (2003). Behavioural strategies in web interaction: A view from eye-movement research. In J. Hyönä, R. Radach & H. Deubel (Eds.), *The mind's eye: Cognitive and applied aspects of eye movement research* (pp. 633-644). Amsterdam, The Netherlands: Elsevier.

Sundar, S. S., & Kalyanaraman, S. (2004). Arousal, memory, and impression-formation effects of animation speed in web advertising. *Journal of Advertising, 33*(1), 7–17.

Wedel, M., & Pieters, F. G. M. (2000). Eye fixations on advertisements and memory for brands: A model and findings. *Marketing Science, 19*(4), 297–312. doi:10.1287/mksc.19.4.297.11794

Wei-Tsung, S., Yau-Hwang, K., & Po-Cheng, H. (2008). A QoS-driven approach for service-oriented device anycasting in ubiquitous environments. *Computer Networks*, *52*(18), 3342–3357. doi:10.1016/j.comnet.2008.09.001

Yaveroglu, I., & Donthu, N. (2008). Advertising repetition and placement issues in on-line environments. *Journal of Advertising*, *37*(2), 32–43. doi:10.2753/JOA0091-3367370203

Ylikoski, T. (2005). A sequence analysis of consumers' online searches. *Internet Research*, *15*(2), 181–194. doi:10.1108/10662240510590351

Yoo, C. Y., & Kim, K. (2006). Processing of animation in online banner advertising: The roles of cognitive and emotional responses. *Journal of Interactive Marketing*, *19*(4), 18–34. doi:10.1002/dir.20047

Zajonc, R. B. (1968). Attitudinal affects on mere exposure. *Journal of Personality and Social Psychology Monograph*, *9*(Supplement), 1–27. doi:10.1037/h0025848

ADDITIONAL READING

Castelli, G., Mamei, M., Rosi, A., & Zambonelli, F. (2009). Extracting High-Level Information from Location Data: The W4 Diary Example. *Mobile Networks and Applications*, *14*(1), 107–119. doi:10.1007/s11036-008-0104-y

Cuff, D., Hansen, M., & Kang, J. (2008). Urban Sensing: Out of the Woods. *Association for Computing Machinery. Communications of the ACM*, *51*(3), 24. doi:10.1145/1325555.1325562

Diesbach, P., & Midgley, D. (2008). Embodied Agents on Commercial Websites: Modeling Their Effects through an Affective Persuasion Route. In H. Oinas-Kukkonen, P. Hasle, M. Harjumaa, K. Segerståhl & P. Øhstrøm (Eds.), *Proceedings of Third International Conference on Persuasive Technology,* June 2008, Oulu, Finland (pp. 283-286), Berlin, Springer-Verlag.

Girelli, M., & Luck, S. J. (1997). Are the same attentional mechanisms used to detect visual search targets defined by colour, orientation and motion? *Cognitive Neuroscience*, *9*(2), 238–253. doi:10.1162/jocn.1997.9.2.238

Heath, R., & Nairn, A. (2008). How Creativity of Advertising Influences Consumer Behaviour. In Proceedings of the Conference on Neuroeconomics, Copenhagen Business School., May 15 -16, Denmark.

Henderson, J. M., & Hollingworth, A. (1999). High-level scene perception. *Annual Review of Psychology*, *50*, 243–271. doi:10.1146/annurev.psych.50.1.243

Horrey, W. J., Wickens, C. D., & Consalus, K. P. (2006). Modeling Driver's Visual Attention Allocation while Interacting with In-Vechile technologies. *Journal of Experimental Psychology. Applied*, *12*(2), 67–78. doi:10.1037/1076-898X.12.2.67

Hyönä, J., Munoz, D., Heide, W., & Radach, R. (Eds.). (2002*) The brain's eye: Neurobiological and clinical aspects of oculomotor research.* Amsterdam: Elsevier Science

Janiszewski, C., Hayden, N., & Sawyer, A. G. (2003). Meta-analysis of the Spacing Effect in Verbal Learning: Implications for Research on Advertising Repetition and Consumer Memory. *The Journal of Consumer Research*, *30*, 138–149. doi:10.1086/374692

Krugman, E. P. (2008). *Consumer Behavior and Advertising Involvement: Selected Works of Herbert Krugman.* New York: Routledge, Taylor & Francis Group.

McDougall, S., & Tyrer, V. (2006). Searching for Signs, Symbols and Icons: Effects of Time of Day, Visual Complexity, and Grouping. *Journal of Experimental Psychology. Applied*, *12*(2), 118–128. doi:10.1037/1076-898X.12.2.118

Movements, E. Evidence from Static and Dynamic Scene Perception. In *Proceedings of the XXVII Conference of the Cognitive Science Society, July 21 - 23, Stresa, Italy* (pp. 2283-2288).

Pashler, H. (Ed., 2004). *Attention.* Hove, East Sussex, UK: Psychology Press

Pieters, R., & Wedel, M. (2008). Informativeness of Eye Movements for Visual Marketing: Six Cornerstones. In M. Wedel, & R. Pieters (Eds.), *Visual Marketing. From Attention to Action* (pp. 43-73). New York: Lawrence Erlbaum Associates, Taylor & Francis Group.

Rosenthal, R., & Rosnow, R. (2008). *Essentials of Behavioural Research: Methods and Data Analysis.* New York: McGraw-Hill

Rye, G., Lim, E. A. C., Tan, L. T. L., & Han, Y. J. (2006). Preattentive processing of banner advertisements: The role of modality, location and interference. *Electronic Commerce Research and Applications*. Elsevier

Schmitt, J., Hollick, M., Roos, C., & Steinmetz, R. (2008). Adapting the User Context in Realtime: Tailoring Online Machine Learning Algorithms to Ambient Computing. *Mobile Networks and Applications, 13*(6), 583. doi:10.1007/s11036-008-0095-8

Shen, L., Callaghan, V., & Shen, R. (2008). Affective e-Learning in residential and pervasive computing environments. *Information Systems Frontiers, 10*(4), 461. doi:10.1007/s10796-008-9104-5

Simons, D. J., & Chabris, C. F. (1999). Gorillas in our midst: sustained inattentional blindness for dynamic events. *Perception, 28*, 1059–1074. doi:10.1068/p2952

Tavassoli, N. T. (2008). The Effects of Selection and Ignoring on Liking. In Wedel, M., Pieters R. (Eds.), *Visual Marketing. From Attention to Action* (pp. 9-43). New York: Lawrence Erlbaum Associates, Taylor & Francis Group.

Velichkovsky B.M., Helmert J. M., & Pannasch, S. (2005). Two Visual Systems and their

Vidnyánski, Z., & Sohn, W. (2004). Learning to suppress task-irrelevant visual stimuli with attention. *Vision Research, 45*, 677–685. doi:10.1016/j.visres.2004.10.009

KEY TERMS AND DEFINITIONS

Ad Types: Online advertisement formats such as banners, skyscrapers, pop-ups located or popping-up on various pages on the Internet sites.

Animation: The essence of animation is motion which is effective in attracting visual attention

Attention Funnel: Augmented reality interface technique to direct users' visual attention to target with bottom-up spatial attention cues

Attention: A state of focused awareness on a subset of the available perceptual information.

Between-Subjects Design: A research design in which different groups of participants are randomly assigned to experimental conditions.

Bottom-Up Processing: Perceptual analyses based on the sensory data available in environment.

Eye Movements: Fixation and saccades are the most common eye movement metrics to evaluate the quantity and spatial locations of visual attention, and also cognitive load during visual search tasks.

Gaze Controlled Interfaces: Interfaces users' can control by their visual gaze, based on inbuilt eye tracking devices.

Recall: A method of retrieval in which an individual is required to reproduce the information previously presented.

Recognition (Memory): A method of retrieval in which an individual is required to identify stimuli as having been experienced before.

Chapter 3
The Feature Extraction Algorithm for the Production of Emotions in Text-to-Speech (TTS) System for an Indian Regional Language

Jagadish S Kallimani
M S Ramaiah Institute of Technology, India

V K Ananthashayana
M S Ramaiah Institute of Technology, India

Debjani Goswami
IBM Technologies, India

ABSTRACT

Text-to-speech synthesis is a complex combination of language processing, signal processing and computer science. Ubiquitous computing (ubicomp) is a post-desktop model of human-computer interaction in which information processing has been thoroughly integrated into everyday objects and activities. Speech synthesis is the generation of synthesized speech from text. This chapter deals with the development of a Text to Speech (TTS) Synthesis system for an Indian regional language by considering Bengali as the language. This chapter highlights various methods which may be used for speech synthesis and also it provides an overview on the problems and difficulties in Bengali text to speech conversion. Variations in the prosody (speech parameters – volume, pitch, intonation, amplitude) of the speech yields the emotional aspects (anger, happy, normal), which are applied to our developed TTS system.

INTRODUCTION

Speech Synthesis is the process of converting input data into spoken language. The goal of a Text to Speech synthesis system is to convert any computer readable text into a human sounding synthetic speech. A text-to-speech system is composed of two parts: a front-end and a back-end. The front-end has two major tasks. First, it converts raw text contain-

DOI: 10.4018/978-1-60566-996-0.ch003

Figure 1. Block diagram of text-to-speech synthesis

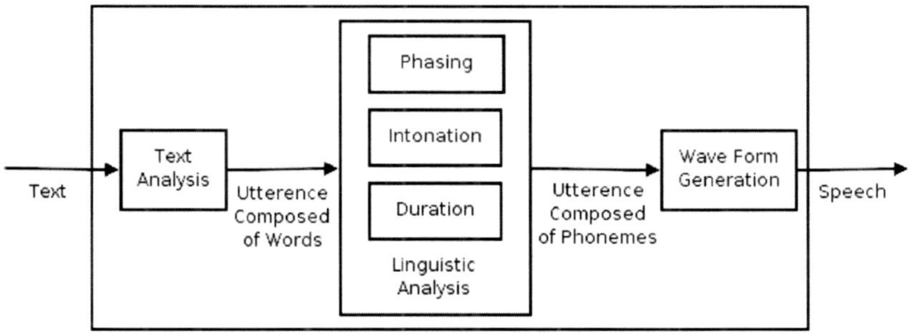

ing symbols like numbers and abbreviations into the equivalent written-out words. This process is called text normalization, pre-processing, or tokenization. The front-end then assigns phonetic transcriptions to each word, and divides and marks the text into prosodic units, like phrases, clauses, and sentences. The process of assigning phonetic transcriptions to words is called text-to-phoneme or grapheme-to-phoneme conversion. Phonetic transcriptions and prosody information together make up the symbolic linguistic representation into an audible sound. The back-end often referred to as the synthesizer—then converts the symbolic linguistic representation into an audible sound. Diagrammatically a typical TTS system can be represented as in Figure 1.

There are several approaches which may be used for the development of TTS. They are concatenate Synthesis, Formant synthesis and Pre-recorded Synthesis systems. In Concatenate synthesis, the text is phonetically represented by the combination of its syllables. These syllables are concatenated at run time and they produce phonetic representation of text. Here, the vocabulary is unlimited and voice quality is good, but cannot produce multiple featured voices and also needs large storage space. Formant synthesis is based on manipulating formants. Formants are the distinguishable frequency components of human speech. Here the voice is generated by simulation of the behavior of human vocal cord, vocabulary is unlimited, storage space is low and can produce multiple featured voices but the voice is robotic, which is not appreciable by the users. In pre-recorded, a database of pre recorded words is maintained. The voice quality obtained here is good but the vocabulary is limited and demands large storage. The Concatenative synthesis may follow several methodologies (Epoch Synchronous Non-Overlapping Add (ES-NOLA) Approach Concatenative Text to Speech Synthesis - A Technical Report, 2005). They are Time Domain Pitch Synchronous OverLap Add (TDPSOLA), Pitch Synchronous Overlap Add (PSOLA), Multi-Band Re-synthesis OverLap Add (MBROLA), and Epoch Synchronous Non Overlapping Add (ESNOLA).

The remaining chapter is arranged as follows: Section 2 presents a brief background on available TTS systems for various languages. The method follows, complexities involved in Bengali TTS system, steps and algorithm adopted are available in Section 3. The procedure for recording the speech and interface developed are also discussed here. Prosodic analysis is discussed in section 4. Conclusion and future works are suggested in Section 5.

BACKGROUND

In the recent years, several works has been carried out in the field of Text to Speech synthesis. The history of speech synthesis dates back to 1939, when Dudley at the Bell Laboratories performed a research work on text to speech synthesis. Other related works was carried out by: Cooper's Pattern Playback in 1951, Fant's OVE in 1953, Lawrence's PAT in 1953, Rosen's DAVO in 1958 and the first full text-to-speech system for English was developed in the Electro technical Laboratory, Japan 1968 by Noriko Umeda. Considerable amount of work has been done in the Text to Speech conversion for languages like English, Japanese, German, Chinese, Russian, French, Spanish, Dutch, Arabic and Portuguese. Of late, lot of work has been done in the field of TTS for Indian Regional Languages. But the complexity associated with Regional languages did not make it much popular. There have been several attempts in the past, where different attempts of Bengali TTS were considered. Recently, *Centre for Development of Advanced Computing* (CDAC) Kolkata, India has produced a user friendly TTS for Bengali using the ESNOLA technique, which is claimed to have high precision and naturalness of phonetic quality. Technology Development for Indian Languages (TDIL) has provided relevant information in January 2005 issue (http://tdil.mit.gov.in/Jan_issue%202005/19-cdac%20kolkata.pdf). A Bengali TTS using Epoch Synchronization and Overlap Add (ESOLA) methodology is discussed in (Sarkar T 2005). An attempt is made to develop a TTS, which takes as input, two Indian languages, Bengali and Hindi. This TTS is also ported on two handheld devices, i.e., iPaq from Compaq and Cassiopia from Casio, both of which run on Microsoft Pocket PC (Mandal S K D, 2002). In (Shyamal Kr, 2002), a TTS was designed to overcome the literacy barrier of the common people. It also aimed at empowering the visually impaired population. The TTS used ENSOLA technique to concatenate basic sound units to produce synthetic speech.

METHODOLOGY

The Method

The synthesis of text to speech consists of several stages like Text normalization, Homograph disambiguation, Word to phoneme conversion, Prosody and Waveform synthesis (Mukhopadhya A, 2005) (see Figure 2).

Bengali TTS

In the text normalization phase, the text entered is converted into a group of spoken words. The next stage is homograph disambiguation. "Homographs" are words with similar spelling but different pronunciation. In Bengali, there are no such words. Each word has a unique rule of pronunciation. In the next stage, i.e. word to phoneme conversion, each word is broken down till the lowest phoneme level is obtained. An example is shown in Figure 3. The prosodic analysis module

Figure 2. Stages of text to speech conversion

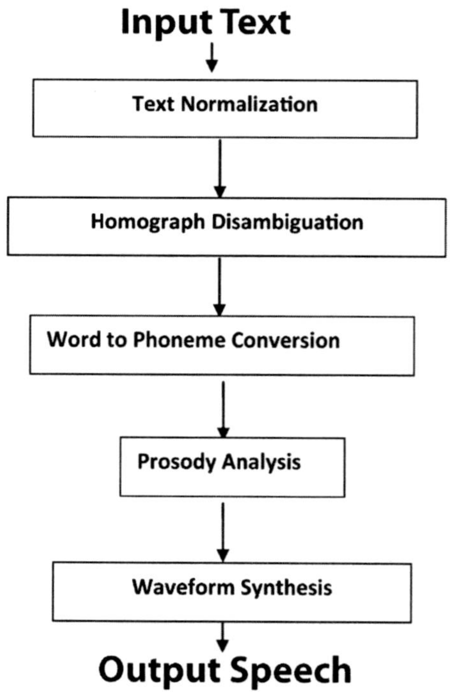

Figure 3.

জীবন

(jybn) is broken down into

জ (j) + ী (y) + ব (b) + ন (n)

then takes the phoneme sequence and assigns to each phoneme the required pitch and duration. The next step waveform generation takes place using the recorded phoneme database. Each of the lowest level of phoneme is mapped with its corresponding wave file. The flowchart showing the sequence in which the Bengali TTS works is shown in Figure 4.

The Algorithm

Bengali Orthography

Bengali orthography supports eleven vowels and thirty nine consonants. Any Bengali word is typically of the form C*VC*, where C is a consonant and V is a vowel. Building Bengali voice using FESTVOX is well explained in the link given. (http://speech.iiit.net/~speech/publications/BengaliTTS.pdf). In our TTS, each of the Bengali letters is represented using its equivalent ASCII. The table below (Figure 5) shows few representations of Bengali letters in ASCII.

Complexities in Bengali Language

Bengali is a language of the Indo-Aryan branch of the Indo-European family of languages. The characteristics and prosodic analysis in Bengali voice is discussed in the below link. (http://bangla.com/Wikipedia/bangla.htm). Bengali is derived from Sanskrit. Bengali lexicon consists of "tatsama", i.e. Sanskrit words that have changed pronunciation, but retained the original spelling. It consists of "tadbhava", i.e. Sanskrit words that have changed at least twice in the process of becoming Bengali (Naushad UzZaman, 2005). Bengali has also been greatly influenced by two non-Aryan languages: Dravidian and Kol. Apart from these, the Bengali language also came under the influence of Arabic, Persian and Turkish, Portuguese, Dutch, French and English. Words from these languages entered Bengali vocabulary, making the vocabulary more complex. If we consider English language, the letter to sound rules are relatively easy due to their phonetic nature, i.e., there is a fairly good correspondence between what is written and what

Figure 4. Flowchart for Bengali TTS

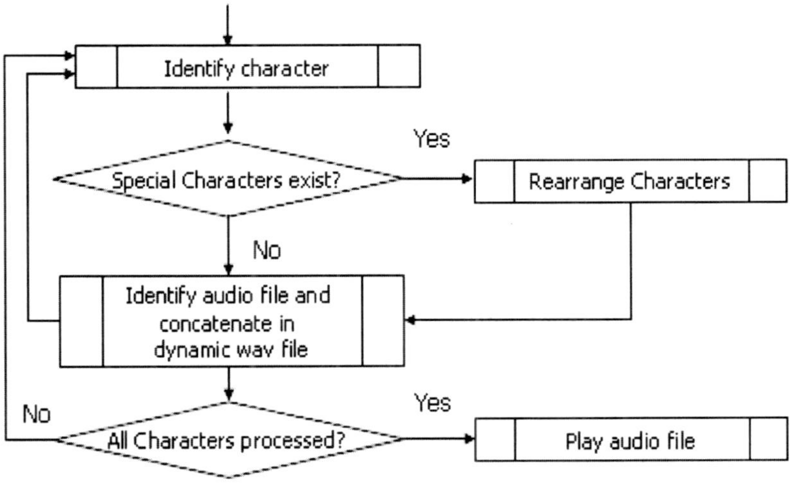

Figure 5. Letter to ASCII mapping

Letter	ASCII	Letter	ASCII	Letter	ASCII
অ	A	ক	k	ঝ	z
আ	Aa	খ	K	ট	T
ই	I	গ	g	ঠ	H
ঈ	Y	ঘ	G	ড	X
উ	U	ঙ	M	ঢ	D
ঊ	W	চ	c	ণ	n
ঋ	>	ছ	C	প	p
এ	E	জ	i	ফ	f

Figure 6.

i. There are several characters in Bengali, which are phonetically similar. For example (n), and (N) where both sound as "Na" or (s), (S), (x) where all sound as "Sha", or (j), (J) which sound as "Ja".

ii. Bengali has many consonant clusters which have unusual pronunciations. For example, (q). (q) = (k) + (x). The word () is pronounced as (Kt) i. e (q) is pronounced as (K) but (x) is not pronounced at all.

iii. Depending on the context, the pronunciation of letters varies. Consider the letter (q). When it appears at the beginning of a word it is pronounced as (kha), whereas when it appears in between other letters it is pronounced as (ka kha) as in (dq).

iv. There are some letters which have multiple pronunciations. For example, (Aahban) can be pronounced in two different ways (Aa)+ (h)+ (ba) + (n) or (Aa)+ (o)+ (va) + (n).

v. There are few words in which the order of pronunciation is different from the order in which they are written. For example in the word ([m&). The sequence of writing is ([) + (m) + (&), but is pronounced as ([) + (&) + (m).

vi. Bengali supports combination of two characters to forma single character. For example (ib]d) is a combination of (ib) + (]d) + (u). Here (] d) is a combination of (n) + (d).

is spoken. However, for Bengali, the rules for mapping of letter to sound are not straight forward (Bandopadhyay A 2002). To build a good text processing module and thus to generate natural sounding speech synthesis in Bengali is relatively difficult. The Bengali orthographic rule makes the language more difficult. Some of the special cases are discussed in Figure 6.

Steps for Bengali Text to Speech

The steps for Bengali text to speech conversion are as follows.

i. Identify the individual words in the sentence. (see Figure 7)
ii. Break down the words into phonemes. (see Figure 8)

Figure 7.

Example: If we consider the sentence আজি যত তারা তব আকাশে (Aaij Jt tara tb akaes), it is broken down into five words আজি (Aaij), যত (Jt), তারা (tara), তব (tb), and আকাশে (Aakaes)

Figure 8.

Example: If we take the word আকাশে (Aakaes), it is broken down into the phonemes আ (Aa) + কা (ka) + শে (es).

Figure 9.

Let us consider the word আজি (Aaij). The individual phonemes for আজি is আ (Aa) + ই (i) + জ (j). While playing the voice files should be reordered and played as আ (Aa) + জ (j) + ি (i)

iii. Identify the voice files for each phoneme.
   - *Example:* Each individual phoneme needs to be mapped with the corresponding voice files.

iv. Arrange the voice files in the order in which it has to be played. (see Figure 9)

v. Create a dynamic file and concatenate the individual voice files.
   - *Example:* Every time a text is entered, an audio file is created dynamically at run time. For each phoneme, the voice files are fetched and concatenated.

vi. Play the dynamic voice file.
   - *Example:* Once each phone has been concatenated, the dynamic file is played.

The Interface

The Interface provides the user with buttons to enter Bengali characters. The characters could also be entered using keyboard. Once the required text has been entered, the user must press the Play button to convert the entered text into speech. A snap shot of the interface is as follows (see Figure 10) (Debjani Goswami, 2008).

Recording of Speech

The voice is recorded using a native Bengali Female speaker using a stand mounted microphone. The speech data was recorded using the a microphone with the following specifications:

Frequency response: 20 Hz – 16 KHz
Impedance: 2.2 K ohm
Sensitivity: 54 dB +/- 3dB
Connector: 3.5mm stereo plug

This is necessary to maintain consistency in the recorded voice (Sridhar Krishna .N, 2002).

Implementation

The Bengali TTS is developed using VB.NET. MS Excel is used for storing the file paths for the phonemes. The TTS system requires keyboard mapping software, *Apona Bangla* in order to

Figure 10. Interface for Bengali TTS

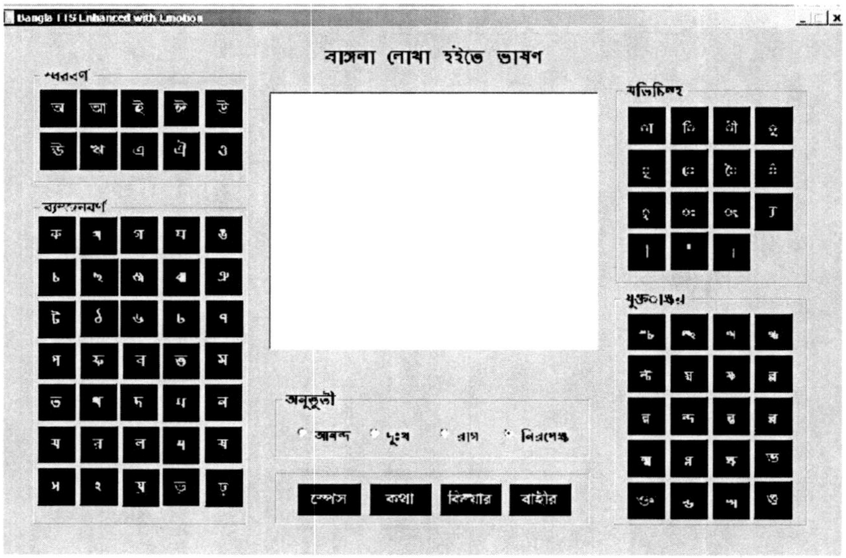

Table 1. The summary of human vocal emotion effects. The effects described are those most commonly associated with the emotions indicated, and are related to neutral speech

	Anger	Happiness	Sadness	Fear	Disgust
Speech rate	Slightly faster	Faster or slower	Slightly slower	Much faster	Very much slower
Pitch average	Very much higher	Much higher	Slightly lower	Very much higher	Very much lower
Pitch range	Much wider	Much wider	Slightly narrower	Much wider	Slightly wider
Intensity	Higher	Higher	Lower	Normal	Lower
Voice quality	Breathy, chest tone	Breathy, blaring	Resonant	Irregular voicing	Grumbled, chest tone
Pitch changes	Abrupt, on stressed syllables	Smooth, upward inflections	Downward inflections	Normal	Wide, downward terminal inflections
Articulation	tense	normal	slurring	precise	normal

be able to enter Bengali text. Microsoft Sound Recorder is used to record the speech files and Audacity is used as the audio editor for displaying .wav file properties.

PROSODIC ANALYSIS

In an ideal condition, read 25 sentences in three emotional styles that were: happiness, anger and sadness. Besides, it is also required to record the same 25 sentences in a neutral way and this last set of signals was used as the baseline for successive elaborations (Enrico Zovato, 2004). The semantic content was rather neutral and therefore could not provoke any particular emotional attitude. Mainly, the emotion expressed in a speech can be controlled by operating three factors: tempo, pitch and power. The emotions are joy, sorrow, anger and surprise that strongly characterize the speech and neutral emotion that is located at center of these emotions (Futoshi Sugimoto, 2004).

Applying the general rules shown in Table 1 to our developed TTS, it has provided the results in Tables 2 and 3.

Table 2. Frequency and duration values for different emotions

	Neutral	Happiness	Sadness	Anger
Frequency (Hz)	22050	23250	21050	22450
Duration (Sec)	2.739602	2.598203	3.763220	2.682164

Table 3. The percentage variations required for producing the effect of emotions

	Happiness	Sadness	Anger
Frequency (Hz)	6%	5%	2%
Duration (Sec)	5%	4%	3%
Loudness	20%	80%	Maximum

RESULTS

The result is analyzed by comparing the synthetic speech output of our TTS to the natural speech output for several samples. The comparison between the natural and concatenated wave files are made by considering the time consumed by each wave file as the prosodic parameter. The figures below shows the waveform generated for the word **(ihmalO)**. Figure 11 shows the waveform for natural speech and Figure 12 shows the waveform for concatenated speech.

If we consider the wave form generated by the TTS Engine in Figure 12, we notice considerable amount of delay between each of the phonemes being spoken. The word is spelt as shown in Figure 13. This delay is one of the inherent characteristics of concatenate synthesis. The delay happens due to concatenation of individual phoneme WAV files. To improve the output, the silent portions of the

Figure 11. Waveform for natural speech

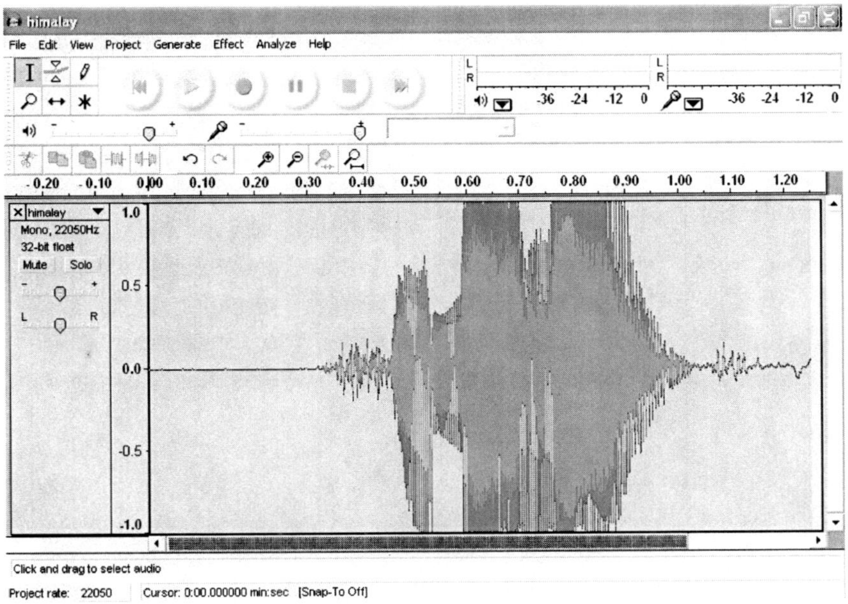

Figure 12. Waveform for speech generated by TTS

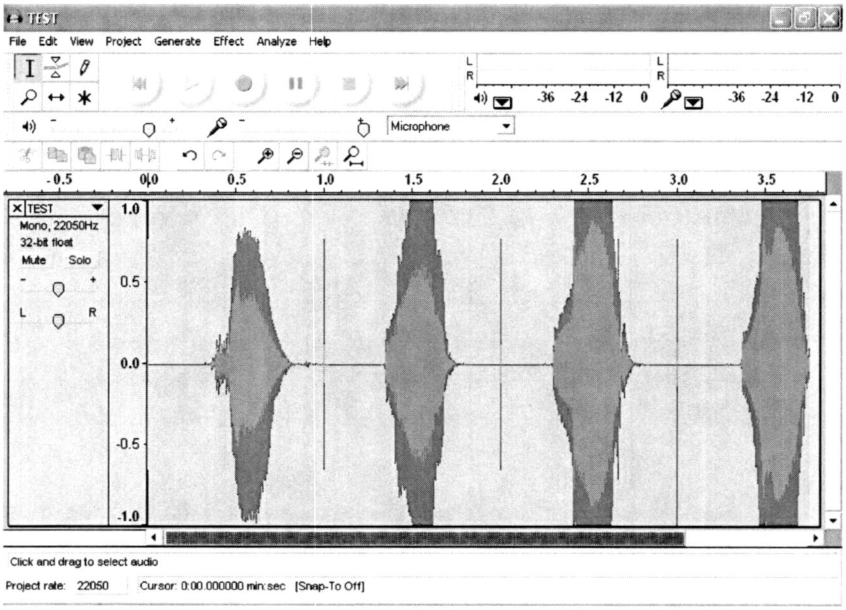

wave file are stripped by using a filter amplitude range. The lower threshold has been set to -30000 and the upper threshold is set to 10000. The output file generated after stripping is as in Figure 14, which considerably improves the performance.

The space at the beginning of each file is due to the 44 bytes of header information. A comparison between the natural, concatenated and stripped files shown in Figure 15. We notice a considerable improvement in time when we compare concatenated vs. stripped.

FUTURE TRENDS

This chapter discusses on the feature extraction algorithm for the production of emotions in Text-To-Speech (TTS) system for an Indian regional language. The dictionary of all .wav files are generated by only one female voice. This can be extended for a male voice, child, aged person and so on. Different speech variations for different types of speech can be achieved. The theme of this chapter is on technology for automated language processing, and thus the emphasis in this work is on representations and computational models of prosody for spoken language processing applications. There are two classes of problems in speech processing for human-computer interactions: speech synthesis and speech understanding. Prosody plays a role in both problems, as is clearly seen in the different papers. Prosodic patterns are determined by the information structure of language and realized in the speech waveform, duration and energy patterns. The overall problem in computational modeling of prosody is to move from one domain to the other, optionally via an intermediate abstract representation. Until

Figure 13.

[illegible] (ih) + [illegible] (ma) + [illegible] (l) + [illegible] (O)

Figure 14. Waveform for speech after stripping

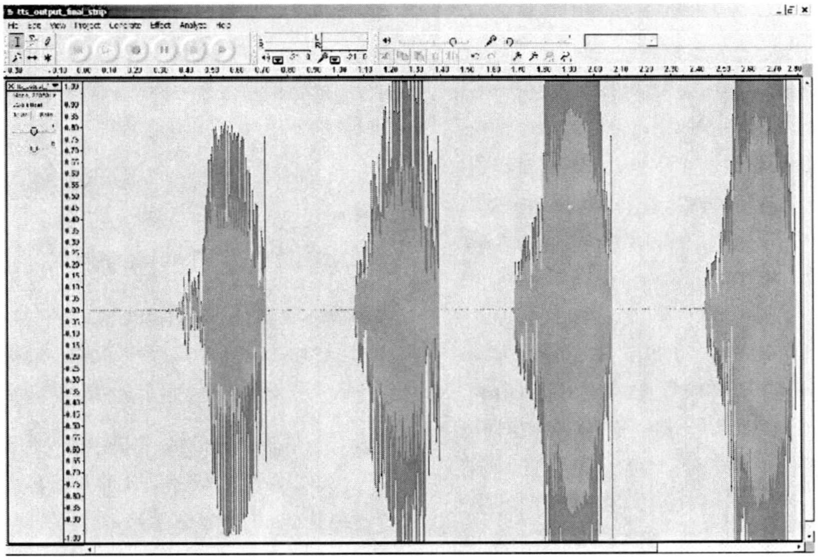

Figure 15. Comparison of output wav files

Word/ Emotion	NATURAL (sec)	CONCATENATED (sec)	STRIPPED (sec)
હિમાલય (ihmalO)	1.500136	3.763830	2.779049
દેવયાની (edbJany)	1.753009	3.988598	2.739602
નારાયણ (naraOn)	1.497693	3.757720	2.699922
મહાવીર (mhabvr)	1.250113	3.995115	2.642628
રઘુવીર (rGubvr)	1.252149	4.001633	2.802114
Average	1.45062	3.9013792	2.732663

recently, almost all research in computational modeling of prosody has been in speech synthesis applications, where it has been claimed that good prosody models are among the most important advances needed for high quality synthesis. The papers by Silverman, van Santen, and Collier *et al.* each address different problems related to prosody synthesis. Silverman attacks the problem of predicting abstract prosodic labels, while van Santen presents a model for predicting duration from text (and optionally abstract labels). Collier *el al.,* on the other hand, analyzes the relation between automatically predicted boundary levels and perceived level in natural speech. Both Silverman and van Santen make the point that good prosody models can improve naturalness, but Silverman also shows that intelligibility can be improved. All recent advances in this direction can be incorporated for the naturalness of the speech output.

CONCLUSION

This paper describes a concatenated Bengali Text to Speech Synthesis system. The paper highlights on the complexities associated with the development of a TTS in Bengali. It talks about the algorithm being used for converting text to speech. A comparative study between natural speech and that produced by the test to speech synthesizer is also shown.

The TTS provides limited and unique voice output in Bengali language. A female voice has been stored to provide the speech output. *Apona Bangla* transliterator is required to enter the Bengali text. The TTS provides an option to select four different emotions – anger, happiness, sadness and neutral. Depending on the selection the output speech varies.

REFERENCES

Bandopadhyay, A. (2002) *Some Important Aspects of Bengali Speech Synthesis System*, Retrieved June 24-25, 2002, from IEMCT, Pane.

Epoch Synchronous Non-Overlapping Add (ESNOLA) Approach Concatenative Text to Speech Synthesis - A Technical Report. (2005, January). Retrieved 2005, from http://tdil.mit.gov.in/Jan_issue%202005/10-EPOCH.pdf

Goswami, D., Kallimani, J. S., & Ananthashayana, V. K. (2008). An Efficient Concatenated Speech Generator for Bengali Language. In *Proceedings of International Congress on Pervasive Computing and Management (ICPCM-2008).*

Mandal, S. K. D., & Pal, B. (2002). *Bengali Text to Speech Synthesis System: A Novel Approach for Crossing Literacy Barrier*. CSI-YITP A (E).

Mukhopadhya, A., Chakraborty, S., Chowdhury, M., Lahiri, A., Dey, S., & Basu, A. (2005) Shruti: an embedded text to Speech system for Indian Languages. *Software Engineering, Special Issue on Microsoft Research.*

Sarkar, T., Keri, V., Santosh, M., & Prahallad, K. (2005) *Building Bengali Voice Using Festvox.* ICLSI 2005, IIIT Hyderabad.

Shyamal, Kr., DasMandal, & Pal, B. (2002). *Bengali text-to-speech synthesis system, a novel approach for crossing literacy barrier*. CSI-YITP.

Sridhar Krishna, N., Murthy, H. A., & Gonsalves, T. A. (2002). *Text-To-Speech (TTS) in Indian Languages*. International Conference on Natural Language Processing.

Sugimoto, F., Yazu, K., Marakami, M., & Yoneyama, M. (2004). *A method to classify emotional expressions of text and synthesize speech.* First International Symposium on Control, Communications and Signal Processing. (pp.611-614).

UzZaman, N., & Khan, M. (2005) A Double Metaphone Encoding for Bangla and its Application in Spelling Checker. In *Proceedings of IEEE International Conference on Natural Language Processing and Knowledge Engineering, IEEE NLP-KE '05* (pp.705-710).

Zovato, E., Sandri, S., Quazza, S., & Badino, L. (2004). *Prosodic analysis of a multi-style corpus in the perspective of emotional speech synthesis.* INTERSPEECH 2004 – ICSLP. Retrieved October 4-8, 2004. 8th International Conference on Spoken Language Processing, Korea.

ADDITIONAL READING

Adell, J., Bonafonte, A., & Escudero, D. (2005). *Analysis of prosodic features: towards modeling of emotional and pragmatic attributes of speech.*

Barbosa, P. A., & Bailly, G. (1994). Characterization of rhythmic patterns for text-to-speech synthesis. *Speech Communication*, *15*, 127–137. doi:10.1016/0167-6393(94)90047-7

Barras, C., Geoffrois, E., Wu, Z., & Liberman, M. (2001). Transcriber: development and use of a tool for assisting speech corpora production. *Speech Communication*, *33*(1), 5–22. doi:10.1016/S0167-6393(00)00067-4

Brugnara, F., Falavigna, D., & Omologo, M. (1993). Automatic Segmentation and Labeling of Speech based on Hidden Markov Models. *Speech Communication*, *12*(4), 357–370. doi:10.1016/0167-6393(93)90083-W

Cutugno, F., D'Anna, L., Petrillo, M., & Zovato, E. (2002). *APA: towards an Automatic Tool for Prosodic Analysis*. Speech Prosody 2002, Aix-en-Provence, pp.231-234.

Eide, E., Bakis, R., Hamza, W., & Pitrelli, J. (2003). Multilayered Extensions to the Speech Synthesis Markup Language for Describing Expressiveness. In *Proc. of EuroSpeech'03* (pp. 1645-1648), September. 2003.

Escudero-Mancebo, D., Gonzalez-Farreras, C., & Cardeñoso, V. (2002). *Quantitative evaluation of relevant prosodic factors for text-to-speech synthesis*. In the Proceedings of ICSLP.

Fujisaki, H., Ohno, S., & Narusawa, S. (2000). Physiological mechanisms and biomechanical modeling of fundamental frequency control for the common Japanese and the standard Chinese. In *the Proceedings of the 5th Seminar on Speech Production* (pp 145-148). Bavaria, Germany.

Iida, A., Campbell, N., Iga, S., Higuchi, F., & Yasumura, M. (2000). A Speech Synthesis System for Assisting Communication. *ISCA Workshop on Speech & Emotion, Northern Ireland 2000* (pp.167-172).

Iriondo, I., Guaus, R., Rodríguez, A., Lázaro, P., Montoya, N., Blanco, J. M., et al. (2000). Validation of an Acoustical Modelling of Emotional Expression in Spanish using Speech Synthesis Techniques. *ISCA Workshop on Speech & Emotion, Northern Ireland 2000* (pp.161-166).

Jagadish, S. Kallimani., & Ananthashayana V K. (2006). Text-to-speech engine for Kannada language. In *Proceedings of national conference on convergence of linguistics, e-governance & IT for making kannada – A tech-savvy language* (pp.78-84).

Jiang, D.-N., Zhang, W., Shen, L.-Q., & Cai, L.-H. (2005). Prosody analysis and modeling for emotional speech synthesis. In *Proceedings of ICASSP 2005*.

Ma, X. J., Zhang, W., Zhu, W. B., et al. (2004). Probability based Prosody Model for Unit Selection. In *Proc. of ICASSP'04, Montreal, Canada* (pp. 649-652), May 2004.

Marumoto, T., & Campbell, N. Control of speaking types for emotion in a speech re-sequencing system [in Japanese]. In *Proc. of the Acoustic Society of Japan, Spring meeting2000* (pp. 213-214).

Murray, I. R., & Arnott, J. L. (1993). Towards the simulation of emotion in synthetic speech: A review of the literature on human vocal emotion. *The Journal of the Acoustical Society of America*, *93*(2). doi:10.1121/1.405558

Murray, I. R., Edgington, M. D., Campion, D., et al. (2000). Rule-Based Emotion Synthesis Using Concatenated Speech. In *Proc. of ISCA Workshop on Speech and Emotion, Belfast, North Ireland* (pp. 173-177).

Murray, I. R., Edgington, M. D., Campion, D., & Lynn, J. (2000). Rule-based Emotion Synthesis Using Concatenated Speech. *ISCA Workshop on Speech & Emotion, Northern Ireland 2000* (pp. 173-177).

Schröder, M. (2001). Emotional Speech Synthesis: A Review. In *Proceedings of EUROSPEECH 2001, Scandinavia* (pp. 561-564).

Schröder, M., Cowie, R., Douglas-Cowie, E., Westedijk, M., & Gielen, S. (2001). Acoustic Correlates of Emotion Dimensions in View of Speech Synthesis. In *Proceedings of EUROSPEECH 2001, Scandinavia* (pp. 87-90).

Stallo, J. (2000). *Simulating Emotional Speech for a Talking Head*, Honours Thesis, School of Computing, Curtin University of Technology, Australia, 2000. Retrieved from http://www.computing.edu.au/~stalloj/projects/honours

KEY TERMS AND DEFINITIONS

Concatenative Synthesis: It is based on the concatenation (or stringing together) of segments of recorded speech. Generally, concatenative synthesis produces the most natural-sounding synthesized speech.

Diphone: In phonetics, a diphone is an adjacent pair of phones. It is usually used to refer a recording of the transition between two phones.

Formant Synthesis: It does not use human speech samples at runtime. Instead, the synthesized speech output is created using an acoustic model. Parameters such as fundamental frequency, voicing and noise levels are varied over time to create a waveform of artificial speech. This method is sometimes called rules-based synthesis.

MBROL: It is an algorithm for speech synthesis. It is the software which is distributed at no financial cost but in binary form only, and a world-wide collaborative project.

Phone: A sound that has definite shape as a sound wave.

Prosody: In linguistics, prosody is the rhythm, stress, and intonation of speech. Prosody may reflect the emotional state of a speaker, whether an utterance is a statement, a question, or a command; whether the speaker is being ironic or sarcastic; emphasis, contrast and focus; and other elements of language which may not be encoded by the grammar.

Speech Synthesis: It is the production of speech from a given input data. Synthesized speech can be created by concatenating pieces of recorded speech that are stored in a database.

Section 2
Pervasive Computing Enabled Manufacturing and Re-Engineering

Pervasive computing has the potential of proving services in complex, hazardous and dynamic manufacturing environment. Its usage can improve the efficiency and effectiveness of the manufacturing processes and lower various risks that may affect workers health. Focusing in Manufacturing and reengineering, this section comprises of two chapters. Chapter 4, "Lean Manufacturing Scenario and Role of Pervasive Computing in Indian SMEs", gives a description of the latest pervasive technologies that can improve the usage of lean manufacturing in SMEs. It also investigates to what extent Small and Medium-Sized Organisations have understood and adopted lean manufacturing and the challenges they face in the implementation of lean manufacturing. Chapter 5, "RMS: A New Linkage with Pervasive Computing", explains the shift of mass production techniques in manufacturing systems to flexible automation techniques. It identifies increasing need of incorporating highly flexible and intelligent reconfigurable manufacturing systems that can maintain effective and efficient manufacturing operations with minimum downtime under conditions of uncertainty. This chapter proposes various research issues related to the development of reconfigurable manufacturing systems with pervasive computing.

Chapter 4
Lean Manufacturing Scenario and Role of Pervasive Computing in Indian SMEs

Deepak Tripathi
Quality Assurance, Ministry of Railways, India

ABSTRACT

Large scale firms have been adopting various management practices to remain competitive in today's global economy. Lean manufacturing is one such initiative, which significantly improves performance in terms of cost, delivery, quality and flexibility. Although small and medium enterprises (SMEs) play a very significant role in overall manufacturing supply network, less is known about the extent to which lean is present in these firms. The present study investigates this issue by exploring the scenario of implementation of lean manufacturing in Indian SMEs. It also examines the constraints, which need to be addressed for real penetration of lean on a wider scale and the role information and communication technologies like pervasive computing play in successful implementation of this initiative. This aspect is considered important as no organization, whether big or small, can afford to neglect it in today's business environment. The study reveals that although lean manufacturing is not implemented as a formal management initiative in SMEs, its elements could be traced with varying degrees in firms. However, a need is felt to improve upon various identified constraints, so that SMEs are able to implement it as formal system and reap maximum benefits. It is also experienced that IT solutions like pervasive computing help in improving lean manufacturing performance but Indian SMEs in general have not taken considerable initiatives in this direction.

INTRODUCTION

Small and medium enterprises (SMEs) play a vital role in Indian economy as more than 50% of country's GDP is contributed by them. SMEs are also the backbone of manufacturing sector as they form critical upstream supply network to the large-scale firms and OEMs. Like their counterparts in other regions of world, Indian SME are characterized with family based businesses with loose manage-

DOI: 10.4018/978-1-60566-996-0.ch004

ment structure, poor investments levels in new technologies and processes, lack of competent manpower, inadequate research and development facilities and constrained financial resources.

These constraints in SMEs have caused them to lag behind large-scale firms in implementing improvement initiatives like Just in Time (JIT), Total Quality Management (TQM), Total Productive Maintenance (TPM) and lean manufacturing. Therefore, such management practices have not received any appreciable attention in SMEs globally (Gunasekaran, 2000). This is despite the importance of improving competencies in small and medium scale industry being emphasized by many experts. For example, need to focus on areas like quality, just in time manufacturing, problem solving and lean management was highlighted by Hall (2005). Lavinson (2002) also stressed upon the inevitability of lean manufacturing in SMEs to face global competition. However, limitations in terms of management style, manufacturing practices and level of expertise have been the major bottlenecks (Little & McKinna, 2005). Therefore, realizing the importance of SMEs for Indian manufacturing industry, this subject is considered to be of important nature.

Lean manufacturing was originally developed in the Japanese auto industry by Taiichi Ohno. Lean or Toyota Production System (TPS) has its origin from the Toyata's unique way of manufacturing. It requires focus on making product flow through value adding process without any interruption - a 'pull system' that cascades back from customer demand to manufacturing to raw material procurements. It intends to eliminate all kinds of waste from any productive system (Liker, 2004). Various important elements of this system include six-sigma quality, visual display, defect prevention, one-piece flow, Kanban, setup time reduction, quality at source, just-in-time supply, preventive maintenance, value analysis and value stream mapping (Womack, Jones & Roos, 1990). Although the origin and development of lean manufacturing is from automotive sector but these elements can be found in any manufacturing environment in varying degrees of importance and intensity. The key issues addressed by lean manufacturing are (Wiele *et al.*, 2006)

- Value – providing the customer with right product and service for right price and at right time
- Value Stream – set of activities from concept to realization, order to delivery
- Flow- seamless movement through a series of value adding activities
- Pull – taking only those actions which satisfy customers
- Perfection – improving value continuously and relentlessly alongwith associated reduction in defects

Therefore, it can be seen that lean manufacturing is combination of a large number of management practices, which are all important for its success. Macduffie (1995) divided these into three parts – buffer minimization or JIT, work systems and practices to support lean and human resource management. Importance of these has been cited by various researchers (Macduffie, 1995). Various elements of these major groups are

A: Just in time or buffer management
1. Pull type of manufacturing system
2. Small lot production
3. Rapid feedback system
4. Waste reduction programs
5. Quick changeover and SMED
6. Mistake proofing

B: Work systems and practices
1. Relationship with suppliers to improve their performance
2. Kaizen and continuous improvements
3. Equipment management
4. Rapid product development
5. Quality assurance and total quality management
6. Information architecture

C: Human resource management
1. Team working
2. Training of employees
3. Employee selection and compensation
4. Multi-skilling and job rotation

The benefits of lean manufacturing or TPS can be enormous to achieve world-class performance standards. It enables organizations to achieve simultaneously the goals of high quality, quick delivery, low costs and high degree of flexibility for quicker response (Korgaonker, 1992). According to Stamm & Gohar (1990), smaller firms can also reap lean benefits, which include reduced inventory levels, better quality, shorter lead times and reduced costs.

However, lean manufacturing has not been able to penetrate into SME for various reasons cited earlier. The important ones are lack of understanding about lean management, lack of commitment from top management, availability of human resource pool, lack of financial resources and investment in old technology and equipment, which do not qualify for implementing lean manufacturing system (Brown & Inman, 1993; Rothenberg & Cost, 2004).

Realizing the importance of lean manufacturing to improve competitiveness of SMEs, some recent research works have been undertaken in global context. These include studies by Rothenberg & Cost (2004), Ray *et. al.*(2006) and Little & Mac Kinna (2005). However, this area still remains to be explored in Indian industry context.

Emergence of e-business and pervasive computing is another important aspect, which has helped in transforming and redefining business processes. These solutions have strong linkages with almost all key result areas of lean manufacturing –productivity, quality, process flexibility, waste, cycle time and costs (Martin & Milway, 2007). Many firms have experienced this through use of tools like RFID, e-tags, mobile communication and broadband. Therefore, it is important for SMEs to adapt these practices to not only improve their businesses, but to also provide strong linkages in extended supply chains of their customers. The specific characteristics of SMEs like flexible working environment, lesser commitments made in IT infrastructure, and resource and financial constraints for large investments can provide better justification for using mobile and pervasive computing (Patten & Passerini, 2007) to improve business performance.

RESEARCH METHODOLOGY AND OBJECTIVES

This research has been done by undertaking in-depth study of eleven SMEs from three different sectors; namely brake lining, rubber and plastics, which are tier I or tier II sources to automotive and engineering firms. These sectors have been chosen for the two important reasons – Firstly, these are directly linked to two most progressive large-scale industries in terms of implementing lean. From this point of view, they truly represent the face of upcoming Indian SMEs. The other important reason is that brake linings, rubber and plastics manufacturing businesses are mostly undertaken by SME sector.

The objective of this study was to answer two basic questions

1. To what extent these SMEs have been able to understand and adopt lean manufacturing in their firms?
2. What are the main constraints in implementation of lean manufacturing in SMEs?

In order to examine these issues, a questionnaire was developed as research instrument, elements of which were determined on the basis of extensive literature review. The questionnaire has three parts - the first part is designed to gather general information, the second part addresses emphasis provided on various elements of lean

Table 1. Level of implementation of elements of lean manufacturing: measures of central tendencies

Elements of Lean Manufactuirng	Mean	Median	Mode
Buffer Management/JIT Manufacturing			
Implementation of pull type manufacturing system	1.2	1	1
Emphasis on small bacth manufacturing	1.9	2	2
Implementation of SMED/Setup reductions	1.6	1	1
Implementation of visual management in your firm	2.0	2	2
Implementation of waste reduction programme	1.9	2	1
Use of Error prevention at source and mistake proofing	1.6	1	1
Work System and Practices			
Use of kaizen and continuous improvement	2.5	3	3
Emphasis on value stream mapping	1.4	1	1
Relationship with suppliers	2.5	2	2
Use of quality assurance and total quality management	2.7	2	2
Use of information system	2.6	2	2
Emphasis on housekeeping and 5S	2.5	2	2
System of equipment management	2.4	2	2
Human Resource Management			
Emphasis on team working for improvement projects	2.0	2	2
Emphasis on training and development of employees and executives	2.5	2	2
Emphasis on selection and compensation based skills and knowledge	2.5	2	2
Emphasis on multi-skilling and job rotation	1.7	1	1

manufacturing and the third part includes constraints on implementation of lean manufacturing in SMEs. It has a 5 points scale for every individual element. Each of the firm was also visited to understand the true nature of implementation of lean elements and to verify data provided by these firms.

The role of information and communication technology (ICT) and pervasive computing in improving performance and enabling implementation of lean manufacturing is also deliberated along with experiences of SMEs selected for this research. This is based available literature on the subject and information collected from firms during site visits.

FINDINGS AND DISCUSSIONS

The data collected from the firms and responses received were plotted against each element as shown in appendix 1. As only 11 firms were taken for study, detailed statistical analysis could not be done. However, In order to demonstrate the extent of emphasis on each of the lean element, mean, median and modes have been calculated, which are given in table 1.

Findings on Implementation Scenario

The data collected indicates significantly low presence of lean manufacturing elements in SMEs as a whole for all three groups i.e. buffer management, work system and practices and human resource management. A vast variation is also noticed among firms with respect to elements of lean manufacturing. While few firms have considerably higher level of implementation maturity, most of them have even not understood and appreciated the concept well.

The implementation of just in time or buffer management in true sense has been limited to few large firms in automotive sector with special focus on assembly lines. In order to feed assembly lines with materials and components in small batches to suit just in time (JIT) requirements, the vendors of these firms are given supply schedules on daily or hourly basis. The vendor firms remain under pressure to ensure timely supply of exact quantity of material with required quality so that assembly line is not hampered. However, only a few firms have been taught to implement lean systems at their end to effectively manage such supply chains. Therefore, in order to meet their customers' requirements, they resort to intensive inspection of their products and also keep large inventories at their cost. The information collected from SME firms reveals that only one firm, out of those studied, has implemented buffer management of JIT, the most important part of lean manufacturing, in their final assembly and finishing section. The firm has implemented pull type production, small batch manufacturing and quick changeover in this section. This firm has plans to extend it upstream, as full benefits of lean are not reaped at present.

The data reveals that pull type production has not yet penetrated in these SMEs, even though some of their customers have implemented it to a considerable level of maturity. This is indicated through mean, median and mode values obtained for this element. However, other elements of buffer management like small batch manufacturing, waste reduction program, set up reduction, mistake proofing and visual management are visible in these firms with varying degrees. The mean, median and mode values obtained are quite low as shown in table 1. These elements, even if not a part of formal lean manufacturing system, are available due to specific characteristics of SMEs. For example smaller inventory levels are considered important due to financial and space constraints, limiting firms to produce in smaller quantities. This is the reason only few firms manufacture entire order quantity as one lot and production quantities are mostly decided as per supply schedules. However, small batch production as element of lean manufacturing in true sense is found in only one firm.

Visual management is an important tool of lean, which helps to reduce time on non-value adding communications and to reduce chances of making errors. Although it is not implemented as a formal program under lean in most of the firms, but various types of visual indicators like painted floor area, visual work instructions, visual indicators for identification and traceability of materials and equipment are seen in shop floors. The mean, median and mode values obtained for this element also support this fact. Waste reduction program is also being practised in some way or the other in almost all SMEs. Most of this is primarily due to pressures from their customers to cut costs and improve product quality. However, implementation of mistake proofing, another tool of lean, is not visible in more than 50% of the firm studied. The low values of central tendencies indicate that quite a few numbers of firms have implemented it only on a smaller scale.

Almost all the firms studied have developed and implemented vendor performance evaluation system based on quality and delivery parameters. Their vendors' performance is reviewed at specified intervals and future orders are determined based of this performance evaluation. Sometimes customers also put a condition on specific vendors from which these SMEs could source their raw materials. For example, SMEs involved in plastics business have to source their requirements from customer recommended vendors only. In addition, less leverage is available to some firms in terms of managing supplier relationships, as they are sandwiched between large firms both on upstream and downstream of their supply chains. The mean, median and mode values obtained are 2.5, 2 and 2 respectively, which support the observations made.

Continuous improvement, with formal or informal kaizen, has been witnessed in different forms in almost all the firms. Some firms have formal kaizen implementation programs, which are monitored by top management. In some other firms, customer driven improvement projects are undertaken with the objective of cost reduction and improvement in quality. Similarly, equipment management largely varies from breakdown maintenance to preventive maintenance. Implementation of advanced maintenance techniques like predictive maintenance, condition monitoring, autonomous maintenance and TPM are generally not visible, except in one firm, which has implemented a full-fledged TPM program.

There is also a wide variation on product development capabilities. Very few of the firms studied have their own research and development facilities. They are largely dependent either on their customers or raw material suppliers or their technical collaborators. For examples firms in rubber sector have their own product development capabilities and they also take help from R&D laboratories and firms in this area. Firms in plastic sector mostly depend on their raw material suppliers for product development and upgradation. In brake lining sector, some firms have their own R&D and product development facilities while others depend on technical collaborations.

One element, which helps in systematic implementation of lean manufacturing, is value stream mapping. It provides a formal identification of different types of wastes in a process so that strategies can be developed for their elimination. This element has been totally ignored in SMEs, probably as they do not formal lean manufacturing system in place.

All the firms studied have ISO 9001: 2000 system certifications, so a formal quality assurance program is already implemented. Some of these firms also make use of statistical quality control, statistical process control and other quality improvement programs. Therefore, the understanding and maturity level of firms on this element is considerably higher. These firms also do have some information system in place. A few of them have implemented ERP system, while some others have intranet facilities to make information available at point of use. Some traces of improved housekeeping and implementation of 5- s to varying degree is also witnessed.

Human resource management has remained a weak area in SMEs with respect to issues like selection, compensation and employee development. These firms seem to be trapped in a vicious circle, as they find it difficult to employ and retain talent due to lower than average salaries they pay. The financial constraints do not allow them to match their compensation with large firms. The emphasis on various human resource issues like team working, employee training and development, multi-skilling and selection and compensations has been quite low except in few firms. Analysis of data on human resource management supports these facts.

Findings on Implementation Constraints

The analysis of data collected on constraints in implementing lean manufacturing is given in appendix 1 and also in figures 1 to 4. Unsatisfactory level of knowledge of management about lean manufacturing, as depicted in figure 1, clearly speaks out that concepts and advantages of lean manufacturing have not percolated from large scale sector even to their tier I vendors in SMEs. Although implementation of lean manufacturing is seen in large-scale auto and engineering companies, a formal movement to spread it down to SME is not visible as it is in case of other initiatives like

Figure 1. Knowledge of management about lean manufacturing

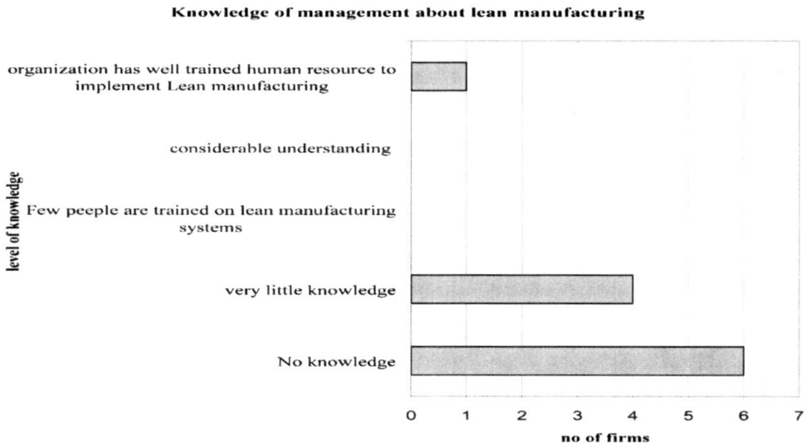

TQM and TPM. However, data shown in appendix 1 indicates that firms with high export content have higher level of implementation of lean elements. The investigations reveal that these firms have been guided and motivated to implement lean or its elements by their foreign customers, whereas level of involvement of Indian firms in developing their vendors has been relatively low.

This lack of appreciation of lean has also resulted in lower level of commitment of management as shown in figure 2.

Availability of competent and experienced human resource has been a major constraint faced by SMEs in almost all spheres of business. The primary reasons have been their low paying capacity as compared to organized large scale sector and relatively higher turnover rate among supervisor and management categories, which leave for better opportunities after gaining adequate work experience. This results in poor motivation of SMEs to invest in training and development of their people.

Nonavailability of adequate financial resources and poor appreciation of long term life cycle advantages of investing in reliable and modern equipment also lead to a tendency to opt for old outdated technology available as lower initial cost. However intense pressures from customers, especially in automotive sector, has resulted in these firms investing in equipment with higher reliability and flexibility. SMEs in plastics and rubber manufacturing have now started installing microprocessor controlled injection moulding machines. Similar is the case in brake linings, where firms have automated mixers, presses and ovens with much higher levels of process controls.

ROLE OF PERVASIVE COMPUTING IN LEAN MANUFACTURING SYSTEM AND SCENARIO IN INDIAN SMES

Applications of information and computing technologies including pervasive computing can support implementation of lean manufacturing by enabling people to have real time access to information and thus empowering them to identify and solve problems quickly. Electronic data logging directly from machines, real time quality checks, electronic display systems and use of mobile communication and emails ensure availability of information at remote locations to make lean management more effective. Further, emergence of concepts like e-commerce, mobile

Figure 2. Commitment of management to implement lean manufacturing

Figure 3. Availability of human resources to implement lean manufacturing

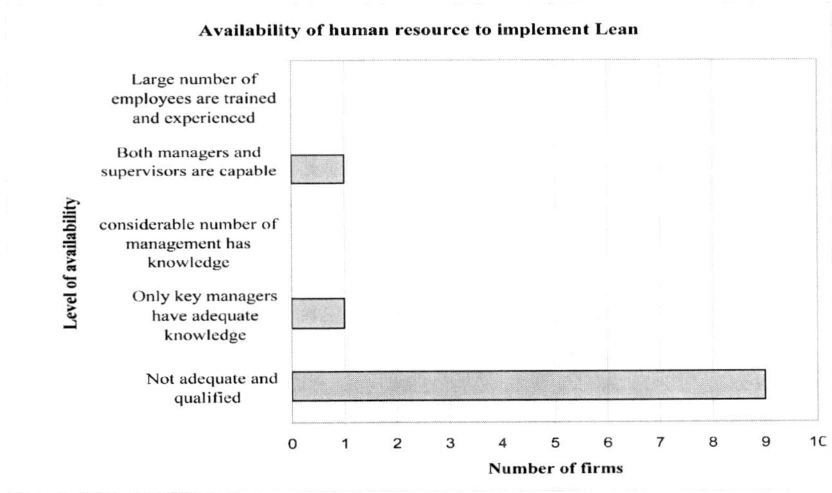

commerce and pervasive commerce have revolutionized businesses and their applications can have multiplier effects of performance of firms (Godara, 2009).

It can be seen from the information provided in table 2 that such information and computing technologies can provide a boost to each element of lean manufacturing – buffer management, work systems and practices and human resource management. For example electronic kanban system and autonomous defect controls at equipment with data logging and analysis can improve the effectiveness of JIT and buffer management. Similarly, monitoring of processes and inventory at suppliers' end and use of advanced software for product and process design help in implementation of work systems to reduce waste and process cycle time and to ensure higher product quality. Use of mobile communication technology aided by database and ERP support provides a virtual

Figure 4. Availability of machinery and plant for lean manufacturing

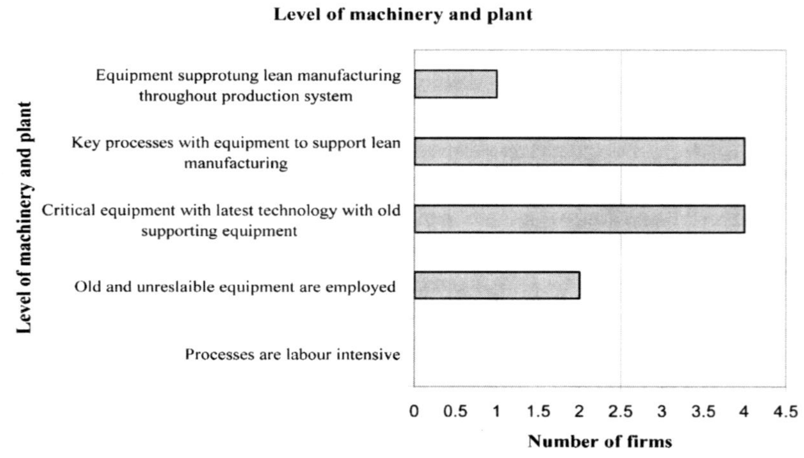

Table 2. Role of information and communication technology in different elements of lean manufacturing

Elements of Lean Manufacturing	Use of Information and Computing Technology
Buffer Management/JIT Manufacturing	• Various planning systems like material requirement subsystem, Kanban planning system, process load planning system, issue of electronic kanbans. • Autonomous defect control system on each machine and checking devices on instruments. • Data logging and transfer devices for condition monitoring of equipment.
Work system and practices	• On line management of inventory and manufacturing processes of suppliers • Product quality and equipment management through devices attached to equipments, assembly points and inspection tools, which monitor equipment and processes performance and transfer logged data for decision making • Use of CAD/CAM and other modeling software for developing products/processes to minimize wastes, cost and time in prototype development
Human resource management	• Mobile communication technology to create virtual workplace and to enable effective team work and communication among employees • Better utilization of human resource through mobile communication • Employees work in virtual spaces. Activities like remote order entry at customer's place and access to company database anytime from anywhere is feasible.

workplace environment, which improves teamwork and empowers employees to implement lean manufacturing more effectively.

The investment in information and communication technology has generally been much lower in Indian SMEs as compared to large firms. The reasons for this are same as in case of lean manufacturing. Some important ones are lack of initiatives from the top, poor appreciation of benefits that could be obtained from such investments and lack of competent manpower to handle such implementation projects (Patten & Passerini, 2007). A wide variation is observed among firms with respect to investments and initiatives taken by them in this direction. This variation is seen across sectors and also within each sector. The status in SMEs selected for this research with respect to implementation of information technology is detailed below.

The three sectors covered in this study are rubber, plastics and composite materials. One of the four firms from rubber sector has implemented advanced computer and microprocessor based manufacturing processes for mixing and moulding. This process and quality data is transferred between its mixing and moulding facility through web based ERP system. The equipment are provided with process control and condition monitoring devices, which control the equipment condition and also feed information for decision making. Another firm has provided microprocessor based injection moulding facility, but in an isolated way with no connectivity with other processes. The other two firms have not taken any appreciable initiatives and work outdated processes and systems. On the contrary, firms in plastics sector have invested uniformly in CNC based injection moulding machines to obtain desired and consistent quality products. These firms work on isolated personal computer based information systems and even no formal ERP system is in place.

One of the firms in brake lining has taken a lead by implementing computerized manufacturing execution system combined with quality checks and condition monitoring system. It is an integrated hardware and software solution for improving manufacturing productivity, addressing on line quality and equipment maintenance problems and communicating such information to remote places and even to customer locations. The hardware includes data collection and data entry terminals, equipment and process monitoring and display devices. The process monitoring information is communicated to its work centers and customers through wireless LAN and internet. This firm provides a good example of its progress towards pervasive computing environment. However, other two firms make conventional use of computers for data entry and processing.

The status of implementation indicates that maturity level of SMEs to attain pervasive computing environment is far from satisfactory. At the same time a few of them have taken some initiatives to reap the benefits of advanced computing and information techniques.

FUTURE DIRECTIONS

Manufacturing of future involves rapidly changing customer requirements leading to need for mass customization, global supply chains requiring virtual and global production networks and continuous improvements in production systems to improve product quality and flexibility with reduced costs and cycle time. SME are most vulnerable to such dynamic environment and they need to learn to respond quickly to these changes by adopting best manufacturing practices and information technologies available to them.

The ever intensifying competition will lead to OEMs and large firms working with their vendors to form extended enterprises through practices like lean manufacturing, as real benefits of lean manufacturing could be realized only if it is implemented to the entire supply chain. Thus ability to adapt lean manufacturing practices will be the key to survival and success of future SMEs.

Further, extended enterprises can be more competitive only with seamless information and knowledge networks among larger firms, OEMs and their vendors. This can help them to jointly take decisions regarding product development, process and quality control as well as supply and inventory management. Therefore, we will witness increasing role of information technology and pervasive computing in future SMEs. As SMEs have relatively smaller human resource base, extensive use of mobile communication technology will be seen to help them improve their effectiveness in areas like sales and remote factory management.

This research is based on empirical data collected on various elements of lean manufacturing from eleven Indian SMEs in automotive and engineering sector. The applications of information and communication technology and its role in reinforcing lean manufacturing systems in context of SMEs has also been deliberated on the basis of information collected from these firms. Future researchers can undertake a structured questionnaire based empirical research on existence of various elements of pervasive computing in firms, capabilities of firms to implement pervasive computing and its impact on lean manufacturing efforts. This study may be done on a larger set of firms to obtain fruitful results. Individual firm based case studies can also be undertaken to create a better insight. As advanced manufacturing and technological solutions like lean manufacturing and pervasive computing are bound to penetrate more and more into SMEs, such research studies will be of much help in coming years.

CONCLUSION

This paper is based on a research to examine the status of lean manufacturing in SMEs and constraints, which need to be addressed to improve lean implementation in these firms. It also addresses the role of information and computing technology to reinforce lean manufacturing.

Although this study has been carried out on few selected firms, but it reveals very interesting facts, which are reiterated below.

The implementation of lean manufacturing in formal way is not found in Indian SMEs except in very few cases, but the practice of lean in terms of its three important elements – buffer management, work practices and human resource management can be seen in varying degrees. In buffer management category, implementation of small batch manufacturing, visual management and waste reduction is more visible than pull production system, error proofing and SMED. However, overall visibility of this component has been quite low. Work system and practices are seen to have been implemented to much larger extent as process and quality improvement projects, information management, quality assurance systems and housekeeping have been employed in most of the firms. Human resource management, the third lean component, needs to be geared up in term of selection, compensation, development and empowerment of management and employees, as they form the backbone for any improvement initiative like lean manufacturing.

Although a change with respect to making equipment capable to implement lean is seen in most of the firms under study, other issues like, appreciation of lean as a transformational tool by top management, making employees capable through training and motivation for its implementation are also important. The OEMs and major customers need to play an important role in this direction.

The role of information technology and pervasive computing to support lean manufacturing and to improve business performance is explained by addressing each element of lean – buffer management and JIT, work system and practices and human resource management. Although use of information and computing technology is seen in almost all SMEs at different maturity levels, a proper framework for their application need to be developed by each firm to support all elements of lean manufacturing.

REFERENCES

Brown, K. L., & Inman, A. R. (1993). Small business and JIT: A managerial overview. *International Journal of Operations & Production Management, 13*(3), 57–66. doi:10.1108/01443579310026032

Godara, V. (2009). Pervasive Computing: A Conceptual Framework. In V. Godara (Ed.), *Risk Assessment and Management in Pervasive Computing* (pp. 1-19). Hershey, PA: Idea Group Inc.

Gunasekaran, A. (2000). World class manufacturing in small and medium enterprises. *International Journal of Manufacturing Technology and Management, 2*(1-7), 777-789.

Hall, K. W. *(2005).* Identifying non-value added practices in manufacturing: An instructional design. *Doctoral dissertation, Illinois State University.*

Korgaonker, M. G. (1992). *Just In Time Manufacturing.* New Delhi: Macmillan India Limited.

Lavinson, W. A. (2002). Lean Manufacturing: Made in USA. *Quality Digest, 22*(2), 64.

Liker, J. K. (2004). *The Toyota Way: 14 Management Principals from World's Greatest Manufacturer.* New York: McGraw Hill Publications.

Little, D., & McKinna, A. (2005). *A lean manufacturing assessment tool for use in manufacturing.* Paper presented at Seventh SMESME International Conference: Stimulating Manufacturing Excellence in Small & Medium Enterprise, University of Strathclyde, Glasgow.

Macduffie, J. P. (1995). Human resource bundles and manufacturing performance: Organizational logics and flexible manufacturing system in world auto industry. *Industrial & Labor Relations Review, 48*(2), 173–188. doi:10.2307/2524483

Martin, R. L., & Milway, J. B. (2007). *Enhancing the productivity of Small and Medium Enterprises through Greater Adoption of Information and Communication Technology.* Ottawa, Canada: Information and Communication Technology Council (ICTC).

Patten, K., & Passerini, K. (2007). *Next Generation Small and Medium Enterprises Mobility Strategy Roadmap.* Paper presented at Sixth Annual ISOnE world Conference, Las Vegas, Nevada.

Ray, C. D., Zuo, X., & Michael, J. H. (2006). The Lean Index- Operational 'Lean' Metrices for Wood Product Industry. Wood and Fibre Science- Society of Wood and Technology, 38*(2), 238-255.*

Rothenberg, S., & Cost, F. *(2004).* Lean Manufacturing in Small and Medium Size Printers. *New York: A Research Monograph, Rochester Institute of Technology.*

Stamm, C., & Golhar, D. (1990). *Can small manufacturing firms successfully implement JIT.* Paper presented at annual conference of Decision Science Institute, California.

Wiele, V. T., Van, I. J., Dale, B. G., & Williams, R. (2006). A comparison of five modern improvement approaches. *International Journal of Productivity and Quality Management, 1*(4), 363–378. doi:10.1504/IJPQM.2006.009092

Womack, J. P., Jones, D. T., & Roos, D. (1990). *Machine that changed the world.* New York: Simon and Schuster.

ADDITIONAL READING

Berger, A.J., & Gattorna, J.L. (2001). *Supply Chain Cybermastry: Building High Performance Supply Chains of the future.* London: Gower Publishing Limited.

Bititci, U. S., & Carrie, A. S. (1998). *Strategic Management of Manufacturing Value Chain.* Boston: Kluwer Academic Publishers.

Burns, P., & Dewhurst, J. (1996). *Small Business and Entrepreneurship.* London: McMillan Business.

Cecelja, F. (2002). *Manufacturing Information and Data System: Analysis, Design and Practice*. London: Penton Press.

Drogosz, J. D. (2002). Applying Lean Above the Factory Floor. *Journal of Ship Production, 18*(3), 159–166.

Dyer, J. H. (2000). *Collaborative Advantage: Winning Through Extended Enterprise Supplier Network*. New York: Oxford University Press.

Eversheim, W., Klocke, F., Pfeifer, T., & Weck, M. (1997). *Manufacturing Excellence in Global Markets*. London: Chapman and Hall.

Fisher, J. G. (2001). *E-Business for Small Businesses*. London: Kogan Page.

Frank, K. A., Gupta, S. K. S., Richard, G. G., & Schwiebert, L. (2005). *Fundamentals of Mobile and Pervasive Computing*. New York: McGraw Hill.

Korgaonker, M. G. (1992). *Just In Time Manufacturing.* New Delhi: Macmillan India Limited.

Lee, J., & Wang, B. (1999). *Computer Aided Maintenance: Methodology and Practices*. Dordrecht: Kluwer Academic Publishers.

Liker, J. K. (2004). *The Toyota Way: 14 Management Principals from World's Greatest Manufacturer*. New York: McGraw Hill Publications.

Medland, A. J., & Burnett, P. (1986). *CADCAM in Practice: A Manager's Guide to Understanding and using CADCAM.* London: Kogan Page.

Milner, D. A., & Vasiliou, V. C. (1986). *Computer Aided Engineering for Manufacturing*. London: Kogan Page.

Moody, P. D., & Morley, R. E. (1999). *The Technology Machine: How Manufacturing Will Work in Year 2020*. New York: The Free Press.

Stokes, D. (2002). *Small Business Management*. New York: Continuum.

Underwood, L. (1994). *Intelligent Manufacturing*. Wok Hingham, England: Addison-Wesley Publishing Company.

Vos, I., & Klein, P. D. (2002). *The Essential Guide to Mobile Business*. Englewood Cliffs, NJ: Prentice Hall.

Wilson, J. R., Cruz, M. D., Cobb, S., & Eastgate, R. (1996). *Virtual Reality for Industrial Applications: Opportunities and Limitations*. Nottingham, England: Nottingham University Press.

Womack, J.P., Jones, D.T., & Roos, Daniel. (1990). *Machine that changed the world*. New York: Simon and Schuster.

Womack, J. P., & Jones, D. T. (2005). *Lean Solutions: How Companies and Customers can Create Value and Wealth Together*. London: Simon and Schuster.

KEY TERMS AND DEFINITIONS

Just in Time (JIT): JIT is a philosophy of continuous improvement in which non-value-adding activities (or wastes) are identified and removed. It also aims to reduce inventory in all forms – raw material, in-process and final product.

Kanban: A system of continuous supply of products, components and raw materials such that a work center gets exactly the quantity it needs at regular time intervals. The word "kan" means "card" in Japanese and the word "ban" means "signal". So kanban refers to "signal cards".

Lean Manufacturing: Lean manufacturing or lean production is a production practice that considers the expenditure of resources for any goal other than the creation of value for the end customer to be wasteful, and thus a target for elimination. Lean manufacturing is a generic process management philosophy derived mostly from the Toyota Production System (TPS).

Mistake Proofing: Mistake proofing or 'Poka Yoke' is one of the main components of Shingo's Zero Quality Control (ZQC) system. It aims to produce zero defective products. It includes small devices that are used to either detect or prevent defects from occurring at the source.

Pervasive Computing: Pervasive computing is a trend towards increasingly connected computing devices in the environment, which has been made possible by a convergence of advanced electronic, internet and mobile communication technologies. Pervasive computing devices are very tiny and even invisible devices, either mobile or embedded in objects including cars, tools, appliances, clothing and various consumer goods. These devices communicate through increasingly interconnected networks.

RFID: Radio frequency identification (RFID) is a tag applied to or incorporated on an object for the purpose of identification and tracking using radio frequency. It is used in product identification in inventory and supply chain management.

Small and Medium Enterprises (SME): Small and medium enterprises (SME) are defined in term of investments made in machinery and plant. In India, a unit with investment upto INR 50 million is termed as small enterprise and upto INR 100 million is termed as medium enterprise.

SMED: Single minute exchange of die (SMED) is a concept to bring setup time on any machine or production system to single digit of minutes (less than 10 minutes). This is an important tool in lean manufacturing to achieve smaller production batch sizes and to improve flexibility.

Value Stream Mapping: Value stream mapping is an important technique used in lean manufacturing to map and analyze material and information flow in a production system. This is used to identify non value adding activities, which need to be curtailed or eliminated

APPENDIX A

Table 3.

		Brake lining				Rubber				Plastics			
	General Information	**B1**	**B2**	**B3**	**R1**	**R2**	**R3**	**R4**	**P1**	**P2**	**P3**	**P4**	**Average**
	Main Customer sector (Auto (A)/Engineering (E)/ Others (O)	A	A	O	A	O	O	O	A	A	E	E	
	Whether Export is Significant (more than 20% of turnover) (Yes/Y or No/N)	Y	Y	N	Y	N	N	N	N	N	N	N	
	Management (Family based (F)/ Professional (P))	P	P	F	F	F	P	F	F	F	F	F	
	In house R&D facilities (Y/N)	Y	Y	N	Y	Y	N	N	Y	N	N	N	
I	**Buffer Management/JIT Manufacturing**												
A	**Implementation of pull type manufacturing systems**												1.2
1	Not implemented		■	■	■	■	■	■	■	■	■	■	
2	Being undertaken as pilot project												
3	Implemented in final assembly area	■											
4	Implemented in main manufacturing work centers												
5	Kanban/pull system employed in entire manufacturing chain												
B	**Emphasis on small batch manufacturing**												1.9
1	manufacture entire order quantity in one lot			■			■	■				■	
2	production quantity is determined based on supply schedules				■	■			■	■	■		
3	batch sizes have been decided based on EOQ		■										
4	invested in flexible production schedules to make small batches	■											
5	lot size of one is possible in the production system												
C	**Implementation of SMED/Setup reductions**												
1	Not implemented anywhere			■	■	■	■	■		■		■	1.6
2	Implemented in one or two work centers								■		■		
3	Implemented at considerable number of work centers		■										
4	Implemented in few production lines	■											
5	Implemented throughout plant covering all production lines												

continued on the following page

Table 3. continued

D	**Implementation of visual management in your firm**												1.8
1	Not implemented			■		■	■	■				■	
2	Implemented in one or two work centers		■							■	■		
3	Implemented at considerable number of work centers	■			■				■				
4	Implemented in few production lines												
5	Implemented throughout plant covering all production lines												
E	**Implementation of waste reduction programme**												1.9
1	Not implemented			■		■	■	■				■	
2	Implemented in one or two work centers								■	■	■		
3	Implemented at considerable number of work centers		■		■								
4	Implemented in few production lines												
5	Implemented throughout plant covering all production lines	■											
F	**Use of Error prevention at source and mistake proofing**												1.6
1	Not implemented			■		■	■	■			■	■	
2	Implemented in one or two work centers		■		■				■	■			
3	Implemented at considerable number of work centers												
4	Implemented in few production lines	■											
5	Implemented throughout plant covering all production lines												

Table 4.

		Brake lining			Rubber				Plastics				
		B1	B2	B3	R1	R2	R3	R4	P1	P2	P3	P4	Average
A	**Use of kaizen and continuous improvement**												2.5
1	No emphasis						■					■	
2	Very small emphasis			■				■		■			
3	Considerable emphasis		■		■	■			■		■		
4	Strong emphasis												
5	Very strong emphasis	■											
B	**Emphasis on value stream mapping**												1.4
1	No emphasis			■	■	■	■	■	■	■	■	■	
2	Very small emphasis		■										
3	Considerable emphasis												
4	Strong emphasis	■											
5	Very strong emphasis												
C	**Relationship with suppliers**												2.5
1	No emphasis on vendor relations												
2	Purchases are made from selected vendors			■			■	■		■	■	■	
3	Vendor evaluation and selection is done		■		■	■			■				
4	Vendors are helped to improve their processes and quality	■											
5	Close relationship and regular communication is kept with vendors												
D	**Use of quality assurance and total quality management**												2.6
1	No quality assurance programme in place												
2	Formal quality assurance programme in place with ISO systems			■		■	■	■		■	■	■	
3	Quality improvement projects are undertaken on limited scale				■				■				
4	SQC/SPC are implemented in processes		■										
5	TQM programme is implemented with involvement of all	■											
E	**Use of information system**												2.6
1	No formal information system is used												
2	Use of computers is made in different sections				■	■	■	■		■	■	■	

continued on the following page

Table 4. continued

3	Information is made available at various points of use in the organization			■					■				
4	ERP system is implemented within organization	■	■										
5	Customers and suppliers are part of computerised information system												
F	**Emphasis on housekeeping and 5S**												2.5
1	No emphasis											■	
2	Very small emphasis			■		■	■	■		■	■		
3	Considerable emphasis		■		■				■				
4	Strong emphasis												
5	Very strong emphasis	■											
G	**System of equipment management**												2.4
1	Breakdown maintenance is frequently used							■				■	
2	Maintenance is done in between production schedules and on holidays			■			■		■	■	■		
3	Proper preventive maintenance is implemented		■		■	■							
4	Predictive maintenance and condition monitoring of critical equipment is also done along with preventive maintenance												
5	TPM is implemented with involvement of all	■											

Table 5.

		Brake lining			Rubber				Plastics				
		B1	**B2**	**B3**	**R1**	**R2**	**R3**	**R4**	**P1**	**P2**	**P3**	**P4**	**Average**
A	**Emphasis on team working for improvement projects**												2.0
1	No emphasis					■	■	■		■	■	■	
2	Very small emphasis			■	■				■				
3	Considerable emphasis		■										
4	Strong emphasis												
5	Very strong emphasis	■											
B	**Emphasis on training and development of employees and executives**												2.5
1	No emphasis							■				■	
2	Very small emphasis			■		■	■			■	■		
3	Considerable emphasis				■				■				
4	Strong emphasis		■										
5	Very strong emphasis	■											
C	**Emphasis on selection and compensation based skills and knowledge**												2.5
1	No emphasis												
2	Very small emphasis			■		■	■	■		■	■	■	
3	Considerable emphasis		■		■				■				
4	Strong emphasis	■											
5	Very strong emphasis												
D	**Emphasis on multiskilling and job rotation**												**1.7**
1	No emphasis			■		■	■	■			■	■	
2	Very small emphasis				■				■	■			
3	Considerable emphasis		■										
4	Strong emphasis	■											
5	Very strong emphasis												

Table 6.

		Brake lining			Rubber				Plastics				
		B1	**B2**	**B3**	**R1**	**R2**	**R3**	**R4**	**P1**	**P2**	**P3**	**P4**	**Average**
A	**Level of knowledge management has about lean manufacturing**												1.7
1	No knowledge			■		■	■	■			■	■	
2	Very little knowledge		■		■				■	■			
3	Few people are trained on lean manufacturing systems												
4	Considerable understanding												
5	Organization has well trained human resource to implement Lean manufacturing	■											
B	**Commitment of management to implement Lean**												1.6
1	No commitment			■		■	■	■		■	■	■	
2	Very little commitment		■		■				■				
3	Considerable level of commitment												
4	Strong commitment												
5	Very strong commitment	■											
C	**Availability of human resource to implement lean management**												1.5
1	Not adequate and qualified to understand and implement lean manufacturing			■	■	■	■	■	■	■	■	■	
2	Only key managers have adequate education and experience		■										
3	Considerable number of management staff has education and experience to implement lean manufacturing												
4	Both managers and supervisors are capable of understanding and implementation												
5	Large number of employees have been trained and have experience of implementing lean manufacturing	■											
D	**Level of machinery and plant to implement lean manufacturing**												3.4
1	Processes are labour intensive and not enough machinery are available												
2	Old equipment are employed which are not very reliable						■	■					

continued on the following page

Table 6. continued

3	Only some critical equipment are available with latest technology but supporting equipment and processes are old			■		■					■	■	
4	Key manufacturing processes have been supported with equipment that support lean manufacturing		■		■				■	■			
5	Invested in equipment with flexibility manufacturing and visual control systems throughout production system	■											

Chapter 5
RMS:
A New Linkage with Pervasive Computing

Vasdev Malhotra
Y.M.C.A. Institute of Engineering, India

Tilak Raj
Y.M.C.A. Institute of Engineering, India

Ashok Kumar
Y.M.C.A. Institute of Engineering, India

ABSTRACT

Today, markets increasingly require more customized products, with shorter life cycles. In response, manufacturing systems have evolved from mass production techniques to the flexible automation. This paper argues that **manufacturing** *systems of the next generation will have to incorporate more flexibility and intelligence, evolving towards reconfigurable manufacturing systems. In particular, the concept of intelligence becomes more relevant because of the need to maintain effective and efficient manufacturing operations with minimum downtime under conditions of* **uncertainty**. *This chapter presents some research issues related to the development of reconfigurable manufacturing systems with pervasive computing.*

INTRODUCTION

Reconfigurable pervasive computing is defined as "an ability to repeatedly configure machine to perform different and varying functions (Batia, 1997).It refers to the ability to customize the architecture to match the computation and data flow of the application (Bondalapati, et al., 2002). Reconfigurable Manufacturing Systems (RMS) can be cost-effectively reconfigured to rapidly adapt the system's manufacturing capacity and machine functionality in a changing marketplace (Koren, et, al., 1996). Reconfigurability and **adaptation** are achieved through flexible control architectures and open information exchange via networks. In achieving these goals, RMS devices must be designed to function modularly and intelligently. Modularity provides standardized units or dimensions for flexibility and variety of device operations, and intelligence enables devices to function independently and to interoperate with other devices to achieve system functionality goals. With the designated RMS devices, machines and systems can be efficiently and quickly reconfigured, both in hardware and software, to meet new task requirements. However, the successful cooperation

DOI: 10.4018/978-1-60566-996-0.ch005

of RMS devices also relies on the reconfigurability of the communication architecture. (Schickhuber, et al., 1997).

The reconfigurable hardware and software are necessary but not sufficient conditions for a true RMS. The core of the RMS paradigm is an approach to reconfiguration based on system design combined with simultaneous design of open architecture reconfigurable controllers with reconfigurable modular machines that can be designed by synthesis of modular machines. The ultimate goal of Reconfigurable manufacturing system (RMS) is to utilize a systems approach in the design of manufacturing processes that allows reconfiguration to achieve cost effective scalablity.

The pervasive computing technique for control systems on machining tools is point-to-point, which has been successfully implemented in industry for decades. However, expanding physical setups and machining systems functionality push the limits of the point architecture. Hence, a traditional centralized point control system is no longer suitable to meet new requirements, such as modularity, decentralization of control, integrated diagnostics, quick and easy maintenance, and low cost (Eccles, 1998).

When configuring sensors, actuators and controllers together in a reconfigurable machine tool, it is important to investigate the impact of the functionality and limitation of these devices on the capability of a network system. This is one of the issues being investigated in a research effort whose primary goal is to develop methodology and tools for assisting the implementation of a networked architecture at the machine level of an RMS.

BACKGROUND

Nowadays the market is characterized by over capacity and large fluctuations in demands. Therefore today's manufacturing systems should enable flexibility in capacity, **responsiveness** in market changes, product verity, adoption and utilization of new technologies and general scalability in a cost **effective** manner (Abdi, et al., 2003)

Cost in Dedicated manufacturing system (DMS) is low as long as they operate a full capacity. This means that demands should exceed supply. Furthermore, DMS are not scalable, as they have fixed cycle time and capacity (Astley, et al., 1996). Clearly, DMS do not offer an efficient solution for the current market conditions. **Advancement** in manufacturing system is the introduction of Flexible Manufacturing System (FMS). FMS are flexible, scalable systems that support product variety. They are however rather complex as they are constructed with all possible functionality built in despite of fact in many cases not all of it is needed. This level of complexity requires highly skilled personnel are to be employed.(Kamimura, et al, 2001) As a result the capital cost and acquisition risk are very high. Although FMS focus on flexibility they are obsolete, as their hardness and software are predetermined and fixed. This means that they are not adequately responsive to change as their capabilities in term of upgrading additions and customization are limited. Moreover FMS were built for low or medium volume productivity, so they are not suitable for large market fluctuations. The new paradigm needed by today manufacturing should incorporate the advantages of FMS but also be similar, responsive and less costly. The reconfigurable manufacturing system (RMS) paradigm attempts to satisfy these requirements and avoid the shortcomings of the previous conventional manufacturing philosophies. RMS, associated with pervasive computing is designed for rapid adjustment of production capacity and functionality in response to new circumstances by rearrangement or change of its components". This definition implies that the benefits of a reconfigurable manufacturing system arise from a constantly changing marketplace. The reconfigurable manufacturing is the latest development in the general field of computer integrated manufacturing system. But reconfigurable manufacturing systems have some barriers also that the advances in reconfigurable manufacturing will not occur without machine tools that have modular structure to provide the necessary characteristics for quick configuration. However the lack of machine tool design methodology and lack of interfaces are the major barriers.

With respect to RMS, these changes include:

- Increasing frequency of new product introductions due to shorter product life cycles,
- Changes in parts for existing products to improve product customizations
- Large fluctuations in the quantity and mix of product demand
- Changes in government safety and environmental regulations

Keeping in view the above advantages of RMS an attempt has been made in this paper to study some important issues related to design and implementation of RMS

REASEARCH ISSUES RELATED TO RECONFIGRUABLE MANUFACTURING SYSTEM (RMS)

The following sections present a review regarding the different research areas critical for developing and integrating reconfigurable and intelligent machines.

Structural Design of Reconfigurable and Machines

The concept of Reconfigurable Machine Tools (RMTs) appeared in the early 1990s as a particular trend that evolved directly from the concept of FMS (Chick, et al. 2000). Machine tools available in today's markets have been designed for flexibility in terms of the types of processes and geometric complexity of the product that can be manufactured (see Figure 1).

Multi-axis machining and turning centers capable of performing different types of operations on multiple planes of a work piece for any given set-up are widely used today.

This flexibility is provided at a high cost, given that only a very limited subset of the machine tool's capabilities are used at any given instant. Clearly, the user has to pay for any **unused** capacity. In response, concepts such as modular machine tool construction were explored and developed during the past 10 years in an effort to reduce costs (Acherkan 2000).

The concept of reconfigurability imposes very specific constraints on the structural design of a machine. According to (Mehrabi, et al., 2002), quick design and realization are important components of this technology, and as a consequence the dimensions that must be incorporated in RMTs are:

- Ease of assembly and integration with monitoring, actuation systems;
- Design for structural **integrity** and dynamic stiffness of machine tool.
- Design for rapid ramp up systems for rapid diagnosis.

Manufacturing Process and Simulation Machines

Machine intelligence is greatly enhanced through the incorporation of manufacturing process models into the controllers. There is extensive research on modeling of manufacturing processes (Saad, 2003).The current trend is gradually incorporating these manufacturing process models into the machine controllers, together with additional machine sensors. With process-oriented controllers, and associated programming systems, there are multiple benefits in the operation of machine tools, for example: increased machine productivity

Figure 1. Network of reconfigurable and intelligent machine (Source De Silva, 2000)

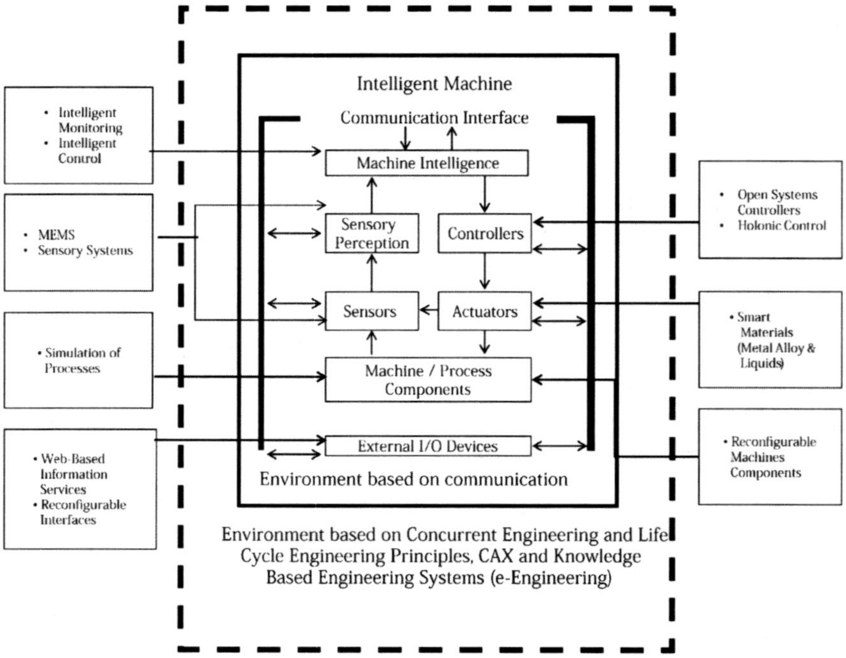

through adaptive control, improved machine reliability through avoidance of process instability.

Micro Electro-Mechanical Devices for Sensors

In pervasive computing the design of new reconfigurable machines will therefore depend on an intelligent use of sensor and actuator devices to reduce cost without compromising capabilities. In that sense, MEMS-based sensors and actuators have an enormous **potential.** According to (Shah, et al., 2003). Microsystems, involve both electronic and non-electronic elements, and perform functions that can include sensing, signal processing, actuation, control and display. MEMS are fabricated either by bulk micromachining or surface micro-machining. There are many advantages of MEMS devices compared with the elements they replace. For example, they can be so small that hundreds of them can fit in the same space as one single macro-device that performs the same function.

Integrated Machine Development Based on Scientific Engineering

In machine development, a synergetic combination of mechanics, electronics, software and computing requires that individuals possess a multidisciplinary understanding of relevant scientific and engineering principles (Selim, et al., 1998). This individual knowledge must be sufficiently comprehensive to be able to create the **innovative** combination, which makes up a mechatronic solution. To support this mechatronic solution, appropriate design methods and tools backed by computer design facilities are needed. The individual software tools for mechanical, electronic and software engineering are all available, and there has been considerable progress in bringing them together to provide a coherent simulation environment by which the performance of a given mechatronic system can be assessed.

Effective Network Control System Solutions

In order to achieve effective NCS solutions for RMS control systems a number of issues must be addressed in addition to the performance **analysis.** One important issue involves the utilization of smart devices which are smart sensors, smart actuators and networked controllers. Smart sensors or actuators have three major features: intelligence, communication ability, and data acquisition or actuation, respectively, Besides network-capable application processors, the major functionalities of networked controllers are to analyze the sensor data, make decisions, and give commands to actuation devices. The control algorithms should handle decentralized information analysis as well as the traditional centralized cases. (Raji, R., 1994)

FUTURE TRENDS

Research in the architecture, configuration and use of dynamic reconfigurable pervasive computing is ongoing. Some of the major challenges involve organizing and interfacing configurable **logic**, designing new concept foe scheduling the computations, developing software tools for designing reconfigurable computer architectures and simulation of reconfigurable pervasive computing system .The future research topics includes:

- Reconfigurable assembly line: The production capacity in **assembly** lines could be increased through **replication** and modularization. (Chow, 1998)
- Reconfigurable material handling, fixturing and grasping devices systems
- Reconfigurable and self reconfigurable robots
- Identification of Reconfigurable computing business needs and formation of new organization strategies.
- Development of reconfigurable pervasive computing control technology for the organization

CONCLUSION

This paper provided the study of key Issues related to design and implementation of RMS. Based on the literature review presented in this paper the authors argue that the following research issues must be addressed to design and integrate reconfigurable and intelligent machines.

- Manufacturing machine concepts: design, manufacturing and integration of reconfigurable machines.
- Application of concurrent engineering and life cycle engineering theories.
- Supporting technologies: design and development of web-based information systems for integrated machine development

REFERENCES

Abdi, M. R., & Labib, A. W. (2003). A design strategy for reconfigurable manufacturing systems (RMS) using Analytical hierarchical process (AHP): A Case Study. *International Journal of Production Research*, *41*(10), 2273–2299. doi:10.1080/0020754031000077266

Batia, D. (1997). Reconfigurable computing technology. *Journal of Design & Manufacturing*, *2*(4), 312–315.

Chick, J., Hooman, & Roosmalenl, O.V. (2000). Modular Control for Machine Tools: Cross-Coupling control with friction compensation. *International Journal of Machine Control*, *2*(21), 455–462.

Chow, W. M. (1998). Assembly lines Design Methodology and Applications. *Journal of Manufacturing Technology*, *1*(2), 61–65.

Desilva, Moon. D. B., Stewart, R. A., Volpe, & Khosla, P.K. (2000). Design of dynamically reconfigurable real-time software using port-based objects. *Journal of Automation & Control*, *1*(23), 759–775.

Ding, Y., Ceglarek, D., & Shi, J. (2002). Fault diagnosis of multistage manufacturing processes by using state space approach. *Journal of Manufacturing Science*, *1*(24), 313–322. doi:10.1115/1.1445155

Haas, E., Schwarz, R. C., & Papazian, J. M. (2002). Design and test of a reconfigurable forming die. *Journal of Manufacturing Process*, *1*(4), 77–86. doi:10.1016/S1526-6125(02)70134-5

Hart, A. J., Slocum, A., & Willoughby, P. (2004). Kinematic coupling interchangeability . *Journal of Manufacturing Engineering*, *1*(28), 1–15.

Kamimura, A., Murata, S., Yoshida, S., Kurakawa, H., Tomita, K., & Kokaji, S. (2001). Selfreconfigurable modular robot-experiments on reconfiguration and locomotion's. *International Journal of Intelligent Robots and Systems*, 606-612

Kondalapati, K., & Prasanna, V. K. (2002). Reconfigurable Computing System. *Journal of Manufacturing Process*, *90*, 1201–1217.

Koren, Y., Pasek, Z., Ulsoy, A., & Benchetrit, U. (1996). Real time Open Control Architectures and System Performance. *Journal of Manufacturing Process*, *1*(45), 377–380.

Landers, R., & Ulsoy, A. (1998). Supervisory Machining Control: Design approach and experiments. *Journal of Manufacturing Technology*, *1*(47), 301–306.

Maier-Speredelozzi, V., & Husoy, J. S. (2002). Selecting manufacturing system configuration based on performance using AHP. *Journal of Robotic and Automation*, *1*(1), 23–28.

McGee, D. (1999). From Craftsmanship to Drafmanship: Naval Architecture and the Three Traditions of Early Modern Design. *Journal of Technology and Culture*, *1*(40), 209–236.

Mehrabi, M. G., Ulsoy, A. G., & Koren, Y. (2000). Reconfigurable manufacturing systems and their enabling technologies. *International Journal of Manufacturing Technology*, *1*(1), 113–130.

Moon, S. K., Moon, Y., Kota, S., & Landers, R. (2001). Screw theory based methodology for design and error compensation of machine tools. *Journal of Computer Aided Manufacturing*, *1*(1), 45–49.

Raji, R. (1994). Smart Networks for Control. *Journal of Robotic and Automation*, *6*(31), 49–55.

Saad, S. M. (2003). The Reconfiguration Manufacturing Systems. *Journal of Materials Processing Technology*, *34*(1), 3–20.

Schick Huber, G., & McCarthy, O. (1997). Distributed Field bus and Control network system. *Journal of Computing & Control Engineering*, *1*(8), 22–32.

Selim, H. M., Askin, R. G., & Vakharia, A. J. (1998). Cell formation in group Technology Review, Evaluation and Direction for Future Research. *Journal of Computers and Industrial Engineering*, *34*(1), 3–20. doi:10.1016/S0360-8352(97)00147-2

Shah, R., & Ward, P. T. (2003). Lean Manufacturing: context, practice bundles and performance. *Journal of Operations Management*, *21*(2), 129–149. doi:10.1016/S0272-6963(02)00108-0

Tilbury, D. M., & Kota, S. (1999). Integrated machine and control design for reconfigurable machine tools. *Journal of Advanced Intelligent Mechatronics*, *1*(1), 629–634.

Walczyk, D., Lakshmikanthan, J., & Kirk, D. (1998). Development of a reconfigurable tools for forming aircraft body panels . *Journal of Manufacturing Systems*, *1*(17), 287–296. doi:10.1016/S0278-6125(98)80076-9

Yigit, A. S., & Ulsoy, A. G. (2002). Dynamic stiffness evaluation for reconfigurable machine tools including weakly non-linear joint characteristics. *Journal of Manufacturing Engineering*, *1*(6), 87–101.

ADDITIONAL READING

Annals of CIRP, Vol 2, pp. 1-114

... *European Journal of Operational Research*, *25*, 58–64. doi:10.1016/0377-2217(86)90159-1

... *International Journal of Flexible Manufacturing Systems*, *16*, 5–9. doi:10.1023/B:FLEX.0000039311.13861.a7

International Journal of Manufacturing Technology, Vol 15, pp. 17-25

... *International Journal of Technology Management*, *8*, 294–298.

... *Journal of Advanced Manufacturing Systems*, *22*, 224–235.

Journal of Dynamic System Measurement Control, Vol 120, pp. 346-351

Journal of Industrial Engineering, Vol 1, pp. 426-431

... *Journal of Intelligent Manufacturing*, *8*, 147–156. doi:10.1023/A:1018560922013

Journal of Machine Design, Vol 114, pp.117-125

Journal of Manufacturing and Service Operations, Vol 2, pp. 32-38

Journal of Manufacturing Science, Vol 4, pp. 91-117

Journal of Production Reseach, Vol 38, pp. 4159-4169

Journal of Robotic and Automation, Vol 2, pp.121-124

Reconfigurable Machine Tool, U. S. Patent 5, 943,750

The FMS Magazine, April, 1984

... *The International Journal of Robotics Research*, *18*, 225–242.

Website, http://www4.gartner.com

Website, http://www. americanmachinist.com

Website, http://www assenblymag.com

KEY TERMS AND DEFINITIONS

Adaptability: This is an approach towards flexibility by characteristic a system ability to deliver intended functionality under varying conditions through the design variables.

Dimensional Flexibility: It is the classification scheme which builds the concept of base dimensions describing flexibility in terms of configuration changes in the design space.

Flexibility: The system that implies changes in both the design and performance.

Modularity: This is an approach achieving mass dimensional flexibility in that those modules comprising a system can be replaced and updated.

Pervasive Computing: Pervasive computing deals with control systems on machining tools to point to point applications.

Reconfigurability: A subset of flexibility in which system configurations can be changed repeatedly and reversibly

Section 3
Pervasive Computing in Quality Control

Section 3 consists of three chapters. Chapter 6, "A Quality Assurance System in a Pervasive Computing Environment", identifies the need of an adaptive quality assurance system using Pervasive computing devices to face competition in complex and dynamic business environment. This system ensures the quality of the final products that takes its parts from various suppliers and is responsive to the existing quality environment at the various sources that contribute to the manufacture of the product or delivery of the service. The chapter further proposes an approach to integrate decision making in the context of the entire supply chain. Chapter 7, "The Role of Computer-Mediated Communication Modes in Enhancing Audit Quality: An Empirical Study", explains how Computer mediated communication can enhance the audit quality and effectiveness of meeting in the Egyptian auditing scenario. It also discusses how Computer-Mediated Communication (CMC) modes can enhance the auditor performance in auditing firms and provide competitive advantage. Chapter 8, "Evaluating the Dimensions of Web-Based Software System Service Quality: An Empirical Study", describes various aspects of appraising the web-based service quality and identifies six web-based service quality dimensions; information quality, responsiveness, web assistance, tangibles, empathy, and call-back.

Chapter 6
A Quality Assurance System in a Pervasive Computing Environment

Amitava Mitra
Auburn University, USA

ABSTRACT

As the competition for products and services continues to grow, with customer satisfaction playing an integral part in this process, organizations are faced with the task of ensuring quality in all of their activities. Since many organizations do not necessarily produce the entire product or deliver the service by themselves, they are dependent on other vital sources, for example, suppliers, that impact quality of the finished product/service. This necessitates development and implementation of a quality management system which can integrate information from the various entities to facilitate decision making in a timely manner. Additionally, it is desirable for such a quality management system to be responsive to the existing quality environment at the various sources that contribute to the manufacture of the product or delivery of the service. This chapter provides a foundation for accomplishing such quality management objectives.

PERVASIVE COMPUTING IN THE 21ST CENTURY

The advent of the twenty first century has experienced a phenomenal growth in the need for processing of data/information on a real-time basis. The notion of "anytime anywhere" goal associated with mobile computing is now replaced by "all the time and everywhere" associated with pervasive computing. Advances in several areas have enabled the realization of such. One is the area of distributed computing, whereby seamless access to remote information resources has been accomplished. Further, such communication is possible with the features of minimum fault tolerance, high level of security, and a high rate of availability (Satyanarayanan (2001)).

Networking ubiquity of the World Wide Web has made it feasible to promote pervasive computing. Access to information is dynamic and has been

DOI: 10.4018/978-1-60566-996-0.ch006

accomplished through the integration of cellular technology with the Web (Saha, Mukherjee, and Bandyopadhyay (2002)). However, there are certain desirable features that are necessary to expand the role of pervasive computing. These include the ability to integrate various devices (traditional input/output devices, speakers, light-emitting diodes, wireless mobile devices, etc.), along with smart devices, that include intelligent appliances and sensors, that automatically collect information, transfer it, and are able to take appropriate actions accordingly. Further, effective pervasive computing will require a "middleware" to interface between the networking structure and the end-user applications (Saha and Mukherjee (2003)). Perhaps, the most utility of pervasive computing will be realized through the use of intelligent devices. Such may encompass enhanced wearable devices, identity transponders, and the like of imbedded devices, which has the potential of major breakthroughs in health care (Tentori, M., & Favela, J. (2008)).

Gone are the days where a product or service is manufactured or delivered by a single entity or organization. There are several reasons for this occurrence. First, the complexity of products has increased tremendously. Second, customer needs are varied and dynamic. Third, competition is on a global basis, necessitating the need for continuous improvement. All of these challenges require integration of information from various sources. Such information must be acquired in a timely manner through pervasive computing means. Further, a static model in quality management does not address the continued quality changes that may take place in the various entities. To overcome this problem, an adaptive model is proposed in this chapter.

Traditional concepts of quality management as advocated by renowned experts (Deming (1982), Crosby (1979, 1989), Juran (1986), Juran and Gryna (1993)) are based on the foundation of a single entity having the major impact on the quality of the product or service. The prescriptions on sound quality management principles from these experts are usually therefore guidelines for management of the particular organization.

Customer needs continue to expand and change with time. Since all organizations are interested in increasing their market share, this can be achieved by meeting customer needs, effectively and efficiently, on a dynamic basis. Product specialization has mandated many conceptual changes in the way processes are designed. For example, to address product customization based on customer requirements, the concept of just-in-time production (JIT) has been adopted by organizations (Womack and Jones (1996)). This has the features of reducing inventory carrying costs and lead time. However, it is also based on certain assumptions that must be held to meet demand, quality, and delivery requirements. For example, it assumes that a quality part or sub-assembly will be available, in the quantity that is required based on customer demand. It also assumes that such quantities will be available when they are demanded so as to not increase the lead time for delivery of the finished product as promised to the customer by the organization. A typical example of such a situation is the assemble to order of computers to satisfy specific needs of the customer.

Complexity and specialization of products has had an impact on the procurement and manufacturing functions. Specific components or sub-assemblies associated with a product could be made by organizations (suppliers) distinct from the original equipment manufacturer (OEM). These suppliers have a niche in the production of the component/sub-assembly, leading to improved quality and a competitive price. Because of such efficiencies, the OEM finds it desirable to sub-contract certain components/sub-assemblies to various providers or suppliers. While it allows the OEM to focus on its core competencies, at the same time, it is able to maintain its edge in quality and cost. An integrated quality management model, as described in this chapter, should therefore address the quality of the components/

sub-assemblies as it will impact the quality of the finished product.

Advances in information technology have made it possible to obtain data and use it for decision making in a timely fashion. This encompasses data from all sources; point of sale data based on customer demand, inventory data at all levels (i.e., OEM as well as in tier-suppliers at various levels), lead time information based on available suppliers, employee productivity, and quality level, along with other types such as financial, and process-related information. With efficient means of data storage, update, and retrieval being available to all the units associated with the product/service, databases are capable of storing current information pertaining to decisions. These current decisions can be used to estimate the existing quality of certain important process parameters, which can be used subsequently for making future decisions. This is the concept of an adaptive model, which is also a unique feature of this chapter.

In the twenty-first century, many business models are global in nature with suppliers and customers geographically dispersed. To accomplish efficiency in operations as well as meet customer needs on a timely basis, organizations are developing business relationships with partners globally. Partners must have the ability to provide a quality product/service at a competitive price thereby allowing the OEM to maintain its competitive edge in the market place. The internet has made it feasible to communicate and share information across all units of the organization as well as its suppliers. Hence, using concepts in pervasive computing will allow organizations of today to function effectively.

Applications of Pervasive Computing in the Enterprise Context

The use of the methodology associated with pervasive computing has witnessed applications in quality assurance systems as well. One example involves automobile manufacturing (Stiefmeier, Roggen, Tröster, Ogris, and Lukowicz (2008)), where it is recommended that a context-aware wearable computing system could support a production or maintenance worker by recognizing the worker's actions and delivering just-in-time information about activities to be performed. Such a system could be used on a proactive basis. They could be used to streamline the training process, whereby wearable systems could provide online instructions to trainees about upcoming assembly steps. Additionally, in the event that the operator does not follow the outlined procedure adequately, a warning signal could be generated that would prompt the operator to make appropriate changes.

Another example of quality assurance through process control is in the semiconductor manufacturing industry. Fabrication facilities that have a strong customer orientation need to be flexible to meet the varying needs of customers on a dynamic basis. This may require a rearrangement of the machinery and other technical equipment. To incorporate such needs, a system that combines active RFID, passive RFID, and ultrasound sensors to track wafer boxes have been used in a chip manufacturing process (Thiesse, Fleisch, and Dierkes (2006)).

Quality management models, for the most part, have focused on addressing issues from an individual organizational point of view (Ahire & Golhar (1996), Ghobadian & Gallear (1996)). As discussed previously, the competitiveness of the organization (OEM) is influenced by entities beyond its physical boundaries. These include suppliers and vendors, customer support and service, stakeholders, and the customer. What is necessary is a holistic approach to information needs of the organization. A pervasive computing approach clearly has an advantage to capture all such informational needs for decision making by management.

Businesses have become global in nature with customers, suppliers, manufacturers, retailers, and distributors located in not only in different parts of a country but also in various countries. There is a multitude of performance measures/metrics that are considered by the entities of the entire supply chain. An effective supply chain has the objective to create an alliance of these various business processes by linking the supplier, manufacturer, distributor, and the customer. Some common performance measures are high quality, low cost, short lead times, high flexibility and responsiveness to customer needs. A good review of decision support models for the design of global supply chains is found in Meixell and Gargeya (2005). Since the performance measures are necessarily not in the same units and may have different priorities associated with them, Talluri and Baker (2002) discuss a multi-phase mathematical programming approach for effective supply chain design. A specific application of pervasive computing and sensor technologies for improving the efficiency of a supply chain in the perishable food industry is found in Ilic, Staake, and Fleisch (2009). A model is formulated that examines the trade-offs between profit maximization and carbon footprint emission minimization.

Management decision making comprises various facets related to product and/or process design, information about the suppliers and their capabilities, production/manufacturing/assembly information and their capabilities, financial information to support the organizational objectives, stakeholders needs and customer related information. Figure 1 shows the importance of creating an enterprise-wide database that captures information from the various sources such that each unit has the ability to contribute, access, and share data and use the related information for decision making. As the enterprise-wide database is updated on a real-time basis, all of the various sub-units, including suppliers and vendors, have access to current information. This facilitates decision making that is not only timely but also based on the most current information. Since the enterprise-wide database has this feature, the concept of developing an adaptive quality model becomes feasible since it can incorporate the most current information and thereby minimizes the risks associated with appropriate decisions.

Supply-chain management literature (Bowersox, Closs, & Cooper (2002)) describes the

Figure 1. Information needs captured by an enterprise-wide database(Mitra, A. (2008). Fundamentals of Quality Control and Improvement, Third Edition. Reprinted with permission of John Wiley & Sons, Inc.)*

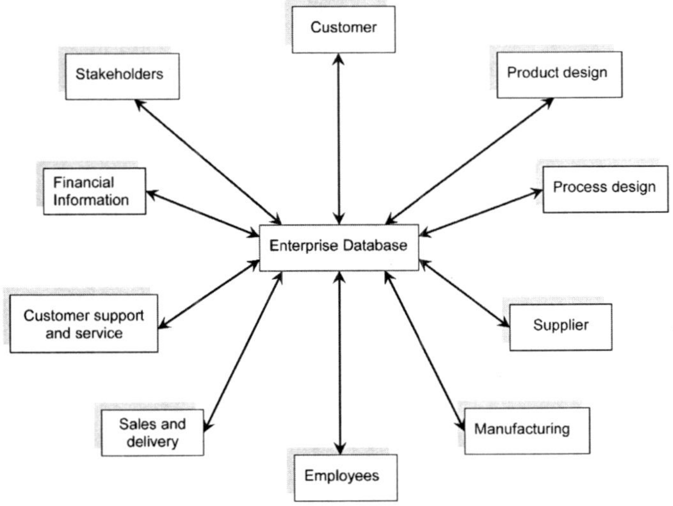

structure whereby companies link to form partnerships with external organizations, which could be vendors, suppliers, and distributors, to increase their operational efficiency as well as leverage their strategic positioning. Since the organization or the original equipment manufacturer (OEM) has certain core competencies, it selects vendors/suppliers that can address its non-core competencies. Hence, an OEM could obtain components or sub-assemblies from suppliers. These suppliers are not necessarily unique to an OEM but could be serving multiple OEMs. Therefore, a situation is created whereby supply chains rather than OEMs compete with each other. Figure 2 shows a supply chain configuration. Note that the customer is still the central theme, whose needs or expectations are to be met or exceeded in order to improve market share. Quality and cost associated with the product are influenced by that of the suppliers, OEMs, and distributors considered collectively.

In order to fully utilize the capabilities of pervasive computing and the enterprise-wide database, access to and updating of information must be conducted on a real-time basis. The enterprise-wide database shown in Figure 1 and the supply-chain configuration shown in Figure 2 need to be integrated. An alternative representation of Figure 2 may be accomplished by constructing a network that demonstrates the linkages between suppliers at various tiers, the original equipment manufacturer and the end customer. Note that there are intermediate customers depending on the links between the various tier suppliers. To grasp the concept of an enterprise-wide database, one needs to now link the databases associated with each supplier and OEM into one database where the network relationships are preserved. Then, process information and customer needs at all tiers can be updated on a dynamic basis. Such information will assist management at individual tiers/phases to determine capacity requirements and plan on updating placement of order requirements. Such a system will have the sensitivity to adapt to end-customer needs and the intermediaries in a responsive manner. It will also alleviate meeting these needs in a timely fashion by utilizing

Figure 2. Supply chain configuration (Mitra, A. (2008). Fundamentals of Quality Control and Improvement, Third Edition. Reprinted with permission of John Wiley & Sons, Inc.)

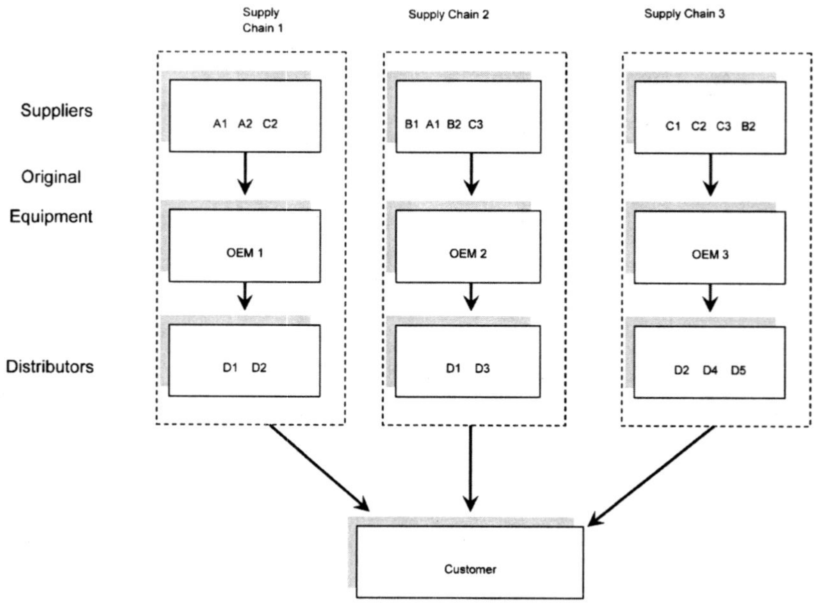

appropriate lead time and order volumes, based on demand and inventory on hand.

In Figure 2, the block diagram depicting the suppliers may be exploded further to demonstrate the hierarchical nature in which components, sub-assemblies, and the finished product is created. The OEM depends on Tier 1 suppliers, who in turn might depend on Tier 2 suppliers, and so forth. So, in making decisions on quality, we wish to incorporate the quality of the tier-level suppliers into the decision framework. Further, we wish to make our model responsive and make decision making at subsequent levels adaptive to quality at prior levels of the hierarchy.

An Adaptive and Integrated Quality Assurance System

A model for monitoring quality is developed assuming that suppliers, from various tiers, submit components/sub-assemblies to the next tier above it, and this scheme continues in a hierarchical fashion. So, a Tier 3 supplier submits to a Tier 2 supplier, a Tier 2 supplier submits to a Tier 1 supplier, and a Tier 1 supplier submits to the OEM. Hence, output quality from the OEM is affected by all of its tiered suppliers as well as the quality systems that prevail at the OEM.

We assume that some form of quality control systems exist at each supplier and OEM, whereby the output from the system is monitored and the process is classified to be in control or not. Such monitoring may take place through various means, such as control charts for the process mean, control charts for the process standard deviation, cumulative sum control charts for monitoring the process mean, among others (Mitra (2008), Montgomery (2004), Woodall & Adams (1993)).

In the basic form of a control chart, the quality characteristic is plotted along the vertical axis, while the horizontal axis represents the samples or subgroups (in order of time) from which the quality characteristic is found. Samples of a certain size are selected and the quality characteristic value is calculated based on the observations in the sample. Examples of the quality characteristic could be the average thickness of a wafer or the average diameter of a part. A typical control chart contains three lines. The centerline, an indication of the process centering, is usually the average value of the characteristic over all the samples. Two other lines, known as the upper control limit and the lower control limit, are used to make decisions about the process. If the plotted points fall within the control limits and do not exhibit any identifiable pattern, the process is deemed to be in statistical control. The placement of the control limits, one on each side of the centerline, is influenced by the level of risks that can be tolerated by the decision maker. The two types of risks are a false alarm and the non-detection of a process that is out-of-control. These two risks are labeled as a Type I error and a Type II error, respectively, and are discussed in detail, subsequently. In this chapter we only consider changes in the process mean to cause out-of-control conditions, even though it is quite possible to include changes in the process standard deviation as being another possible cause. The primary reason is to keep the model simple.

For simplicity, we assume that there is only one supplier per tier. At each tier, based on observations obtained from the process, using an appropriate control chart, a decision is made on the status of the process, i.e., whether it is in control or not. If the process is deemed to be out-of-control, it is assumed that the identification of causes for such will be investigated and remedial actions will be subsequently suggested.

Note that in making decisions on the status of the process, based on observed samples, two types of error may be committed. A Type I error occurs when we conclude that a process is out of control, when it is really in control. Conversely, a Type II error is made when we conclude that a process is in control, when it is really out of control. The relative degree of importance placed on these two types of errors are dependent on the organization, the type of product that they sell, and the type of protection that they wish to allocate for their processes.

Many organizations choose a risk level for a Type I error to be about 0.26%, by using control charts for the mean that have control limits at three standard errors from the center line (Mitra (2008)). A Type I error is a false alarm. If an organization wishes to reduce the probability of a false alarm, the control limits could be moved further out from the center line (say, four standard errors). On the contrary, a Type II error represents the inability to detect a change in the process parameter, in this case the process mean, when there has been one. For critical parts or components, where it is essential that the part be functional, it is desirable to keep the probability of a Type II error to be small. The probability of a Type II error is dependent on the degree of shift of the process parameter. So, for small changes in the process mean from a desirable target, the probability of a Type II error could be large, since detection of such changes could take place with a small probability. However, for large changes in the process mean, the chance of non-detection will decrease. It is known that, for a given sample size of observations, the probability of a Type I error and that of a Type II error are inversely related (Wadsworth, Stephens, & Godfrey (2001)).

In decision making using control charts, the null hypothesis is - H_o: process is in control, while the alternative hypothesis is - H_a: process is not in control. Observe that, based on the decision made at a given phase, only one type of error can be committed for that phase. Hence, if H_o is rejected, only a Type I error may be committed, while if H_o is not rejected, a Type II error may be committed.

We now develop an integrated model for monitoring quality in the entire supply chain that includes suppliers and OEM. An assumption is made that the suppliers operate independently. Further, we desire an adaptive model that reacts to decisions at prior stages. Our objective is to stay within a tolerable risk, at the overall level, and provide a decision making framework.

The following notation is used to develop the model:

p = number of tiers of suppliers where OEM is at tier p
α_i = probability of a Type I error in tier i
β_i = probability of a Type II error in tier i
$\hat{\mu}_i$ = estimate of the process mean in tier i
α = overall desired level of a Type I error
μ_{oi} = target level of process mean in tier i
σ_i = process standard deviation in tier i
Φ = cumulative distribution function of the standard normal distribution

Let us first develop a model for quality management decision making at each phase, where an overall level (α) of Type I error is specified. With only one tier supplier and OEM, the probability of aType I error is calculated as follows:

Tier 1 level: If H_o is rejected, P (Type I error in tier 1) = a_1
OEM level: If H_o is rejected at this level, P (overall Type I error) = $1 - (1\text{-}\alpha_1)(1\text{-}\alpha_2)$.

Hence if an overall level of Type I error rate (α) is specified, we may adjust the individual Type I error levels (α_i), to accomplish the desired overall level. In general, this concept may be extended to a system with p tiers. The overall Type I error rate is given by

$$\alpha = 1 - \prod_{i=1}^{p} (1 - \alpha_i). \tag{1}$$

The more the number of tier-suppliers, the greater the chance of a false alarm. False alarms, in many organizations, result in a wasted effort in identifying special causes in processes when there really is none. It can be seen that with suppliers at three tiers and the OEM, if the false alarm rate at each stage is selected to be 5%, the overall

Type I error is about 19%. This may not be an acceptable level. Conversely, if we were to select an acceptable overall false alarm rate of 5%, one can determine what the Type I error rates at the tier levels would have to be, so as to satisfy this requirement. Assuming equal false alarm rates at each tier level and the OEM, this would be about 1.27% at each level. The impact of such a level would be to impact the control limits in the corresponding tier levels. To decrease the false-alarm rate, the control limits would move outward.

Another approach could be to base the selection levels of the Type I error at a certain tier *i* based on the outcome that occurred in the previous tier (*i*-1). This approach utilizes information at the prior phase and chooses the parameters on an adaptive basis. Suppose in tier (*i*-1), the decision was to not reject H_o. Given this outcome, the chances of an error are of Type II. So, at the level of tier *i*, we may place more emphasis on detecting a process change, if there is one. In order to detect changes with a higher probability, the control limits will be tighter around the center line.

Now, let us examine the sequential nature of the decision making process:

Tier 1 level: If H_o is rejected, P (Type I error in tier 1) = α_1

OEM level: If H_o is not rejected at this level, P (joint decision) = $\alpha_1\beta_2$

Table 1 shows the probability of a joint decision based on a single tier supplier and the OEM, when the decision at the Tier 1 level is to reject H_o. Note that if the process is in control (H_o is true) at the Tier 1 level, an error in decision making occurs when H_o is rejected. Similarly Table 2 shows the probability of a joint decision, when the decision at the Tier 1 level is to not reject H_o. Only one of the four outcomes in the two tables may occur, the probabilities of which will be influenced by the quality level of the individual tier suppliers and OEM. However, once an outcome occurs at a prior stage, say Tier 1, we can identify the branches of the subsequent outcome. This may then help us determine the degree to which the control limits should be placed relative to the process mean for the next tier, making the decision making process adaptive.

Let us amplify this adaptive model. Suppose for Tier 1, we started with a chosen level of Type I error of 5% (α_1=0.05), an acceptable level of a false alarm rate for this supplier. Using the Φ() tables, it can be seen that the control limits for a control chart for averages should be placed 1.96 standard errors away from the center line. Now suppose, after obtaining samples from the process of Tier 1 supplier, the decision is to reject H_o, i.e., conclude that the process is not in-control. The possible error that could be made is that of a false alarm, which will happen 5% of the time. Given the decision to reject H_o at this stage, it will force management to look for special causes in the process and thereby identify remedial actions, if any. Thus, at the Tier 1 level, this decision provides a signal to rectify the process and bring it to a state of control.

Using this decision at the Tier 1 supplier level as a guideline for the next phase at the OEM level, since we concluded that our process was out-of-control, we will now place more importance on detecting process changes at the OEM level. Thus,

Table 1. Probability of a joint decision with one tier supplier and OEM, when decision is to reject H_o at tier 1

Tier	Decision Reject H_o	Decision Do Not Reject H_o
Tier 1	α_1	–
Tier 2 (OEM)	$\alpha_1\alpha_2$	$\alpha_1\beta_2$

on a relative scale, false alarms will be considered less important. So, we can relax the level of a Type I error (α_2) by moving the control limits at the OEM level closer to each other, to reduce the probability of non-detection. This will have the effect of reducing β_2. In other words, at the OEM level, we may increase the power of detection of changes in the process mean. If α_2 is chosen to be 10%, the control limits at the OEM level will be placed at 1.645 standard errors away from the center line. This explains the adaptive nature of the control limits. They are influenced by the outcome at the previous stage.

Note that the sum of α_2 and β_2 is not necessarily one. The probability of non-detection of a shift in the process mean at the OEM level (β_2) is influenced by the magnitude of the shift. It may be computed using the following rationale. We assume that an estimate of the process standard deviation at the OEM level (σ_2) is known and that the distribution of sample means is normal. The distributional assumption may be justified by the Central Limit Theorem (Mendenhall, Reinmuth, & Beaver (1993)). An estimate of the process mean at the OEM level ($\hat{\mu}_2$) is obtained from the center line on a control chart for the average. Suppose the process mean has shifted upward from the target value of μ_{02}.

The adaptive control limits at the OEM level, on a control chart for means, for a selected Type I error level of α_2, are given by:

$$\mathrm{UCL}_2 = \mu_{02} + z_{\alpha_2/2} \frac{\sigma_2}{\sqrt{n}} \tag{2}$$

$$\mathrm{LCL}_2 = \mu_{02} - z_{\alpha_2/2} \frac{\sigma_2}{\sqrt{n}},$$

where n represent the sample size at this stage.

With the process mean shifted to $\hat{\mu}_2$, the probability of non-detection is obtained as:

β_2 = P (non-detection at OEM level)

$$= \Phi\left[\frac{(UCL_2 - \hat{\mu}_2)}{\sigma_2/\sqrt{n}}\right] - \Phi\left[\frac{(LCL_2 - \hat{\mu}_2)}{\sigma_2/\sqrt{n}}\right]. \tag{3}$$

One can conduct a trade-off analysis between the relative risks of α_2 and β_2, and eventually the costs associated with them to determine suitable values. Additionally, the corresponding control limits at this appropriate level may also be found. The above concept may be applied to the general situation when there are several tiers of suppliers along with the OEM.

An alternative approach to quality control decision making at the various tiers of suppliers may be followed when the process spread is much smaller than the spread between the specifications. For supplier at tier i, this implies that:

$$6\sigma_i \ll (USL_i - LSL_i) \tag{4}$$

where USL_i and LSL_i represent the upper and lower specification limits of the characteristic at tier i. We assume that the process variability is stable. The objective here is to determine bounds on the process mean such that the proportion of nonconforming product does not exceed a desir-

Table 2. Probability of a joint decision with one tier supplier and OEM when decision is to not reject H_o at tier 1

Tier	**Decision Reject H_o**	**Decision Do Not Reject H_o**
Tier 1	–	β_1
Tier 2 (OEM)	$\beta_1\alpha_2$	$\beta_1\beta_2$

able value δ_i. Note the process can drift out of control and still produce a product that conforms to specifications.

Figure 3a shows the distribution of the individual values of the characteristic, assuming normality. Two locations of the process mean are shown, μ_L and μ_U, the lowest and highest allowable mean. Let z_δ denote the standard normal value corresponding to a tail area of δ. The process mean should be maintained within the bounds $\mu_L \leq \mu_i \leq \mu_U$, so that the fraction nonconforming does not exceed δ. From Figure 3a, we have:

$$\mu_L = LSL_i + z_{\delta_i}\sigma_i \quad (5)$$

$$\mu_U = USL_i - z_{\delta_i}\sigma_i .$$

Figure 3b shows the distribution of the sample means, since control charts are maintained for the means of observations drawn from the process. Note that the standard error of the sample means is $\sigma_{\bar{x}} = \sigma_i / \sqrt{n}$. To maintain the proportion nonconforming at δ_i, the process means are restricted by the bounds μ_L and μ_U. Assuming a Type I error rate of α_i at tier *i*, the control limits are given by:

$$UCL_i = \mu_U + z_{\alpha_i}\sigma_i / \sqrt{n} \quad (6)$$

$$LCL_i = \mu_L - z_{\alpha_i}\sigma_i / \sqrt{n} .$$

Combining equations (5) and (6), we get, for a modified control chart, for tier *i*, the control limits are:

$$UCL_i = USL_i - (z_{\delta_i} - z_{\alpha_i} / \sqrt{n})\sigma_i \quad (7)$$

$$LCL_i = LSL_i + (z_{\delta_i} - z_{\alpha_i} / \sqrt{n})\sigma_i .$$

Given that the number of tiers, including the OEM, is *p*, an estimate of the rolled throughput yield (RTY) which is the proportion of acceptable product with no defects at the finished goods level is given by:

$$\text{RTY} = \prod_{i=1}^{p} (1 - \delta_i) . \quad (8)$$

Organizations definitely like to monitor RTY at the OEM level. This, however, requires scrutiny at the tier-level suppliers, as observed from equation (8). Through information available from all tier suppliers, by the adoption of an enterprise-wide database, this becomes feasible. Thus, for a certain desired level of RTY at the OEM level, this will place restrictions on yields at the individual tier levels. Knowledge of the capability of individual suppliers may determine whether we will be capable of meeting the RTY at the OEM level. For example, suppose there is one supplier and an OEM. It is known that the supplier at tier 1 has a yield of 98% and cannot improve further. If the desired level of RTY is 95%, the OEM has to come up with a process that has a yield of 96.9%. This may necessitate certain changes in the process at the OEM level.

The concept of the adaptive nature of decision making in the hierarchical process, as explained previously, may be used in this context as well. Consider the example in the previous paragraph. Note that if $\delta_i = 0.02$, it will influence the bounds (μ_{L1} and μ_{U1}), within which the process mean for the supplier may be allowed to vary. Further, based on a chosen acceptable risk of a Type 1 error (α_1), the control limits for decision making (UCL_1, LCL_1) at the supplier level will be affected. As before, we could adopt decision making at the OEM level, based on the outcome at the supplier level.

FUTURE TRENDS

Access to global suppliers and global markets is of prime importance in the twenty-first century. Such a business model has revolutionized the

Figure 3. Modified control chart limits(Mitra, A. (2008). Fundamentals of Quality Control and Improvement, Third Edition. Reprinted with permission of John Wiley & Sons, Inc.)

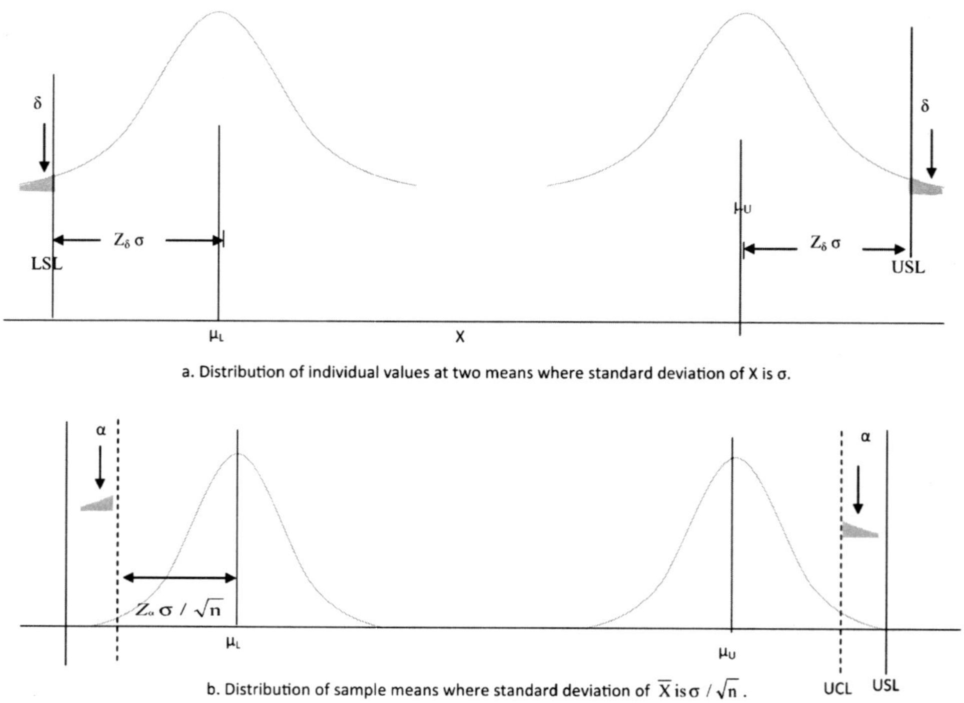

manufacturing/service industry. Consequently, flow of materials/components/goods and flow of information are critical to being effective and efficient in the entire supply chain. Since decision making, and thereby information needs are at various levels and linked to each other, organizations will find a growing need to use models that are pervasive in nature.

Based on this growing need, there is the scope to study various networking models and use of application-oriented software. While the proposed approach in this chapter is somewhat reactive, at the upper tier, based on the outcomes at a lower tier, future research could focus on decision making being proactive. A major benefit in using "intelligent" equipment is to sense when something is going astray and recommend/take remedial action. This would reduce nonconformance rate, reduce downtime, minimize manufacturing costs, and reduce lead time.

CONCLUSION

A majority of the quality control methods do not incorporate the sequential nature of operations, by suppliers, that are inherent in creating a finished product. Quality management decision making is therefore influenced by the outcomes of those at prior stages or levels.

It is known that errors in decision making in quality control fall into two categories. A Type I error is essentially a false alarm whereby it is inferred that a process is out of control, when it is really in control. On the other hand, a Type II error occurs when it is inferred that a process is in control, when it is really out of control. The criticality of these two errors is dependent on the nature of the business and the type of product.

This chapter has proposed an approach to integrate decision making in the context of the entire supply chain, i.e., suppliers and the original equipment manufacturer. Further, an adaptive model is proposed that chooses the parameters of a quality control policy via selecting appropriate Type I or Type II error rates and hence control limits for control charts for averages. This approach would not be feasible in practice had it not been for the advances in the information technology field. Modern developments make it promising to collect data at the enterprise-level and use this data for informed decision making processes by all entities. Since collection of data is on a real-time basis, decision making at all levels is also accomplished on a dynamic basis.

REFERENCES

Ahire, S., & Golhar, D. (1996). Quality management in large versus small firms. *Journal of Small Business Management*, *34*(1), 1–13.

Bowersox, D. J., Closs, D. J., & Cooper, M. B. (2002). *Supply chain logistics management*. New York: McGraw-Hill.

Crosby, P. B. (1979). *Quality is free*. New York: McGraw-Hill.

Crosby, P. B. (1989). *Let's talk quality*. New York: McGraw-Hill.

Deming, W. E. (1982). *Quality, productivity, and competitive position*. Cambridge, MA: Center for Advanced Engineering Study, Massachusetts Institute of Technology.

Ghobadian, A., & Gallear, D. N. (1996). Total quality management in SME. *Omega*, *24*(1), 83–106. doi:10.1016/0305-0483(95)00055-0

Ilic, A., Staake, T., & Fleisch, E. (2009). Using sensor information to reduce the carbon footprint ofperishable goods. *IEEE Pervasive Computing / IEEE Computer Society [and] IEEE Communications Society*, *8*(1), 22–29. doi:10.1109/MPRV.2009.20

Juran, J.M. (1986). The quality trilogy. *Quality Progress*, August, 19-24.

Juran, J. M., & Gryna, F. M., Jr. (1993). *Quality planning and analysis: From product development through use* (3rd ed.). New York: McGraw-Hill.

Meixell, M. J., & Gargeya, V. B. (2005). Global supply chain design: A literature review and critique. *Transportation Research Part E, Logistics and Transportation Review*, 531–550. doi:10.1016/j.tre.2005.06.003

Mendenhall, W., Reinmuth, J. E., & Beaver, R. J. (1993). *Statistics for management and economics* (7th ed.). Belmont, CA: Duxbury.

Mitra, A. (2008). *Fundamentals of quality control and improvement* (3rd ed.). Hoboken, NJ: Wiley.

Montgomery, D. C. (2004). *Statistical quality control* (5th ed.). Hoboken, NJ: Wiley.

Saha, D., & Mukherjee, A. (2003). Pervasive computing: A paradigm for the 21st century. *Computer*, (March): 25–31. doi:10.1109/MC.2003.1185214

Saha, D., Mukherjee, A., & Bandyopadhyay, S. (2002). *Networking infrastructure for pervasive computing: Enabling technologies and systems*. Dordrecht, Kluwer Academic.

Satyanarayanan, M. (2001). Pervasive computing: Vision and challenges. *IEEE Personal Communications*, *8*(4), 10–17. doi:10.1109/98.943998

Stiefmeier, T., Roggen, D., Tröster, G., Ogris, G., & Lukowicz, P. (2008, July). Wearable activity tracking in car manufacturing. *IEEE Pervasive Computing / IEEE Computer Society [and] IEEE Communications Society*, *7*(2), 42–50. doi:10.1109/MPRV.2008.40

Talluri, S., & Baker, R. C. (2002). A multi-phase mathematical programming approach for effective supply chain design. *European Journal of Operational Research, 141*(3), 544–558. doi:10.1016/S0377-2217(01)00277-6

Tentori, M., & Favela, J. (2008). Activity-aware computing for healthcare. *IEEEE Pervasive Computing, 7*(2), 51–57. doi:10.1109/MPRV.2008.24

Thiesse, F., Fleisch, E., & Dierkes, M. (2006). LotTrack: RFID-based process control in the semiconductor industry. *IEEE Pervasive Computing / IEEE Computer Society [and] IEEE Communications Society, 5*(1), 47–53. doi:10.1109/MPRV.2006.9

Wadsworth, H. M., Jr., Stephens, K. S., & Godfrey, A. B. (2001). *Modern methods for quality control and improvement* (2nd ed.). New York: Wiley.

Womack, J. P., & Jones, D. T. (1996). *Learn thinking – Banish waste and create wealth in your corporation*. New York: Simon & Schuster.

Woodall, W. H., & Adams, B. M. (1993). The statistical design of cusum charts. *Quality Engineering, 5*(4), 559–570. doi:10.1080/08982119308918998

ADDITIONAL READING

Alshuwaikhat, H. M., & Abubakar, I. (2008, November). An integrated approach to achieving campus sustainability: Assessment of the current campus environmental management practices. *Journal of Cleaner Production, 16*(16), 1777–1785. doi:10.1016/j.jclepro.2007.12.002

Amin, S. H., & Razmi, J. (2009, May). An integrated fuzzy model for supplier management: A case study of ISP selection and evaluation. *Expert Systems with Applications, 36*(4), 8639–8648. doi:10.1016/j.eswa.2008.10.012

Baïna, S., Panetto, H., & Morel, G. (2009, April). New paradigms for a product oriented modelling: Case study for traceability. *Computers in Industry, 60*(3), 172–183. doi:10.1016/j.compind.2008.12.004

Bei, W., Wang, S., & Hu, J. (2006, October). An analysis of supplier selection in manufacturing supply chain management. *International Conference on Service Systems and Service Management, 2,* 1439-1444.

Bevilacqua, M., Ciarapica, F. E., & Giacchetta, G. (2009, July). Business process reengineering of a supply chain and a traceability system: A case study. *Journal of Food Engineering, 93*(1), 13–22. doi:10.1016/j.jfoodeng.2008.12.020

Bottazzi, D., Montanari, R., & Rossi, G. (2008, August). A self-organizing group management middleware for mobile ad-hoc networks. *Computer Communications, 31*(13), 3040–3048. doi:10.1016/j.comcom.2008.02.027

Brewer, J., & Dourish, P. (2008, December). Storied spaces: Cultural accounts of mobility, technology, and environmental knowing. *International Journal of Human-Computer Studies, 66*(12), 963–976. doi:10.1016/j.ijhcs.2008.03.003

Celik, M. (2009). Establishing an Integrated Process Management System (IPMS) in ship management companies. *Expert Systems with Applications, 36*(4), 8152–8171. doi:10.1016/j.eswa.2008.10.022

Chatfield, D. C., Harrison, T. P., & Hayya, J. C. (2009, July). SCML: An information framework to support supply chain modeling. *European Journal of Operational Research, 196*(2), 651–660. doi:10.1016/j.ejor.2008.03.027

Chatterjee, S., Chakraborty, S., Sarker, S., Sarker, S., & Lau, F. Y. (2009, February). Examining the success factors for mobile work in healthcare: A deductive study. *Decision Support Systems, 46*(3), 620–633. doi:10.1016/j.dss.2008.11.003

Cortellessa, V., Marinelli, F., & Potena, P. (2008, October). An optimization framework for "build-or-buy" decisions in software architecture. *Computers & Operations Research*, *35*(10), 3090–3106. doi:10.1016/j.cor.2007.01.011

Evers, L., & Havinga, P. (2007, October). Supply chain management automation using wireless sensor networks. *IEEE International Conference on Mobile Adhoc and Sensor Systems*, 1-3.

Francas, D., & Minner, S. (2009, August). Manufacturing network configuration in supply chains with product recovery. *Omega*, *37*(4), 757–769. doi:10.1016/j.omega.2008.07.007

Gunasekaran, A., & Ngai, E. (2009, June). Modeling and analysis of build-to-order supply chains. *European Journal of Operational Research*, *195*(2), 319–334. doi:10.1016/j.ejor.2008.03.026

Hsu, S-F., & Chiang, C-H. (2007, August). Wireless Technology: A challenge toward supply chain management. *Portland International Center for Management of Engineering and Technology* (pp. 2361-2364).

Ilic, A., Andersen, T., & Michanelles, F. (2009). Increasing supply-chain visibility with rule-based RFID data analysis. *IEEE Internet Computing*, *13*(1), 31–38. doi:10.1109/MIC.2009.10

Joo, J., & Lee, S. M. (2009, April). Adoption of the semantic web for overcoming technical limitations of knowledge management systems. *Expert Systems with Applications*, *36*(3), 7318–7327. doi:10.1016/j.eswa.2008.09.005

Junglas, I., Abraham, C., & Ives, B. (2009, February). Mobile technology at the frontlines of patient care: Understanding fit and human drives in utilization decisions and performance. *Decision Support Systems*, *46*(3), 634–647. doi:10.1016/j.dss.2008.11.012

Karthik, V. N. (2006, June). An integrated supplier selection methodology for designing robust supply chains. *IEEE International Conference on Management of Innovation and Technology*, 2, 906-910.

Lee, A., Kang, H.-Y., Hsu, C.-F., & Hung, H.-C. (2009, May). A green supplier selection model for high-tech industry. *Expert Systems with Applications*, *36*(4), 7917–7927. doi:10.1016/j.eswa.2008.11.052

Lee, C. H., & Rhee, B.-D. (2008, September). Optimal guaranteed profit margins for both vendors and retailers in the fashion apparel industry. *Journal of Retailing*, *84*(3), 325–333. doi:10.1016/j.jretai.2008.07.002

Lee, D.-E., Lim, T.-K., & Arditi, D. (2009, May). Automated stochastic quality function deployment system for measuring the quality performance of design/build contractors. *Automation in Construction*, *18*(3), 348–356. doi:10.1016/j.autcon.2008.10.002

Lee, Y.-W., Leung, K.-S., & Satyanarayanan, M. (2002). Operation shipping for mobile file systems. *IEEE Transactions on Computers*, *51*(12), 1410–1422. doi:10.1109/TC.2002.1146707

Legner, C., & Thiesse, F. (2006). RFID-based maintenance at Frankfurt airport. *IEEE Pervasive Computing / IEEE Computer Society [and] IEEE Communications Society*, *5*(1), 34–39. doi:10.1109/MPRV.2006.14

Michnik, J., & Lo, M.-C. (2009). The assessment of the information quality with the aid of multiple criteria analysis. *European Journal of Operational Research*, *195*(3), 850–856. doi:10.1016/j.ejor.2007.11.017

Roussos, G., & Kostakos, V. (2009, February). RFID in pervasive computing: State-of-the-art and outlook. *Pervasive and Mobile Computing*, *5*(1), 110–131. doi:10.1016/j.pmcj.2008.11.004

Sanchez, D., Tentori, M., & Favela, J. (2008). Activity recognition for the smart hospital. *IEEE Intelligent Systems*, *23*(2), 50–57. doi:10.1109/MIS.2008.18

Sarkis, J., & Talluri, S. (2004). Evaluating and selecting e-commerce software and communications systems for a supply chain. *European Journal of Operational Research*, *159*(2), 318–329. doi:10.1016/j.ejor.2003.08.018

Satyanarayanan, M. (2002). Wearable computing: Is it just hype? *IEEE Pervasive Computing / IEEE Computer Society [and] IEEE Communications Society*, *1*(2), 2–3. doi:10.1109/MPRV.2002.1012328

Shin, H., Benton, W. C., & Jun, M. (2009, August). Qualifying suppliers' product quality and delivery performance: A sourcing policy decision model. *Computers & Operations Research*, *36*(8), 2462–2471. doi:10.1016/j.cor.2008.10.005

Soroor, J., Tarokh, M. J., & Shemshadi, A. (2009, July). Initiating a state of the art system for real-time supply chain coordination. *European Journal of Operational Research*, *196*(2), 635–650. doi:10.1016/j.ejor.2008.03.008

Tan, W., Li, S., & Yang, F. (2005, September). Zero-time enterprise modeling with component assembly and process model optimization techniques. *The Fifth International Conference on Computer and Information Technology* (pp. 1135-1139).

Tentori, M., Favela, J., & Rodriguez, M. D. (2006). Privacy-aware autonomous agents for pervasive healthcare. *IEEE Intelligent Systems*, *21*(6), 55–62. doi:10.1109/MIS.2006.118

White, C. (2008, October). Trends and research directions in supply chain & logistics engineering. *IEEE International Conference on Service Operations and Logistics, and Informatics*, 1, XII.

Xiao, L. (2009, May). An adaptive security model using agent-oriented MDA. *Information and Software Technology*, *51*(5), 933–955. doi:10.1016/j.infsof.2008.05.005

Xie, J., & Wei, J. C. (2009, September). Coordinating advertising and pricing of a manufacturer-retailer channel. *European Journal of Operational Research*, *197*(2), 785–791. doi:10.1016/j.ejor.2008.07.014

Yuan, Q., Xiaokang, Z., & Qiong, Z. (2008, August). Key technology and system design in mobile supply chain management. *International Symposium on Electronic Commerce and Security* (pp. 258-262).

Zarokostas, N., Dimitropoulos, P. D., & Soldatos, J. (2007, September). RFID middleware design for enhancing traceability in the supply chain management. *IEEE 18th International Symposium on Personal Indoor and Mobile Radio Communications* (pp. 1-5).

Zhang, X., Song, H., & Huang, G. Q. (2009). Tourism supply chain management: A new research agenda. *Tourism Management*, *30*(3), 345–358. doi:10.1016/j.tourman.2008.12.010

Zhang, Z., & Tao, L. (2008, December). Multi-agent based supply chain management with dynamic reconfiguration capability. *IEEE/WIC/ACM International Conference on Web Intelligence and Intelligent Agent Technology*, 2, 92-95.

Zhao, F., He, Z., & Wu, D. (2008, September). Quality assurance of mass customization: A state-of-the-art review. *IEEE Symposium on Advanced Management of Information for Globalized Enterprise* (pp. 1-3).

Zhao, X., Zhao, H., & Hou, J. (2006, June). E-business and information integration in supply chain management. *IEEE International Conference on Service Operations and Logistics, and Informatics*, 919-924.

KEY TERMS AND DEFINITIONS

Adaptive Model: A model where decision making is influenced by outcomes at prior stages.

Control Chart: A graphical tool, based on statistical theory, that monitors a process to determine if special or assignable causes exist that require remedial action.

Integrated Decision Making: A framework that utilizes the links that exist between various entities in the system to make informed conclusions from a systems perspective.

Parameter Estimation: The use of sample information, collected from a process, to arrive at a value of the unknown parameter associated with the process.

Quality Assurance: A system that ensures that all procedures/processes have been designed, planned, and followed accordingly.

Supply Chain Management: A system that links various suppliers, manufacturers, retailers, distributors, and the customer and creates an integrated framework to manage the entire process.

Type I Error: In the context of decision making from control charts, this error occurs when a conclusion is made that the process is out of control, when it is really in control. This also represents a false alarm.

Type II Error: In the context of decision making from control charts, this error occurs when a conclusion is made that the process is in control, when it is really out of control.

Chapter 7
The Role of Computer-Mediated Communication Modes in Enhancing Audit Quality:
An Empirical Study

Mohamed Hegazy
American University in Cairo, Egypt

Rasha Hamdy
Principal Bank of Development and Agricultural Credit, Egypt

ABSTRACT

The circumstances and variables surrounding the auditing environment like the International Trade Agreement (ITA) and the probability of the entrance of foreign auditing firms in the auditing field in Egypt resulted in pressure to enhance the audit effectiveness and quality of Egyptian auditing firms' performance. The main focus in this research study is on the Computer-Mediated Communication (CMC) modes to be used in the communication process in auditing firms to enhance the auditor performance. A survey strategy is conducted by using questionnaires, which are distributed among a number of Egyptian auditing firms, to collect the required data and then the collected data is analyzed logically and statistically. These logic and statistical analyses are made to test the study hypotheses. The results of this research study supported the acceptance of all study hypotheses. The results revealed that CMC modes effectiveness increases the audit work effectiveness and audit quality. Also, the results indicate the contradiction between the users' perception of the effect of using CMC modes on the audit effectiveness and the real application of traditional communication modes in auditing firms.

INTRODUCTION

A major influence on the technological development over the last decade has been the pressure to improve audit effectiveness and efficiency. The concentration on communication to exchange information and experiences between the audit team individuals can be considered a primary axis for development of the quality of audit work. Communication is the lifeblood of business. Without the ability to interact with internal and external parties for more than a short period of time, an organization is unable to

DOI: 10.4018/978-1-60566-996-0.ch007

operate and therefore, decreases its chances for success (Mascha et al., 2004). Auditing firms have responded to this incentive by using advanced communication modes in the communication between the audit team individuals through the audit process. Also, it is clear in numerous surveys, that one of the most important motivators in the workplace is feeling like the member is part of the team or being involved. By promoting this feeling, there will be a creation of a positive atmosphere for work success (Atwood, 2007). So, the need for using communication modes in auditing firms is necessary. If communication within the organization is not effective, chances are slim that communication outside of the organization will ever be noticed (Atkinson, 2007). In past decades, auditing firms focused on using traditional communication modes such as Face-to-Face (FTF) meetings, Fax, Telephone, and Mail to exchange data and documents, but prior research studies evidenced their ineffectiveness (e.g., Dennis, 1996; Straus1996; and Murthy and Kerr, 2004). Today, the main direction toward Information Technology (IT) increases rapidly. As a result of technological development, the advanced communication modes such as Computer-Mediated Communication (CMC) modes including e-mail, Chat, Bulletin-board and Web-based systems had great acceptance as effective communication modes in many firms. CMC modes are considered the most advanced modes to be applied in auditing firms since the use of these modes offer significantly improved audit effectiveness and efficiency. Most organizations today, including public accounting firms, use some of these modes in exchanging information (Murthy and Kerr, 2004).

The use of Information Technology to support audit team work in decision making and problem solving has been the subject of ongoing research. While the majority of this research has been in using advanced communication modes to improve the audit effectiveness. Several surveys on the use of advanced communication modes have been carried out (e.g., Kerr and Murthy, 1994; Bamber et al., 1996; Dennis, 1996; and Murthy and Kerr, 2004). The current research study surveys whether alternative forms of CMC tools affect the ability of audit teams to resolve problems or make decisions that require team individuals to exchange and process information.

Employing a survey strategy, the researchers used the questionnaire technique to collect the data, where 121 applications were distributed among some Egyptian auditing firms. Only the data of 80 questionnaires can be considered valid to be analyzed using logic and statistical data analyses. According to the results of these analyses, the study results concluded that there is a general agreement with the effect of the type of used communication mode on the audit work effectiveness, where using effective communication modes in auditing firms increases the audit effectiveness. The communication mode that has received much attention in information systems literature is of CMC mode. This research study has found that using CMC modes in the communication system in auditing firms improves the auditor performance as well as increasing the audit effectiveness. Also, it has been found that CMC modes are extensively preferred by auditors to be used in auditing firms, particularly by larger auditing firms, as they have gained users' satisfaction. The real application of CMC modes in Egyptian auditing firms is already existed but still the traditional modes are applied in some of those firms more than CMC modes. While auditing firms may increase their use of CMC modes and replace traditional modes, with expectation of effectiveness and efficiency gains, these may be realized at present only partially.

This study contributes to existing studies on the effect of using alternative communication modes on the audit effectiveness in the following dimensions. First, it provides evidence on the effect of the type of communication modes, which are used in the communication process, on the audit work effectiveness, where using CMC modes increases the audit effectiveness compared with traditional communication modes. Prior research studies concluded that groups using CMC modes outperformed FTF groups (e.g., Valacich et al., 1993; Straus, 1996; Murthy and Kerr, 2004; Butschi and Steyn, 2006 and O'Kane et al (2007)). Second, it helps in identifying the effect of using CMC modes on the audit effectiveness. Third, it measures the users' satisfaction with using both traditional and advanced communication modes. CMC modes facilitated greater and more equalized participation by group members than FTF (Olaniran et al., 1996; and Brown, 2004). This paper revealed that CMC modes have gained users' satisfaction rather than traditional communication modes. Finally, it facilitates identifying the general direction toward the preference of CMC modes and the application of traditional and advanced communication modes in Egyptian auditing firms.

The remainder of the paper is organized as follows. The next section provides a background discussion of CMC research and reviews prior work in this line of research. Thereafter the research hypotheses are presented, followed by a description of the research methodology. The survey results are then presented, after which the concluding section summarizes the results of the hypotheses' testing and then provides some possible directions for future research.

PROFESSIONAL BACKGROUND AND HYPOTHESES

As a result of the challenges that face auditors, the Auditing Standard Board (ASB) of the American Institute of Certified Public Accountants (AICPA) issued Statement on Auditing Standards (SAS) No. 99, Consideration of Fraud in a Financial Statement Audit, in October 2002. The purpose of this new standard is to enhance the auditor's effectiveness in addressing fraud in financial statements audit (Casabona and Grego, 2003). SAS No. 99 provides guidance to auditors in fulfilling their responsibility, as it relates to fraud, in an audit of financial statement conducted in accordance with Generally Accepted Auditing Standards (GAAS). Although the new standard has the same name as its predecessor, it is clearly more far-reaching than SAS No. 82, as it provides auditors with expanded guidance for detecting material fraud and will result in a substantial change in auditor performance. Section 110, Responsibilities and Functions of the Independent Auditor, states that "The auditor has a responsibility to plan and perform the audit to obtain reasonable assurance about whether the financial statements are free of material misstatement whether caused by error or fraud" (AICPA, 2002). The relevant requirements of SAS No. 99 were introduced by AICPA (2002) such as: discussion among engagement personnel regarding the risks of material misstatement due to fraud, obtaining the information needed to identify risks of material misstatement due to fraud, and communicating about fraud to management; the audit committee; and others.

The Statement on Auditing Standards No. 99 provided main evidence on the importance of commutation with the auditing firms. Another support for the importance of communication in auditing firms is the increase in the amount of work which is completed outside the conventional office. The communication became necessary to exchange the information and experiences through the audit team. Of interest in the current study are two types of communication modes: (1) Traditional modes (Face-To-Face, Telephone, Fax, and Mail), and (2) Advanced modes (CMC modes such as: e-mail, Chat, Bulletin-board and Web-based systems). These alternative configurations can affect team members' ability to access and process information shared during group discussion (Murthy and Kerr, 2004). The study by Atkinson (2007) presented the philosophies and strategies of three executives for making sure that all of the reciprocal communication between themselves and their staff is effective. One of those executives stated that, in most instances, the primary form of communication is e-mail, especially for information that is communicated to a large number of people. Also, this executive has found conference calls to be particularly effective. The other executive has found that it is important to make the effort to communicate with the people in other facilities on a regular basis. The last executive asserted using all forms of communication, including FTF meetings, e-mail, phone calls, conference calls, faxes, and web in corporations. The present study discussed the characteristics of both traditional and advanced modes to identify the most effective modes to be used in the communication process in auditing firms in order to increase the audit effectiveness. Some prior studies were consistent with the results of this study, where they revealed the ineffectiveness of traditional modes and the opposite of advanced modes (e.g., O'Kane et al, 2007; Butschi and Steyn, 2006; Brown, 2004; Murthy and Kerr, 2004; Grimshaw et al, 2002; Huang, 2002; and Olaniran, 1996). Drawbacks inherent in FTF meetings such as personality conflicts can have a detrimental effect on individual members' performance (Rapoza, 2001). Telephone can transmit sound only, it will not enable users to send or receive papers or files containing data. Fax machine disables users to make databases of the data sent. Also, sending documents by mail may need more time.

The technology development has great impact on communication field. People may have FTF meetings, but also they may exchange information at any time through their computer (Lumsden and Lumsden, 2000). A few studies investigated whether the use of CMC modes can improve the effectiveness of teams' performance, but with mixed results. Straus (1996) found that no significant difference in information sharing or performance between CMC groups and FTF groups. While Dennis (1996) found that the use of CMC modes may increase the amount of information exchanged. A study by Valacich (1993) has explained how the use of computer-assisted communication will continue to grow; based upon the understanding of how these new media influence group communication processes and outcomes. Thus, it has investigated the effect of two important and manipulable elements of these media on group process and performance: the communication channel used and the physical proximity of group members. Its objectives were to gain a better understanding of different technology-based group work environments for a specific task. Results of this study have found that, for small groups in decision-making or problem-solving situations, the medium used for communication makes a difference, and these differences have been found to be heavily dependent on task type. It has focused on a task with relatively low ambiguity as idea generation. The interest was to identify how differences in the richness of the communication media influence group idea generation. The general research question was: how do difference in the richness of the group communication media influence group performance when addressing a task of low ambiguity, such as idea generation. It hypothesized that groups using electronic communication will be more effective at generating ideas than groups using verbal communication and groups whose members are distributed from one another will be more effective at generating ideas than groups whose members are Face-to- Face. It has found that groups using computer mediation outperformed groups using verbal or FTF communication. The results of Walsh and Bayma (1996) suggested that fields that consist of tightly coupled but geographically dispersed work groups tend to adopt CMC more heavily than other groups. According to Murthy and Kerr (2004), in auditing, especially on audits with multiple locations, hidden-profile type tasks can arise when different team members possess relevant information, the integration of which is necessary for the team to reach an optimal decision. The current study investigated the relationship between the auditor tasks and CMC modes. The effects of CMC on decision-making, problem-solving, or idea generation behavior in auditing have been the focus of recent research (Kerr and Murthy, 2004; Arnold et al., 2000; Bamber et al., 1996; Kerr and Murthy, 1994; and Valacich et al., 1994). The results of these studies have been mixed with some reporting improved performance from CMC tools and others finding the opposite. CMC tools, also known as Group Support System (GSS), provide a structured environment that allows participants in a collaborative team to interact simultaneously and anonymously to generate ideas, make decisions, and solve problems (Jessup et al., 1990). Such interaction is expected to increase in the future as technology and groupware increase the opportunities for simultaneous interaction among team members in geographically dispersed locations (Kerr and Murthy, 2004). The study by Karau and Kelly (1992) examined the impact of time limits on group interaction process and performance quality. It concluded that time limits had strong influences on group interaction and group performance. This, in turn, will lead to group decision making to overcome the time pressure that faces auditors and its impact on the group performance. Also, working in groups and applying GSS in auditing firms will improve the audit performance quality and solve the problem of time pressure. Arnold et al., (2000) represented an exploratory study into the interrelated effects of time pressure and GSS on group decision making in an audit task domain. They examined the impact of opportunity-cost-time pressure on group decision making during completion of an audit judgment task where communication was assisted through the use of a GSS. The result of their study indicated that the use of GSS led to slower processing of information cues and a corresponding increase in time required reaching a group decision. Also, the GSS may have impeded the decision quality. They have found that the use of GSS led to slower processing information cues and may have impeded the decision quality. While Kerr and Murthy (1994) found that tasks in the GSS-mediated groups were performed significantly more than tasks in FTF groups.

Huang (2002) investigated supervisor-subordinate relationships and discovered that those who frequently used e-mail to communicate had much better interpersonal relationships. He referred such findings to increased communication resulting in higher levels of social information being transmitted as well as the opportunity for misunderstandings to occur was decreased, and additional ways of social networking were introduced. He noted that it was an increase in actual communication instances that led to an improvement in relationship.

O'Kane et al (2007) provided insights into the polymorphic role of email, particularly the way in which it is adapted by individuals within the organizations. They interrogated the day to day role of email in explicating, influencing and shaping social and information interactions within an organization. Based upon a series of in-depth interviews which were undertaken to elicit employee opinions on their email adaptation, experiences, and practices, the research contributed to the study of computer mediated communication (CMC) showing how every day interactions are used to understand employee reactions to email communications, and hence faster an atmosphere in which these interactions assist organizational development. The paper met Gimshaw et al (2002) and Butschi and Steyn's (2006) call for more research to theoretically engage with and consider the individual idiosyncrasies of email practices within organization in order to understand fully how employees manage their email communications. O'kane et al (2007) confirmed the CMC benefits that the speed, a synchronicity and "one to many" aspects of email can lead to efficiencies such as reduced office administration and avoidance of "telephone tag" (a succession of unsuccessful interactions between colleagues) leading to both time saving and management rewards. They believed that as with many channels of communications, e-mail can directly explicate, influence and shape the nature, function and effectiveness of the message.

O'Kane et al (2007) findings were presented in the development of five case areas in which a role for email was established namely: information management, contact management, Personal (in) effectiveness, Social interaction and E-mail composition. Under those five interrelated themes, the authors deduced 23 Sub-themes, which demonstrated e-mail's polymorphic role. They proposed a necessary interdependence between the elements in order to manage email, role within Knowledge creation. The interaction of the developed tool (i.e., the polymorphic nature of email adaptation) with day to day work activities and tasks stimulates and moves knowledge through improved connections, while also simultaneously introducing disruptive relationships behavior. In the study, employee ties, were seem to develop through increased access opportunities and ease of contact, whereas disabling consequences resulted from negative communication incidents.

Cheung et al (2008) discussed the Web creation of electronic word-of-mouth (eWOM) communication through electronic media, such as online discussion forums, electronic bulletin board systems, news groups, blogs, review sites, and social networking sites. The use of eWOM communication through electronic media may allow a group of users who might be geographically dispersed, to obtain information related to a particular topic or issue. The researchers indicated in their study of information usefulness and reliability that WOM is more effective than traditional marketing tools by individual selling and conventional advertising media. Electronic word of mouth communication according to Henning-Thurau et al (2004) is any positive or negative statement made by potential, actual, or former customers about a product or company which is made available to a multitude of people and institutions via the internet. It is seen as the latest extension of traditional interpersonal communication into the new generation of cyberspace. Cheung et al (2008) reviewed past researches including the elaboration likelihood model (ELM) and proposed a theoretical model of information adoption to explain how people are influenced to adopt information posted in computer-mediated communication (CMC) contexts. They discussed the notion that ELM posits that a message can influence people's attitudes and behaviors in two ways: centrally and peripherally. Centrally is associated with the nature of arguments in the message. Peripherally relates to the issues or themes that are not directly related to the subject matter of the message. When applied in a CMC context, the information adoption model (Cheung et al, 2008) has two key propositions. The first is the information quality represented in argument quality which is the central influence. The second is the source credibility reflecting the peripheral influence. The findings of the above research study provided some advice to the organizers of on-line communities in order to help them better manage their website for the purpose of presenting useful information. Also, they found that information relevance and information comprehensiveness were the most vital elements for influencing information usefulness.

Moreover, the interaction between the communication modes and group tasks, which may affect the group performance, has great attention of prior research. Valacich et al. (1993) found that, for small groups in decision-making or problem-solving situations, the medium used for communication makes a difference, and these differences have been found to be heavily dependent on task type. Also, Chidambaram and Jones (1993) indicated that Electronic Meeting System (EMS) can improve decision-making performance, given proper Task Technology Fit (TTF) theory, which is proposed by Goodhue (1995) and Goodhue and Thompson (1995) in the context of *individual* performance and by Zigurs and Buckland (1998) in the context of *group* performance, a good "fit" between CMC technology tools and task requirements will result in the best performance. Prior CMC research has typically employed (TTF) theory to examine the fit between task type and

CMC technology; the results were consistent with (TTF) theory in some studies. Dennis et al. (2001) developed a new model for interpreting GSS effects on performance (a Fit-Appropriation Model), which argues that GSS performance is affected by two factors. The first is the fit between the task and the GSS structures selected for use. The second is the appropriation support the groups receive in the form of training, and facilitation to help them effectively incorporates the selected GSS structures into their meeting process. They used this model to organize previous research to better understand and interpret GSS effects on performance by examining both the fit between GSS capabilities and tasks, and the appropriation of these capabilities by group. They found that when this model was used appropriately (i.e., there is a fit between the GSS structures and the task, and the group receives appropriation support), GSS use increased the number of ideas generated, took less time, and led to more satisfied participants than if the group worked without the GSS. Fitting the GSS to the task had the most impact on outcome effectiveness (decision quality & ideas); while appropriation support had the most impact on the process (time required and process satisfaction). In addition, Murthy and Kerr (2004) provide evidence that, for tasks requiring the exchange and processing of information, CMC results in significantly more effective problem-solving performance than FTF interaction.

The main focus, in this paper, is on evaluating the effectiveness of FTF meeting as a traditional mode and CMC mode as an advanced mode to identify the most effective mode and the effect of those communication modes on the participant's satisfaction. In general, when CMC compared with FTF meeting, the result is that CMC modes are less costly than FTF meeting which may require traveling; CMC is rapid and took less time than FTF which need more time; CMC is more reliable than FTF; CMC makes the information available at any time and any place; and it provides accurate information than FTF meeting.

Given the aforementioned advantages of CMC over FTF communication, CMC modes should be superior to FTF modes. A considerable amount of research has evaluated FTF meetings and CMC modes and most of them presented the main advantages and superiority of CMC modes over FTF meetings (Straus, 1996; Olaniran et al., 1996; Bordia, 1997; and Brown, 2004). According to Straus (1996) the direct and indirect cost savings of using the medium for groups that are distributed by time space may outweigh any disadvantages of CMC over FTF interaction. CMC offers a number of advantages, such as rapid information, convenience and increased accessibility to co-worker and information. The main benefit of using CMC in the communication process is that it allows users to form databases from data exchanged and access to information easily at any time. Face-to-Face and Computer-Mediated Communication are compared in four defined properties of group discussions and making decisions in a study by Olaniran et al. (1996): (1) Participation: where CMC facilitated greater and more equalized participation by group members than FTF. Advantages of CMC were the ability to communicate concurrently, and an increased willingness of members to participate. (2) A synchronicity and record, storage, and retrieval: where CMC enables a synchronous communication, allowing for any time, any place discussions. This method also provides a record of discussions. (3) Training: CMC may seem more tedious to members if they are unfamiliar with this medium and need training in protocol. (4) Time binding, time and physical location: where CMC groups take more time to reach consensual agreements and make decisions. However, CMC groups also do not incur expenses such as travel to meeting attendance.

Also, Brown (2004) summarized comparisons of CMC and FTF communication in the following: CMC is less inhibited than FTF where people using CMC communicate more openly, especially on group tasks, it also increases the participation equality in group tasks where CMC provides greater opportunity for equal participation because of the limited FTF interaction, it provides flexibility in cutting across department, hierarchical, and geographical lines, and it increases speed and flow of communication, information access, rapid feedback, and rapid diffusion of message. As a result of the medium's effect on participation equalization, there can be an effect of selecting a specific mode on the participant's satisfaction. Thus, the emphasis in CMC research is on the best performance resulted from using CMC modes. Also, CMC modes increase the participant's satisfaction that improves the audit effectiveness. The current study is directed toward achieving audit effectiveness to increase audit quality by employing audit tasks and comparing the performance of CMC and FTF groups.

Hypotheses

In the present study, the researchers extend prior research on Computer-Mediated Communication effectiveness by investigating the performance and characteristics of CMC groups compared with FTF groups. According to prior research and TTF theory, it is expected that there is an effect of using CMC modes on the auditor performance, and group tasks. Also, CMC groups may outperform FTF groups and affect the participant's satisfaction. That leads to set the following hypotheses.

Hypothesis 1: The effectiveness of the audit work performed depends on the type of the communication modes.

Hypothesis 2: There is a relationship between the auditor procedures and electronic communication modes.

Hypothesis 3: There is an effect of the selection of a specific communication mode on the participants in the audit engagement satisfaction.

According to Hypothesis 1, the type of the communication modes, which are used, is expected to affect the audit effectiveness and that may require identifying the effective communication mode to be used. Hypothesis 2 proposes a relationship between audit tasks whether decision making or problem solving and the communication modes based on TTF theory and the interaction between the task and communication mode. Hypothesis 3 expects that using CMC modes will increase the participant's satisfaction.

RESEARCH METHODOLOGY

This study is conducted to assess the effect of using CMC modes on the audit effectiveness. So, a field study was designed to test the study hypotheses. The researchers used a questionnaire survey to collect the data, where a pre-performed questionnaire was designed containing 15 questions focusing on data arising mainly from reviewing academic research on FTF and CMC modes. The questionnaire was distributed among selected sample of auditors. The population of the study is auditors in various Egyptian auditing firms, where 121 applications were distributed among

Table 1. Results of questionnaires distribution

Questionnaire State	Number	Percentage %
Distributed	121	100%
Uncollected	37	30.5%
Rejected	4	3.3%
Accepted	80	66%

the sample, which has been chosen judgmentally, and only 80 applications were valid. Table 1 and illustrative graph (1) provide the number of distributed, uncollected, rejected, and accepted questionnaires.

In order to collect accurate and large amount of data, the survey strategy was used. So, the questionnaire was designed and most questions could be answered either by indicating "yes" or "no"; or by rating alternatives on a five-point likert-type scale; or by ranking modes in rank order; or by choosing one option from available two. Using close-ended questions helps in providing high response rate and save the time of respondents.

SURVEY RESULTS

The number of received questionnaires was about 84 applications but only 80 applications were valid, resulting in a response rate of 66%. The researchers performed both logic and statistical analyses, by using SPSS, to test the hypotheses' relationships and verify the hypotheses acceptance or rejection. Statistical analysis has two forms, which are descriptive and non-descriptive analysis through calculating Mean, Standard Deviation, and Coefficient of Variation for the sample data; and non-descriptive analysis through the use of Spearman's Correlation and Chi-Square test.

Non-descriptive or hypotheses' testing is conducted through using Spearman's Correlation to test the correlation between two variables at a specific significance level because this technique determines the level of correlation through the Correlation Coefficient (r); and Chi-Square was used to test the relationship between the tested variables at specific significance level, where this technique measures the strength of the relationship between tested variables through the Contingency Coefficient (C.C). In other words, using both Spearman's Correlation technique and Chi-Square test in the hypotheses' testing is to identify the correlation or relationship between the tested variables whether positive or negative and its strength at a specific level of significance. Each technique is used for specific data based on the nature of tested data, where Spearman's Correlation technique is more suitable for Likert-Scale questions and Chi-Square tests are more suitable for nominal questions.

The Effect of Communication Modes on Audit Effectiveness

The respondents were asked to indicate the effect of the type of used communication mode on the audit effectiveness. Also, they were asked about the characteristics of both traditional and advanced communication modes to identify the effectiveness of each type. In addition, ranking a number of communication modes according to the effectiveness of each one was required. In order to test Hypothesis 1, the collected data was analyzed using Spearman's Correlation technique as in the following correlation tables.

There is a relationship between the auditor tasks and the communication modes.

The result of Table 2 indicates that there is a high positive correlation between auditor tasks and the used communication modes, where there is a strong positive relationship at a significance level of .01 between the auditor tasks whether making a decision or solving a problem and the

Table 2. the Correlation between Q1.3 and Q1.2

Question	r	Sig.
The communication mode is used in the communication process to exchange the information and experiences.	0.35**	0.002

** Correlation is significant at the .01 level (2-tailed).

communication modes which are used in exchanging information and experiences with a positive correlation (r) of .35.

Based on this result, it can be concluded that the strong correlation between the auditor tasks and the used communication mode statistically supports the dependence of the audit work performed effectiveness on the used communication modes.

The communication mode, which is used by the audit team, affects the audit performance

The results of table 3 indicate that there is a significant positive correlation between the auditor performance and the use of communication modes in exchanging information and experiences at a significance level of .05, with a positive correlation (r) of .26. Also, the results in the above table indicate a high strong positive correlation between the auditor performance and the communication modes at a significance level of .01, with a positive correlation (r) of .32. It can be said that, the correlations between the auditor performance and communication modes are statistically significant.

According to these results, there is a strong effect of the communication modes on the effectiveness of audit work performed, where using effective communication modes in the auditing firm can positively affect the auditor performance.

From all of the above, it can be summarized that the results of testing Hypothesis(1) statistically evidence that the effectiveness of the audit work performed depends on the type of communication modes, supporting the acceptance of this hypothesis, in line with the logic and descriptive data analyses results.

The Effect of E-Communication Modes on Audit Tasks

The researchers investigated the opinions of respondents about using various e-communication modes in auditing firms and the effect of those modes on the auditor performance and audit process. The collected data was analyzed by using Spearman's Correlation technique and Chi-Square test to test Hypothesis 2. The results are provided in the following tables.

The agreement of using the computer in the communication between the auditing firm and the client or the partner through the audit process increase audit effectiveness.

The result of table 4 indicates that there is a high significant correlation between the audit process effectiveness and using e-communication modes in auditing firms. There is a high positive strong relationship between the increased use of e-communication modes between audit team and the increase of the audit process effectiveness at a significance level of .01 with a correlation (r) of .38.

So, it can be said that, the audit process effectiveness is positively related to the use of e-communication modes at a level of 99% confidence. In other words, there is a relationship between the audit process and e-communication modes and this relationship is direct and strong.

Using the web sites in obtaining information or getting a specific audit standard will improve the auditor performance.

Table 3. the Correlation between Q1.4 and Q1.2; Q1.3

Question	r	Sig.
The communication mode is used in the communication process to exchange the information and experiences.	0.26*	0.019
There is a relationship between the auditor tasks and the communication modes.	0.32**	0.004

** Correlation is significant at the .01 level (2-tailed).
* Correlation is significant at the .05 level (2-tailed).

Table 4. the Correlation between Q6 and Q7

Question	r	Sig.
If you are using the computer in the communication between audit team, since when did you start to use it: less than one year, 1-3 years, or more than 3 years?	0.38**	0.002

** Correlation is significant at the .01 level (2-tailed).

The results of Table 5 indicate that the positive contingency between the effect of using web sites (as e-communication mode) on the auditor performance and the effect of using e-mail (as e-communication mode) on the audit process with a Chi-Square of 3.4 and a Contingency Coefficient (C.C.) of .20 at a level of 90% confidence. This contingency supports the strong positive relationship between e-communication modes and the audit process effectiveness.

Also, there is a high positive contingency between the effect of using web sites on the auditor performance and the preferred type of communication modes to be used in auditing firms, which is CMC modes as advanced modes, where Chi-Square is 5.48 with a Contingency Coefficient (C.C) of .25 at a significance level of .01. This strong contingency indicates the significant positive relationship between the auditor performance improvement and CMC mode as a preferred type of communication mode to be used in auditing firms.

All of the above results indicate the existence of a positive relationship between the audit process and e-communication modes. So, it can be concluded that hypothesis statistical testing results support the relationship between the audit process and e-communication modes and are consistent with the logic data analysis that evidenced the acceptance of this hypothesis.

The Effect of Communication Modes on Participant's Satisfaction

The effect of both traditional and advanced communication modes on the user's satisfaction was measured through surveying the opinions of respondents about the effect of each mode on the participation equality, the preference and application of each one. That is clear in testing Hypothesis 3 through using Chi-Square tests as in the following tables.

The negative effect of using traditional communication modes in the communication process in auditing firms on the participants' satisfaction.

The result of table 6 indicates that there is a high strong contingency between the negative effect of using traditional communication modes in audit process on the participants' satisfaction and the preference of using CMC modes in auditing firms and that contingency confirms the relationship between the selection of the communication mode to be used in the audit process and the participants' satisfaction where Chi-Square is 6.07 and this relationship is strong with a Contingency Coefficient (C.C) of 0.26 at a level of 99% confidence because the negative effect of

Table 5. the Contingency between Q10 and Q9; Q14

Question	Chi-Square	C.C.	Sig.
Using E-mail in the communication between the supervisor and staff to answer the inquiries will affect the audit process.	3.4	0.20	0.06
The preferred type of communication mode to be used in auditing firms is (CMC mode).	5.48	0.25	0.01

Table 6. the Contingency between Q12 and Q14

Question	Chi-Square	C.C	Sig.
The preference of CMC mode to be used in auditing firms.	6.07	0.26	0.01

using traditional communication modes on the participants performance, by disabling equal participation, reduces their satisfaction.

On the contrary, the positive effect of using advanced communication modes which increase the participation equality and decisions quality on the participants' performance strongly increase their satisfaction and that leads users to prefer using CMC modes. All of that support the effect of selecting a specific communication mode to be used in the audit process on the participants' satisfaction whether the communication mode is traditional, which may decrease their satisfaction, or advanced modes which may increase their satisfaction.

That means the sample data supports the effect of the selection of a specific communication mode on the participants' satisfaction. Based on this result, the hypothesis is accepted statistically which in line with logic analysis and results within the selected sample data. According to the results of the non descriptive analysis for the sample data, all the research study's hypotheses are valid so they can be accepted.

CONCLUSION

The auditing environment formulated the aim of this research study, which is identifying the effect of using communication modes whether traditional or advanced modes on the auditor performance. This identification can help in determining the most effective communication modes to be used in the audit process in auditing firms to achieve the audit effectiveness and efficiency through ensuring high quality of audit process and improving the auditor performance (effectiveness) and control extra audit costs (efficiency). This study examines the effect of CMC modes on the audit effectiveness. Surveying prior research on the effect of e-communication modes on the audit performance, this research hypothesized that the effectiveness of the audit work depends on the type of the communication mode. It also predicted the existence of a relationship between the audit process and e-communication modes. In addition, this research suggested that there is an effect of selecting specific communication modes to be used on the participants' satisfaction.

Based on the logic and statistical analyses for the selected sample data, the findings suggest that the traditional communication modes are less effective as a result of their disadvantages while the advanced modes are the most effective ones to be used in auditing firms and that, in turn, affect the audit work effectiveness. The ineffectiveness of the traditional modes negatively affects the participants' satisfaction. On the contrary, the advanced modes effectiveness positively affects the participants' satisfaction by allowing users to equally participate and improve the auditor's performance.

The results of logic and statistical data analyses, including descriptive and non descriptive analyses, are consistent and show that the type of the communication mode, which is used by audit team, affects the audit effectiveness. Also, they support the direct relationship between the audit process effectiveness and e-communication modes, and evidence the positive effect of selecting e-communication modes to be used on the participants' satisfaction and all of that support the study hypotheses.

It should be noted that CMC modes offer important benefits relative to FTF meetings. A significant advantage over traditional modes, from a cost-benefit perspective, is supporting geographically dispersed teams, permitting any time/any place meetings. As a result, the CMC mode has gained acceptance as a valid and effective form of communication. It has been found that the main direction is toward the preference of using e-communication modes in Egyptian auditing firms. However, the trend toward the real application of traditional communication modes in those firms is ensured. That raises questions about the reasons of the contradiction between the preference of using advanced modes and the real application of traditional modes in local auditing firms. Although the users' perception of the effectiveness of e-communication modes and their effect on the audit effectiveness is evidenced, there may be some constraints impeding total application of advanced modes in auditing firms.

It is suggested that there are some problems which may face the users of advanced modes. So, it has been found that, many factors should be taken into consideration during the use of CMC modes as the wide access to the communication system, the large volumes of data which can be processed and stored, the complexity of computer systems, and the need for continuous development and maintenance for computer systems. Also, users should have experience in using computers for interaction and dealing with CMC tools through training and repeated use of those modes.

FUTURE RESEARCH

There are numerous avenues for **future research** exploring the use of CMC modes by audit teams. This study focused on the interaction between audit team members rather than other communicating parties including management and government bodies, future research could explore the effect of interaction between audit teams and the other communicating parties using CMC modes on the information exchanging. Also, future research can provide additional investigation about the advanced communication modes effectiveness concentrating on a specific communication mode which may increase the audit quality and improve the auditor performance. In addition, future research could explore the effect of CMC modes on the audit effectiveness after the replacement of traditional modes with the CMC modes in Egyptian auditing firms. The researchers recommend the analysis and assessment of the cost perspective on the practical use of the various CMC modes taking into consideration the financial capabilities of local auditing firms compared with those with international affiliation.

REFERENCES

American Institute of Certified Public Accountants (2002). *Consideration of Fraud in a Financial Statement Audit*, Statement on Auditing Standards No (99). New York: AICPA.

Arnold, V., Sutton, S., Stephen, C., Hayne, S., & Smith, C. (2000). Group decision making: The impact of opportunity-cost time pressure and group support systems. *Behavioral Research in Accounting, 12*, 69–96.

Atkinson, W. (2007). Communicating with your risk managers. *Risk Management, 54*(11), 28–32.

Atwood, C. (2007). Implementing your succession Plan. *Training & Development, 61*(11), 54–55.

Bamber, E. M., Watson, R. T. & Hill, M.C. (1996). The effects of group support system technology on audit group decision making. *Auditing: A Journal of Practice & Theory, 15*(1), 122-134.

Bordia, P. (1997). Face-to-Face versus Computer-Mediated Communication: A synthesis of the experimental literature. *The Journal of Business Communication*, *34*(1), 99–120. doi:10.1177/002194369703400106

Brown, J. L. (2004). How does Face-to-Face communication differ from online communication? *OMBA 600*, Assignment 2. Retrieved from http://www.mtholyoke.edu

Butschi, G., & Steyn, B. (2006). Theory on Strategic Communication Management is the key to Unlocking the Board Room. *Journal of Communication Management*, *10*, 106–109. doi:10.1108/13632540610646436

Casabona, P. A., & Grego, M. J. (2003). Consideration of fraud in a financial statement audit. *Review of Business, Jamaica*, *24*(2), 16–21.

Cheung, C., Lee, M., & Rabjohn, N. (2008). The Impact of Electronic Word-of-Mouth: The Adoption of Online Opinions in Online Customer Communities. *Internet Research*, *18*(3), 229–247. doi:10.1108/10662240810883290

Chidambaram, L., & Jones, B. (1993). Impact of communication medium and computer support on group perceptions and performance: A comparison of face-to-face and dispersed meetings. *MIS Quarterly*, *17*(4), 465–491. doi:10.2307/249588

Dennis, A. R. (1996). Information exchange and use in group decision making: You can lead a group to information, but you can't make it think. *MIS Quarterly*, *20*(4), 433–457. doi:10.2307/249563

Dennis, A. R., Wixom, B. H., & Vandenberg, R. J. (2001). Understanding fit and appropriation effects in group support systems via Meta analysis. *MIS Quarterly*, *25*(2), 167–193. doi:10.2307/3250928

Goodhue, D. L. (1995). Understanding user evaluations of information systems. *Management Science*, *41*(12), 1827–1844. doi:10.1287/mnsc.41.12.1827

Goodhue, D. L., & Thompson, R. T. (1995). Task-Technology Fit and individual performance. [Retrieved from http://www.misq.org - http://www.highbeam.com/library]. *MIS Quarterly*, *19*(2), 213–236. doi:10.2307/249689

Grimshaw, D., Cooke, F. L., Grugulis, I., & Vincent, S. (2002). New Technology and Changing Organizational forms: Implications for managerial Control and skills. *New Technology, Work and Employment*, *17*, 86–203. doi:10.1111/1468-005X.00104

Henning-Thurau, T., Gwinner, K. P., Walsh, G., & Gremler, D. D. (2004). Electronic Word-of-Mouth via Consumer-opinion platforms: What motivates consumers to articulate themselves on the Internet? *Journal of Interactive Marketing*, *18*(1), 38–52. doi:10.1002/dir.10073

Huang, A. H. (2002). E-mail communication and supervisor-subordinate exchange quality: an empirical study. *Human Systems Management*, *21*, 193–204.

Jessup, L. M., Connolly, T., & Tansik, D. A. (2004). *Toward a theory of automated group work: The deindividuating effects of anonymity, 1990*. In D. S. Kerr & U. S. Murthy (Eds.), *Divergent and convergent idea generation in teams: A comparison of Computer-Mediated and Face-to-Face Communication, Group Decision and Negotiation* (Vol. 13, pp. 381-399).

Karau, S. J., & Kelly, J. R. (1992). The effects of time scarcity and time abundance on group performance quality and interaction process. *Journal of Experimental Social Psychology*, *28*(6), 542–571. doi:10.1016/0022-1031(92)90045-L

Kerr, D. S., & Murthy, U. S. (1994). Group decision support systems and cooperative learning in auditing: An experimental investigation. *Journal of Information Systems*, *8*(2), 85–96.

Kerr, D. S., & Murthy, U. S. (2004). Divergent and convergent idea generation in teams: A comparison of Computer-Mediated and Face-to-Face Communication. *Group Decision and Negotiation*, *13*, 381–399. doi:10.1023/B:GRUP.0000042960.38411.52

Lumsden, G., & Lumsden, D. (2000). *Communicating in Groups and Teams* (3rd ed.). Wadsworth Thomson Learning.

Mascha, M. F., Bellovary, J., & Matczynski, M. (2004). The Benefits and Risks of Data Communication Methods. *American Accounting Association Conference, Aug. 7* (pp. 23-26).

Murthy, U. S. & Kerr, D. (2004). Comparing audit team effectiveness via alternative modes of Computer-Mediated Communication. *Auditing: A Journal of Practice & Theory, 23*(1), 141-151.

O'Kane, P., Palmer, M., & Hargie, O. (2007). Workplace Interactions and the Polymorphic Role of e-mail. *Leadership and Organization Development Journal*, *28*(4), 308–324. doi:10.1108/01437730710752193

Olaniran, B. A., Savage, G. T., & Sorenson, R. L. (1996). Experimental and experiential approaches to teaching Face-to-Face and Computer-Mediated Group Discussion. *Communication Education*, *45*(3), 244–260. doi:10.1080/03634529609379053

Rapoza, J. (2001). Will Face-to-Face meetings be replaced? *Enterprise News & Reviews*.

Straus, S. G. (1996). Getting a clue: The effect of communication media and information distribution on participation and performance in computer-mediated and face-to-face groups. *Small Group Research*, *27*(1), 115–142. doi:10.1177/1046496496271006

Valacich, J. S., Dennis, A. R., & Connolly, T. (1994). Idea generation in computer-based groups: A new ending to an old story. *Organizational Behavior and Human Decision Processes*, *57*(3), 448–467. doi:10.1006/obhd.1994.1024

Valacich, J. S., Paranka, D., George, J. F., & Nunamaker, J. F. Jr. (1993). Communication concurrency and the new media: A new dimension for media richness. *Communication Research*, *20*(2), 249–276. doi:10.1177/009365093020002004

Walsh, J. P., & Bayma, T. (1996). Computer networks and scientific work. *Social Studies of Science*, *26*(3), 661–703. doi:10.1177/030631296026003006

Zigurs, I., & Buckland, B. K. (1998). A theory of task-technology fit and group support systems effectiveness. *MIS Quarterly*, *22*(3), 313–334. doi:10.2307/249668

ADDITIONAL READING

Abbasi, Ahmed & Chen, Hsinchun. (2008). Cybergate: A Design framework and System For Text Analysis of Computer-Mediated Communication. *MIS Quarterly*, *32*(4), 811–837.

Advances in Consumer Research. (2008). The Value of Human Warmth: Social Presence Cues and Computer-Mediated Communications. *North American Conference Proceedings* (Vol. 35, pp. 793-794).

Berry, G. (2006). Can Computer-Mediated, Asynchronous Communication Improve, Team Processes and Decision Making? *Journal of Business Communication*, *43*(4), 344–366. doi:10.1177/0021943606292352

Bertacco, M. (2007). Social Norms and Behavioral Regulation in Asynchronous Communication: The Shift of Attention During Speed Communication. *Human-Computer Interaction*, *22*(3), 299–324.

Braun, Robert. L., & Davis, Harold. E. (2003). Computer-assisted audit tools and techniques: analysis and perspectives. *Managerial Auditing Journal*, *18*(9), 725–731. doi:10.1108/02686900310500488

Byron, K., & Baldridge, D. C. (2007). E-Mail Recipients' Impressions of Senders' Likability. *Journal of Business Communication*, *44*(2), 137–160. doi:10.1177/0021943606297902

Carbonara, J. (2008). It's time for Technology. *Foodservice Equipment & Supplies*, *61*(7), 28–36.

Cherng-Jyh, Y., & Chih-Hsiung, T. (2008). Online Social Presence: A Study of Score Validity of the Computer-Mediated Communication Questionnaire. *Quarterly Review of Distance Education*, *9*(3), 297–310.

Christensen, J., & Hughes, B. (2007). Voice-enabled IT transformation: The new Voice technologies. *IBM Systems Journal*, *46*(4), 763–775.

Dabbish, L., Hsieh, G., Kraut, R., & Hudson, S. (2007). Prioritization in Computer-Mediated Communication: Influences of Urgency, Notification, and Identity. *Academy of Management Proceedings* (pp.1-6).

Dowling, C., Leech, S. A., & Moroney, R. (2008). Audit Support System Design and the Declarative Knowledge of Long-Term Users. *Journal of Emerging Technologies in Accounting*, *5*, 99–108. doi:10.2308/jeta.2008.5.1.99

Hancock, J. T., Curry, L. E., Goorha, S., & Woodworth, M. (2008). On Lying and Being Lied To: A Linguistic Analysis of Deception in Computer Mediated Communication. *Discourse Processes*, *45*(1), 1–23. doi:10.1080/01638530701739181

Kerr, D. S., & Murthy, U. S. (2009). The effectiveness of Synchronous Computer-Mediated Communication for solving hidden-profile problems: Further empirical evidence. *Information and Management*. Available at http://www.elsevier.com/locate/im

Lai, Y., & Burchell, B. (2008). Distributed work: communication in an officeless firm. *New Technology, Work and Employment*, *23*(1-2), 61–76. doi:10.1111/j.1468-005X.2008.00203.x

Lo, S.-K. (2008). The Nonverbal Communication Functions of Emoticons in Computer-Mediated communication. *Cyberpsychology & Behavior*, *11*(5), 595–597. doi:10.1089/cpb.2007.0132

Mraovic, B. (2003). Social audit and accountability in IT management. *Managerial Auditing Journal*, *18*(3), 166–179. doi:10.1108/02686900310469943

Munzer, S., & Borg, A. (2008). Computer-mediated communication: synchronicity and compensatory effort. *Applied Cognitive Psychology*, *22*(5), 663–683. doi:10.1002/acp.1387

Nigrini, M. J., & Johnson, A. J. (2008). Using Key Performance Indicators and Risk Measures in Continuous Monitoring. *Journal of Emerging Technologies in Accounting*, *5*, 65–80. doi:10.2308/jeta.2008.5.1.65

Pomeranz, F. (2004). The US General Accounting office: Is freedom of audit access imperiled? *Managerial Auditing Journal*, *19*(3), 394–399. doi:10.1108/02686900410524391

Sanchez-Franco, M. J., & Roldan, J. L. (2005). Web acceptance and usage model: A comparison between goal-directed and experiential web users. *Internet Research*, *15*(1), 21–48. doi:10.1108/10662240510577059

Saritas, T. (2008). The Construction of knowledge Through Social interaction via Computer-Mediated Communication. *Quarterly Review of Distance Education*, *9*(1), 35–49.

Song, M., Berends, H., Van der Bij, H., & Weggeman, M. (2007). The effect of IT and Co-location on Knowledge Dissemination. *Journal of Product Innovation Management*, *24*(1), 52–68. doi:10.1111/j.1540-5885.2006.00232.x

Till Johnson, J. (2008). The many modes of communication. *New World (New Orleans, La.)*, *25*(34), 24–24.

Turner, T., Creighton, S., Nudurupati, S., & Bititci, U. (2004). Implementing a web enabled Performance measurement system. *Measuring Business Excellence*, *8*(2), 40–54. doi:10.1108/13683040410539427

van den Hooff, B., & de Ridder, J. A. (2004). Knowledge sharing in context: the influence of organizational commitment, communication climate and CMC use on Knowledge sharing. *Journal of Knowledge Management*, *8*(6), 117–130. doi:10.1108/13673270410567675

Yang, D. C., & Guan, L. (2004). The evolution of IT auditing and internal control standards in financial statement audits: The case of the United States. *Managerial Auditing Journal*, *19*(4), 544–555. doi:10.1108/02686900410530547

KEY TERMS AND DEFINITIONS

Audit Effectiveness: refers to improving the performance of the audit team and enhancing the quality of the audit process.

Communication: is the process of using verbal and nonverbal cues to negotiate a mutually acceptable meaning between two or more people within a particular context and environment.

Computer-Mediated Communication: is a form of interaction that has become extremely prevalent in many people's social lives. The interaction is to share the information and collaborate with others through electronic technologies.

Electronic Meeting System (EMS): is a system which provides instant communication capabilities and help coordinate dispersed decision-making activities.

Electronic Word-of-Mouth (eWOM): means of communication through electronic media such as on line discussion forums, electronic bulletin board systems, news groups, blogs, review sites, and social networking sites.

Group Support System (GSS): provides a structured environment that allows participants in a collaborative team to interact simultaneously and anonymously to generate ideas, make decisions, and solve problems.

Task Technology Fit (TTF): is a theory assuming that a good "fit" between CMC technology tools and task requirements will result in the best performance.

Chapter 8
Evaluating the Dimensions of Web-Based Software System Service Quality:
An Empirical Study

Ülkü Şişik
Hacettepe University, Turkey

Leyla Özer
Hacettepe University, Turkey

Muhammet Mustafa Cerit
Banking Regulation and Supervision Agency, Turkey

ABSTRACT

The purpose of this study is to evaluate Web-based service quality. First related literature is reviewed and then a survey is conducted to measure Web-based service quality which is provided by a Turkish firm. Study results have indicated six Web-based service quality dimensions; information quality, responsiveness, Web assistance, tangibles, empathy, and call-back. Average values of information quality and responsiveness dimensions are highest indicating that these are valued highly by respondents in determining the software firm's service quality. Also, average values of all dimensions being greater than 3, indicates that respondents evaluated service quality as good. Dimensions do not predict overall service quality, indicating that respondents independently evaluate each dimension and the overall service quality. Overall service quality and dimensions are found as distinct constructs and overall quality affected user satisfaction.

INTRODUCTION

Today, the percentage of service sector in national income is not very high in developing countries as in the developed ones. Service sector is relatively labor intensive and investment cost is less. In addition, service sector productivity is low while cost and price are high.

Quality became a very powerful tool of competition for the firms in today's world (Smith 1995). While goods quality is tangible, service quality is

DOI: 10.4018/978-1-60566-996-0.ch008

abstract (Hoffman and Bateson, 1997). Because of the distinctive properties of service, custumer perception quality is important for fims in addition to presented quality. Perceived service quality is viewed as the degree and direction of discrepancy between consumers' perceptions and expectations (Parasuraman, et al., 1988).

Information technology had significant effect on producing and delivering services. Using information technology some of the service characteristics were changed. The changes in information technology progressed from traditional business computing to mobile and pervasive computing (Okunoye, 2004).

Web-based services as well as Web-based service quality have gained a great importance in recent years. Web-based services have many properties such as to establish firm images, inform customers, provide interaction with customers, distributed service, effective and efficient online communication (Waite, 2006). These properties may be strategic tools to increase competitive power and become necessity for most of Web-based services. Therefore, beyond presenting high quality service upon competitors, higher level quality service should be provided to satisfy customers and increase the perceived service quality level which will bring in measuring perceived Web-based service quality, and accordingly to result correction and betterment on quality.

There is discrepancy between measuring **Web-based service quality** and traditional service quality. According to Tan, et al. (2003) such differences are Web-based service reach broad crew less cost, discrepancy of customer and customer profile is different. Kuo et al. (2005) study points out two differences between traditional service and Web-based services. Web-based service being more efficient then traditional one, and Web-based service customers are not passive. Li et all. (2002) study also mensions two differences between traditional service and Web-based services. First is the communication between service and customer being two ways and, second is Web-based services no phsical interaction so that non tangibles dimensions are more important.

The objectives of this study are (1) to determine Web-based service quality dimensions, and (2) to evaluate relationship between dimensions and overall service quality, and (3) to evaluate relationship between overall service quality and satisfaction. For this purpose; first, related literature is reviewed, second, a model devoloped (See Figure 1), and then the methodology applied.

BACKGROUND

Parasuraman, Zeithaml, and Berry (1985), review the definitions of the service quality before defining servqual. New definition of service quality which is directed to consumer contains many of service quality definitions and also the source of their model.

Servqual which is developed by Parasuraman et al. (1988), for measuring service quality concentrates on perceived quality. Perceived quality refers to a consumer's judgment about a product's overall excellence (Zeithaml, 1987). Through research conducted with focus groups, the researchers asked about the characteristics a service provider should have in order to have high quality. They found out that consistently all of the members of the focus group had similar criteria. With these findings, they created 10 quality dimensions. Researchers found that some of these 10 dimensions overlapped and customers could only distinguish 5 dimensions. These dimensions are tangibles, reliability, responsiveness, assurance and empathy (Parasuraman et al., 1988).

Web-based service is different from the traditional one and this also results in some differences in dimensions. There has been considerable confusion in defining and interpreting service quality for Web-based services. The main reason is because there are various types of Web-based services, such as e-commerce, Web portals and

Figure 1. Conceptualization of the model

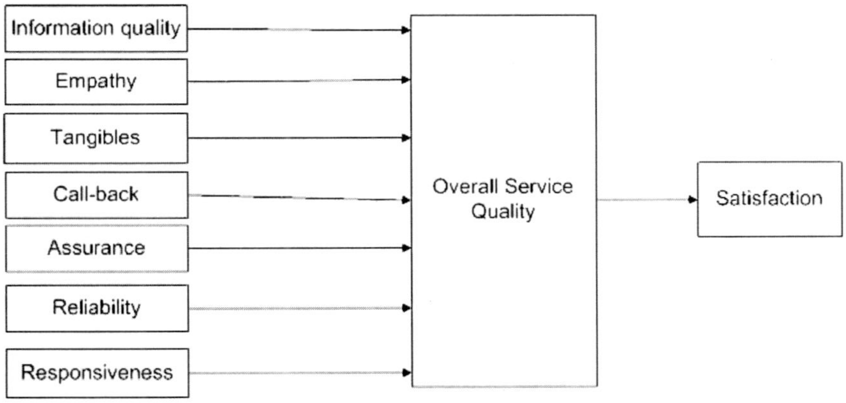

search engine. Consequently, service quality dimensions differ according to the Web-based services (Yang et al., 2005).

Several studies have been conducted to develop measurement scales for Web-based service quality. Table 1 lists some examples of studies on Web-based service quality, including the dimensions of e service quality.

In the preparation of Table 1, dimensions used by different studies are either consolidated, or renamed. Some others are divided into two dimensions. For example 'Ease of Navigation' and 'Usability' dimensions combined under the name of 'Ease of Use' dimension. 'Assurance and Trust' renamed as 'Assurance' dimension, and 'Accessibility' as 'Access' dimension. 'Privacy and Security' divided into two dimensions 'Privacy' and 'Security', and 'Appearance' converted into 'Webpage Design and Content'.

Zhu and Chen (2002), in their study on information technology based services, have added information technology dimension to original servqual dimension. This dimension includes ease of use, conservation of time, privacy and accuracy.

Li et al. (2002) combined some of servqual dimension and came up with 6 dimensions which are responsiveness, competence, empathy, quality of information, Web assistance and call-back systems.

In a later study, Li et al. (2003) found 11 dimensions on Web-based information system research. New dimensions are added to servqual dimension and some modifications are made. Result of research dimensions are reliability, responsiveness, access, flexibility, ease of navigation, efficiency, assurance/trust, security, site aesthetics, customization/personalization and quality of information.

Iwaarden and Wiele (2003) in their study noticed that servqual dimensions equally useful in Web-based service. They use tangibles, reliability, responsiveness and assurance of servqual dimensions and change the definition of the dimensions according to service.

Kuo (2003) has prepared survey questions according to five dimensions of servqual. While evaluating the survey, new dimensions are added to dimension list. New dimensions are advertising mail management, customer service management, online quality and information safety, Webpage design and content, extra function and service.

On e-service quality research Santos (2003) found 11 dimensions. These dimensions group into incubative and active dimensions. Incubative includes the proper design of Web site. The majority of the elements in Incubative can be developed prior to a Web-site being launched. Active dimension includes the good support, fast speed, and attentive maintenance of a Web-site.

Table 1. Web-based service quality dimensions in literature

	Parasuraman et al. (1988)	Zhu et al. (2002)	Li et al. (2002)	Kuo (2003)	Iwaarden and Wiele (2003)	Lie et al. (2003)	Santos (2003)	Tan (2003)	Webb & Webb (2004)	Badri et all. (2005)	Kuo et al. (2005)	Yang et al.(2005)	Parasuraman et al. (2005)	Coller & Bienstock (2006)	Ho & Lie (2007)	Swaid & Wigand (2007)	Bandyopadhyay & Natarajan (2008)	Connally & Bannister (2008)	Raman et al. (2008)	Liu et al. (2009)
Tangibles	X	X			X				X	X										
Reliability	X	X			X	X	X	X	X	X						X	X		X	
Responsiveness	X	X	X		X	X		X	X	X			X		X	X		X		
Assurance	X	X			X	X		X	X	X						X				
Empathy	X	X	X		X				X	X	X									
Competence			X																	
Quality of Information			X			X		X	X		X				X	X				
Ease of Use		X				X	X	X			X	X		X		X	X		X	X
Privacy		X											X	X				X		X
Accuracy		X												X						
Security						X		X							X					X
Conservation of Time		X												X						
System Availability													X					X		
Convenience		X																		
Website Functionality														X	X					
Multifunctional Capabilities		X		X																
Incentive							X												X	
Customer Service Management				X																
Advertising Mail Management				X																
Fulfilment													X					X		
Compensation													X					X		
Personalization						X		X								X			X	
Web Assistance			X																	
Call-back System			X																	
Customer Relationship															X					

continued on the following page

Table 1. continued

	Parasuraman et al. (1988)	Zhu et al. (2002)	Li et al. (2002)	Kuo (2003)	Iwaarden and Wiele (2003)	Lie et al. (2003)	Santos (2003)	Tan (2003)	Webb & Webb (2004)	Badri et all. (2005)	Kuo et al. (2005)	Yang et al.(2005)	Parasuraman et al. (2005)	Coller & Bienstock (2006)	Ho & Lie (2007)	Swaid & Wigand (2007)	Bandyopadhyay & Natarajan (2008)	Connally & Bannister (2008)	Raman et al. (2008)	Liu et al. (2009)
Interaction							X					X					X		X	
Contact													X					X		
Access						X		X			X	X								
Flexibility						X		X												
Efficiency						X		X					X					X		
Online Quality and Information safety				X																
Webpage Design and Content				X		X	X	X						X			X		X	X
Usefulness of Content												X								
Adequacy of Information												X								X

Tan at all. (2003) in their study have defined attributes and dimensions related to Web-based service quality as reliability, responsiveness, access, flexibility, ease of navigation, efficiency, assurance/trust, security, site aesthetics, customization/personalization, quality of information.

Webb and Webb (2004) pointed out that Web-based service measured by using union of servqual dimension and information quality dimension. Information quality dimension includes accessibility quality, contextual quality, representational quality and intrinsic quality.

Kuo et al. (2005) in their study on Web portals determined dimension of service quality as empathy, ease of use, information quality and accessibility.

Badri et al. (2005) prepared survey question according to five dimensions of servqual. At the end of their study, they conclude that investigating expectation is enough instead of gap analysis between expectation and perception.

Yang et al. (2005) in their study on service quality of information in Web portals suggested using quality of information, ease of use adequacy of information, customization, technical adequacy and privacy and security as an initial measurement dimension. At the end of research, they found usability, usefulness of content, adequacy of information, accessibility and interaction as a dimension.

Coller and Bienstock (2006) in their study measured e-retailing service quality. They found three groups of dimensions: process quality, outcome quality and recovery. Process quality group included functionality, information accuracy, design, privacy and ease of use. Outcome quality includes order accuracy, order condition and time. Recovery group included interactive fairness, procedural fairness and outcome fairness.

Ho and Lie (2007) identified the dimensions of e-travel service quality as information quality, security, Website functionality, customer relationship, responsiveness and fulfilment.

Swaid and Wigand (2007) study have concentrated on e-commerce, e-service quality dimensions and found out Website usability, information quality, reliability, responsiveness, assurance and personalization dimensions. They also have investigated, dimension relationship to satisfaction and loyalty.

Bandyopadhyay and Natarajan (2008) measured the service quality of educational Websites as perceived by students by using conceptual model developed by Santos (2003). Ease of use, content, reliability, privacy, and interaction were used to prepare the survey. All of them except privacy were found to have a significant effect on service quality.

Connally and Bannister (2008) measured following quality dimension on e - tax filing and service by using survey. Used quality dimensions were: efficiency, system availability, fulfilment, privacy, responsiveness, efficiency, compensation, contact, perceived value, loyalty intentions

Raman et al. (2008) study on internet banking and commerce, used ease of use, appearance, reliability, customization, communication and incentive dimension as a part of e-service quality.

Liu et al. (2009) study on service quality of general portals. At the end of their study, they found out that information quality and quantity play important role in internet portals.

Service quality dimensions need to be customized to each kind of services (Carman 1990). Above some of Web-based service research are reviewed. These studies show that, some of added and subtracted service quality dimensions are common. Commonly added dimension is information quality. In addition there is need to add some dimensions which are related to general quality of system such as ease of use, aesthetics, security.

In some studies tangible dimension is omitted because it seemed unimpotant for Web-based service quality. To provide a continuous Web-based service requires investment on computer hardware. To increase service quality firms must establish necessary infrastructure (Bharatti and Berg, 2003). For this reason, tangible dimension may be considered as important as the others. Its importance will be tested in our study, as well as the necessity of information quality dimension.

CONCEPTUALISING WEB-BASED SERVICE QUALITY

In literature review, service quality is measured by using different dimensions (See Table 1). However research in Zeithaml et al. (2002) suggested that the necessity to understand the importance of different dimensions and perceptual attributes to overall electronic service quality and its consequences. Ho and Lie (2007) in e-travel service quality study suggested that online purchasers evaluated e-travel service quality both on the basis of the five dimensions and the overall e-travel service quality. The authors investigated which dimensions represent overall quality. The study of Collier and Bienstock (2006) stated that, Web site factors have an impact on the overall e-service quality.

In some other studies, a relation is founded between service quality and customer satisfaction. Wolfinbarger and Gilly (2003) showed a positive link between electronic service quality dimensions and customer satisfaction. Yang et al. (2005) showed that overall service quality had a positive, important influence on user satisfaction. The study of Ho and Lie (2007) found that service quality had a direct effect on satisfaction. In this context, service quality dimension may imply the evaluated **overall service quality** and service quality may affect the satisfaction.

Based on the above discussion, our conceptualization of model is shown in Figure 1.

METHODOLOGY

We focus on measuring Web-based service quality by using servqual and based on Li et al. (2002) study. In servqual service quality is measured by the gap between expectation and perception. In our study, customer perception is measured because of two reasons (Li et al., 2002): first customer does not express exactly his/her expectation, and second, errors in customer expectation create problems to measure the gap between expectation and perception.

Scale Item Development

Based on the review of related literature and Li et al. (2002) study, our conceptual framework was tested on Web-based service. Li et al. (2002) prepared 25 questions of six dimensions in their study. Because of the service surveyed in our study, some modifications (extraction, adding and restatement) are made on their original Li et al. (2002) survey. These changes/alterations are explained below in detail.

Since the selected service in our study is not open to public (it is used only by authorized firms) there is no need to advertise Web site address. Therefore the first question of responsiveness dimension 'Website addresses are included in all existing documentation, publicity and advertising channels are extracted from scale.

There is no payment process in this service, the fourth question of the competence dimension in Li et al study 'Offer options on mode of payment.' also dropped from scale.

Service is used only in Turkey; there is no other country or region. Therefore the fourth question of the information quality dimension in the original study 'Offer language or geographic options.' is also omitted.

In Li et al. (2002) study, question of tangibles dimension 'Integrate graphics, sound and video to make the Website visually appealing.' did not appear as a dimension, although it was among the questions, and was extracted. In our study, because of the necessity of hardware system for the continuity of the service and the visual attractiveness of the software are considered important. Therefore we decided to use this dimension in our study.

After modification and subtractions we have 23 questions, 5 of empathy, 5 of responsiveness, 2 of assurance, 2 of reliability and 2 of tangibles. In parallel with Li et al. (2002) study, 4 for information quality, and 3 call-back system questions are added to the scale.

Introductory part of our survey explains the aim of the study to the customers, and how to answer the questions. First part of the survey includes Web-based service quality 23 questions. All questions scored by five-point Likert scale. Second part of the survey includes some questions about overall service quality and customer satisfaction. Third part contains questions about some demographic characteristics and experience on the software of customer.

Data Collection

The chosen service is not open to public but only to the firms which have access authority. Responders use this service as part of their job. Service is used by authorized approximately 50 firms. Prepared Survey questions were sent to by e-mail firms' personnel who use software as part of their jobs. Survey was answered by 102 customers via internet. Because of each responder uses software system as a part of job, all responses are accepted as valid.

Table 2 shows, the characteristics of the respondents. The majority of respondents are male (41.2% female, 58.8% male). When examining the education of respondents, 9.8% is high school graduate and 6.9% have two years degree, 73.5%

Table 2. Sample properties

		Frequency (n)	Percentage (%)
Gender	Female	42	41.2
	Male	60	58.8
	Total	102	100.0
Education	High school	10	9.8
	Two year degree	7	6.9
	Bachelor degree	75	73.5
	Master	10	9.8
	Total	102	100.0
Age	20 – 29	18	18
	30 – 39	66	65
	40 or over	16	15
	Invalid	2	2
	Total	100	100.0

bachelor degree and 9.8% master. Respondents' age distribution is 18% 20-29, 65% 30-39 and 15% 40 or over. 2 of respondents did not answer the age group question.

Data Analysis and Results

The reliability of analysis was tested by using Alpha model. Reliability coefficient which is known as Cronbach Alpha is 0.902.

To identify Web-based service quality dimensions, a principle component factor analysis with a "Varimax Rotation" was conducted. After 16 iterations six factors are obtained. Resulting values about factor analysis are exhibited in Table 3.

Kaiser-Meyer-Olkin (*KMO*) test value was found 0.747, degree of freedom was found 231 and significance level was found 0.000. Therefore the data was suitable for factor analysis. Variables explained 71.296% of total variance.

The first factor (dimension), **the quality of information**, consists of eight questions related to the quality of the information put forward and access to this information. With the quality of the information, at what level the customer needs are met with the information presented by the software is evaluated; with information access, the factors such as security, confidentiality, speed and ease of use of the system are evaluated. One of the results of the factor analysis, with respect to the company which is subject to the research, was whether the quality of the information should be evaluated without considering the factors related with access to the information. If the access to the information is not secure, then there cannot be a guaranteed about the reliability of the information, and the quality of the information presented to the customer may be affected.

The second dimension, **responsiveness**, consists of four questions. In this dimension, ability to come with a solution to the customer struggles, and the user-friendliness of the software is evaluated. In the research of Li at al. (2002), user friendliness is also dealt with in responsiveness dimension.

The third dimension, **Web assistance**, consists of four questions. In this dimension, the help of frequently asked questions and answers sent to the customers about their requirements via e-mail to solve the problems themselves is evaluated.

The fourth dimension, **tangibles**, consists of two questions. With this dimension, the availability of the service and the visual appealing

Table 3. Result of factor analysis

Factor groups	Average	Standard Deviation	Factor Loading
FACTOR 1: Information Quality (Cronbach Alpha = 0.88)	4.16		**0.806**
Information contained on the software system is current and timely.	4.04	0.83	**0.806**
Information contained on the software system is accurate and relevant.	3.92	0.97	**0.755**
Software system speed is sufficient.	4.13	0.82	**0.679**
Security of arrangements and privacy is stated on the Website.	4.05	0.71	**0.663**
Information contained on the software system is rich in detail.	4.03	0.71	**0.629**
Firewall, certificates, password etc. are used to guarantee transaction security.	4.42	0.65	**0.623**
Intuitive on-page navigation improves ease of use.	4.33	0.69	**0.616**
The tone of message is consistently courteous.	4.38	0.69	**0.508**
FACTOR 2: Responsiveness (Cronbach Alpha = 0.76)	4.13		**0.792**
E-mail systems are both inbound and outbound to deal with customer complaints.	4.23	0.72	**0.792**
Privacy statement and e-mail notification accompany while posting form process.	4.28	0.68	**0.752**
Form posting process is simple.	4.08	0.88	**0.648**
Offer personal e-mail responses and Web pages.	3.93	0.79	**0.585**
FACTOR 3: Web Assistance (Cronbach's Alpha = 0.81)	3.61		**0.753**
The answers from the software system come fast.	3.23	1.03	**0.753**
E-mail responses are relevant and accurate, and software system content is appropriate to customer requirements.	3.96	0.82	**0.639**
Relevant FAQ (Frequently Asked Questions) helps customer to solve problems by themselves.	3.66	0.85	**0.639**
Various FAQs help different customers.	3.58	0.79	**0.620**
FACTOR 4: Tangibles (Cronbach Alpha = 0.70)	3.53		**0.826**
Integrate graphics, sound and video to make the Website visually appealing.	3.10	0.97	**0.826**
The software system is available all the time.	3.95	1.07	**0.711**
FACTOR 5: Empathy (Cronbach Alpha = 0.70)	3.83		**0.761**
E-mails or questionnaires are used to conduct customer satisfaction surveys.	3.99	0.81	**0.761**
The achievable service level is stated on the software system.	4.01	0.76	**0.647**
E-mail system tells customers exactly when the required service will be performed.	3.500	0.85	**0.508**
FACTOR 6: Call-back	3.32		**0.787**
Feedback is continuously changed in response to customers.	3.32	1.04	**0.787**

of the software user interface are evaluated. The high availability of the software systems is mostly relevant with the investment made to the hardware. The software services will be kept available in proportion to the competent hardware investment. The other issue of the tangibles dimension is the appealing of the user interface of the software system. In comparison of two software systems, the one which is supported with visual interface components will be preferred more. The importance of the tangibles in terms of the company subject to the research is included as a result of the factor analysis.

The fifth dimension, **empathy**, consists of three questions. With this dimension, providing supplying customer satisfaction, measuring cus-

Figure 2. The measurement model

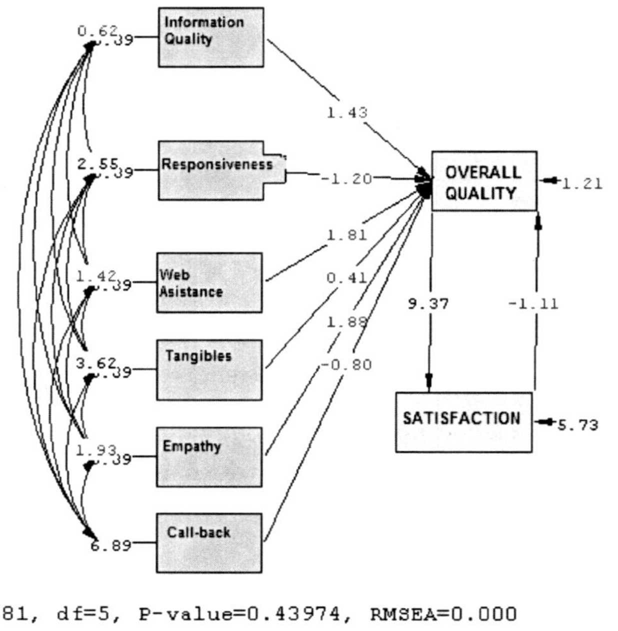

tomer satisfaction level to solve possible problems and the continuity level of the provided service are evaluated.

The sixth dimension, **call-back**, consists of just one question. With this dimension the feedback provided to the customer is evaluated.

Table 3 shows that the average values of all factors are greater than 3, which can be interpreted as the respondents' perceived service quality rating as good and satisfied. In addition, according to results of factor analysis, information quality and responsiveness average values (4.16 and 4.13) are greater than the others indicating that these two factor play an important role in determining of service quality. To increase customer perception, more importance needs to be attached to these factors and other factors were needed.

Average values of empathy, Web assistance and tangibles' dimensions (3.38, 3.61 and 3.52 respectively) were relatively high. These average values show the importance of dimensions.

The average value of call-back dimension is low (3.32), indicating that to increase the service quality this factor needs to be improved.

The 6 dimensions of Web-based service quality; information quality, responsiveness, tangibles, Web assistance, empathy and call-back are assumed to predict overall quality and satisfaction. To test our hypothesis we used Lisrel, and found that the coefficient is 8.51. The hypothesized model is presented in Figure 2.

Figure 2 is prepared to exhibit our model: six factors (quality, responsiveness, Web-assistance, tangibles, empathy and call back) were expected to predict overall service quality perceived by users, which in turn was expected to affect satisfaction. This model was supported in terms of Satorra-Bentler scaled $\chi 2$ and adjusted goodness of fit index (AGFI), $\chi 2$ (5, N= 122) = 4.81, $p>.05$, ADGFI= 0.92. Other fit indices indicated that the data fit the model well (e.g. normed fit index (NFI) = 0.98, RMSEA = .00)

When hypothesized relationships were examined in detail, it was seen that six factors could not predict overall service quality as it was expected ($p>.05$). In line with expectations, overall service quality affected the satisfaction (standardized coefficient = 0.98, t (122) = 9.37; $p<.05$). In other

Table 4. General evaluation of overall service quality and satisfaction level

Overall service quality	**Very Bad**	**Bad**	**Normal**	**Good**	**Very Good**
Frequency (n)	0	0	11	77	14
Percentage (%)	0	0	10.8	75.5	13.7
Satisfaction Level	**Never Satisfied**	**Do not Satisfied**	**Not Sure**	**Satisfied**	**Highly Satisfied**
Frequency (n)	0	0	7	79	16
Percentage (%)	0	0	6.9	75.5	15.7

words, as perceived quality increases, satisfaction derived from the service also increases. Yet, the reverse was not found to be true. That is, satisfaction did not have any effect on overall service quality ($t(122) = 1.11$; $p > .05$)

Average value of overall service quality which is taken in part two of the survey was 4.029 So that respondents evaluated software system service quality as good. Average value of service satisfaction level was 4.088. Related statistical data shown in Table 4.

DISCUSSION

The study has determined 6 dimensions of Web-based service quality as information quality, responsiveness, tangibles, Web assistance, empathy and call-back. There was a difference between the dimensions before and after the factor analysis.

The quality of the information dimension after the factor analysis included two assurance questions about access to the information. With this study, questions related to the assurance dimension resulting from servqual dimensions are found within the scope of quality of the information. In addition, a question related to the user friendliness of the system which comes from responsiveness dimension and another question related to the politeness of the language used within the messages which comes from the empathy dimension are also found within the scope of the quality of the information.

The seventh question (intuitive on-page navigation improves ease of use.) which is thought to be in the responsiveness dimension at first sight, has appeared in the simplicity of usage thereby increasing the quality of the information. It is also understandable that the competence of the tools (security of arrangements and privacy is stated on the Website.) which keep the security of the software to the right, are included in the quality of the information dimension. The finding that the question (the tone of message is consistently courteous) related with the politeness of the language used in the software system and which is expected to be covered in the empathy dimension, is meaningful because the information is provided by the Web site instead of a human being. A polite tone of message will result in a pleasurable impact on respondents.

There were no differences in tangibles dimensions before and after the factor analysis.

The call-back dimension is reduced to one question after the factor analysis.

The question related to the personalized e-mail answers which were considered in empathy dimension before the application is included in responsiveness dimension after the factor analysis. It is found meaningful to be included in responsiveness dimension considering the enthusiasms of the service providers to provide better service to the customer.

The Web assistance dimension which was not included to the study and comes after the factor analysis, consists of two questions from empathy, one from call-back, and one from the responsiveness dimensions. It is not meaningless that the following questions which are covered in empathy dimension before the application are included in Web assistance dimension, withstanding the level of the desire to help to the customer with using the Web pages:

- Relevant FAQ (Frequently Asked Questions) helps customer to solve problems by themselves.
- Various FAQs help different customers..

Same way, it is shown that, the question within the responsiveness dimension "E-mail responses are relevant and accurate, and software system content is appropriate to customer requirements." which proves the actuality and uprightness of the e-mail messages sent to the customers can be interpreted in Web assistance dimension. Also it is meaningful to put the question "The answers from the software system come fast." -which is included in the call-back dimension- into Web assistance dimension because the question is related with the speed of the answers to the customer.

General interpretation and comparison with other studies; the quality of the information dimension is not included in the original servqual model. If it is thought that either a function is interpreted or information is put forward in the Web sites, this domain research points out the necessity of the quality of the information for Web-based services. As a matter of fact, Li et al. (2003), Webb and Webb (2004), Kuo at al. (2005) and Li at al. (2002) also stressed the necessity of the quality of the information in measurement of the quality of Web-based services. With this study, the definition of the quality of the information is expanded by adding factors related with the information access process. In this study, the assurance dimension of servqual dimensions takes part in quality of the information dimension because it is related to information access.

The questions from Li at al. (2002) one of which takes part in the empathy dimension as "Software system speed is sufficient." and the other takes part in the responsiveness dimension as "Intuitive on-page navigation improves ease of use." are included in the quality of the information dimension in this study. Also the questions which takes part in the competence dimension as "The tone of message is consistently courteous.", "Security of arrangements and privacy is stated on the Website." and "Firewall, certificates, password etc. are used to guarantee transaction security." are included in the quality of the information dimension in this study. This is based on the relation with these questions on information access.

In the study of Li at al. (2002), the questions take part in the tangibles dimension of servqual dimensions were considered as unimportant because they have not taken part in any factor group. But in this study, tangibles dimension is reached with two questions after factor analysis. The question as "The software system is available all the time." is taken part in tangibles dimension which was in responsiveness dimension in the study of Li at al. (2002). As the service is provided by using software system, the availability of the services depends on the hardware systems and the backup systems on which the software is run. And because of the hardware and backup systems are physical devices, this result found meaningful by the company which provides the software system service.

The Web assistance and call-back dimensions which do not take part in the servqual model are found necessary in measurement of the quality of the Web-based services as a result of this research. Even at first sight, these two dimensions seem to be under same dimension, they come out as separate dimensions after the application. This result is the same in the study of Li at al. (2002). As a result of this research, the questions "The answers from the software system come fast.", "E-mail responses are relevant and accurate, and software system content is appropriate to customer requirements." which took part in the responsiveness dimension take part in Web assistance, and the other one as "Feedback is continuously changed in response to customers." which took part in empathy dimension takes part in call-back dimensions.

The questions of Li at al. (2002) are employed in this research. One of the differences between Li at al. (2002) and this study can be this reimplementation, and the other is that research of Li at al. (2002) is an international research in terms of the participator companies and researchers while the application area of this study is a single country and a single software company.

After these studies two dimensions of servqual responsiveness and empathy were needed to measure Web-based service quality. This result is the same in the study of Li at al. (2002). As a result of this research, the questions as "Form posting process is simple." and "Privacy statement and e-mail notification accompany while posting form process." which took part in the competence dimension take part in responsiveness, "The achievable service level is stated on the software system." which took part in competence and "E-mail system tells customers exactly when the required service will be performed." which took part in call-back dimension take part in empathy dimensions.

For the selected company, survey result shows that assurance and reliability dimensions are not direct part of Web-based service quality dimension, but information quality, Web assistance and call-back dimensions are added as Web-based service quality dimension. In addition, tangibles dimension which was found as unimportant in Li at al. (2002) study is taken into consideration in this study.

The results of testing our model can be summarized as: a) dimensions do not predict overall service quality, indicating that respondents independently evaluate each dimension and the overall service quality, b) overall service quality and dimension are found as distinct constructs, and c) overall quality affect user satisfaction.

CONCLUSION

A number of Web-based services are increasing such as e-commerce, job application systems, online publications systems, e-government etc. Some of the reasons for these increases are Web-based service cost is relatively low, 7/24 access is possible and may be most importantly firms want to place themselves on internet whose usage is increasing rapidly.

This study aimed at a) to determine Web-based service quality dimensions, b) to examine the relationship between dimensions and overall service quality, and the relationship between overall service quality and satisfaction. After an extensive review of the related litterateur, we measured the Web-based service quality which is provided by a Turkish firm. We carried out the survey by sampling. On line survey was answered by 102 respondents. Data were collected about demographic profile, service quality perception and satisfaction.

In this study Web-based service quality is measured, factor analysis was used. The result of factor analysis showed 6 dimensions of Web-based service quality for research base firm; information quality, responsiveness, tangibles, Web assistance, empathy and call-back. Average values of information quality and responsiveness dimensions are highest indicating that these dimensions played important role in determination of software firm service quality. In addition, average values of all dimensions are greater than 3. It shows that respondents evaluated service quality as good.

In this study, finding information quality as a factor shows that information quality dimension is a necessity for measuring Web-based service quality. Information quality dimension includes question about criterion of the information access and servqual dimension of assurance. Tangibles dimension is not much important as information quality, but for the reason of the availability of the services depends on the hardware systems and the backup systems on which the software is run, some question about tangible dimensions are added to survey. In conclusion, one of the findings of this study is that tangible dimension is obtained as a result of factor analysis.

Our findings show that dimensions do not predict overall service quality, indicating that respondents independently evaluate each dimension and the overall service quality . Therefore overall service quality and dimension are found to be distinct constructs, as previous research had found. In other words, overall quality affects user satisfaction.

This study has included only one firm in Turkey, so results may be related to this firm. If this study were extended to other firms in Turkey, which serve Web-based services, results may change. In addition, data about demographic profile and labour experience were collected through survey. Relation between these data and customer perception of service quality may be investigated in another research. Furthermore, number of sample size may change the results.

In summary, since Web-based service has certain information, adding information quality dimension to servqual is needed. In addition, tangible dimension which seems as unimportant in some research is needed for measuring service quality.

FUTURE TRENDS

Internet and internet based applications, which are the result of rapid technological change, are increasing quickly, and pressuring the competition among firms. Customer focused firms, in order to capture a greater portion of the market, aim to meet the customer needs earlier than their competitors. Speediness and therefore time becomes a key element of competition. Time is important for customers also. Instead of face to face commerce, they prefer to work at home, run their errands while traveling or even walking.

The importance of time for firms and customers is expected to stimulate further research and development on existing new products such as mobile phones or wristwatches endowed with new features to serve for e-operations as pocket PCs, or completely new products will be produced, new Web-based services ("mobile" Web-based services) will be provided to meet the need for mobile e-services. New products and new "mobile" Web-based services require further researches on mobile services and their quality.

REFERENCES

Badri, M. A., Abdulla, M., & Al-Madini, A. (2005). Information technology center service quality assessment and application of SERVQUAL. *International Journal of Quality & Reliability Management*, *22*(8), 819–848. doi:10.1108/02656710510617247

Bandyopadhyay, S., & Natarajan, V. (2008). Service quality of educational Websites: an empirical study. *Journal of Business & Economics Research*, *6*, 49–54.

Bharatti, P., & Berg, D. (2003). Managing information systems for service quality: a study from the other side. *Information Technology & People*, *16*, 183–201. doi:10.1108/09593840310478685

Buttle, F. (1996). SERVQUAL: review, critique, research agenda. *European Journal of Marketing*, *30*, 8–32. doi:10.1108/03090569610105762

Carman, J. M. (1990). Consumer perception of service quality: an assessment of the servqual dimensions. *Journal of Retailing*, *66*(1), 33–55.

Collier, J. E., & Bienstock, Carol C. (2006). Measuring service quality in e-retailing. *Journal of Service Research*, *8*, 260–275. doi:10.1177/1094670505278867

Connolly, R., & Bannister, F. (2008). eTax filing & service quality: the case of the revenue online service. Proceedings of World Academy of Science. *Engineering and Technology*, *28*, 313–317.

Coulthard, L. J. M. (2004). Measuring service quality a review and critique of research using servqual. *The Market Research Society*, *46*, 479–497.

Ho, C. I., & Lee, Y. L. (2007). The development of an e-travel service quality scale. *Tourism Management*, *28*(6), 1434–1449. doi:10.1016/j.tourman.2006.12.002

Hoffman, K. D., & Bateson, J. E. G. (Eds.). (1997). *Essentials of services marketing*. Fort Worth, TX: Dryden Press.

Iwaarden, J. V., & Wiele, T. V. D. (2003). New research applying servqual to Web sites: an exploratory study. *International Journal of Quality & Reliability Management*, *20*, 919–935. doi:10.1108/02656710310493634

Kuo, T., Lu, I., Huang, C., & Wu, G. (2005). Measuring users' perceived portal service quality: an emprical study. *Total Quality Management*, *16*(3), 309–320.

Kuo, Y. (2003). A study on service quality of virtual community Website. *Total Quality Management*, *14*(4), 461–473.

Li, Y. N., Tan, K. C., & Xie, M. (2002). Measuring Web-based service quality. *Total Quality Management*, *13*(5), 685–700. doi:10.1080/09544120220000002072

Li, Y. N., Tan, K. C., & Xie, M. (2003). A service quality framework for Web-based information systems. *Total Quality Management*, *15*(3), 164–172.

Liu, C., Du, T., & Tsai, H. (2009). A study of the service quality of general portals. *Information & Management*, *46*, 52–56. doi:10.1016/j.im.2008.11.003

Okunoye, A. (2004, June). *Increase in Computing Capability and its Influence on Service Provision*. Paper presented at the meeting of the Proceedings of the 37th Hawaii International Conference on System Sciences Technologies, Processes, and Institutions, Bled, Slovenia.

Parasuraman, A., Zeithaml, A. V., & Berry, L. L. (1985). A conceptual model of service quality and its implications for future research. *Journal of Marketing*, *49*, 41–50. doi:10.2307/1251430

Parasuraman, A., Zeithaml, A. V., & Berry, L. L. (1988). SERVQUAL: a multiple-item scale for measuring consumer perception of service quality. *Journal of Retailing*, *64*(1), 12–40.

Parasuraman, A., Zeithaml, V. A., & Malhotra, A. (2005). ESQUAL: a multipleitem scale for assessing electronic service quality. *Journal of Service Research*, *7*(3), 213–234. doi:10.1177/1094670504271156

Raman, M., Stephenaus, R., Alam, N., & Kuppusamy, M. (2008). Information technology in Malaysia: e-service quality and uptake of internet banking. *Journal of Internet Banking and Commerce*, *13*, 2–18.

Santos, J. (2003). E-Service quality: a model of virtual service quality dimensions. *Managing Service Quality*, *13*(3), 233–246. doi:10.1108/09604520310476490

Smith, A. M. (1995). Measuring service quality: is SERVQUAL now redundant? *Journal of Marketing Management*, *11*, 257–276.

Swaid, S. I., & Wigand, R. T. (2007 June). *Key Dimensions of E-commerce Service Quality and Its Relationships to Satisfaction and Loyalty*. Paper presented at the meeting of 20th Bled eConference eMergence: Merging and Emerging Technologies, Processes, and Institutions, Bled, Slovenia.

Tan, K. C., Xie, M., & Li, Y. N. (2003). Service quality framework for measuring Web-based information systems. *The TQM Magazine*, *15*(3), 164–172. doi:10.1108/09544780310469262

Waite, K. (2006). Task scenario effects on bank Web site expectations. *Internet Research*, *16*(1), 7–22. doi:10.1108/10662240610642514

Webb, H. W., & Webb, L. A. (2004). SiteQual: an integrated measure of Web site quality. *The Journal of Enterprise Information Management*, *17*(6), 430–440. doi:10.1108/17410390410566724

Wolfinbarger, M., & Gilly, M. C. (2003). eTailQ: Dimensionalizing, measuring and predicting retail quality. *Journal of Retailing*, *79*(3), 183–198. doi:10.1016/S0022-4359(03)00034-4

Yang, Z., Cai, S., Zhou, S., & Zhou, S. (2005). Development and validation of an instrument to measure user perceived service quality of information presenting Web portals. *Information & Management*, *42*(4), 575–589. doi:10.1016/S0378-7206(04)00073-4

Zeithaml, V. A. (1987). *Defining and relating prices, perceived quality and perceived value*. Marketing Science Institute, Cambridge, MA.

Zeithaml, V. A., Parasuraman, A., & Malhotra, A. (2002). Service quality delivery through Web sites: a critical review of extant knowledge. *Journal of the Academy of Marketing Science*, *30*(4), 362–375. doi:10.1177/009207002236911

Zhu, F. X., Wymer, W., & Chen, I. (2002). IT- Based services and service quality in consumer banking. *International Journal of Service Industry Management*, *13*(1), 69–90. doi:10.1108/09564230210421164

ADDITIONAL READING

Aladwani, A., & Palvia, P. (2002). Developing and validating an instrument for measuring user-perceived Web quality. *Information & Management*, *39*(6), 467–476. doi:10.1016/S0378-7206(01)00113-6

Cao, M., Qingyu, Z., & Seydel, J. (2005). B2C e-commerce Web site quality: an emprical examination. *Industrial Management & Data Systems*, *105*(5), 645–661. doi:10.1108/02635570510600000

Cox, J., & Dale, B. G. (2001). Service Quality and e-commerce: an exploratory analysis. *Managing Service Quality*, *11*(2), 121–131. doi:10.1108/09604520110387257

Cristoal, E., Flavian, C., & Guinaliu, M. (2007). Perceived eservice quality: Measurement validity and effects on consumer satisfaction and Web site loyalty. *Managing Service Quality*, *17*(3), 317–340. doi:10.1108/09604520710744326

Cronin, J. J. (2003). Looking back to see forward in services marketing: some ideas to consider. *Managing Service Quality*, *13*(5), 332–337. doi:10.1108/09604520310495813

Dabholkar, P. (1996). Consumer evaluations of new technology based self-service options: An investigation of alternative modes of service quality. *International Journal of Research in Marketing*, *13*(1), 29–51. doi:10.1016/0167-8116(95)00027-5

De Ruyter, K., Bloemer, J., & Peeters, P. (1997). Merging service quality and service satisfaction: an emprical test of an integrative model. *Journal of Economic Psychology, 18*, 387–406. doi:10.1016/S0167-4870(97)00014-7

Durvasula, S., Lysonski, S., & Mehta, S. C. (1999). Testing the SERVQUAL scale in the business-to-business sector: The case of ocean freight shipping service. *Journal of Services Marketing, 13*(2), 132–150. doi:10.1108/08876049910266040

Field, J. M., Heim, G. R., & Sinha, K. K. (2004). Managing quality in the eservice system: Development and application of a process model. *Production and Operations Management, 13*(4), 291–306.

Hwang, Y., & Kim, D. J. (2007). Customer self-service systems: The effects of perceived Web quality with service contents on enjoyment, anxiety, and e-trust. *Decision Support Systems, 43*, 746–760. doi:10.1016/j.dss.2006.12.008

Jiang, J. J., Klein, G., & Carr, C. L. (2002). Measuring information system service quality: SERVQUAL from the other side. *MIS Quarterly, 26*(2), 145–166. doi:10.2307/4132324

Lee, G., & Lin, H. (2005). Customer perceptions of e-service quality in online shopping. *International Journal of Retail & Distribution Management, 33*(2), 161–176. doi:10.1108/09590550510581485

Lee, Y., & Kozar, K. (2006). Investigating the effect of Website quality on e-business success: an analytic hierarchy process (AHP) approach. *Decision Support Systems, 42*, 1383–1401. doi:10.1016/j.dss.2005.11.005

Liu, C., & Arnett, K. P. (2000). Exploring the factors associated with Web site success in the context of electronic commerce. *Information & Management, 38*(1), 23–33. doi:10.1016/S0378-7206(00)00049-5

Llosa, S., Chandan, J., & Orsingher, C. (1998). An emprical study of SERVQUAL's dimensionality. *The Service Industries Journal, 18*(2), 16–44. doi:10.1080/02642069800000017

Madu, C. N., & Madu, A. A. (2002). Dimensions of e-quality. *International Journal of Quality & Reliability Management, 19*(3), 246–258. doi:10.1108/02656710210415668

Parasuraman, A., & Grewel, D. (2000). The impact of technology on quality-value-loyalty chain: a research agenda. *Journal of the Academy of Marketing Science, 28*(1), 168–174. doi:10.1177/0092070300281015

Teas, K. R. (1993). Expectations, performance evaluation and consumers' perceptions of quality. *Journal of Marketing, 57*(4), 18–24. doi:10.2307/1252216

Van Riel, A. C. R., Liljander, V., & Jurriens, P. (2001). Exploring consumer evaluations of eservices: a portal site. *International Journal of Service Industry Management, 12*(4), 359–377. doi:10.1108/09564230110405280

Yang, Z., & Fang, X. (2004). Online service quality dimensions and their relationships with satisfaction: a content analysis of customer reviews of securities brokerage services. *International Journal of Service Industry Management, 15*(3), 302–326. doi:10.1108/09564230410540953

Yang, Z., & Jun, M. (2002). Consumer perception of eservice quality: from internet purchaser and nonpurchaser perspectives. *The Journal of Business Strategy, 19*(1), 19–41.

Yang, Z., Jun, M., & Peterson, R. T. (2004). Measuring customer perceived online service quality: scale development and managerial implications. *International Journal of Operations & Production Management, 24*(11), 1149–1174. doi:10.1108/01443570410563278

Yoo, B., & Donthu, N. (2001). Developing a scale to measure the perceived quality of an internet shopping site (Sitequal). *Quarterly Journal of Electronic Commerce*, *2*(1), 31–46.

Zeithaml, V. A., Parasuraman, A., & Malhotra, A. (2002). Service quality delivery through Web sites: a critical review of extant knowledge. *Journal of the Academy of Marketing Science*, *30*(4), 362–375. doi:10.1177/009207002236911

Zhang, X., & Prybutok, V. (2005). A consumer perspective of e-service quality. *IEEE Transactions on Engineering Management*, *32*(4), 461–477. doi:10.1109/TEM.2005.856568

KEY TERMS AND DEFINITIONS

Customer Satisfaction: is a customer judgement about product/service being met or exceed the customer's expectations and needs.

Servqual: which is developed by Parasuraman et al. (1988), for measuring service quality, concentrates on perceived quality. Perceived quality refers to a customer's judgement about a product's overall excellence (Zeithaml, 1987).

Software System Quality: is related to how well the software system is desined, and how well the software conforms to its design.

Web-Based Service Quality: In this paper Web-based service quality is defined as the extend to which services based on the Web technology, facilitating the effective online communication, purchase and delivery of products/services

Section 4
Pervasive Computing and Human Resource Management

Focusing on Human Resource Management this section contains 3 chapters. Chapter 9, "The Human Factor in Quality – Examining the ISO 9000 and Business Excellence frameworks in selected GREEK Organizations", discusses issues related to quality improvement, human resource, the excellence movement, ISO 9000:2000 and EQA on HR in the context of Greek industrial organizations. It further talks about still very traditional status of HR department and tendency of avoiding the involvement of HR department on either certification or the EQA.Chapter 10," Speed of technology adaptation in connection to organizational change and ownership concentration – study in Croatia", explains the importance of planned planned organisational change when technology is changing very fast. It discusses Organizational change as change in technology, organizational structure, organizational culture, strategy, employees' structure and/or in products and services. From the study of Croatian companies, it further describes how to manage organizational change in computing environment and relationship between ownership concentration and various factors such as corporate control, pattern of organisation change, etc. Chapter 11, "Strategic Human Resource Management & Organizational Performance", describes the importance of strategic human resource management and its effect on organisational performance. It discusses the future trends in HR management that are very crucial for high performance of organisations in the coming times and proposes action plan for HR functionaries and the organization itself to enhance the strategic fit between the various HR practices and the overall organizational strategic plan.

Chapter 9
The Human Factor in Quality: Examining the ISO 9000 and Business Excellence Frameworks in Selected Greek Organizations

Fotis Vouzas
University of Macedonia, Greece

ABSTRACT

The aim of this chapter is to theoretically investigate the implications of ISO 9000:2000 and EQA on HR issues in selected Greek industrial organizations in their road to quality improvement. The study sample consists of two selected industrial organizations that were judged as normal, ordinary, and representative. The data gathering was carried out through extensive and in-depth interviews in the two organizations asking several multiple informants. The study shows that organizations approach to quality is of great influence to effective human resource utilization. There is a tendency to avoid the involvement of HR department on either certification or the EQA and also it is clear that HR department status and role is still very traditional. The small sample does not allow making any generalizations for the majority of Greek organizations in all sectors of the economy. This is the first step towards an understanding of the current context and content of HRM in organizations moving towards total quality management implementing ISO 9000:2000 or EQA model. However, further studies needed to investigate similarities and differences in an international basis. The chapter provides a basis for understanding the present status of HRM implementation under ISO 9000 implementation and EQA model of selected Hellenic organizations and the results can be helpful for academics and practitioners. The author suggests that in order to have a reliable and objective depiction of the effect and influence of ISO 9000:2000 and EQA to the context and content of HRM, a thorough examination and analysis of relevant studies should be conducted which will include all the various approaches, practices and perceptions recorded so far in the literature -some of them based on empirical data and some deriving from rhetoric and "good-stories" or "how things ought to be" perspective.

DOI: 10.4018/978-1-60566-996-0.ch009

INTRODUCTION

The word quality in recent year is becoming very popular among organizations and academics and it is widely used in annual reports, in advertisement and even in government initiatives all over the world. However, although the true meaning and the value of quality is gaining ground in all over the world, the figures said a different story. Organizations are facing enormous quality problems in production (defects, scrap), in marketing (customer satisfaction), in logistics (response time, reliability), in finance (quality costs) and in most of their functions, even though the "Quality Revolution" has started according to many authors long time ago.

Having that in mind it is obvious that there is an oxymoron in the quality literature. Some authors argue that quality is about rhetoric and good stories in order for organizations to promote sales and create a "customer-orientation" profile. In United States and in Europe awards were established to promote awareness and provide a basis and a model for TQM implementation. However, the organizations both in US and in Europe were not so enthusiastic about the awards and the numbers are very small in all categories. On the other hand the certification with the new ISO 90000:2000 series of standards is gaining ground and especially in Asia the increase in certified organizations is beyond expectations. But still, many authors state that ISO 9000 is not equal to Total Quality Management but is just a third part quality audit that is not related to final product quality mainly used by organizations as a commercial tool. So what is "right path" to quality improvement and to customer satisfaction? Why quality is so desirable but very few organizations are willing to be involved in the quality journey?

In Greece, according to Dervitsiotis (1999) quality "had been of paramount importance in Greek culture since antiquity often mentioned as "areti (virtue) by Aristotelians and was at the center of all cultural and political activities in the ancient Greek civilization. Over the last twenty years the efforts of Greek industrial organizations for quality improvement were simply focused in the use of statistical methods in the production area and the introduction of quality assurance systems certified by third party (ISO 9000 series). However, the "technical" and "process-oriented" approach seems that does not provide the basis for the establishment of company-wide quality culture that covers all functions of the organization and focus on internal and external customer satisfaction. (IPM, 1993 Blackburn&Rosen, 1992).

On the contrary, moving from a traditional quality assurance system to a new philosophy of continuous improvement in which responsibility for quality is at the hands not of quality professional but all people within the organization is a challenge for Greek Industrial organizations that external and internal conditions will force them to implement.

The new ISO 9000:2000 and the Business Excellence movement through the American and European Quality Awards are the prevailing approaches to quality improvement according to the majority of Quality academics. Both seemed to provide a basis for the implementation of a TQM philosophy, which provides a unique way of improving organizational performance and attaining competitive advantage. The TQM rhetoric calls for a cultural shift, emphasises self-control, autonomy and have a significant effect in the way people are managed. In the context of these awards and the new ISO 9000:2000, new realities and perspectives emerge for the effective utilization of the organization's human resources. In the literature, aligning Quality Improvement programmes and initiatives with human resources effective utilization requires radical changes in the way the organizations perceive their "human capital" and the way the organizations' HR function operate (Hart&Schlesinger, 1991; Blackburn&Rosen, 1993). In the quality literature the importance of the "human or people element" in the quality improvement efforts are often been overlooked and according to Wilkinson, et.al (1991) organizations are often engaged in a "production-oriented" perspective of Total Quality. Until recently, academics and practitioners seemed to be preoccupied with the study and implementation of the "hard" elements of quality improvement (mainly ISO 9000 certification), and the evidence is on the few books and articles published in the 90's and the following years. Only recently a number of authors suggested that the shift on thinking about quality has major implications for the management of labor and has occurred in parallel to a shift in thinking about Strategic Human Resources Management (Hart&Schlesinger, 1991; Blackburn&Rosen, 1993 Beaumont, at.al, 1994; Baruch, 1997; Vouzas, 2004; Conti, 2002; Soltani, 2003; Soltani, et.al, 1994). It has been argued that TQM cannot be applied in isolation. TQM is a total philosophy involving all organizational members and has high personnel content.

THE NEW ISO 9000:2000 AND BUSINESS EXCELLENCE (QUALITY AWARDS).

Since the introduction of ISO 9000 fifteen years ago there were a series of controversies and doubts over the role and the significance of ISO 9000 series on improving product and service quality, achieving internal and external customer satisfaction, and improving performance (Tsiotras&Gotzamani, 1996; Dick, 2000; Van der Wiele et al., 2000; Withers and Ebrahimpour, 1998; Magd & Curry, 2003; Stevenson and Barnes, 2001;Kartha, 2002.) According to Douglas, et.al (2003) "ISO 9000 is a multi-million-pound industry with many individuals and organizations reliant on it for their livelihood, including quality consultants, lead auditors, internal auditors, supplier auditors, quality representatives/managers and software designers/sellers as well as the numerous training companies and certification bodies and their employees". However, other authors and among them Kartha (2002) argues that the new standards main purpose is to assist organizations to "identify mistakes, streamline their operations, and be able to guarantee a consistent level of quality".

The new revised standard was launched at the end of 2000 and according to Beckford (2002), is "an attempt to harmonize all the standards and remove the manufacturing bias. Several authors stated that the new ISO9000: 2000 is directed towards performance rather than conformance (Najmi&Kehoe, 2000). Coleman&Douglas (2003) argue that organizations in order to achieve the new ISO 9000:2000 should demonstrate that have quality processes and procedures in place, but they are skeptical about what happens after ISO 9000 certification. Casadesús &Karapetrovic (2005) studying the relationship between the "new" and the "old" ISO found that "the evaluation of the new ISO 9001: 2000 standard is generally positive". Vouzas&Gotzamani (2005) argue that there is no really negative impact but mention that the perceived benefits are less than the previous standard and that the level of reported benefits of ISO 9001/2/3: 1994 decreases with time, evidenced by two empirical studies conducted in 1998 and 2002. Overall argue that there is "an erosion of the perceived usefulness of ISO 9001: 2000 in the future, especially in terms of short-term benefits". Martínez-Lorente & Martínez-Costa (2004) further argue that organizations certified by ISO 9000 "may have gone a part of the way to TQM. However, the authors claim that it is only the "first part of the way, not its end, because there is a large amount of TQM requirements that ISO 9000 does not satisfy". Research on ISO 9000:2000 all over the world is still going on and the perceived benefits and its integration to other quality initiatives is expected to clear the picture and provide a basis for further improvement of the standard (Laszo, 2000; McAdam& Jackson, 2002; Najmi & Kehoe2000,).

According to Vouzas&Gotzamani (2005), "careful analysis of the ISO 9000:1994 standards' requirements compared to the basic principles of TQM and the requirements of the two most representative business excellence awards, the European Quality Award and the Malcolm Baldrige National Quality Award, reveals several main shortages of the ISO 9000:1994 standards. The authors stated that lack of strategic quality planning, absence of top management commitment; lack of focus on customer satisfaction, lack of systematic training in quality. Furthermore HR competitiveness, benchmarking, and quality cost measurement are absent, as well as issues related to health, safety and the environment in a study in Greek EQA awarded organizations. However, many authors believe that the new revised ISO 9000:2000 series of standards is a significant improvement on the previous version in terms of its conceptual simplification, its process-based vision and its acknowledgement of the importance of customer satisfaction as a key requirement for verifying the effectiveness of the quality system (Conti, 1999). The basic principles on which the new standards' requirements are based (as found in the ISO 9000:2000 document) are much more TQM oriented.

On the other hand, Business Excellence literature is mostly based on rhetoric and "good stories" on EQA and MBNQA awarded organizations in Europe and USA. Bohoris (1995) in a comparative analysis of the two main awards stated that "Quality Awards' assessment procedures seem to be the only comprehensive means available to date by which TQM initiatives can be thoroughly monitored and assessed, providing any business with a competitive internal mechanism necessary to face the imposition of future new barriers to trade in the form of technical or quality standards requirements. However, the criticism over "excellence models and awards" is growing (Dale, et.al, 2000; Laszlo, 1996; van der Wiele, et, al, 2000; McDonald, et.al, 2002; Hewitt, 1997; Steventon, 1994) According to Dale,et.al (2000) the EQA "acted in response to the perceived tarnished image of TQM, whilst the consultancies sought to address the diminishing demand and increasing competition for their services".

QUALITY IMPROVEMENT AND "HUMAN RESOURCES:" A LITERATURE REVIEW

As mentioned earlier, only recently quality experts, researchers, academics and practitioners realized that "human resources" issues can be at the core of the quality philosophy and that employee involvement and commitment is essential for the successful introduction and implementation of quality initiatives, programmes or practices and techniques (Blackburn&Rosen, 1993; IPM, 1993; Hart& Schlesinger, 1992;Soltani, et.al, 2004;Soltani, 2003Boselie & van der Wiele2002). It is widely accepted that Total Quality Management has a high human resource context and that quality movement recognizes the importance of human resources utilization and states a conceptual and well-defined image concerning human behaviour and motivation (Pfeffer, 1994). Wilkinson et al., (1991) state "putting human resources issues in the top management agenda is a prerequisite for the effectiveness of all quality improvement efforts". Research evidence suggest that as TQ improvement efforts proceeds, a change in the corporate culture occurs, resulting in the establishment of a work climate in which participation, trust, responsibility for goal achievement and employee involvement takes place (Lawler, 1994).

ISO 9000 Series Implementation and Human Resources

The literature on Human Resources utilization and quality improvement efforts is rather limited, especially when the focus is on the relationship and the impact of the implementation of the ISO 9000 series. The majority of these studies is descriptive in nature, with many generalizations, and basically put the basis for a better understanding of the role of the personnel function in quality improvement efforts. TQM is often confused with quality initiatives, short-term projects and ISO 9000 series certification (Soltani,et.al, 2003; Hill&Wilkinson, 1995; Ho, 1994).

The launch and implementation of the new ISO 9000:2000 series of standards increases even more the companies' expectations and the likelihood that the new systems will bring firms one step closer to TQM and Business Excellence Vouzas&Gotzamani (2005). The introduction of the five building blocks and the introduction of the process-based approach are an attempt by ISO to reduce the amount of documentation required. Even more, the new elements that it introduces to the certified companies belong to the "soft elements" of TQM, that have been proved to be the fundamental ones in the TQM system, with a very strong effect in improving company results (Costa & Martinez-Lorente, 2003). However, up to now there is no major research done on the effects and impact of the new ISO 9000:2000 series of standards in Strategic HRM. The relationship between SHRM and ISO 9000 series certification is often seen as part of the HR function involvement in the design, introduction and implementation of a quality assurance system certified by an external evaluator. Wilkinson, et, al (1991) and the IPM (1993) study suggest that HR function actually plays an important role in the design and implementation phase of a quality assurance system. On the other hand, there are cases in which a quality assurance system had been implemented within the HR department.

Furthermore, in the literature, it was found that in many organizations the human resource function plays an important role in the design and implementation of a quality assurance system (Blackburn and Rosen, 1993; Wilkinson et al., 1991). On the other hand there are cases in which a quality assurance system had been implemented within the human resource department. Its integration with human resource management is increasingly recognized as all level managers' and employees' commitment is a major component of success. Another striking finding is that HR professionals are willing to digest and implement the fundamental principles and practices of quality into their HRM practices. They also strongly believe that quality improvement efforts and the ISO 9000 series certification is one of the major challenges in their job (Lawler, 1994).

Research evidence shows that when quality management evolves from quality control or quality assurance, it tends to focus on the "process" (technical) aspects of quality rather than on the "human" aspects (IPM, 1993; Kufidu&Vouzas, 1998). Thus, organizations being engaged in a quality assurance approach to quality improvement, do not usually allow sufficient room for staff contributions, and training is targeting only towards people involved in the production process. The personnel department usually is a peripheral function with a very traditional role. The IPM study shows that organizations placing emphasis on a ¨process¨ approach to quality tend to exclude human resource department from the design and implementation of quality assurance system such as ISO 9000 series. In most of the cases its role is limited and oriented towards increasing the awareness of the quality standard and handling the administrative aspects of quality efforts (IPM, 1993). Human Resources professionals seem to participate in the various phases of quality initiatives and play a vital role (usually a facilitator role) in these efforts. Overall, the involvement of HR function in quality improvement efforts usually is materialized in three ways a) by participating in the design, introduction and maintenance of various quality initiatives b) by changing traditional personnel practices in order to support a total quality culture and c) by establishing a quality orientation within the function itself. However, we have to consider that the quality stage or level an organization is, instantly influences the embodied organizational changes, which in turn affect the way human resources considerations are formed in relation to strategic quality goals.

The Excellence Movement and the "Human Resources" Element

Hendick&Triplett (1989), suggest that implementing Total Quality initiatives requires continuous adjustments of every facet of work environment and corporate culture and the effective utilizations of organization's human resources through the HR department can play an important role in TQM assessment, planning and implementing process as well as in annual monitoring and review. Furthermore, improving quality, meeting customer's needs according to the literature is part of everybody's job and everybody should feel responsible. Quality efforts should be based on a long-term perspective and be part of the overall business strategy including people-related issues such as education and training, performance appraisal, employee involvement, recognition and improving quality of work life. Absolutely necessary is also a quality policy that is understood and easily applicable by organizational members through a use of a common language.

It is widely suggested that successful TQM implementation changes the dominant values, organizational structures, the way people work together and the way they feel about participation (van Donk&Sanders, 1993). The above support the argument made by many authors stating that quality improvement efforts should become part of everybody's job and everybody should feel responsible. Quality improvements should be based on a long-term perspective and be part of the overall business strategy. In this context people should be considered as assets rather than as additional cost upgrading that way the role of the human resource function. Research in the US shows that in organizations, which were awarded the MBNQA, the human resource function's role was essential, but the overall rating on the HR utilization category was not satisfactory. In these cases the personnel professionals were part of the top management team and fully participated in the design and implementation of the organization's quality strategy. (Blackburn&Rosen, 1993).

There are limited studies concerning the HR element of the European Quality Award and the reason is that in the academic community the EQA framework is not considered synonymous with Total Quality Management but rather such as a business audit approach and a technique within TQM. (McAdam&O'Neill, 1999; Mc Donald, et.al, 2002) A study in Denmark shows that "Danish companies are acting in order to improve the use of human resources in the company and to keep up with competition in the market. The increase in the resource score reflects that companies are also more focused in 1996 on the effective use of non-human resources in such a way that company goals and strategies are supported" Kristensen & Jørn Juhl (1999). Hamzah & Zairi (1996) in a study of British organizations winning the EQA give the following statement concerning people in one of the organizations studied " LL Bean Inc. is about people and respect for people. This is a way of respecting the talents within the organization. A lot of companies see people as the problem. We saw people as part of the solution" Xerox a winner of the European Quality Award uses extensively benchmarking for HR in the areas of "management development, recruiting, compensation and other personnel processes with the world class competitors" (Sherer, 1995). Vouzas& Gotzamani (2005) in a study in Greece found that "EQA seems to provide a new platform for introducing new practices and upgrading the role of the HR function. Management and utilization of people is at the core of the EQA and it seems that the sample organizations are striving to focus on specific issues and measures, covering all HR-related activities.

In some organizations the strategic role of people is still not dynamic. It is considered to be very costly and complex, while respondents realize that there were still high opportunities for improvement in this area. It is obvious that human resources issues were not at the center of the quality strategy formulation and implementation within the sample companies."

QUALITY IMPROVEMENT AND HUMAN RESOURCES ISSUES IN GREECE: A LITERATURE REVIEW

Quality Improvement Efforts and the Greek Industry

The quality movement in Greece started in the late 80's with the organization of a series of conferences and seminars on quality and followed in the early 90's with the introduction of the first "quality year" from the former Ministry of Development in the year 1993. In modern Greece, quality is still in an infant stage, but there are exceptions and Greek organizations and quality managers are at the top of Europe in terms of quality awards. In the past three years (2001-2003) the European Quality Manager of the year was Greek and one Greek medium-sized, family-owned organization was awarded the European Quality Award. On the other hand, ISO 9000:2000 certification awareness is growing due to government and EU initiatives and quality is at the lips of almost all Greek general managers.

Dervitsiotis paper "Quality in Greece" published in 1999 in the TQM Magazine is the only paper portraying the overall quality picture in Greece. There are of course a number of academic papers on quality but all of them focused on specific industry sectors such as textile (Vlachos, et, al, 2000), construction (Zantanidis &Tsiotras, 1998), food (Efstratiadis, et, al, 2000), and Tsekouras,et,al (2002) on a number of industry and service organizations. Furthermore there are also some "quality specific" papers addressing ISO 9000 series certification (Tsiotras&Gotzamani, 1996; Gotzamani&Tsiotras, 2002; Lipovatz, et, al, 1999), EFQM and ISO (Vouzas& Gotzamani, 2005) leadership and quality (Lipovatz, 1998), financial performance and quality (Dimara, et, al, 2004; Tsekouras,et,al (2004) and human resources and quality (Kufidu&Vouzas,1998; Vouzas2004; Dimitriades,2000,2001)

According to Stavroulakis (1997) "The dominant form of business is the small-sized family enterprise, co-existing with a ubiquitous public sector; both suffer from absence of flexibility, of entrepreneurial spirit and of a long-term perspective". The basic philosophy and principles of quality improvement as well as its significance and its context were almost unknown in the majority of the Greek Industrial organizations up to the 1960's. According to the Stafilidis (1995) although quality was perceived as a major element of each business partnership, no specific techniques or practices were used in order to assure quality of raw material or semi-final products among manufacturers and suppliers. The use of extensive and systematic implementation of quality procedures and use of statistical methods were rarely used.

During that era, organizations' customer orientation was focused in domestic markets, while the customer's demands for quality products and services were not a primary concern of the company. The same period competitive pressures were minimal, and price was the basic criterion for the acquisition of products, and finally the "sense of" householder was the one that determined the appropriateness of product and the "degree of" quality. In the mid 1970's the lack of quality specifications became obvious. Industrial organizations produced products applied Quality Control principles and methods initially with high complexity and high cost. A Karvounopoulos (1994) report that in the early 80's the significance of quality in the Greek industry was closely related with the significance of standardization. The pioneer industries of that era - mainly subsidiaries of foreigner multinational enterprises - saw the challenges and the opportunities of quality improvement and began to adopt specifications in order to ensure final product quality. In 1978 the Greek Organization for Standardization (EL.O.T) was founded, aiming at the development of specifications, the guarantee of quality of Greek products, and the support of export activities" (Booklet ELOT, 1991). The focus on bigger markets at international level, the sensitivity of consumers on quality issues, and the surge of products from European and other countries forced Greek industrial organizations to come out from their "quality sleep" in which they had fallen. The big foreigner enterprises were the leaders in that effort followed by Greek not-traditional industrial enterprises. Tsiotras&Gotzamani (1996) state that in Greek industry, companies first began to develop quality assurance systems in the 1990s. Most of these companies were subsidiaries of foreign organizations with certified quality assurance systems, and were forced to follow the quality strategy dictated by their mother company. The main reason for this was the inclusion of ISO 9000 certification within the EC procedures for the certification of industrial products, and the demand of already certified companies to their suppliers (domino effect).

On the other hand, Lipovatz et.al (1999) argue that the most important reason for the introduction of quality assurance systems in the Greek enterprises refers to the external, (i.e. the adjustment to the demands of the international and/or domestic market) and not to the internal impact of certification (i.e. the improvement of the organisational structure and the reduction of the production costs). According to Dervitsiotis (1999) "Performance improvement with quality management in the new tradition, using the guidelines of the European Quality Award, has been receiving increasing attention in Greece at the highest levels of government, industrial organizations for most sectors, universities and others". Lipovatz (1998) argues that Greek leadership has generally not embraced the principles of quality so as to be able to drive the process of change towards total quality

Quality and HR Utilization in Greece

It is argued that the majority of the Greek enterprises have neglected the human resources issues (Kufidu&Vouzas, 1998; Papalexandris, 1993; Kanellopoulos, 1990). Only recently SHRM issues have been thoroughly examined by academics. Studies conducted in the 80's and 90's revealed that in Greek industrial organizations, well-organized personnel departments is a recent phenomenon, and consequently personnel managers seemed to be a rare breed, appearing only over the last fifteen years. The investigation of the current level of SHRM implementation in Greek organizations was mainly covered by the Cranfield survey covering several European countries including Greece (Papalexandris, 1993). The survey was conducted three times (1993,1996 and 1999) and the sample was 150 organizations, which employed more than 200 employees. According to that survey, during the 90's, Greek organizations tried to adopt methods and techniques already successfully applied by multinational. The main emphasis was on the increasing importance of training, the effort to link training to the firm's strategy, the higher involvement and collaboration with line managers. Furthermore, the Cranfield study argues that there is a tendency of Greek organization to adapt their HRM practices to international trends (Papalexandris&Chalikias, 2002).

The literature on the Total Quality Management/ISO 9000 and its relationship to Strategic HRM is rather limited and is focus on commentaries from academics and practitioners and in a few studies. The reasons for such lack of interest can be traced as mentioned above to the small number of certified organizations and the lack of organized HR departments in the majority of the certified organizations. Furthermore quality professionals seemed to ignore or depreciate the "human" elements of the new ISO 9000:2000. The majority of studies shows that the main approach used by the majority of Greek industrial organizations were the adaptation of a quality

Table 1. Successful Greek organizations in the Categories of the European Quality Award 2004-2005 (Source: EFQM)

European Quality Award Categories	Number of organizations	Sector	Award Year	Size	Ownership
Committed to Excellence	16	Service: 11 (in which 2 public) Manufacturing: 5	2004: (8) 2005: (6)	Large: 7 SME's: 9	Foreign: (1) Greek: (18)
Recognized for Excellence	2	Service Organizations	1 in 2004 1 in 2005	SME's	All Greek
Award Winner	1	Manufacturing	2004	SME	Greek
Prize Winner (same company)	1	Manufacturing	2004	SME	Greek

assurance system through the ISO 9000 series certification (Lipovatz, 1998; Vouzas, 2005; Vouzas&Gotzamani, 2005;Deligianakis, 2000). Kufidu&Vouzas (1998) in the first attempt to investigate these issues found that "concerning quality improvement efforts, emphasis also seemed to be given to the "system" side ofTQM in the majority of the Greek industrial organizations and the reason for that could be traced in the ISO 9000 series certification campaign in Europe and recently in Greece - in many cases reinforced by European Union - and to the fact that most Greek organizations are moving from a quality control phase towards a quality assurance phase.

SURVEY OBJECTIVES AND METHODOLOGY

In this paper, the author suggests that in order to have a reliable and objective depiction of the human resources element in the Business Excellence and ISO 9000:2000 quality improvement frameworks, a thorough examination and analysis should include all the various approaches and perceptions recorded in literature -some of them based on empirical data and some deriving from rhetoric and "good-stories" or "how things ought to be" perspective. The sample consists of two selected industrial organizations (one Greek and one multinational company) that were judged as normal, ordinary, and representative, one being certified with the new ISO 9000:2000 series and the other took the EQA award of the EFQM. The data gathering was carried out through extensive and in - depth interviews in all two organizations asking several multiple informants i.e. the plant manager, the production manager, the personnel manager, using a semi-structured questionnaire with open - ended questions. The main purpose was to collect data and produce basic information, enabling qualitative observations concerning organizations' Quality and HRM efforts, the role and the status of Quality and HR professionals, and the implementation of various human resource initiatives from people being directly involved. Each site was written up as an integrated case study, with the focus on drawing out the commonalties of meaning and understanding each site. The data analysis provides some ground for generalizations, even though subjective judgments were also made from the analysis of the cases (see Table 1).

FINDINGS

Excellence Company A

The company A is the only Greek organization that had won the European Quality Award in the past five years. Company's A journey to quality started through ISO 9000 and ISO 14000 series

Table 2. Profile of sample organizations

	Quality Approach	HR Philosophy, Goals and Vision	HR practices	HR dep't Involvement to Quality
Company A	EQA Winner ISO9001:2000	HR vision and goals part of the corporate strategy embedded in line management	Corporate Social Responsibility Performance-based pay EEO Employee development plans, employee participation strong people-driven culture	Education and Training for EQA Awareness Building Team design and support Internal and External communication HR Processes justification and measurement
Company B	ISO9000:2000	Absence of a written policy and Vision for HR Not quantitative long-term HR goals	Traditional/bureaucratic HR practices HR function plays peripheral and supportive role	Minimal, training program Awareness building HR manager not in quality steering committee

certification and continued with the EQA (first attempt was on 1997). The main reason for going for the EQA was the organization's effort to establish a very good brand name domestically and abroad and to move a step forward on its quality improvement efforts. The ingredients of success according to quality manager were the high top management commitment and the participative approach used to design, implement and communicate the various elements and requirements of the EQA framework. However, emphasis was also on improving competitiveness and increasing productivity mainly through financial management techniques (cost reductions). The organization is on a spectacular development stage and a very strong export orientation and establishing strategic supplier alliances abroad.

The organization is a champion in providing Equal Employment Opportunities (70% of personnel are expatriates from the former Soviet Republics and there is also a large amount of disabled employees). Some of the organizations best practices concerning HR issues are the continuous encouragement for employee involvement through suggestion and improvement plans, the open and sincere communication between employees and top management in monthly meetings, employee satisfaction surveys on regular basis, competence-based training, zero accidents (SAFE award from the EU) and family working environment. The HR function implements a series of non-financial rewards such as financial support (loans), Sunday trips, and flexible working hours for disabled employees, special awards and happenings and recognition schemes to valuable employees (see Table 2). Based on the above policies and practices the organizations display a spectacular improvement in many areas. According to company data ninety five percent (97%) of employees consider working in a safe and pleasant working environment, the working hours lost in last two years decreased significantly, career opportunities and career development had been more systematic, almost ninety percent (90%) of employees believe that the products they produce are of highest quality and finally expressed happiness and satisfaction form the training and development programs participated in. The HR function is involved in annual employee attitude surveys aiming at improving working conditions and enhancing employee morale and commitment. However, top management is reluctant to upgrade the HR function and the HR manager role and this is due to the small size of the organization and the predominant role of the owners of the company in all aspects of business activities.

The involvement and the role of the HR function in quality efforts and especially in the

European Quality Award was essential for achieving the award and for setting a new standard for improvement in the issues related to management of people. A series of HR practices were re-evaluated, documented and measured such as performance appraisal and rewards and others were better utilized i.e. internal communication methods, recruitment &selection and employee training. The most challenging task for the HR was the to support the organization toward building quality awareness for all functions and changing the existing corporate quality culture by incorporating HR issues to all quality procedures and by creating a climate of trust and commitment.

ISO 9000:2000 Company B

Company B is a multinational organization operating in Greece for many years with a very recognizable brand name and a big market share in its sector. Its main approach to quality improvement is ISO 9000:2000 and is considered very successful in achieving high quality products and increasing productivity. The main reason for ISO 9000:2000 certification was firstly the pressure from the "mother" organization and the increased competition and secondly quality improvement and efficiency in operations. Speaking with the quality manager, the HR manager and the Managing Director it was clear that all considered employees to be very valuable resource and that played a key role in achieving strategic quality goals and objectives. This of course is contradictory with the overall picture of the organization's HRM practices, the role of the HR department and the lack of a vision and mission for the personnel.

Formal written HR strategy, policy or quantitative goals regarding the management of human resources were absent and this was due to the focus of the organization to other "strategic" areas such as marketing, operations, and public relations. The involvement of the HR manager to the design and launch of ISO 9000 certification was minimal and covered only the development of training programs for quality and awareness building. The HR manager had no authority to review and adjust HR procedures in order to support ISO 9000:2000, to analyze and re-examine past job descriptions, to evaluate previous performance standards for employees, to suggest training methods and learning activities and ways to increase motivation. The HR manager mentioned that he took part in meetings regarding ISO certification (after certificate granted) and received information regarding quality strategic orientation, but he was not part of the quality steering committee. The quality manager claimed that a written policy or quantitative goals for personnel is not prerequisite for ISO 9000:2000 certification and considered as unnecessary and costly. A serious obstacle to the involvement of HR department to ISO 9000:2000 certifications was also the existence of serious interdepartmental communication problems as well as internal disputes and conflicts. Having that in mind it was extremely difficult for the HR professional to develop a sound, clear and integrated HR policy that can support the certification process and the establishment of an "ISO culture".

The HR department role in the organization can be characterized as a "peripheral" or "supportive" representing the average small and medium Greek enterprise. The HR department had only two employees, one secretary and one accountant and its most common HRM practices were administrative in nature such as, data filling, employee payroll, employee complaints, disciplinary action, and traditional HR practices (such dismissals, demotions, transfers, working hours and shift patterns). There were no major indexes and matrixes for HR issues (turnover rates, employee satisfaction, evaluation of education and training programs, induction, labor productivity, etc) and core HR practices like performance appraisal system, rewards and recognition schemes were absent for employees at the shop floor. The above come to support research evidence that when "hard" approach to quality is adopted combined with a weak

HR department with no strategic orientation, then "people" issues are often neglected and the quality improvement efforts are partially satisfied. The argument is more realistic since top management commitment in ISO certified organizations is poor and furthermore top level management is probably not aware of the advantages the "new strategic HRM" practices and the effect these practices might have to the organization's overall quality effectiveness and efficiency. Furthermore, in the organization studied the existing organizational HR culture and generally the overall corporate philosophy of human resources utilization seemed to promote quality improvement efforts through ISO 9000 series in a rather bureaucratic manner in which there is no innovation, promotion of new ideas, opportunities to be gained and best practices to be implemented.

CONCLUSION AND FUTURE TRENDS

It is quite obvious from the above analysis that there is an enormous distance between the HR requirements of the awards and those of ISO 9000. The ISO 9000:2000 is no more than an "audit of procedures" with not substantial HR context and content and on the other side the awards are concerned with HR both in relation to people management and satisfaction/results. The ISO 9000:2000 seemed to represent the minimum effort on HR practices and policies an organization should present in order to achieve third party certification but quality award and specifically EQA award requires proof of systematic design and implementation of HR policies and practices. However, many argue that a company cannot win one of the quality awards without first being able to satisfy the requirements of the ISO 9000.

It seems that ISO 9000:2000 certified organizations although are aware of the fundamental principles and tools of continuous quality improvement but still are in the early stages of a company-wide approach to quality improvement. The author believe that one of the most prevailing factors contributing to the delay of the establishment of a "quality-based" culture and a move towards strategic Total Quality Management are the short period of systematic implementation of quality assurance systems and the preoccupation with the so-called "hard" aspects of quality.

The existence of vision and a mission for Human Resources followed by systematic design and implementation of Strategic HRM practices seemed to be the main issues that differentiate ISO 9000:2000 organizations from EQA organizations according to the literature. However, according to other studies EQA organizations problematic area is that of Human Resources (Vouzas&Gotzamani, 2005; McAdam&O'Neill, 1999). The prevailing HR practices absent from the ISO 9000:2000 organization are the communication to employees of the corporate quality mission, designing and implementing programmes for employee empowerment and developing or applying TQM principles, practices and techniques within the HR function.

REFERENCES

Baruch, Y. (1997). Evaluating quality and reputation of human resource management . *Personnel Review*, *26*(5), 377–394. doi:10.1108/00483489710176057

Beattie, K. R., & Sohal, A. S. (1999). Implementing ISO 9000: a study of its benefits among Australian organisations. *Total Quality Management*, *10*(1), 95–106. doi:10.1080/0954412998090

Beaumont, P. B., Hunter, L. C., & Phayre, R. M. (1994). Human Resources and Total Quality Management Some Case Study Evidence. *Training for Quality*, *2*(1), 7–13. doi:10.1108/09684879410056166

Beckford, J. (2002). *Quality* (2nd ed.). New York: Routledge.

Beer, M., Spector, B., Lawrence, P. R., Quinn Mills, D., & Walton, R. E. (1984). *Managing Human Assets*. New York: The Free Press.

Blackburn, R., & Rosen, B. (1993). Total Quality and Human Resources Management: Lessons learned from Baldrige award-winning companies. *The Academy of Management Executive, 17*(3), 49–66.

Bohoris, G. (1995). A comparative assessment of some major quality awards . *International Journal of Quality & Reliability Management, 12*(9), 30–43. doi:10.1108/02656719510101178

Boselie, P., & van der Wiele, T. (2002). Employee perceptions of HRM and TQM, and the effects on satisfaction and intention to leave . *Managing Service Quality, 12*(3), 165–172. doi:10.1108/09604520210429231

Brewster, C., & Larsen, H. H. (1992). Human resource management in Europe: evidence from ten countries. *International Journal of Human Resource Management, 3*(3), 409–434.

Casadesús, M., & Karapetrovic, S. (2005). The erosion of ISO 9000 benefits: a temporal study. *International Journal of Quality & Reliability Management, 22*(2), 120–136. doi:10.1108/02656710510577198

Cheng, S. P., & Tummala, R. (1998). An employee involvement strategy for ISO 9000 registration and maintenance: a case study for Hong Kong and China companies. *International Journal of Quality & Reliability Management, 15*(8/9), 860–891. doi:10.1108/02656719810198980

Coleman, S., & Douglas, A. (2003). Where next for ISO 9000 companies? *The TQM Magazine, 15*(2), 88–92. doi:10.1108/09544780310461099

Conti, T. (2002). Human and social implications of excellence models: are they really accepted by the business community? *Managing Service Quality, 12*(3), 151–158. doi:10.1108/09604520210429213

Costa, M., & Martinez-Lorente, A. R. (2003). ISO 9000: The past, The Present and The Future. A case study in the Spanish Industry. In *Proceedings of the 8th International Conference on ISO 9000 and TQM, Montreal, Part II.*

Dale, B. G., Zairi, M., Van der Wiele, A., & Williams, A. R. T. (2000). Quality is dead in Europe - long live excellence - true or false? *Measuring Business Excellence, 4*(3), 4–10. doi:10.1108/13683040010377737

Dick, G. P. M. (2000). ISO 9000 certification benefits, reality or myth? *The TQM Magazine, 12*(6), 365–371. doi:10.1108/09544780010351517

Douglas, A., Coleman, S., & Oddy, R. (2003). The case for ISO 9000. *The TQM Magazine, 15*(5), 316–324. doi:10.1108/09544780310487712

Grant, M. R., Shani, R., & Krishnan, R. (1994). TQM's Challenge to Management Theory and Practice. *Sloan Management Review*, (Winter): 25–35.

Hackman, J. R., & Wageman, R. (1995, June). Total Quality Management: Empirical, Conceptual, and Practical Issues. *Administrative Science Quarterly, 40*, 309–342. doi:10.2307/2393640

Hamzah, A., & Zairi, M. (1996). People management: where is the evidence of best practice? Part III. *Training for Quality, 4*(4), 37–44. doi:10.1108/09684879610149026

Hart, C., & Schlesinger, L. (1991). Total Quality Management and the HR professional: Applying the Baldrige Framework to human resources. *Human Resource Management, 30*(4), 433–454. doi:10.1002/hrm.3930300402

Hendricks, C. F., & Triplett, A. (1989). TQM: Strategy for 90's management. *The Personnel Administrator*, *34*(12), 42–48.

Hill, S. (1991). How do you manage the flexible firm? The Total Quality Model. *Work, Employment and Society*, *5*(3), 397–416. doi:10.1177/0950017091005003005

Hill, S., & Wilkinson, A. (1995). In search of TQM. *Employee Relations*, *17*(3), 8–25. doi:10.1108/01425459510147002

Hunt, V. D. (1993). *Managing Quality: Integrating quality and business strategy*. Homewood, IL, Irwin

IPM. (1993). *Quality: People Matters*. London: IPM.

Kanellopoulos, C. (1990). *Personnel Management and Personnel Managers in Greece*. Greek Productivity Centre, Athens

Kartha, C.P. (2002). ISO 9000:2000 quality management systems standards: TQM focus in the new revision. *The Journal of American Academy of Business, September,* 1-6.

Kristensen, K., & Juhl, H. J. (1999). Five years with quality awards in Denmark. *The TQM Magazine*, *11*(2), 80–83. doi:10.1108/09544789910257019

Kufidu, S., & Vouzas, F. (1998). Human Resources aspects of quality management: evidence from MNEs operating in Greece. *International Journal of Human Resource Management*, *9*(5), 818–830. doi:10.1080/095851998340810

Laszo, G. P. (1996). Quality awards - recognition or model? *The TQM Magazine*, *8*(5), 14–18. doi:10.1108/09544789610145999

Laszo, G. P. (2000). ISO 9000-2000 version: implications for applicants and examiners. *The TQM Magazine*, *12*(5), 336–339. doi:10.1108/09544780010341941

Lawler, E. E. (1994). Total Quality Management and Employee Involvement: Are they compatible. *The Academy of Management Executive*, *8*(1), 68–76.

Legge, K. (1995), *Human Resource Management: Rhetorics and Realities*. Chippenham: Macmillan Business.

Lipovatz, D. (1998). Leadership performance in Greek enterprises using the EQA framework . *The TQM Magazine*, *10*(3), 194–203. doi:10.1108/09544789810214792

Magd, H., & Curry, A. (2003). ISO 9000 and TQM: are they complementary or contradictory to each other? *The TQM Magazine*, *15*(4), 244–256. doi:10.1108/09544780310486155

Martínez-Lorente, A. R., & Martínez-Costa, M. (2004). ISO 9000 and TQM: substitutes or complementaries? An empirical study in industrial companies. *International Journal of Quality & Reliability Management*, *2*(3), 260–276. doi:10.1108/02656710410522711

McAdam, R., & Jackson, N. (2002). A sectoral study of ISO 9000 and TQM transitions: the UK and Irish brewing sector. *Integrated Manufacturing Systems*, *13*(4), 255–263. doi:10.1108/09576060210426958

McAdam, R., & O'Neill, E. (1999). Taking a critical perspective to the European Business Excellence Model using a balanced scorecard approach: a case study in the service sector. *Managing Service Quality*, *9*, 191–197. doi:10.1108/09604529910267091

McDonald, I., & Zairi, M., Mohd Ashari Idris. (2002). Sustaining and transferring excellence A framework of best practice of TQM transformation based on winners of Baldrige and European Quality Awards. *Measuring Business Excellence*, *6*(3), 20–30. doi:10.1108/13683040210441959

Najmi, M., & Kehoe, D. F. (2000). An integrated framework for post-ISO 9000 quality development . *International Journal of Quality & Reliability Management, 17*(3), 226–258. doi:10.1108/02656710010300117

Papalexandris, N. (1993). Human resource management in Greece. In C. Brewster & A. Hegewisch (Eds.), *European Developments in HRM* (pp. 163-180). London: Kogan Page.

Papalexandris, N., & Chalikias, J. (2002). Changes in training, performance management and communication issues among Greek firms in the 1990s: intercountry and intracountry comparisons. *Journal of European Industrial Training, 26*(7), 342–352. doi:10.1108/03090590210432697

Pfeffer, J. (1994) *Competitive advantage through people*. Boston, MA: Harvard Business School Press.

Sohal, A., & Marriot, F. (1993). Manufacturing Management in Australia: The Human Resource Management Implications. *International Journal of Manpower, 14*(9), 13–20. doi:10.1108/01437729310048263

Soltani, E. (2003). Towards a TQM-driven HR performance evaluation: an empirical study, *Employee Relations . International Journal (Toronto, Ont.), 25*(4), 347–370.

Soltani, E., Gennard, J., van der Meer, R. B., & Williams, T. (2004). HR performance evaluation in the context of TQM A review of the literature. *International Journal of Quality & Reliability Management, 21*(4), 377–396. doi:10.1108/02656710410530082

Spencer, B. (1994). Models of organization and TQM: A comparison and a critical evaluation. *Academy of Management Review, 19*, 446–471. doi:10.2307/258935

Stavroulakis, D. (1997). Quality circle autonomy: evidence from a Japanese subsidiary and a Western subsidiary . *International Journal of Quality & Reliability Management, 14*(2), 146–159. doi:10.1108/02656719710165419

Stevenson, T. H., & Barnes, F. C. (2001). Fourteen years of ISO 9000: impact, criticisms, costs and benefits. *Business Horizons, 44*(3), 45. doi:10.1016/S0007-6813(01)80034-3

Steventon, D. (1994). Quality Awards - a Means to an End or an End in Themselves? *The TQM Magazine, 6*(5), 7–8. doi:10.1108/09544789410067952

Thomason, G. (1991). The management of personnel. *Personnel Review, 20*(2), 3–10. doi:10.1108/00483489110000390

Tsiotras, G., & Gotzamani, K. (1996). ISO 9000 as an entry key to TQM: the case Greek industry. *International Journal of Quality & Reliability Management, 13*(4), 64–77. doi:10.1108/02656719610114407

Van der Wiele, T., Dale, B., & Williams, R. (2000). ISO 9000 series and excellence models: fad to fashion to fit . *Journal of General Management, 25*(3), 50–66.

Van der Wiele, T., Dale, B., & Williams, R. (2000). Business improvement through quality management systems. *Management Decision, 38*(1), 19–23. doi:10.1108/00251740010311799

van Donk, P. D., & Sanders, G. (1993). Organizational culture as a missing link in quality management . *International Journal of Quality & Reliability Management, 10*(5), 5–15.

Vloeberghs, D., & Bellens, J. (1996). Human resource aspects of ISO 9000 in Belgian organizations. *International Journal of Human Resource Management, 7*(2), 413–435.

Vouzas, F. (2004). HR Utilization and Quality Improvement: the Reality and the Rhetoric – the case of Greek Industry. *The TQM Magazine*, *16*(2), 125–135. doi:10.1108/09544780410523026

Vouzas, F., & Gotazamani, K. (2005). Best Practices of Selected Greek Organizations on Their Road to Business Excellence: The Contribution of the New ISO 9000:2000 Series of Standards. *The TQM Magazine*, *17*(3), 259–266. doi:10.1108/09544780510594225

Wilkinson, A., Allen, P., & Snape, E. (1991). TQM and the Management of Labour. *Employee Relations*, *13*(1), 24–31. doi:10.1108/01425459110002349

ADDITIONAL READING

Aktouf, O. (1992). Management and theories of organizations in the 1990s: Towards a critical radical humanism? *Academy of Management Review*, *17*, 407–431. doi:10.2307/258717

Braddick, C., Pfefferle, M., & Gandossy, R. (1993). How Malcolm Baldrige winners reward employee performance. *Journal of Compensation and Benefits*, *9*, 47–52.

Chen, W. H. (1997). The human side of TQM in Taiwan: leadership and human resources management. *International Journal of Quality & Reliability Management*, *14*(1), 24–45. doi:10.1108/02656719710156761

Ebrahimpour, M., & Cullen, J. B. (1993). Quality Management in Japanese and American Firms operating in the United States: A comparative study of styles and motivational beliefs. *Management International Review*, *33*(1), 23–38.

Lawler, E. E. (1994). Total Quality Management and Employee Involvement: Are they compatible. *The Academy of Management Executive*, *8*(1), 68–76.

Mann, R., & Kehoe, D. (1995). Factors affecting the implementation and success of TQM. *International Journal of Quality & Reliability Management*, *12*(1), 11–23. doi:10.1108/02656719510076212

Patel, A. (1993). Total Quality Management: Paving the way for future training. *Industrial and Commercial Training*, *25*(2), 23–32. doi:10.1108/00197859310036161

Roth, W. F. (1989, November). Quality through people: A hit for HR. *Personnel*, 50–52.

Shani, A. B., Mitki, Y., Krishnan, R., & Grant, R. (1994). Roadblocks in a quality management implementations: a cross-cultural investigation. *Total Quality Management*, *5*(6), 407–416.

Tuttle, T. C. (1992). *Building HRM systems that support Total Quality*. Maryland Centre for Quality and Productivity

Walley, P., & Kowalski, E. (1992). The role of training in Total Quality Implementation. *Journal of European Industrial Training*, *16*(3), 25–31. doi:10.1108/03090599210008644

Wynne, R., & Lancaster, J. (1992). The importance of understanding the concept of TQM and the consequent training needs. *Total Quality Management*, *2*(1), 19–29.

Xu, Q. (1994). *The making of TQM: History and Margins of the Hi(gh)-story*. Working paper presented at British Academy of Management Annual Conference at Lancaster, September, 1994

Yearout, S. (1992). The international Quality study reveals which countries lead the race for total quality . *Journal of European Business*, *3*(4), 27–30.

KEY TERMS AND DEFINITIONS

Business Excellence: The use of quality management principles and tools in business management. It is the systematic improvement of business performance based on the principles of customer focus, stakeholder value, and process management

Corporate Social Responsibility (CSR): Also known as corporate responsibility, corporate citizenship, responsible business and corporate social opportunity is a form of corporate self-regulation integrated into a business model. Ideally, CSR policy would function as a built-in, self-regulating mechanism whereby business would monitor and ensure their adherence to law, ethical standards, and international norms.

Equal Employment Opportunity (EEO): Some use it as a descriptive term for an approach intended to provide a certain social environment in which people are not excluded from the activities of society, such as education, employment, or health care, on the basis of immutable traits.

European Quality Award: is now referred to as the EFQM Excellence Award. This distinction is awarded annually by the European Foundation for Quality Management to the organization that is the best proponent in Europe of Total Quality Management.

Human Capital: refers to the stock of skills and knowledge embodied in the ability to perform labor so as to produce economic value. It is the skills and knowledge gained by a worker through education and experience

Human Resource Management: (HRM) is the strategic and coherent approach to the management of an organization's most valued assets - the people.

Human Resources Strategy: The Human Resources Strategy sets out plans to ensure the recruitment, development and retention of the best quality staff in all staff groups, in order to fulfil the organization's Mission and thereby meet its strategic aims and objectives.

ISO 9000 certification: A company or organization that has been independently audited and certified to be in conformance with ISO 9001 may publicly state that it is "ISO 9001 certified" or "ISO 9001 registered". Certification to an ISO 9000 standard does not guarantee any quality of end products and services; rather, it certifies that formalized business processes are being applied. Indeed, some companies enter the ISO 9001 certification as a marketing tool.

ISO 9000: is a family of standards for quality management systems. ISO 9000 is maintained by ISO, the International Organization for Standardization and is administered by accreditation and certification bodies.

Quality Assurance System: A quality assurance system comprises assessment and remediation action in a closed circle

Quality Improvement: There are many methods for quality improvement. These cover product improvement, process improvement and people based improvement. In the following list are methods of quality management and techniques that incorporate and drive quality improvement

Quality: The common element of the business definitions is that the quality of a product or service refers to the perception of the degree to which the product or service meets the customer's expectations. Quality is a perceptual, conditional and somewhat subjective attribute.

Strategic Human Resources Management: is a general approach to the strategic management of human resources in accordance with the intentions of the organization on the future direction it wants to take. It is concerned with longer-term people issues and macro-concerns about structure, quality

Total Quality Management: (TQM) is a new management philosophy aimed at embedding awareness of quality in all organizational processes.

Chapter 10
Speed of Technology Adaptation in Connection to Organizational Change and Ownership Concentration:
Study in Croatia

Lovorka Galetic
University of Zagreb, Croatia

Najla Podrug
University of Zagreb, Croatia

Domagoj Hruska
University of Zagreb, Croatia

ABSTRACT

This chapter investigates technology adaptation in Croatian companies in connection to organizational changes. Furthermore, this chapter investigates how levels of ownership concentration in Croatian companies form patterns of organizational change. Organizational change is conceptualized as changes in technology, organizational structure, organizational culture, strategy, changes in employees' structure and changes in products and services. The above-mentioned patterns of organizational change are analyzed in terms of their frequency and effects on corporate performance. In this empirical analysis, the authors take in consideration three forms of organizational control: (1) control by one dominant shareholder; (2) control by coalition of several large blockholders and (3) managerial control. Each type of control corresponds with ownership concentration measured with percentage of capital held by the largest shareholder. This chapter observes how different levels of ownership concentration and control influence determinants of organizational change.

DOI: 10.4018/978-1-60566-996-0.ch010

INTRODUCTION

As computing devises become more pervasive, it is becoming obvious that it has great effects on individuals as well organizations. As nature of interactions between users and computers evolve, consequently changes also evolve at the organizational level. Today, as never before, organizations are facing dynamic environment that is changing rapidly and in which resources, from financial and human resources to network connectivity and software services, frequently vary. The task facing managers is to help organizations respond and adjust to the changes taking place. Organizational change is the process by which organizations move from their present state to some desired future state to increase their effectiveness. The goal of planned organizational change is to find new or improved ways of using resources and capabilities in order to increase on organization's ability to create value and improve returns to its stakeholders (Porras & Silvers, 1991). The ownership concentration dictates the distribution of power and control between managers and owners. Empirical work on the subject of influence of large shareholders in corporate governance is focused on trends of ownership dispersion, causes and consequences of reducing the influence of owners.

Planned organizational change is normally targeted at improving effectiveness at one or more of four different levels: technological capabilities, human resources, functional resources and organizational capabilities (Jones, 2004). These four levels at which change can take place are obviously interdependent, it is often impossible to change one without changing other. Human resources are an organization's most important asset and ultimately, an organization's distinctive competences lie in the skills and abilities of its employees. These skills and abilities give an organization a competitive advantage; organizations must constantly monitor their structures to find the most effective way of motivating and organizing human resources to acquire and use their skills. An organization can improve the value that its functions create by changing its structure, culture and technology. Technological capabilities give an organization an enormous capacity to change itself in order to exploit market opportunities. The ability to develop a constant stream of new products or to modify existing products so that they can continue to attract customers is one of an organization's core competences. Similarly, the ability to improve the way goods and services are produced in order to increase their quality and reliability is the crucial organizational capability. At the organizational level, an organization has to provide the context that allows it to translate its technological competences into value for its stakeholders. This task often involves the redesign of organizational activities. Through the design of organizational structure and culture an organization can harness its human and functional resources to take advantage of technological opportunities. Organizational change often involves changing the relationships between people and functions to increase their ability to create value. Changes in structure and culture take place at all levels of the organizations and include changing the routines an individual's uses to greet customers, changing work group relationships, improving integration between divisions and changing corporate culture by changing the top management team.

The influence of ownership concentration on the performance of a company is theoretically very complex and questionable. Basically, a dense ownership concentration can improve a company's performance through a more intensive supervision. On the other hand, the drawback of dense ownership concentration that is mentioned most often is that big owners can use their control rights to worsen the position of small shareholders. Even the fear of bad treatment of small shareholders itself can limit the possibility that a company with dense ownership concentration collects money. One more potential bad trait of a dense ownership concentration is that management's initiatives can be blocked because of intensive monitoring from their owners.

A big number of minority owners are trying to increase the separation between ownership and control–it is traditionally the main characteristic of business systems - corporations (Berle & Means, 1932). A large dispersion of ownership - nonexistence of one large principal, leads to a stronger influence of management which enhances the agency problem. The main question of the American system of corporate governance is the one about collective influence of dispersed owners trying to discipline management. The problem of corporate governance is emphasized in American business practice due to the fact that the owner structure is quite dispersed (Warshow, 1924). While the ownership structure in the United States is quite dispersed, the domination of large shareholders is present in the rest of the world (*blockholders*) (La Porta, Lopez-de-Silanes & Shleifer, 1999).

Managing Organizational Changes in Computing Environment

The effects of change can be studied over different time scales and they can be studied at different levels. However, because of its pervasive nature, change at any one level is interrelated with changes at other levels, and it is difficult to study one area of change in isolation.

An organization can only perform effectively through interactions with the broader external environment of which it is part. The structure and functioning of the organizations must reflect, therefore, the nature of the environment in which it is operating. There are factors which create an increasingly volatile environment, such as: uncertain economic conditions, globalization and fierce world competition, the level of government intervention, political interests, scarcity of natural resources, rapid developments in new technology and the information age. In order to help ensure its survival and future success the organization must be readily adaptable to the external demands placed upon it. But change also originates within the organization itself. Much of this change is part of a natural process of ageing and can be managed through careful planning; however the mail pressure of change is from external forces (Mullins, 2005).

In Goldsmith and Clutterburk's study, one of the critical issues of the high-performance companies is evolutionary versus revolutionary change. Although recognizing that occasionally radical changes is necessary and sometimes it is necessary to push through tough measures with urgency, the companies tend to be cautious but deliberate innovators, and balance the need for continuous change against the need to conserve core values. They have a very strong preference for evolutionary change, for a whole variety of reasons. It enables you to identify wrong turnings before too much damage is done; it gives time for both employees and customers to adopt; and it is less likely to disrupt people's attention to the core activities and values. They can, however, take rapid action when it is needed in response to unpredictable changes in their environment, because they usually have an in—built nimbleness (Goldsmith & Clutterbuck, 1998).

Improvements, innovation and the adoption of new technologies are critical to the health of any economic sector. According to Mellor and Hyland (2005, p. 858) manufacturing is one of the most important economy drivers in countries prosperity. Therefore academic societies in cooperation with the practitioners constantly improve management concepts in order to gain competitive advantage. One of the means of achieving a competitive advantage is to constantly innovating products and manufacturing processes. Hamel and Prahalad (1989), more than a decade ago suggested that innovations, improvement programs and adoption of new technologies is a "strategic context" rather than a set of highly defined top down plans (Price, 1996, p. 38).

Innovations and modernisation works through the introduction of knowledge into the economy (and into the society at large). It requires active learning by individuals and organisations taking part in processes of innovation of different kinds. The efficiency of these learning activities and, hence, the performance of the innovation systems depends of economic, political and social infrastructures and institutions. It also depends on past experiences as they are reflected in the tangible and intangible aspects of the structure of production (Lundvall et al., 2002, p. 225). The authors researched the influence of government innovation initiatives on Danish production and found a significant positive correlation.

Porras and Robertson have provided very useful distinction for understanding organizational change thoroughly: planned versus unplanned and first-order versus second order change (Porras & Robertson, 1992). Planned change is deliberate, conscious decision to improve the organization in some manner or perhaps to change the system in a deeper, more fundamental way. Unplanned change represents response to some unanticipated external change, for example, creation of a whole new technology that affects the very core of business. First-order change involves what we refer to as "continuous improvement" (kaizen), and second-order change is radical, more fundamental change. Weick and Quinn organized their report according to episodic (discontinuous, transformational, and revolutionary) and continuous change (continuous improvement, transactional and evolutionary) (Weick & Quinn, 1999).

According to Cooper (1996, p. 104) it is not important whether a company commits to radical or continuous improvement, as long as there exists commitment to innovation programmes. There is also a significant difference in cultures in initiating innovation programs. The collectivist cultures, such as Japan, facilitate the feeding of the functional groundwork into the final decisions to be made at management level. That means that shop floor workers give suggestion for improvement but the final decision is made by the upper management. In contrast, in individualistic cultures such as US, facilitates a decentralized decision-making by engineers at functional levels (Cristiano et al., 2000, p. 292).

The content of the change process is composed of various stages which are all interrelated. Literature offers a number of well established models for the transformation of organizations like Lewin's and Greiner's models of organizational change. The most important steps are (Bonne & Kurtz, 1992., Lewis, Goodman & Fandt, 1998):

- perception of the need for change and awareness of the inevitable termination of the present situation. Lewin called this first stage „unfreeze" and stressed that the biggest mistakes are made at this stage of terminating the present situation. At this stage of the change process, crucial decisions are taken regarding the directions and goals of transformation as well as regarding the methods used to implement the change (Kovač, 2000).
- process of realization is carried out at various levels - from unperceivable and unrecognizable (e. g. at personal level) to perceivable and recognizable (e.g. in the change of place). The management has to be thoroughly prepared for this part of the change process, with necessary and possible alternatives prepared in advance. The realization of changes is a process limited in time and must, therefore, be executed without interruptions. Every longer-lasting interruption may result in failure of the entire change process. The second step involves moving toward the new desired level of behavior and moving might take form of (a) training managers to behave differently toward their subordinates in order to improve customer service or (b)

implementing action plans for changing work processes or improving information systems (Burke, 2002).

- checking the results of the change and consolidation of the new situation. In Lewin's terminology this last stage is called "refreeze". By using this term, he underlined the importance of the absolute break with the old situation. It often happens that we carry out all necessary steps in the change process and, after some time, find out that the staff is working and acting according to previous rules. Therefore, the change process is concluded only after we can, with certainty, claim that the new mode of operation is prevailing throughout the organization. The above statement is important for the managers, particularly with regard to the true conclusion of the change process. The managers must be well aware of the fact that the change process has not been concluded with the introduction of changes alone. Shein identifies two parts in refreezing stage: (1) personal and individual – helping the organizational member feel comfortable with the new behavior that is required to make the change succeed, that is, to link the new behavior with one's self-concept and (2) interpersonal – making sure that the new behavior fits well with others who are significant in the organization and that these significant individual are conformable with the new behaviors from the "changed" person (Shein, 1987).

Organizational change has been a central and enduring quest of scholars in management and many other disciplines. Change has been the subject of a large number of studies ever since the seminal consideration of Hannan and Freeman raised interest in the relationship between change, inertia and the failure of organizations (Hannan & Freema, 1984). At the outset studies examined the consequences of change, concentrating on the risk of organizational failure as a consequence of change (Barnett & Carroll, 1995. and Clegg, Hardy & Nord, 1996), and later studies on organizational change also investigated the causes of change. Within this research field, the effect of prior change has become a popular topic and there is consensus, both in the theoretical and the empirical literatures, that change increases the likelihood of further change (Amburgey, Kelly & Barnett, 1993. and Dobrev, Kim & Hannan, 2001. and Kelly & Amburgey, 1991). Consequently, change is considered to be a self-reinforcing process; this view has been called the "repetitive momentum hypothesis" (Beck, Bruderl & Woywode, 2008).

Ownership Concentration and Corporate Control

The characteristic that mostly separates German from the Anglo-American system of corporate governance is dense ownership concentration (La Porta, Lopez-de-Silanes & Shleifer, 1999). Nearly all German corporations have one or more large owners. Usually the owners are rich families, other companies or banks.

According to a study of Böhmer and Becht dating from 2001, during the 90s two thirds of German corporations had an owner with a share larger than 25% (Schmidt, 2003). As we emphasized before, owners with more than 25% of stake have the right to call a veto on every major decision. This means that corporative control (voting rights) is even more concentrated than ownership. Study shows that only one owner has more than one forth of voting rights and this is true for even one fifth of corporations listed on stock exchange (Schmidt, 2003).

According to a study of Frank and Mayer dating from 1995, almost 85% of 170 largest German corporations that were listed have one owner with a stake of at least 25% of total ownership; at the same time, this applies to only 16% of 170 largest companies in the Great Britain (Edwards & Nibler,

2000). Second study on German corporations dating from 2001 shows again high level of ownership concentration (Franks & Mayer, 2001).

USA has a very low level of ownership concentration - Shleifer and Vishny have found out that the average of an American corporation is 1, 4 blocks of 5% or more shares (Shleifer & Vishny, 1986). Nevertheless, in empirical and theoretical analysis of each mechanism of American corporate governance system authors have tendency to ignore the existence of the other center of power (Turnbull, 2000).

A study of Becht and Röell on a sample of French corporations shows that the mean concentration of one owner's share block is approximately 20%, in Spain 34%, in Netherlands 43.5%, in Austria, Belgium, Germany and Italy is from 45 to 55%, in Great Britain median is only 9.9%, and below 5% for NYSE and NASDAQ (Becht & Röell, 1999). On a sample of Turkish companies Demirag and Serter have found out that big owner in average has a share capital of 45.1% (Demirag & Serter, 2003).

In analysis of ownership concentration on a sample of Baltic corporations, Pajuste and Olsson discover that the biggest ownership concentration is in Estonia, where large shareholder in average has 61% of shares, then in Latvia, where the largest share block is in average 49.5% and Lithuania where the largest shareholder has just a little below 45% of shares (Pajuste & Olsson, 2001). Authors also give a review of ownership concentration of several other transition countries. Research in Czech Republic and Poland shows that the largest shareholder has 51.9% and 50.3%, whereas this number in Slovenia is 27.4% and in Finland 32.8% (Grosfeld & Hashi, 2005. and Gregorič, Prašnikar & Ribnikar, 2000. and Maury & Pajuste, 2002).

Share of the biggest owner in Croatia is at the same level as in the majority of other transition countries. Concentration of ownership is smaller than in Czech Republic, but bigger than in Slovenia. Basically, we can see that ownership concentration, measured by the share of the largest owner, is moving between these two marginal cases- from 40% to 50% of total capital. Ownership concentration in European Union countries is also moving in this frame, while in countries of Anglo-American business circle we can notice a high dispersion of ownership (Figure 1).

Static measures of concentration do not function well in measuring control. In situations when other corporative control mechanisms (market of corporate control and collective actions of small shareholders) function well, managerial discretion rights are small. On the other hand, no matter what the size of shareholder's share (concentration) is, impact of the investor is small if shareholders are not protected by the legal frame. Dynamic measures of concentration – the ones that refer to the wider context of management – owner relations, take into account power indicators and not just ownership concentration but are not research subjects too often (Leech, 1987). Various ways of managerial control can also be mentioned. What is the degree of managerial control? Ownership dispersion consequences reflect on corporate control through an increase in management influence. Berle-Means measure of the degree of managerial control is frequently used as an object of research.

Ownership Concentration as Determinant of the Pattern of Organizational Change

How does corporate control that comes out of ownership concentration affect the performance of a company? The possible effect of ownership concentration on the performance of a company is the main question in research about corporate governance, but the results of these relations are different.

According to theory, a higher level of ownership concentration has a positive effect on the success of a company. Namely, when control separates from ownership, the value of the com-

Figure 1. Ownership stake of biggest and second biggest shareholder in different countries (Sources: Barca, F. & Becht, M. (2001) The Control of Corporate Europe. Oxford: Oxford University Press. In: Kryštof, M. (2005) Corporate Governance and Ownership Concentration in the Czech Republic. Prague: University Karlova.; Pajuste, A. & Olsson, M. (2001) Ownership concentration: the case of the Baltic States, Conference Corporate Governance and Disclosure in the Accession Process. Portorož: CEPR/ University of Ljubljana.; Gregoric, A., Prasnikar, J. & Ribnikar, I. (2000) Corporate Governance in Transitional Economies: The Case of Slovenia, Economic and Business Review, 2; Maury, C. B. & Pajuste, A. (2002) Controlling Shareholders, Agency Problems, and Dividend, Policy in Finland, LTA 1/02.)

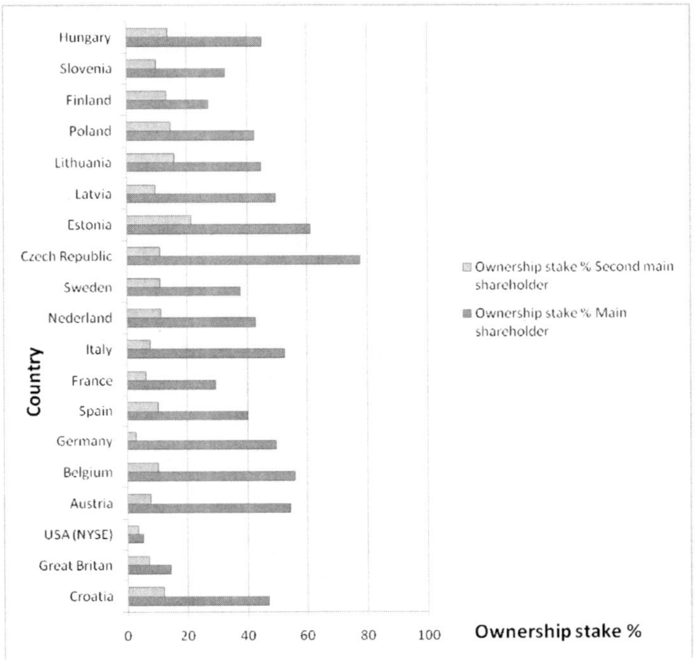

pany will decrease because there is an increasing divergence in interests- managers on one side and owners on the other (Jensen & Meckling, 1976). A large number of shares in the hands of one owner increases the supervision of management and in that way decreases the agency problem. The ownership concentration also has an effect on the low diversification of the investors' portfolios in capital markets, bad situation for shareholders, the lack of transparency in accounting practices, the linkage of groups in the company through networks of joint ownership and possible favoring of certain options in making decisions and hiring management (Shleifer & Vishny, 1997. and Johnson, Bonne, Breach & Friedman, 2000).

Empirical studies relating relationship of performance and ownership concentration have provided very different results. In a study made for some American corporations, Demsetz and Lehn conclude that there is no effect of ownership concentration on the accounting profit (Demsetz & Lehn, 1958). McConnell and Serves have concluded on the same sample of companies that there is no connection between ownership concentration and the relation of market value and replacement property costs (Tobin's q) (McConnell & Servaes, 1990). Research made by Wruck in 1989 has provided interesting results (Wruck, 1989). According to these results, an abnormal positive market return occurred in situations when ownership concentration was low, it was reduced at medium level of ownership concentration, and increased again at a dense ownership concentration. This interpretation implies a U-curve, which is somewhat specific for relations of management ownership's level which as described by Morck and others (Morck, Shleifer & Vishny, 1988).

Claessens and Djankov anticipate an inverse U-relation in Czech Republic (Claessens & Djankov, 1999). Leech and Leahy find inconsistence in the sample of British corporations that refers to a negative relationship when performance is measured using profitability (Leech & Leahy, 1991). In a sample of German corporations Gorton and Schmith find that ownership concentration amplifies the relationship between market and accounting values (however statistically insignificant) and return on investment (Gorton & Schmid, 2000). Prowse has not found a connection between profitability and ownership concentration in Japan, and Hovey and others have not found a connection between concentration and Tobin's q in Chinese companies (Earle, Kucsera & Telegdy, 2005).

Research which was conducted by Earle and others on a sample of corporations from the Budapest stock market quotations shows that there is a positive and statistically significant effect on a company's success only in the case when concentration is measured as a percentage of the share of the largest shareholder. These results strongly prove the hypothesis that the agency problem decreases with increasing ownership concentration, when the biggest shareholder is the only one we consider. On the other hand, research has shown that when there are additional large shareholders *(blockholders),* it is possible than a decrease in value appears, probably as a result of conflicts between these large shareholders (Earle, Kucsera & Telegdy, 2005).

Research Sample

Major goal of the paper is to investigate how differences in ownership concentration influence patterns of organizational change. However, implementation of change is under depends of company size. Since small companies, in early entrepreneurial stage of development are more likely to implement different patterns of change, our intent was not to take these companies in consideration in our research. By concentrating our efforts on bigger companies, with more than 100 employees, we want to avoid possibility of wrong interpretation of change patterns.

The study that is the basis for this paper was conducted during the first half of 2008 in Croatia. The sample covered 500 Croatian enterprises in all branches of the economy. The study questionnaire consisted of basic information about the firm and questions in the areas of organizational structure and culture, strategy, integrations and organizational changes. 63 questionnaires were received (questionnaire return rate: 12,6%), which is satisfactory for the purpose of our study. Out of 63 companies, 2 of them (3%) have more than 5000 employees. 10 companies have between 1000 and 5000 employees. Further on, the sample consists of 11 companies with number of employees between 500 and 1000. 13 companies have between 300 and 500 employees. Biggest number of companies (14) are the ones between 200 and 300 employees. 13 companies have between 100 and 200 employees (Figure 2).

Companies in the sample come from several industries (Table 1). Most of companies are from manufacturing industry which comprises 35% of the sample and this is extremely beneficial for analysis of changes since today's challenges to manufacturing companies are much fiercer. The global market is characterized by more rapid change than experienced in the expansive last decade. This reality requires a strategy with a stronger emphasis on creativity and innovation than previously and on lean systems involved in mass production (Rose-Anderssen et al., 2005, p.1093). Besides manufacturing, industries that are represented in the sample (Table 2 and Figure 3) are: construction (14%), communal infrastruc-

Figure 2. Number of employees in companies in the sample

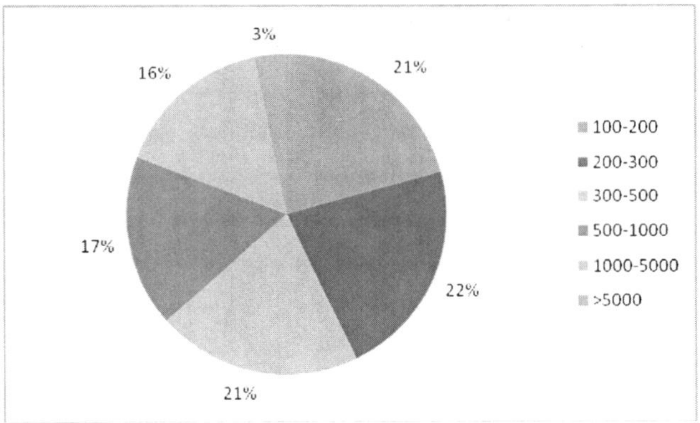

ture (7%), hospitality and tourism (10%), trade (9%), electrical sector (5%) and other industries (16%).

DISCUSSION

Organizational change is conceptualized as changes in technology, organizational structure, organizational culture, strategy, changes in employees' structure and changes in products and services. Above mentioned patters of organizational change are analyzed in terms of their frequency and effects on corporate performance. Evidently, the changes in technology and human resources take place every two to three years and represent the most frequent changes. This conclusion is connected with dominant industry (manufacturing and construction) of the analyzed companies in the sample. As presented it the following exhibit (Figure 4), 5,00 represents changes within one-year time scale; 4,00 represents changes that happen every two years; 3,00 represents changes that happen every three years; 2,00 in period of five years or more and 1,00 stands for changes that never occur. Structural changes, changes in products and services and changes in strategy are recognized as changes that happen within three to five years. Changes in organizational culture stand for evolutionary change and are product of all above mentioned changes. Therefore the rate of recurrence is the lowest (mean=2,56) for changes in organizational culture.

The role of employees within the framework of organizational changes is measured from manager's perception on five – point Likert scale (1-strongly disagree, 2-disagree, 3-neither agree nor disagree, 4-agree, 5-strongly agree). Table

Table 1. Number of employees in companies in the sample

Number of employees	Number of companies
100-200	13
200-300	14
300-500	13
500-1000	11
1000-5000	10
>5000	2
Σ	**63**

Table 2. Industry of companies in the sample

Industry	Number of companies
Manufacturing	22
Construction	9
Trade	6
Hospitality and tourism	6
Communal infrastructure	7
Electricity	3
Other	10

Figure 3. Industry of companies in the sample

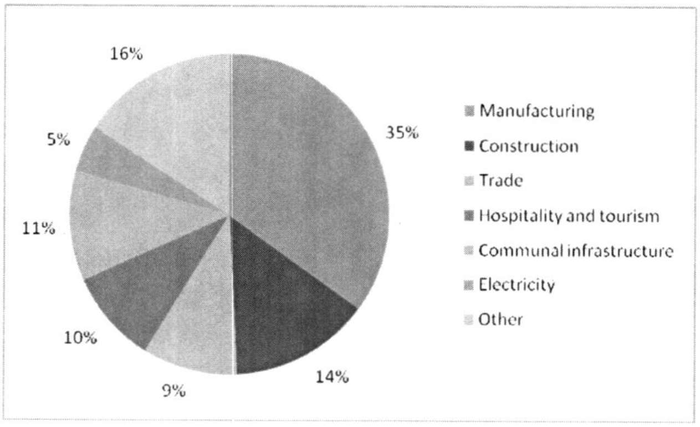

3 presents results (means and standard deviations) for all items concerning employees' role in organizational changes' process. Noticeably employees are perceived as vital element for successful organizational changes and are being trained and educated before and during the process, and consequently they do not resist strongly the organizational change. Training and learning is the mode for enhanced reception of changes, but the explanation is also connected with the type of changes, since the most frequent changes are technological changes that require improved and various new skills and knowledge.

The effect of organizational changes on corporate performance is imperative issue. The *raison d'être* for changes in technology, strategy, structure etc. is to upgrade market value, market share and competitive position, to increase revenues and reduce costs in addition to entrance in new markets. The outcome of organizational changes are measured in terms of non, partial and total influence on revenue, costs, new markets, market share, market value and competitive position. The Table 4 and Figure 5 illustrate the results from the survey (1-no effect, 2-partial and 3-total effect). Organizational changes do have some positive effect on corporate performance particularly on improvement of competitive position and revenues.

There is a large number of different ownership concentration measures. Many authors use Demsetz and Lehn research as a basis for their own. Demsetz and Lehn measure ownership concentration related to a group of owners, usually as total number of shares owned by certain number of owners (e.g. 5 – 20 of the biggest owners) (Demsetz & Lehn, 1958). In other studies, Holderness and Sheen observe only major

Figure 4. Frequencies of organizational changes

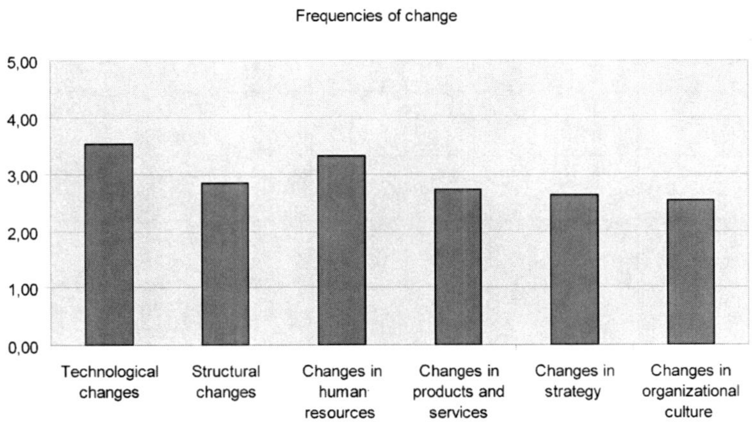

owners while Wruck measures concentration as total share in managers' ownership, and on the other hand also all share blocks (with 5 or more % of ownership) (Holderness & Sheehan, 1988. and Wruck, 1989). Prowse, Howey and others consider only five biggest shareholders when measuring concentration (Prowse, 1992. and Hovey, Lee & Naughton, 2003). Claessens as well as some other authors take into account only the share of the largest shareholder (Earle, Kucsera & Telegdy, 2005). The concentration measure that is used in our research is also the share of the largest shareholder.

The final result is mostly influenced by the way the ownership concentration is measured.

Earle and other authors point out the relevance of the way in which we measure ownership concentration (Earle, Kucsera & Telegdy, 2005). According to these authors, whether we use a group of owners or only the biggest one in our analysis, it makes a difference. In fact, the largest number of owners cannot face the problem of interaction or can draw moves that benefit to them and not to other companies. Not giving enough attention to the possibilities of interaction between owners is one of the possible causes of the conflicted results of the research about the impact of ownership concentration on the company performance.

Ownership concentration is divided in three categories, according to ownership stake of the biggest shareholder (Table 5).

In first group are companies in which biggest shareholder have share of more than 95% which under Croatian laws can be considered absolute control. Number of companies from the sample which fall in this group is 22 or 35%. Most of the companies (28 or 44%) fall in group of where biggest shareholder have share between 50% and

Table 3. The role of employees in organizational changes' process

The manager's perception:	*Results:*
1. Employees participate in process of organizational change.	*mean value* = 3,46 $\partial = 1.03$
2. Employees are being trained and educated before and during the process of organizational change.	*mean value* = 3,82 $\partial = 0.99$
3. Employees resist the organizational change.	*mean value* = 2,82 $\partial = 1.2$

Table 4. The rank of effects of organizational changes on corporate performance

Rank of organizational changes' effects:	*Results:*
1. Better competitive position	*mean value* = 2,25 $\partial = 0.71$
2. Increase in revenues	*mean value* = 2,24 $\partial = 0.60$
3. Increase in market value	*mean value* = 2,22 $\partial = 0.68$
4. Decrease in costs	*mean value* = 2,17 $\partial = 0.72$
5. Entrance in new markets	*mean value* = 2,04 $\partial = 0.78$
6. Increase in market share	*mean value* = 2,03 $\partial = 0.75$

Figure 5. The effects of organizational changes on corporate performance

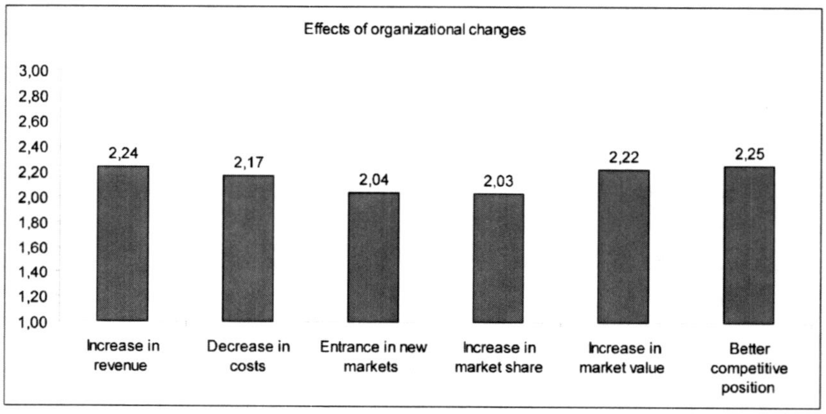

95%. 21% of the companies in the sample fall in the group where dominant shareholder have less that 50% of shares.

Table 6 shows frequency of organizational change in respect to level of ownership concentration. It is interesting to observe how different levels of ownership concentration influence organizational change. Especially interesting are changes in human resources and in organizational culture. It seems that lower levels of ownership concentration bring higher frequency of changes in ownership concentration policies. The situation is same in the case of changes in organizational culture.

Technological changes are the most frequent in companies where the biggest shareholder's stake is higher than 95% and between 50 and 95%. In these companies technological changes occur every two year, followed by changes in human resources that arise every three years time period. In companies with ownership stake of biggest shareholder less than 50% changes in human resources are the most frequent (3,83) followed by technological changes.

In terms of frequency of organizational change generally conclusions are very similar patters in companies with ownership stake of biggest shareholder higher than 95% and in companies

Table 5. Ownership concentration of the sample

Share of biggest shareholder	Number of companies in the sample	% of companies in the sample
More than 95%	22	35
Between 50 and 95%	28	44
Less than 50%	13	21
Total	63	100

with ownership stake of biggest shareholder between 50 and 95%. In both categories the most infrequent changes are in organizational culture. In companies with ownership stake of biggest shareholder less than 50% the frequencies are different to some degree. Changes in products and services as well as changes in strategy are the most sporadic in companies without one dominant shareholder while the changes in human resources are the most regular changes.

The Figure 6 illustrates the employees' role in process of organizational changes. Evidently, employees are being trained and educated before and during the process of organizational changes in all studied companies, regardless of ownership concentration in studied companies. The imperative role of employees is recognized in companies with ownership stake of biggest shareholder between 50 and 95%. Insignificant difference is identified in first two categories of companies concerning participation of employees in process of organizational change as well as in training and education before and during the same process.

The effects of organizational changes on corporate performance are also studied in companies regarding corresponding ownership concentration. Table 7 indicated consistent results of partial effect of organizational changes on corporate performance. The companies with ownership stake of biggest shareholder less than 50% evidently experience the weakest effects on corporate performance. Regardless the consistent results of partial effects, the ranking of particular effects in sub-samples are inconsistent. In companies

Table 6. Frequency of organizational change in respect to level of ownership concentration

Ownership concentration	Frequency of organizational change					
	Technological changes	Structural changes	Changes in human resources	Changes in products and services	Changes in strategy	Changes in organizational culture
Ownership concentration, ownership stake of biggest shareholder higher than 95%	3,58	2,95	3,21	2,62	2,57	2,25
Ownership concentration, ownership stake of biggest shareholder between 50 and 95%	3,58	2,79	3,17	2,96	2,77	2,64
Ownership concentration, ownership stake of biggest shareholder less than 50%	3,33	2,75	3,83	2,5	2,5	2,92

Figure 6. The role of employees in organizational changes' process regarding ownership concentration

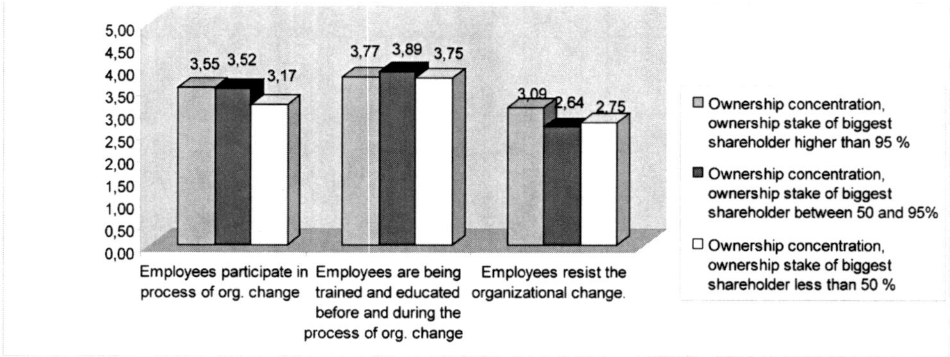

with biggest shareholder having more than 95% shares, maximum effect is confirmed in terms of increased market value; in companies with biggest shareholder having more than 50% shares is increase in revenue while in the rest of analyzes companies maximum effect is defined as effect in decrease of costs.

If we look at influence of concentration ownership on effectiveness of organizational changes (Table 7) we can find interesting results in increase in market value. This finding brings us to conclusion that increase of ownership concentration can be connected to organizational change which, in effect, brings higher levels of market value. In conclusion, the observed companies find increased market share as the most difficult to achieve in the course of organizational change process.

Correlation analysis did not confirm the hypothesis that differences in ownership concentration influence patterns of organizational change (Table 8). Evidently there are significant correlations between different types of organizational changes, but the imperative of this research was to determine the contribution of ownership concentration to the process of organizational change. Even though there are theoretical indication about the connection and impact between these analyzed phenom-

Table 7. Effect of organizational change and ownership concentration

Rank of organizational changes' effects:	**Ownership stake of biggest shareholder higher than 95%**	**Ownership stake of biggest shareholder between 50 and 95%**	**Ownership stake of biggest shareholder less than 50%**
1. Increase in revenues	*mean* = 2,24 ∂ = 0.62	*mean* = 2,32 ∂ = 0.63	*mean* = 2,08 ∂ = 0.51
2. Decrease in costs	*mean* = 2,09 ∂ = 0.81	*mean* = 2,15 ∂ = 0.67	*mean* = 2,33 ∂ = 0.65
3. Entrance in new markets	*mean* = 2,00 ∂ = 0.86	*mean* = 2,16 ∂ = 0.69	*mean* = 1,83 ∂ = 0.83
4. Increase in market share	*mean* = 2,05 ∂ = 0.80	*mean* = 2,16 ∂ = 0.75	*mean* = 1,75 ∂ = 0.62
5. Increase in market value	*mean* = 2,38 ∂ = 0.59	*mean* = 2,16 ∂ = 0.80	*mean* = 2,08 ∂ = 0.51
6. Better competitive position	*mean* = 2,33 ∂ = 0.66	*mean* = 2,27 ∂ = 0.72	*mean* = 2,08 ∂ = 0.79

ena – ownership concentration and organizational change, there is no empirical confirmation within this survey.

CONCLUSION AND FUTURE RESEARCH

Primarily aim of this paper was to analyze organizational changes in computing landscape as well as to determine relationship between organizational change and different levels of ownership concentration in Croatian companies.

The technological changes do represent the most significant aspect of organizational changes. Knowing that it is related with dominant industry – manufacturing, opens many opportunities for future implementation, adaption and integration of different technological solutions. Researches on the subject of ownership concentration and performance have not provided an answer on the question if ownership concentration effects the company's value on a positive or negative way, nor how high is that influence. Companies' performances are related with the tendency to conduct changes as well as with types of changes

Table 8. Correlation analysis of organizational change and ownership concentration

	Ownership concentration	Technological changes	Structural changes	Changes in human resources	Changes in products and services	Changes in strategy	Changes in organizational culture
Ownership concentration - Pearson correlation - Sig. (2.tailed) - N	 1,000 , 62	 -0,067 ,628 55	 -0,072 ,592 58	 0,132 ,335 55	 -0,006 ,965 57	 -0,006 ,967 55	 0,220 ,110 54
Technological changes - Pearson correlation - Sig. (2.tailed) - N		 1,000 , 55	 0,358** ,008 54	 0,152 ,227 53	 0,312* ,021 54	 0,259 ,064 52	 0,122 ,389 52
Structural changes - Pearson correlation - Sig. (2.tailed) - N			 1,000 , 58	 0,451** ,001 54	 0,434** ,001 56	 0,603** ,000 55	 0,285* ,037 54
Changes in human resources - Pearson correlation - Sig. (2.tailed) - N				 1,000 , 55	 0,330* ,015 54	 0,177 ,204 53	 0,211 ,130 53
Changes in products and services - Pearson correlation - Sig. (2.tailed) - N					 1,000 , 57	 0,288* ,033 55	 0,257 ,060 54
Changes in strategy - Pearson correlation - Sig. (2.tailed) - N						 1,000 , 55	 0,351** ,009 54
Changes in organizational culture - Pearson correlation - Sig. (2.tailed) - N							 1,000 , 54

by which a company wants to modify their business activities according to the requirements of a changeable environment.

The study about ownership concentration and change patterns within computing environment was conducted during the first half of 2008 in Croatia. In our correlation analysis we did not found sufficient evidence to confirm the hypothesis that differences in ownership concentration influence patterns of organizational change. Partial explanations may be in transition processes that Croatian companies faced in last twenty years. Privatization has been one of the most important characteristics of the countries in transition and Croatian companies conducted many changes in order to enhance their competitiveness. In our opinion future studies, with completed transition period, could more clearly determine connections between ownership concentration and change. However, we did find significant correlations between different types of organizational changes. Even though there is no empirical confirmation on the connection and impact between these analyzed phenomena – ownership concentration and control and organizational change our paper represents one step further in understanding this important research question.

REFERENCES

Amburgey, T. L., Kelly, D., & Barnett, W. P. (1993). Reseting the clock. The dynamics of organizational change and failure. *Administrative Science Quarterly*, *38*, 51–73. doi:10.2307/2393254

Barnett, W. P., & Carroll, G. R. (1995). Modeling internal organizational change. *Annual Review of Sociology*, *21*, 217–236. doi:10.1146/annurev.so.21.080195.001245

Baum, J. A. C. (1996). Organizational Ecology. In S. R. Clegg, C. Hardy, & W. R. Nord (Eds.), *Handbook of organization studies* (pp. 77-114). London: Sage Publications.

Becht, M., & Röell, A. (1999). Blockholdings in Europe: An International Comparison. *European Economic Review*, *43*, 1049–1056. doi:10.1016/S0014-2921(98)00113-5

Beck, N., Bruderl, J., & Woywode, M. (2008). Momentum or deceleration? Theoretical and methodological reflections on the analysis of organizational change. *Academy of Management Journal*, *51*(3), 413–435.

Berle, A. A., & Means, G. C. (1932). *The Modern Corporation and Private Property*. New York: Macmillian.

Bonne, L., & Kurtz, D. (1992). *Management*. New York: McGraw-Hill.

Burke, W. W. (2002). *Organization Change: Theory and Practice*. Thousand Oaks, CA: Sage Publications.

Claessens, S., & Djankov, S. (1999). Ownership Concentration and Corporate Performance in the Czech Republic. *Journal of Comparative Economics*, *27*(3), 498–513. doi:10.1006/jcec.1999.1598

Cristiano, J. J., Liker, J. K., & White, C. C. III. (2000). Customer-driven product development through quality function deployment in the U.S. and Japan. *Journal of Product Innovation Management*, *17*, 286–308. doi:10.1016/S0737-6782(00)00047-3

Demirag, I. S., & Serter, M. (2003). Ownership Patterns and Control in Turkish Listed Companies. *Corporate Governance*, *11*, 40–51. doi:10.1111/1467-8683.00300

Demsetz, H., & Lehn, K. (1958). The Structure of Corporate Ownership. *The Journal of Political Economy*, *93*, 1155–1177. doi:10.1086/261354

Dobrev, S. D., Kim, T. Y., & Hannan, M. T. (2001). Dynamics of niche width and resource partitioning. *American Journal of Sociology*, *106*, 1299–1337. doi:10.1086/320821

Earle, J., S., Kucsera, C. & Telegdy, Á. (2005). Ownership Concentration and Corporate Performance in the Budapest Stock Exchange: do too many cooks spoil the goulash? *Corporate Governance, 13*, 254–264. doi:10.1111/j.1467-8683.2005.00420.x

Edwards, J., & Nibler, M. (2000). Corporate Governance in Germany: the Role of Banks and Ownership Concentration. *Economic Policy, 15*(31). doi:10.1111/1468-0327.00062

Franks, J., & Mayer, C. (2001). Ownership and Control of German Corporations. *Review of Financial Studies, 14*, 943–977. doi:10.1093/rfs/14.4.943

Goldsmith, W., & Clutterbuck, D. (1998). *The Winning Streak Mark II*. London: Orion Business Books.

Gorton, G., & Schmid, F. A. (2000). Universal Banking and the Performance of German Firms. *Journal of Financial Economics, 58*, 29–80. doi:10.1016/S0304-405X(00)00066-0

Hannan, M. T., & Freema, J. (1984). Structural inertia and organizational change. *American Sociological Review, 49*, 149–164. doi:10.2307/2095567

Holderness, C. G., & Sheehan, D. P. (1988). The role of majority shareholders in publicly held corporations: An exploratory analysis. *Journal of Financial Economics*, 20.

Hovey, M., Lee, L., & Naughton, A. (2003). The Relationship Between Valuation and Ownership of Listed Firms in China. *Corporate Governance: An International Review, 11*, 112–122. doi:10.1111/1467-8683.00012

Jensen, M. C., & Meckling, H. W. (1976). Theory of firm. Managerial Behaviour, Agency Costs and Ownership Structure. *Journal of Financial Economics, 3*(4), 305–360. doi:10.1016/0304-405X(76)90026-X

Johnson, S., Boone, P., Breach, A., & Friedman, E. (2000). Corporate Governance in the Asian Financial Crisis. *Journal of Financial Economics, 58*(1/2), 141–186. doi:10.1016/S0304-405X(00)00069-6

Jones, G. J. (2004). *Organizational Theory, Design, and Change, Text and Cases* (4th ed.). New Jersey: Pearsons Education.

Kelly, D., & Amburgey, T. L. (1991). Organizational inertia and momentum. A dynamic model of strategic change. *Academy of Management Journal, 34*, 591–612. doi:10.2307/256407

Kovač, J. (2000). Dimensions of organizational change. *Management, 5*(1), 73–81.

La Porta, R., Lopez-de-Silanes, F., & Shleifer, A. (1999). Corporate Ownership around the World. *The Journal of Finance, 54*(2), 737–778.

Leech, D. (1987). Ownership Concentration and the Theory of the Firm: a Simple Game Theoretic Approach. *The Journal of Industrial Economics, 35*(3), 225–240. doi:10.2307/2098631

Leech, D., & Leahy, J. (1991). Ownership Structure, Control Type Classifications and the Performance of Large British Companies. *The Economic Journal, 101*, 1418–1437. doi:10.2307/2234893

Lewis, P. S., Goodman, S. H., & Fandt, P. M. (1998). *Management, Challenges in the 21st Century*. Ohio: South-Western College Publishing.

Lundvall, B., Johnson, B., Andersen, E. S., & Dalum, B. (2002). National systems of production innovation and competence building. *Research Policy, 31*, 213–231. doi:10.1016/S0048-7333(01)00137-8

McConnell, J., & Servaes, H. (1990). Additional Evidence on Equity Ownership and Corporate Value. *Journal of Financial Economics, 27*, 595–612. doi:10.1016/0304-405X(90)90069-C

Morck, R., Shleifer, A., & Vishny, W. R. (1988). Management Ownership and Market Valuation: An Empirical Analysis. *Journal of Financial Economics*, *20*, 293–315. doi:10.1016/0304-405X(88)90048-7

Mullins, L. J. (2005). *Management and Organizational Behaviour* (7th ed.). Harlow: Prentice Hall.

Pajuste, A., & Olsson, M. (2001). *Ownership concentration: the case of the Baltic States*. Conference Corporate Governance and Disclosure in the Accession Process. Portorož: CEPR/ University of Ljubljana.

Porras, J. I., & Robertson, P. J. (1992). Organizational development: Theory, practice and research. In M. D. Dunnette & L. M. Hough (Eds.), *Handbook of industrial and organizational psychology* (2nd ed., pp. 719-822). Palo Alto: Consulting Psychologists Press.

Porras, J. I., & Silvers, R. C. (1991). Organization Development and Transformation. *Annual Review of Psychology*, *42*, 51–78. doi:10.1146/annurev.ps.42.020191.000411

Price, R. M. (1996). Technology and strategic advantage. *California Management Review*, *38*(3), 38–56.

Prowse, S. D. (1992). The Structure of Corporate Ownership in Japan. *The Journal of Finance*, *47*, 1121–1140. doi:10.2307/2328979

Rose-Andersen, C., Allen, P. M., Tsinopoulos, C., & McCarthy, I. (2005). Innovation in manufacturing as an evolutionary complex system. *Technovation*, *25*(10), 1093–1105. doi:10.1016/j.technovation.2004.03.006

Schmidt, R. H. (2003). *Corporate Governance in Germany: An Economic Perspective, Center for Financial Studies*. Frankfurt am Main: Johann Wolfgang Goethe-Universität.

Shein, E. H. (1987). *Process consultation: Vol. 2. Its role in organizational development*. 2nd ed. Reading: Addison-Wesley.

Shleifer, A., & Vishny, R. W. (1986). Large Shareholders and Corporate Control. *The Journal of Political Economy*, *95*, 461–488. doi:10.1086/261385

Shleifer, A., & Vishny, R. W. (1997). A Survey of Corporate Governance. *The Journal of Finance*, *52*, 737–783. doi:10.2307/2329497

Turnbull, S. (2000). Corporate Governance: Theories, Challenges and Paradigms. *Social Science Research Network Electronic Paper Collection*.

Warshow, H. T. (1924). The Distribution of Corporate Ownership in the U.S. *The Quarterly Journal of Economics*, *39*, 15–38. doi:10.2307/1883952

Weick, K. E. (1999). Organizational change and development. *Annual Review of Psychology*, *50*, 361–386. doi:10.1146/annurev.psych.50.1.361

Wruck, K. H. (1989). Equity ownership concentration and firm value: Evidence from private equity financings. *Journal of Financial Economics*, *23*, 3–28. doi:10.1016/0304-405X(89)90003-2

ADDITIONAL READING

Barnard, C. (1938). The Functions of the Executive. *Harvard University Press*.

Chang. S. & Mayers. D. (1995). *Who Benefits in a Negotiated Block Trade?* (Working Paper, University of California at Riverside).

Coase, R. (1937). The Nature of the Firm. *Economica, New Series, IV*

Coffee, C. (1999). The Future as History: The Prospects for Global Convergence in Corporate Governance and its Implications . *Northwestern University Law Review*, 93.

Demsetz, H., & Lehn, K. (1958). The Structure of Corporate Ownership. *The Journal of Political Economy*, 93.

Franks, J., & Mayer, C. (1994). *Corporate Control: A Comparison of Insider and Outsider Systems* (Working Paper, London Business School).

Franks, J., & Mayer, C. (2001). Ownership and Control of German Corporations. *Review of Financial Studies*, 14.

Jensen, C., Michael, M., & Kevin, J. (1990). CEO incentives – it's not how much you pay, but how. *Harvard Business Review*, *86*(3).

Jensen, M., & Murphy, J. (1990). Performance Pay and Top management Incentives. *The Journal of Political Economy*, 98.

Kočenda, E. (2002). Ownership structures and corporate performance: Czech firms vaucher sheme. *An Enterprise Odyssey: Economics and Business in the New Millennium 2002, International Conference, University of Zagreb, Graduate School of Economics and Business, Zagreb.*

LaPorta, R., Lopez-de-Silanes, F., Schleifer, A., & Vishny, R. (1998). Law and Finance. *The Journal of Political Economy*, 106.

Leech, D., & Leahy, J. (1991). Ownership Structure, Control Type Classifications and the Performance of Large British Companies. *The Economic Journal*, 101.

Mitchell, R., Agle, B., & Wood, D. (1997). Toward a theory of stakeholder identification and salience: defining the principle of who and what really counts. *Academy of Management Review*, 4.

Morck, R., Shleifer, A., & Vishny, R. (1998). Management Ownership and Market Valuation: An Empirical Analysis. *Journal of Financial Economics*, 20.

Roe, M. (1992). Some Differences in Corporate Governence in Germany, Japan and America. *The Center for Law and Economic Studies, Columbia University School of Law.*

Shleifer, A., & Vishny, R. (1986). Large Shareholders and Corporate Control. *The Journal of Political Economy*, 95.

Stiglitz, J. (1999). Quis custodiet ipsos custodes? Corporate governance failures in the transition. *Annual bank conference on development economics-Europe, Paris.*

Williamson, O. (1981). The Economics of Organization: The Transaction Cost Approach. *American Journal of Sociology*, 87.

Williamson, O. (1985). *The Economic Institutions of Capitalism: Firms, Markets, Relational Contracting*. The Free Press.

Williamson, O. (1991). Comparative Economic Organization: The Analysis of Discrete Structural Alternatives. *Administrative Science Quarterly*, 36.

KEY TERMS AND DEFINITIONS

Corporate Control: is integrative concept of corporate governance which describes position in which one entity can enforce its goals as goals of the whole corporation.

Dynamic Measures of Concentration: the ones that refer to the wider context of management – owner relations, take into account power indicators and not just ownership concentration.

Organizational Change: is the process by which organizations move from their present state to some desired future state to increase their effectiveness.

Planned Change: is deliberate, conscious decision to improve the organization in some manner or perhaps to change the system in a deeper, more fundamental way.

Static Measures of Concentration: are the ones which simply represent percentage of stocks owned by specific shareholder at specific point in time.

Technological Capabilities: are the ability to develop a constant stream of new products or to modify existing products so that they can continue to attract customers is one of an organization's core competences; give an organization an enormous capacity to change itself in order to exploit market opportunities.

The Goal of Organizational Change: is to find new or improved ways of using resources and capabilities in order to increase on organization's ability to create value and improve returns to its stakeholders.

The Ownership Concentration: dictates the distribution of power and control between managers and owners.

Unplanned Change: represents response to some unanticipated external change, for example, creation of a whole new technology that affects the very core of business.

Chapter 11
Strategic Human Resource Management & Organizational Performance

P.C. Bahuguna
University of Petroleum & Energy Studies, India

P. Kumari
Kanya Gurukul Mahavidyalaya, India

ABSTRACT

The discipline of human resource management has progressed significantly over a period of time. Today it is being considered as the most critical source of competitive advantage to the firm. It has progressed to a strategic business partner. Various approaches and models of strategic human resource management have been developed within the framework of strategic human resource management. Like many theories of organization, none are complete. Rather being right or wrong each approach points to different aspect of the process needed to develop effective strategic human resource functions. The issue of fitting HR practices to business strategy has become increasingly relevant over few years. Therefore in the present study we have made efforts to highlight various issues which are relevant to the strategic HRM in the changing scenario of business environment. The present chapter has been divided into five sections. In the first part, the changes occurring in the business environment and its implications for human resource functionaries have been discussed. In the second section we have highlighted the changing role of human resource management. Historical background of strategic human resource management, its role in addressing the challenges of changing business scenario and determinants of strategic fit have also been presented in the second section. In the third section issues regarding the relationship of strategic human resource management with business performance have been discussed. In the fourth section we have made efforts to bring into notice those emerging future trends which might become key issues for high performance in the organization of new era. At last conclusions have been drawn that what needs to be done on the part of the HR functionaries and the organization itself to enhance the strategic fit between the various HR practices and the overall organizational strategic plan.

DOI: 10.4018/978-1-60566-996-0.ch011

Figure 1.

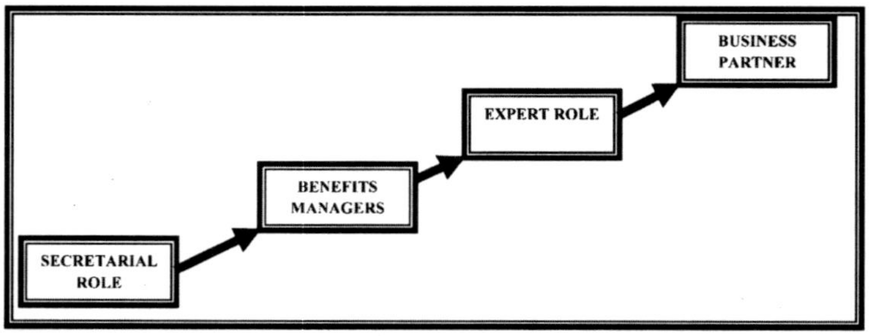

INTRODUCTION

The industrial revolution in the nineteenth century brought about the automation in the manufacturing process putting the muscle power to the back seat and focusing mainly on production of goods. The focus later on shifted to marketing considerations putting customer satisfaction on the top. The information technology revolution of the twentieth century along with globalization has brought the drastic changes in the working environment i.e. putting people as the most important resource. The importance of human resources can be traced back to ancient Hindu texts such as Kautilya's Arthashastra, which provides the evidence of existence of systematic management of people as early as 320 B.C. (Khanka, 2003). However, the first evidence of origin of human resource management (HRM) practices has its roots in the industrial revolution of the 17th century. The technical advancements during this period created the need for better work methods, productivity and quality. Smith (1776) in his book 'An Enquiry into Nature and Causes of Wealth of Nations' talked about the economic advantages of the division of labour. He proposed that work could be made more efficient through specialisation. From the division of labour he saw three advantages: the development of skills, time saving, and the possibility of using specialised tools. The importance of people in the business performance can be traced from the work of Owen (1825). He argued that money spent on developing people was one of the best investments that management can make. Babbage (1832) examined and expanded upon the division of labour in his work and concluded that it allows a more careful matching of people's skills and physical abilities with specific tasks. Land mark revolution came in the field of people management practices when Taylor (1911) attempted to formalize the processes, methods, workers experiences and tacit skills into objective rules and formulae. The path breaking studies that revolutionized the human resource management practices were conducted from 1927 – 1932 by Mayo and his associates to study the relationship between productivity and the working environment followed by the studies carried out by Barnard (1938), and others. All these studies have identified commitment, communication, employee motivation, leadership and learning as the antecedents of organizational success. The nature, status and role of human resource management have progressively become broader and strategic since the days of industrial revolution (Figure 1).

Today human resource management is not just about hiring and firing people, administering wages and salaries, designing and implementing benefit programmes, and implementing the strategic intentions of the top management, rather it is playing an active role in formulating the business strategies. The advent of the era of globalization and liberalization accompanied by the information technology revolution has transformed the world around us. This has made possible the free flow of people, technology, and goods across the globe. Business activities are no more limited and confined to the geographical boundaries of the countries. According to Ulrich and Brockbank (2005) there has been exponential growth in international movements of goods and services. The traditional jobs have become blurred. The economies across the globe are experiencing new order. Globalization is an important factor that influences organizations that compete for customers with high expectations for performance, quality, and low cost. The most pressing competitive issues facing firms are globalisation, embracing new technologies, managing change, developing human capital, responding to the market and optimization of costs. As more and more companies go abroad or operate internationally, the impact on various business functions and in particular on human resource management have become more evident. Effective and strategic human resource management is essential as the international businesses place additional stress on human resource functionaries. Human resources are being viewed as an input, which can provide sustained competitive advantage to the organizations. Over the years, organizations' expectations from their HR champions and departments have changed considerably. The function was and still is expected to ensure that its policies, practices and procedures shape the culture of the organization in a way that is consistent with its values and vision. People management practices need to acknowledge and work within the context and reflect a broader perspective. Human resource policies and practices need to facilitate the work process across time, distance and cultures. The reality today is that most companies consciously or unconsciously experience one or more aspects of international management. Despite the fact that the core principles of human resource management also apply to global human resource management, it presents some unique challenges. Managing people in global settings requires human resource professionals to address broader range of issues such as taxation, exchange rates, compensation plans, dealing with foreign governments and religious groups. Recently terrorism added many anxieties to employees, their families and the employers which further had accentuated the need to manage human resources effectively to gain competitive advantage in the global market place. To achieve this, organizations require an understanding of the factors that can determine the effectiveness of various HR practices and approaches. This is because countries differ along a number of dimensions that influence the attractiveness of investments in each country. These differences determine the economic viability of building an operation in a foreign country and they have a particularly strong impact on HRM in that operation. There are a large number of factors such as culture, economic systems, political systems and the legal framework etc. that affect HRM in global markets. The objectives of the chapter are to highlight

1. The role of human resources as a source of competitive advantage.
2. Strategic role of human resource management in enhancing the organizational performance.
3. Strategic challenges and issues for human resource management to become a strategic business partner.

STRATEGIC HUMAN RESOURCE MANAGEMENT

Role of HR

In the seventies and eighties the business function responsible for people was called "The Personnel Management." The responsibility of this function was to employ people, pay them, and fire them. Subsequently the ever increasing competition forced organizations to take the more planned and calculated approach to management as a result there has been growing interest in the strategic management which further compelled the sub functions of the organizations to redefine their roles in this process. Since human resource management was no exception, it also had to re identify its role. Later efforts were made to integrate it into strategic management process and as a result the function progressed to strategic human resource management. In late eighties and early nineties it was realised that HR function has a much larger role: recruiting the right people, training them, helping the business design jobs and structures, develop compensation packages including benefit plans and serving as a central point of communication for employee health and happiness. In this role, the HR department now became more than a business function: it is a business partner, reaching out to support business processes. The strategic role of HR includes enhancing organizational performance, get involved in corporate planning, decision making on mergers, acquisitions and downsizing, redesigning organizations and work processes and ensuring financial accountability for HR results. In view of the soaring competition and increased expectations of the top management, HRM has certain strategic challenges. The fundamental challenge faced by HR community is to provide a set of services that are in line with the company's strategic plan. HR managers need to support the organizational productivity and performance management efforts and must be involved in designing strategic plans not just executing them.

Strategic HRM and Changing Landscapes of Business Environment

SHRM is considered a relatively new concept, despite its continuous development over the past two decades. Although there is no agreement on a precise definition of SHRM among researchers and academicians, broad consensus has been reached on its basic functions, which involves designing and implementing a set of reliable policies and practices to ensure that the human resource of a firm contributes to the achievement of its business objectives (Schuler and MacMillan, 1984; Baird and Meshoulam, 1988; Jackson and Schuler, 1995). Essentially, SHRM emphasises developing the firm's capacity to respond to the external environmental threats through a better utilization of human resources. Since strategy is the course of action of a business firm to deal with and to meet the challenges of the environment, a human capital reservoir with a wide variety of skills that are complementary to the corporate strategy, is a catalyst for fulfilling the strategic goals through promoting desired behaviour among employees. Strategic human resource Management (SHRM) is a set of human resource strategies designed and implemented to ensure that business objectives are achieved (Baird & Meshoulam, 1988; Delery & Doty, 1996; Huselid, et al., 1997; Jackson & Schuler, 1995). Strategic human resource management (SHRM) is a strategic approach to manage human resources of an organization. It is the linkage between the HRM and strategic goals and objectives to improve business performance and develop organizational culture that foster innovation and flexibility. By combining the HRM function with business strategy, SHRM reflects a more flexible arrangement and utilisation of human resources to achieve the organizational goals, and accordingly help organizations gain a competitive advantage (Wei, 2006). Hendry & Pettigrew (1986) view, SHRM as a logical approach to people management which is based on the organizational philosophy and the strategy wherein people are considered as the strategic resource for creating competitive advantage. The linkage between HR practice and business strategy has been emphasised in studies related to SHRM (Miles and Snow, 1984; Baird & Meshoulam, 1988; Wright and McMahan, 1992; Kazmi and Ahmad, 2001; Devanna et al., 1981; Torrington and Hall, 1995). Strategic view of HRM can be explained as shown in Figure 2.

Figure 2.

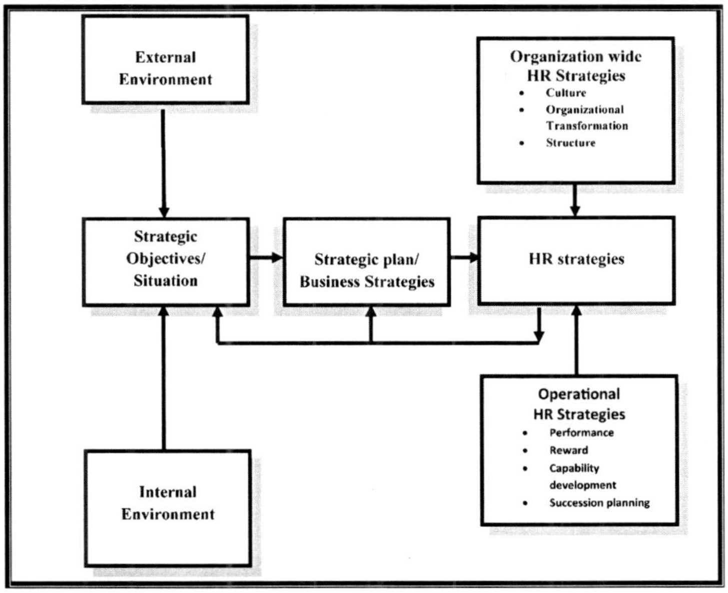

Theoretical Foundations of Strategic HRM

A number of theoretical **models** have been developed for the design and implementation of human resource practices and processes. There are general models named as universalistic, the contingency and configurational (Delery and Doty, 1996) or as best practice and best fit and configurational (Richardson and Thompson, 1999) and particular models namely high performance management, high commitment management and high involvement management. As emphasized by Armstrong and Baron (2004), the best practice approach focuses on adopting a set of universally effective HR practices whereas the best fit focuses on situational factors as there cannot be any universal prescription for HRM policies and practices. The configurational approach is concerned with adopting a set or bundle of HR practices rather than any single HR program or policy. MacDuffie (1995), Richardson and Thompson (1999) concluded that a firm with bundles of HR practices should have a higher level of fit with its corporate strategy. But the problem with this approach is how to decide which bundle of HR practices better suites the organization. High performance working model involves the development of a number of interrelated approaches, which together make an impact on the performance of the firm through its people. The organizational effectiveness is achieved by enhancing the skills and engaging the enthusiasm of the employees (Stevens, 1998). The high commitment management model emphasizes on the importance of enhancing mutual commitment. Walton (1985) and Wood (1996) define high commitment management as a style of management which aims at obtaining a commitment so that behaviour is primarily self regulated rather than controlled. The high commitment management model is concerned with creating high levels of trust within the organizations. The high involvement management model involves treating employees as partners in the enterprise whose interests are respected and who have a say in the matters related to them. Scholars have identified a clear evidence that high involvement work practices result in superior performance. Which theoretical model is correct and practically possible, probably answer to this question is not simple. Each model points out the different aspects of the process needed for developing SHRM. Best fit is perhaps more useful in developing the HR strategies. **Strategic fit** refers to the utilisation of human resources to help the organization to achieve its goals. It is the pattern of planned human resource deployments and activities intended to enable the firm to achieve its goal (Wright and McMahan, 1992). Scholars suggest that there are two kinds of fit: straight or horizontal fit and upright or vertical fit. Horizontal fit is the fit among the number of HRM practices and policies. It refers to the alignment among the various HRM practices (Baird & Meshoulam, 1988). The vertical fit refers to the alignment of HRM practices with the strategic management processes of the firm (Schuler & Jackson, 1987). Vertical fit is viewed as a vital step towards attaining the organizational goals through formulating the human resource practices that are aligned with firm's objectives, while horizontal fit is essential when making good use of these resources. The concept of fit can be explained as shown in Figure 3.

The linkage between HR practices and strategy has been studied by various researchers and scholars (Wright and McMahan, 1992; Wright and Snell, 1998). Due to the lack of in depth empirical evidence, it is debated that this linkage is weaker as compared to the relationship ps among internal HR practices. However, from the perspective of the resource based view (RBV) of the firm (Barney, 1986, 1991), researchers advocate that the HR system which is aligned with the firm's strategy is helpful for creating competitive advantage. Resource based model (Barney, 1995) is based on the idea that organizations gain competitive advantage when they possess resources that are valuable, rare and difficult for competitors to imitate. The aim of the RBV is to improve the capability of resources. It can develop strategic capability i.e. achieving strategic fit between resources and opportunities and obtaining added value from the effective deployment of resources (Barney, 2001). Furthermore, the linkage of organizational resources and firm strategy cannot be easily identified and imitated by other firms due to the complexities and causal ambiguity (Barney, 1991; Boxall, 1998). Thus, the integration of human resources with the appropriate strategy can generate a sustained competitive advantage for the firm. A fundamental problem faced by a firm is: how to decide and formulate the bundle or package of human resource practices necessary for its strategy and overall performance. Now the question is what are the issues or factors influencing the achievement of horizontal fit and vertical fit? Since achieving both kinds of fit is necessary for the performance of the organization, an examination of the relevant determinants of fit is helpful to better understand the nature of SHRM as well as its contribution to organizational performance.

Determinants of Fit

An apparent question here is: How can organizations effectively adopt, implement and make best use of HRM practices for significant firm level outcomes? i.e. how can firms increase the probability that the HRM practices, they adopt and implement will lead to organizational performance. There are a number of factors that influence the congruence among the various human resource practices as well as the alignment between HR practices and the organizational strategic plan. The determinants of fit can further be classified as HR system related factors, individuals related factors and organizational level factors. The system related factors refer to the factors that are related to the HR subsystem – its philosophy, policy and position in the organization. The individuals related factors refer to the personal capabilities or strengths, weaknesses, leadership style, conceptual skills, business orientation etc. of the individuals who are responsible for formulating and implementing the HR strategies. The organizational level factors refer to the overall organizational focus, the organizational objectives, structure and the organizational culture. Bundle or choices of the

Figure 3.

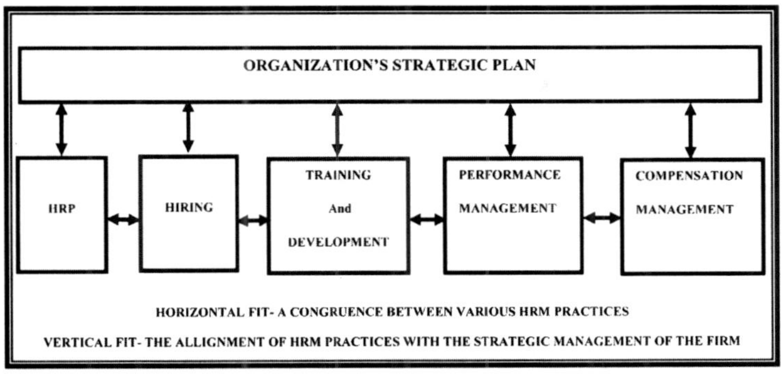

practices available with the human resource department provide the options to the human resource functionaries to decide upon the best suitable practices. Bhattacharya and Wright (2005) suggested that human resource option could be useful in this regard. Investment (direct and indirect) in human resource development is another important factor that determines the congruence among various HRM practices (Pfeffer and Slancik, 1978). With regard to individual or personal factors, the various researches (Lado and Wilson, 1994; Lado, Boyd and Wright, 1992; Wie and Lau, 2005) suggest that personal factors such as personal capabilities, leadership style, commitment, knowledge and skills are important factors that determine the strategic fit among the various HR practices as well as the business strategic plan. To ensure that HRM plays an important role in achieving the strategic objectives of the organization, the human resource professionals need to have certain competencies. Members of the HR function should have the appropriate competencies to increase the likelihood of effective implementation of HRM practices (Huselid, et al., 1997). The concept of determinants of strategic fit can be explained as shown in Figure 4.

The figure clearly outlines the various factors or determinants of strategic fit that influence the congruence among different HR practices and their alignment with the over all organizational strategic plan. With regard to vertical fit, besides system and individual related factors, the organizational factors also play an important role. The types of strategy, organizational culture, the value system, and the organizational philosophy are important determinant of vertical fit (Schuler and Jackson, 1987). The influence of nature of strategy has been demonstrated by Martell, Gupta and Carroll (1996). Organizational culture and values shape the HRM practices (Wie and Lau, 2005). The strategic fit is also influenced by the economic conditions, structure of the industry, the supply of human resources etc. (Lengnick and Hall, 1998). Truss and Gratton (1994) refer to the external environment as the one that provides opportunities and constraints for HR managers. Sparrow & Pettigrew (1987) identify the external factors like technology, political, social and economic conditions as that influence the HR practices. They also point out that organizational philosophy, culture, structure interact with the external environment in the process of HRM.

STRATEGIC HRM AND BUSINESS PERFORMANCE

Researchers have evidenced the strong relationship between HRM practices and **organizational performance** (Huselid, 1995; Pfeffer, 1998). A survey conducted by Guest et al (2000b) revealed that there was a strong association between human

Figure 4.

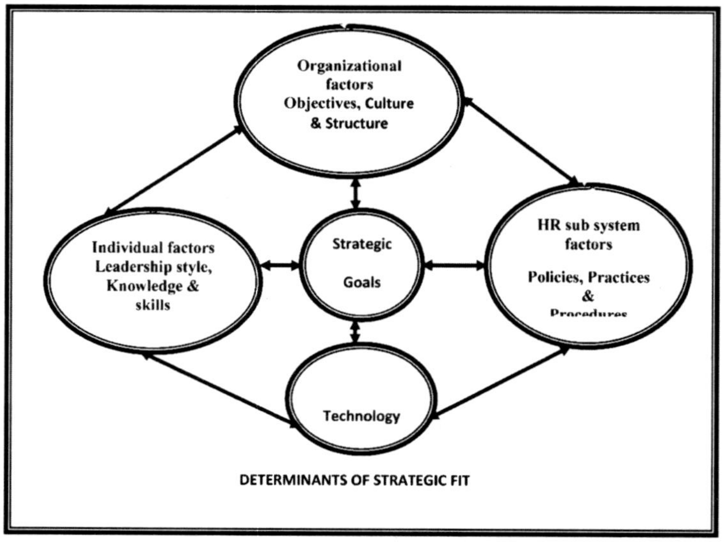

resource management and performance of the organization. In consistent with the aforementioned objectives to investigate the key dimensions of strategic human resource management, besides the analysis of the various models of SHRM, a pilot survey was also carried out through an unstructured interview with the executives of Oil and Gas industry. After analyzing the interview findings, we have concluded that strategic human resource management is not just about procuring, developing and retaining the high potential individuals rather it is about creating a system that aligns the organizational strategic plan with the human resource strategies of the organization. In essence it entails creating a strategy centric organization. Coherent and integrated strategic human resource management system is likely to be developed only if the organization recognizes and proceeds with the strategic importance associated with management of people in the organization. Strategic human resource management addresses organization wide issues (cultural priorities, structural priorities and transformational issues) along with the core areas of human resource management. From the discussions, the following issues emerge.

1. There is considerable evidence that HR has the strategic value for the organizations.
2. There is a considerable relationship between strategic HRM practices and employee behaviour.
3. There is a considerable relationship between strategic HRM practices and organizational performance.
4. There is comparatively high degree of strategic fit between HRM practices and the organizational objectives in the high performing firms from those in the low performing firms.
5. Finally, environmental context variables like firm size, technology and union status affect the extent of implementing HRM practices.

Essential elements in developing strategic human resource management and thereby contributing to the organizational performance are:

1. **Transforming the HR functionaries** - Based upon the resource based view of the firm, Huselid, Jackson and Schuler (1997) differentiated traditional HRM activities

from strategic HRM activities. In the traditional role, staff members need to be specialist in certain personnel functional activities such as attracting high quality employees, placing them in appropriate positions, training them to work in the firm's specific way, and motivating them to devote more efforts to organizational goals. Strategic fit will be enhanced if the HR staff members and other functionaries are well equipped with the organizational development concept, tools and techniques. They need to share responsibility for performance and profitability, be customer driven, focus on solutions not on activities, be strategic, initiate, and lead.

2. **Restructuring of HR department and enhancing administrative efficiency** – As with many other forms of organizational restructuring, a key issue in designing strategic human resource is to determine which activities should be centralized and which should be decentralized. Companies like Warner – Lambert, Motorola, and Coca cola have created new organization structure to realign the roles. Beer et al, (1984) and Walton (1985) describe a high level of functional flexibility, with the abandonment of potentially rigid job descriptions, a heavy reliance on team structure, structuring work and problem solving are some of the ways for high commitment. Restructuring of HR department and enhancing its administrative efficiency is very essential for effective strategy formulation, strategic fit and strategy implementation.
3. **Integrating HR into strategic planning** – In order to achieve the strategic fit (Horizontal as well as vertical fit) HR must play a role of the partner in the strategic planning or strategy formulation process. Ulrich (1998) is of the view that HR executives should impel and guide serious discussion of how the company should be organized to carry out its strategy. Tyson (1985) discusses HR should integrate their activities closely with top management and ensure that they serve a long term strategic purpose. HR people have the capability to identify business opportunities, to see the broad picture, and to see how their HR role can help to achieve the company's business objectives. The same is also evidenced by Armstrong (2001). One important aspect of integrating the HR with strategic planning is to decide about the role, position and status of the HR executives in comparison to other top executives. The strategic fit will be enhanced when the HR functionaries play a role of a partner in strategic planning process.
4. **Developing partnership with line managers** – It is impossible for HR activities to have a significant impact of HR practices and to enhance the strategic fit if those performing the HR functions do not work closely with line managers. Development of partnership between line managers and HR staff is critical. Lucent Technologies provide a very good example of partnership between HR and line management. To become a business partner the HR managers must learn the firm's business, be more responsive about the needs and direction of the business and demonstrate how critical HR is to the success of the business.
5. **Measuring and benchmarking the HRM impact** – In order to make the contribution to the organizational performance or to enhance the contribution of HR practices to the organizational performance, the HR activities or practices are to be measured in terms of return on investment. Customer reaction approach can also be a useful tool for this purpose. It is very important for HR to carry out a customer (other departments) survey to evaluate the effectiveness of its practices. An example of Kodak is

very relevant to mention, it uses a variety of measures and approaches to measure the impact of its HRM practices.

FUTURE TRENDS

The organizations have entered a new era: the emergence of **talent management,** wherein the business is facing a new set of strategic issues that have stemmed out of the changed landscapes of business environment. Shift in the demographic composition of societies, increase in the expectations of people from the business, political and economical instability in certain regions, terrorism, inadequate infrastructure and substandard quality education in the developing countries are some of the critical issues faced by the organizations that have led them into the war for talent. There is a great need for systems and processes that can address the challenges.

Since 1997 when McKinsey coined the term war for talent, it has become a buzz word in the board rooms, among consultants, service and technology providers etc. A survey conducted by Society for Human Resource Management reports that, as many as 53% of the organizations have specific talent management initiatives in place. Out of these companies 76% have talent management on top priority and 85% of human resource functionaries in these companies work in close coordination with top management to implement talent management strategies. Every organization irrespective of the industry is talking about talent management and its contribution in creating high performance work system. Talent management is now being viewed as a key business process and a driver for organizational success. Over a decade since McKinsey initiated the talk on talent management, a lot has been written by the consultants, practiceners and the technology providers without much understanding and clarity about the topic. The term has been defined from different perspectives. All of which give different establishment of meaning to the same set of practices within different organizations. Therefore a need emerges for the future research in the area of talent management. Besides this, the technological advancements such as mobile computing and **pervasive computing** have also changed the nature of business, as a result new terms like E- Business and pervasive business have emerged. Human resource management being the integral part of business has to embrace such technological advancements if it really wishes to be considered as a strategic business partner. These advancements further open new areas of research such as human centered pervasive computing i.e to make the interactions of human beings and computing devices very natural. The time is not very far when the vision of Mark Weisers will become a reality. Many projects on pervasive computing have already begun. Oxygen at MIT, Aura at Carnegie Mellon, and Endeavour at UC Berkley are some of the examples of recent research work in the area of pervasive computing. Pervasive computing soon may help the organizations to make their human resource practices more efficient so that they have the right talent at the right place at the right time so that everyone performs at their highest standard. There is a great possibility that pervasive computing may help the human resource function to become a pervasive function. Research on the application of pervasive computing in human resource management will help to develop new models of strategic human resource management.

CONCLUSION

On the basis of overwhelming evidences we may conclude that progressive human resource practices improve business performance. Organizations gain competitive advantage when they adopt a strategic and rational approach to people management. The new economic order has provided an opportunity as well a challenge to human resource management and its functionaries to play an important role in achieving the strategic objectives of the organization. They are not required to implement the organizational strategies only but to play an active role in designing and formulating the strategies. For this they need to have a multidisciplinary approach and an understanding of the business goals. HR functionaries have got to play significant role in addressing challenges of fast changing business scenario as well as enhancing the strategic fit between the HR practices and organizational strategic plan. Taking the strategic approach to human resource management involves making the function of managing the human assets the most important priority in the organizations and integrating all human resource policies and procedures with the company strategy.

REFERENCES

Armstrong, M. (2001). *A Handbook of Human Resource Management Practice* (8th ed.). London: Kogan Page.

Armstrong, M., & Baron, A. (2004). Strategic HRM: *The key to improved business performance. Encyclopedia of Human Resource Development* (Vol. 5). Mumbai: Jaico Publication.

Babbage, C. (1832). *On the Economy of Machinery and Manufacturers*. London: Charles Night.

Baird, L., & Meshoulam, I. (1988). Managing two fits of strategic human resource management. *Academy of Management Review, 13*(1), 116–128. doi:10.2307/258359

Barnard, C. I. (1938). *The Functions of the Executive*. Cambridge, MA: Harvard University Press.

Barney, J. (1986). Types of competition and the theory of strategy: Toward an integrative framework. *Academy of Management Review, 11*(3), 791–800. doi:10.2307/258397

Barney, J. (1991). Firm resources and sustained competitive advantage. *Journal of Management, 17*(1), 99–120. doi:10.1177/014920639101700108

Barney, J. (1995). Looking inside for competitive advantage. *The Academy of Management Executive, 9*(4), 49–61.

Barney, J. (2001). Is the resource-based view a useful perspective for strategic management research? Yes. *Academy of Management Review, 26*, 41–56. doi:10.2307/259393

Beer, M., Spector, B., Lawrence, P., Quinn-Mills, D., & Walton, R. (1984). *Managing Human Assets*. New York: The Free Press.

Bhattacharya, M., & Wright, P. M. (2005). Managing human assets in an uncertain world: Applying real options theory to HRM. *International Journal of Human Resource Management, 16*(6), 929–948.

Boxall, P. (1998). Achieving competitive advantage through human resource strategy: Towards a theory of industry dynamics. *Human Resource Management Review, 8*(3), 265–288. doi:10.1016/S1053-4822(98)90005-5

Delery, J. E., & Doty, D. H. (1996). Modes of theorizing in strategic human resource management: Tests of universalistic, contingency, and configurational performance predictions. *Academy of Management Journal, 39*, 802–835. doi:10.2307/256713

Devanna, M. A., Fombrun, C., & Tichy, N. M. (1981). Human resource management: A strategic perspective. *Organizational Dynamics, 9*(3), 51–68. doi:10.1016/0090-2616(81)90038-3

Guest, D., Michie, I., Sheehan, M., & Conway, N. (200b). *Employee relations, HRM & Business Performance: An analysis of the 1998 Workplace Employee Relations Survey*. London: Institute of Personnel & Development.

Hendry, C., & Pettigrew, A. (1986). The practice of strategic human resource management. *Personnel Review*, *15*, 2–8. doi:10.1108/eb055547

Huselid, M. A. (1995). The impact of human resource management practices on turnover, productivity, and corporate financial performance. *Academy of Management Journal*, *38*(3), 635–672. doi:10.2307/256741

Huselid, M. A., Jackson, S. E., & Schuler, R. S. (1997). Technical and strategic human resource management effectiveness as determinants of firm performance. *Academy of Management Journal*, *40*(1), 171–188. doi:10.2307/257025

Jackson, S. E., & Schuler, R. S. (1995). Understanding human resource management in the context of organizations and their environments. In J. T. Spence, J. M. Darley & D. J. Foss (Eds.), *Annual review of psychology, 46* (pp. 237–264). Palo Alto, CA: Annual Reviews, Inc.

Kazmi, A., & Ahmad, F. (2001). Differing approaches to strategic human resource management. *Journal of Management Research*, *1*(3), 133–140.

Khanka, S. S. (2003). *Human Resource Management* (1st ed.). New Delhi: S.Chand & Co.

Lado, A. A., Boyd, N. G., & Wright, P. (1992). A competency-based model of sustainable competitive advantage: Toward a conceptual integration. *Journal of Management*, *18*(1), 77–91. doi:10.1177/014920639201800106

Lado, A. A., & Wilson, M. C. (1994). Human resource systems and sustained competitive advantage: A competency-based perspective. *Academy of Management Review*, *19*(4), 699–727. doi:10.2307/258742

Lengnick-Hall, C. A., & Lengnick-Hall, M. L. (1998). Strategic human resource management: A review of the literature and a proposed typology. *Academy of Management Review*, *13*(3), 454–470. doi:10.2307/258092

MacDuffie, J. P. (1995). Human resource bundles and manufacturing performance: Organizational logic and flexible production systems in the world auto industry. *Industrial & Labor Relations Review*, *48*(2), 197–221. doi:10.2307/2524483

Martell, K., Gupta, A., & Carroll, S. J. (1996). Human resource management practices, business strategies, and firm performance: A test of strategy implementation theory. *Irish Business and Administrative Research*, *17*(1), 18–35.

Miles, R. E., & Snow, C. C. (1984). Designing strategic human resource management systems. *Organizational Dynamics*, *28*(3), 62–74.

Owen, R. A. (1825). *A New View of Society*. New York: E.Blis & White.

Pfeffer, J. (1998). *The Human Equation: Building Profits by Putting People First*. Boston: Harvard Business School Press.

Pfeffer, J., & Salancik, G. (1978). *The external control of organizations: A resource dependence perspective*. New York: Harper & Row.

Richardson, R., & Thompson, M. (1999). *The Impact of People Management Practices on Business Performance: A literature review.* London: Institute of Personnel and Development.

Schuler, R. S., & Jackson, S. E. (1987). Linking competitive strategies with human resource management practices. *Academy of Management Executive*, *1*(3), 207–219.

Schuler, R. S., & MacMillan, I. C. (1984). Gaining competitive advantage through human resource management practices. *Human Resource Management*, *23*(3), 241–256. doi:10.1002/hrm.3930230304

Smith, A. (1776). *An Enquiry into the Nature and Causes of Wealth of Nations*. Oxford: Clarendon, 1976.

Sparrow, P. R., & Pettigrew, A. M. (1987). Britain's training problems: The search for a strategic human resource management approach. *Human Resource Management*, *26*(1), 109–128. doi:10.1002/hrm.3930260107

Stevens, J. (1998). *High Performance Working is for Every One*. London: Institute of Personnel and Development.

Taylor, F. W. (1911). *Principles of Scientific Management*. New York: Harper & Brothers.

Torrington, D., & Hall, L. (1995). *Personnel Management: Human Resource Management in Action*. London: Prentice-Hall.

Truss, C., & Gratton, L. (1994). Strategic human resource management: A conceptual approach. *International Journal of Human Resource Management*, *5*, 663–686.

Tyson, S. (1985). Is this the very model of a modern personnel manager? *Personnel Management*, *26*, 35–39.

Ulrich, D. (1998). A new mandate for human resources. *Harvard Business Review*, *76*(1), 124–135.

Ulrich, D., & Brockbank, W. (2005). *The HR Value Proposition*. Boston: Harvard Business School Press.

Walton, R. E. (1985). From control to commitment in the workplace. *Harvard Business Review*, *63*, 76–84.

Wei, L. (2006). Strategic human resource management: Determinants of fit. *Research and Practice in Human Resource Management*, *14*(2), 49–60.

Wei, L., & Lau, C. M. (2005). Market orientation, HRM importance and HRM competency: Determinants of SHRM in Chinese firms. *International Journal of Human Resource Management*, *16*(10), 1901–1918. doi:10.1080/09585190500298586

Wood, S. (1996). High commitment management and organisation in the UK. *International Journal of Human Resource Management*, (February): 41–58.

Wright, P. M., & McMahan, G. C. (1992). Theoretical perspectives for strategic human resource management. *Journal of Management*, *18*(2), 295–320. doi:10.1177/014920639201800205

Wright, P. M., & Snell, S. A. (1998). Toward a unifying framework for exploring fit and flexibility in strategic human resource management. *Academy of Management Review*, *23*(4), 756–772. doi:10.2307/259061

ADDITIONAL READINGS

Barney, J. (1996). The resource-based theory of the firm. *Organization Science*, *7*, 469. doi:10.1287/orsc.7.5.469

Becker, B. E., & Gerhart, B. (1996). The impact of human resource management on organizational performance: Progress and prospects. *Academy of Management Journal*, *39*, 779–802. doi:10.2307/256712

Becker, B. E., & Huselid, M. A. (1998). High performance work systems and firm performance: A synthesis of research and managerial implications. *Research in Personnel and Human Resources Management*, *16*, 53–101.

Becker, B. E., & Huselid, M. A. (2006). Strategic human resources management: Where do we go from here? *Journal of Management*, *32*(6), 898–925. doi:10.1177/0149206306293668

CIPD. (2001b). *The change agenda: People management and business performance*. London, Charted Institute of Personnel and Development.

Decenzo, D. A., & Robbins, S. P. (2005). *Fundamentals of Human Resource Management* (8th ed.). New Delhi: Wiley India.

Delery, J. E. (1998). Issues of fit in strategic human resource management: Implications for research. *Human Resource Management Review, 8*(3), 289–310. doi:10.1016/S1053-4822(98)90006-7

Dessler, G. (2008). *Human Resource Management* (10th ed.). New Delhi: Dorling Kindersley.

Ferris, G. R., Hochwarter, W. A., Buckley, M. R., Harrell-Cook, G., & Frink, D. D. (1999). Human resource management: Some new directions. *Journal of Management, 25*(3), 385–415. doi:10.1177/014920639902500306

Huang, T. (1998). The Strategic level of human resource management and organizational performance: An empirical investigation. *Asia Pacific Journal of Human Resources, 36*(2), 59–72. doi:10.1177/103841119803600206

Jyothi, P., & Venkatesh, D. N. (2006). *Human Resource Management*. New Delhi: Oxford University Press.

Katz, R. H., Long, D., Satyanarayanan, M., & Tripathi, S. (1996, October). *Workspaces in the Information Age*. In report of the NSF Workshop on Workspaces in the Information Age. Leesberg,VA.

Khilji, S. E., & Wang, X. (2006). Intended and implemented HRM: The missing linchpin in strategic human resource management research. *International Journal of Human Resource Management, 17*(7), 1171–1189. doi:10.1080/09585190600756384

Mathis, R. L., & Jackson, J. H. (2003). *Human Resource Management* (10th ed.). Bangalore: South Western.

Pfeffer, J. (1994). *Competitive Advantage through People*. Boston: Harvard Business School Press.

Pfeffer, J. (2005). Producing sustainable competitive advantage through the effective management of people. *The Academy of Management Executive, 19*(4), 95–106.

Ployhart, R. E. (2006). Staffing in the 21st Century: New Challenges and Strategic Opportunities. *Journal of Management, 32*(6), 868–898. doi:10.1177/0149206306293625

Satyanarayanan, M.(2001). *Pervasive Computing: Vision and Challenges*. IEEE personal Communications.

Singh, K. (2003). Strategic HR orientation and firm performance in India. *International Journal of Human Resource Management, 14*(4), 530–543. doi:10.1080/0958519032000057574

Tyson, S. (2006). *Essentials of Human Resource Management* (5th ed.). New Delhi: Elsevier.

KEY TERMS AND DEFINITIONS

Competitive Advantage: an edge that a firm enjoys or has over another firm. It is an inimitable or incomparable ability of the organization that creates the value and distinguishes it from the competitors.

Human Resource Management (HRM): HRM refers to the people management practices that the organizations adopt to ensure that people perform at the optimum level. Human resource management encompasses all the activities that are undertaken right from recruitment to separation of the people. It is concerned with the initiating a system (Policies, plans and practices) to ensure effective and efficient utilization of the human capital to accomplish the strategic intentions of the organization.

Human Resource: refers to all men and women working in the organization. It includes the qualitative (knowledge, skills and abilities) and quantitative (numbers) aspects of people.

Strategic Fit: refers to the appropriateness of various organizational strategies to achieve the strategic intentions of the organization. In case of strategic human resource management, it refers to the suitability of human resource management policies, practices and strategies to achieve the overall organizational objectives. Generally there are two types of strategic fit; vertical and horizontal. Vertical fit refers to the alignment of HRM practices with the strategic objectives of the organization whereas horizontal fit is the congruence among various HRM strategies.

Strategic Human Resource Management (SHRM): designing and implementing a set of internally consistent policies and practices that ensure the human capital of a firm contributes to the achievement of its business objectives. Essentially, SHRM emphasises developing the firm's capacity to respond to the external environment through a better deployment of human resources. SHRM seeks to link the human resource management practices with strategic goals to improve business performance.

Strategy: A plan of action that the organization assumes based on its strategic position and intentions.

Section 5
Pervasive Computing and Financial Systems

Section 5 includes five chapters. Chapter 12, "Automatic Trading System Design", describes ATS principles and the lifecycle of design of Automatic Trading System that can support various processes such as investment decision making process, defining Future contracts and various trading states, etc. The chapter explains various phases focusing on the proper environment selection, appropriate set of tools selection, and the automatic trading system creation which has to follow rules of money (risk) management and trading psychology. Finally it covers testing and optimization concepts. Chapter 13, "Pervasive Computing, Firm Characteristics, and Environmental Factors Conductive to the Adoption of Activity-Based Costing: Evidence from Bahrain", provides evidence on the contextual features of firms adopting Activity-Based Costing (ABC) compared to those not adopting ABC. It looks at organisational and business environment variables which appear to have influenced the adoption of ABC including computing usage. Chapter 14, "The effects of innovative instruments to market participants and the financial system: The particular role of information technologies", focuses on risk management in financial institutions and discusses various financial innovations that triggered new ways in which financial institutions and Corporate cope with credit risk since the advent of credit derivatives. The chapter explains how advanced computerization is by large the most important factor for the wide use of credit derivatives and what are its benefits to banks, such as more efficient loans portfolio management, further business expansion and confidentiality, etc. Chapter 15, "Bivariate causality between FDI inflows and economic growth in India since 1990", describes the direct relationship between the flow of FDI and economic development and analyses the existence and nature of causalities, between FDI and economic growth in India since 1990, where growth of economic activities and FDI has been one of the most pronounced. Chapter 16, "Regional and Sectoral Disparities in Inflow of FDI in India-An Empirical Analysis", depicts the disparity between states in India and a shift from primary and secondary sectors to tertiary sectors and pervasive computing areas. It explains that during the last two decades, Foreign Direct Investment (FDI) has become most important source of finance and therefore increasingly important in the developing world and lots of developing countries including India are willing to attract substantial amounts of inward FDI. This chapter analyses the regional and sectoral disparities in Inflow of FDI in India since 1990.

Chapter 12
Automatic Trading System Design

Petr Tucnik
University of Hradec Kralove, Czech Republic

ABSTRACT

This chapter will focus on the problem of design of automatic trading system for futures trading, specifically its design lifecycle. This is a task that can be divided into several phases. In this chapter we focus on the selection of proper environment (i.e. choose the right market and commodity), choosing appropriate set of tools (fundamental or technical analysis indicators) and creating the automatic trading system itself, which has to follow rules of money (risk) management and trading psychology. The chapter stresses the importance of the system's acceptability for the user. The last phase covers the topic of testing and optimization. This chapter provides a general overview of each of these phases together with a discussion of typical issues.

INTRODUCTION

The futures trading became electronic business when widespread use of internet technologies occurred. There exist many electronic markets since 90's and at present day they are equal in both size (quantity) and importance to the traditional trading. When the electronic trading became possible, the computing power of computers allowed many tasks to be automated. It is possible to automatically process market data and to perform the analysis very quickly, automating part of the decision-making process and leaving only small part of the work to be handled by trader.

From the point of view of electronic trading, it is trading of stocks that are in the centre of interest of scientific community. There are several differences between stock trading and futures trading. Discussion about the differences can be found in e.g. (Williams, 1979, pp. 17-20). But there is much in common for both types of trading and we will not be strictly separating stock trading from commodities (futures) trading. In the following text whenever the notion "trading" is mentioned, it is a

DOI: 10.4018/978-1-60566-996-0.ch012

futures trading that we have in mind. Many (not all) indicators useful for the futures markets are useful for trading stocks as well and vice versa. The principle is usually similar.

This chapter is focused on lifecycle of design of automatic trading system. Its purpose is to present and summarize rules of design, important notes on the topic and discussion of typical issues. No specific automatic trading system will be presented in this text. However, as we hope, it may bring some interesting insights into this problem area.

The investment decision-making process consists basically of two parts. First part of this process is fundamental analysis, second part is technical analysis. For the purpose of automatic trading it is a technical analysis that is more important for us. But best outcome is archived when both parts takes place in the decision-making process. Because this matter will be discussed in the following text for the moment it could be said that fundamental analysis represents the "what", while technical analysis is the "when". The concept of fundamental analysis in commodity trading is covered in (Dunsby, 2008). Dunsby (2008) is focused on selected categories of commodities only – energies, grains and oilseeds, livestock, industrial materials, softs. However, this publication gives reader the right perspective of fundamental analysis importance and application on real-life situations.

The cycle of steps of system design is usually done during the mentioned investment decision-making process (IDMP), allowing some part of this process to be automated. It is not necessary to have automated the whole IDMP. An automatic trading system (ATS) may cover only the technical analysis part and provide the best outcome of the applied indicators to the user in order to allow him to make the final decision. It is also possible to leave whole process to the ATS itself, but the former solution is usually preferred by traders.

In the following text, we would refer to trader as to "him", instead of "him or her", as it would be more appropriate. By this, we do not mean any disrespect to female traders. This simplification is used in order to make reading easier.

Futures Market Environment

Before we will discuss the topic of ATS design, it is necessary to provide the explanation of terms and mechanisms used for description of futures market environment. These terms will be used in the following parts of this chapter. Readers already familiarized with the topic may proceed to the next part. The books that stand out as good sources of general information for beginners in the area are (Carter, 2006), (Elder, 1993), (Elder, 2002) or (Williams, 1979).

Futures Contracts

The gain of profit is realized by buying or selling futures contracts. Futures contract is a standardized contract to buy or sell a certain underlying instrument at a certain date in the future at a specified price. Futures contracts (or simply futures) are traded on futures exchange and are exchange traded derivatives. The trade is made with actual, not future, price of the commodity.

For differentiation of trading states we use terms open position and closed position. We are in the "open position" when we are in the middle of the trade. I.e. we have the open position when we have either bought some contract(s) and we are waiting for the right moment to sell them (this is called "long position") or we have sold some contract(s) and are waiting for the right moment to buy them back ("short position"). In other words: A long (resp. short) position entails the purchase of futures contracts in anticipation of rising (resp. lower) prices. As soon as the long or short position is terminated it is called the "closed position" and the trade is finished.

The standardization of futures contracts ensures liquidity and marketability. Each country has certain supervisory authorities (regulators),

Table 1. Symbols for futures contract months

Month	Symbol	Month	Symbol	Month	Symbol	Month	Symbol
January	F	April	J	July	N	October	V
February	G	May	K	August	Q	November	X
March	H	June	M	September	U	December	Z

for example in United States it is Commodity Futures Trading Commission (CFTC), National Futures Association (NFA), Futures Industry Association (FIA), Securities and Exchange Commission (SEC) or National Association of Securities Dealers (NASD). For more information see respective web sites. As a result, we may rely on standardized rules of trading and the environment of futures markets can be mechanically processed by an ATS.

It has been said before that futures contract is standardized. This means the futures contract has a finite set of given attributes, defining its properties. Every futures contract may be traded (bought or sold unlimited number of times) in a certain time frame. Together with its name and price, the temporal validity of the contract is one of the most important information.

The validity of the futures contract is limited by two important dates. First is the First Notice Day (FND), second is the Last Trading Day (LTD). The former one refers to the notification of the fact that the futures contract will cease trading in one week and the latter is the last day when the contract may be traded. Usually, there are also certain contract months specified. These define months in which this commodity is traded. Symbols for the contract months are in the Table 1.

Other important attribute of each futures contact is a margin. The margin is amount of money used as refundable deposit for each contract. The margin is used to allow trade with large quantities of commodities hidden in each contract. With this relatively small deposit of money, trader may trade with considerably larger amount or merchandise then he could normally do, if he had to pay full price for it. Statistics showed that small speculators focus on relatively small profits, in order of magnitude of $1000 USD. The margin allows these speculators to participate and enhance the market liquidity. The margin height depends on the type of commodity and generally it is higher for more expensive commodity and lower for the cheaper ones. The margin blocks some money on the investment account and it is important to keep it in mind when conducting business.

We distinguish two types of margins:

- Initial margin – it is inserted when the trader enters the open position.
- Maintenance margin – ensures that in the case of unfavorable development is lost only a part of the investment account. It is a minimal amount of money that must remain on the account. When this limit is reached, the broker will do so-called margin-call. Margin-call is a request to raise the amount of money on the account. If no money is added, the broker will close all open positions automatically. This situation must be avoided.

To get an idea what other information could futures contract contain, see Figure 1. As you may see, there is a number of characteristics and it is well beyond the scope of this chapter to discuss it in full detail. More detailed description of all of futures contract's attributes may be found many sites on the web or in (Nesnídal & Podhajský, 2006). Some software trading platforms may omit some of the attributes or display some others not mentioned here, but the most important set

Figure 1. An example of futures contract

Label	Value
Symbol:	C
Name:	Corn (Open Outcry)
Group:	GRAINS
Exchange:	CBOT
Contract Size:	5 000,00
Contract Units:	Bushels
Tic Size:	1 / 4
Minimum Move:	0,250000
Tic Units:	Cents
Full Point Value:	50,00
Init. Margin:	1 350,00
Maint. Margin:	1 000,00
FND: First Notice Day:	29.2.2008
LTD: Last Trading Day:	14.3.2008
Market Open:	09:30:00
Market Close:	13:15:00

One contract represents 5 000,00 Bushels.

A tick, or minimum move is 1 / 4 (0,250000) Cents per Bushels and worth $12.50 per contract.

A full point movement is 1 (1.00) Cents per Bushels and worth $50,00 per contract.

of attributes as it was described above is always present.

Futures Markets

There are many futures markets in the world, but among the most important are futures markets in the United States (specifically Chicago and New York). Environment of these large markets is suitable for the use of ATS because there are many traders present. We have to have ensured high level of liquidity and volume of realized trades in order to process the market with technical analysis tools with success.

The commodity price is usually presented in the form of a graph. Although there are several choices about how to represent the price, the bar chart or candlestick charts are the most popular. Figure 2 is representing price in chosen timeframe (commentary see below).

There are four points of interest:

- High – this is the highest level of price in the given timeframe.
- Low – this is the lowest level of price in the given timeframe.
- Open – this is the initial (opening) price for the given timeframe.
- Close – this is the final (closing) price for the given timeframe.

The timeframe is chosen by the user (trader). In intraday trading (during one day) one bar usually represents several minutes or seconds, in position trading it could be a day or week. The resolution depends on the trader preferences, but the high-definition (intraday) data is usually more expensive.

When applying technical indicators, we are always dealing when applying technical indicators with a probability under 100%. Each indicator has a different level of dependability and absolute certainty cannot be achieved. When there are many traders present on the market then the probability of the price movement is predictable to some degree. But when there is only a small number of traders, the price can be easily influenced and statistical tools cannot be used.

The trade is done by pairing of trading orders. Each order either to buy or sell has to be paired with another order of the opposite kind to conclude the trade. The pairing is made either by the stock market server (electronic trading) or by human trader in the trading pit. Electronic pairing is faster and has lower transaction cost, but many traders still prefer traditional way. During pairing there could occur some delays, it is not done in real-time. This must be taken into account when planning business. This is also another reason why to choose large, well-established futures markets. The pairing is simple when there are thousands of traders – there is always someone who want buy or sell.

Figure 2. The bar chart

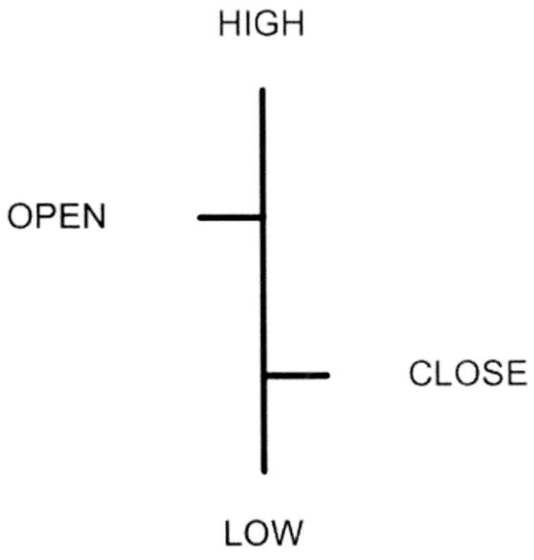

The behavior of the market price is completely dependable on people. Each bar on the graph represents the mood of a big crowd of people. This fact is well described in (Stevens, 2002, p. 9) where the importance of human psychology is stressed. Traders form groups when trading and therefore, group psychology could and should be applied. The outcome of human interaction is realized in form of patterned behavior which can be predicted. Moreover, (according to (Stevens, 2002, p. 9)) since markets are trying to anticipate development in economic and social fundamentals, precise use of technical analysis can help predict those fundamentals.

Other authors (e.g. Elder, 1993) or (Elder 2002) are often emphasizing the psychological aspect of futures trading. In fact, the mood of people is forming the trend. A trend exists when price is continually rising or falling over time. There are three types of trends. Uptrend – each rally and decline reaches higher than the previous one. Downtrend – each decline falls to lower low than the previous decline and each rally stops at lower level than previous one. Trading range – rallies stop at approximately same high and declines stop at approximately same low.

It is much easier to follow the trend than to try to trade against it. Technical analysis tools help recognize crucial moments in the trend development. Therefore, it is necessary to focus on the analysis of the market which is described in the following part.

Technical and Fundamental Analysis

The notions of technical and fundamental analysis were mentioned in the introduction. Both approaches are closely connected because they are trying to describe the same thing – the behavior of the futures contract's price. Excellent source of information on this topic is (Murphy, 1999).

The fundamental analysis is application of deep understanding and knowledge about the selected commodity in order to predict its behavior (price change). E.g. farmer knows everything about the corn he grows – influence of weather, yield, fertilizer effects, treatment price, etc. It is usually difficult and time consuming to obtain this kind of knowledge. Sometimes, the fundamental analysis is also defined as retrogressive comparison of supply and demand. We are interested in the "intrinsic value" of commodity. By comparison of price from the past with actual prices, it is possible to decide whether the actual price is high or low. Other sources of fundamental knowledge are government institutions. E.g. in United States, the Commodity Futures Trading Commission releases the Commitments of Traders (COT) report once a week. This report shows open interest (open positions) of all major groups of traders (commercials, non-commercials and non-reportable positions). The COT is an excellent example of a fundamental indicator. In general, fundamental indicators are worse for machine processing than technical indicators.

The technical analysis is using only the price graph as an input and by application of technical indicators identifies important moments of price behavior. Kaufman (2005, p.1) states that technical analysis is the systematic evaluation of market parameters (such as price, volume, etc.) for the purpose of price forecasting.

Every trading decision should be supported by some technical indicators. Technical analysis is easily made on computers. Apart from mathematical indicators, to the category of technical analysis also belong the graph formations. These formations are recognizable simply by look into the chart – these are special shapes and patterns. It is empirically verified that when some graph formations occur (such as double top, double bottom, head and shoulders, etc.) the market will with high probability move predictably. The graph formations may signal some excellent trading opportunities.

The indicators (both fundamental and technical) form up a powerful set of tools. There are dozens of indicators and many of them have adjustable parameters. According to (Elder, 1993, p. 120) there are three types of indicators:

- Trend-following indicators – this type of indicator is following the trend and in the moment it changes, the trend will change as well. This group includes: moving averages, MACD, MACD-Histogram, Directional System, On-Balance Volume, Accumulation/Distribution, etc.
- Oscillators – help identify turning points. They are running with the trend and their development often changes before the change of prices. They include: Stochastic, Rate of Change, Smoothed Rate of Change, Momentum, RSI, Elder-Ray, Force Index, William %R, Commodity Channel Index, etc.
- Miscellaneous indicators – provides insight into the intensity of bullish (rising trend) or bearish (descending trend) market opinion. They are running with the trend of in front of it. They include: New High-New Low Index, Put-Call Ratio, Bullish Consensus, Commitment of Traders, Advance/Decline Index, Trader's Index, etc.

This list of indicators is not complete, but it is sufficient to get the idea. Because there is such a wide range of tools available, any ATS may be customized to fit the style of trading of its user perfectly. It is a matter of optimization. However, senior experts often warn about the effect of over-optimization. Usually, the strongest systems are also very simple, well-ordered and transparent. Making changes in order to optimize the system may lead to worse performance.

Every trading platform provides a slightly different set of indicators. As we will not discuss details of each of them in this text, any books related to the topic of technical analysis may serve as a source of valuable information. From our list of references, we may recommend (Murphy, 1999), (Elder, 1993), (Nesnídal & Podhajský, 2006), (Williams, 2007), (Aronson, 2007), (Kirkpatrick, 2005) or (Stevens, 2002).

Commissions and Slippage Barrier

In order to generate a profit, we have to overcome a barrier in the form of commissions and slippage and other fees. In fact, every part of the chain connecting trader with the futures market is taking some money from him. See Figure 3 for details.

The chain represents usual way of trading order processing. The first arrow between trader and trading platform is labeled "data and software purchase". Every trader has to pay for data. Although there are some data sources for free, these usually do not provide necessary time resolutions, e.g. for intraday trading. Most of the software trading platforms are also available for a price. These are expenses that have to be taken into account.

The second arrow is labeled "commissions, margins, consultations" – these are payments for services provided by brokers. For every ex-

Figure 3. The payments made by trader

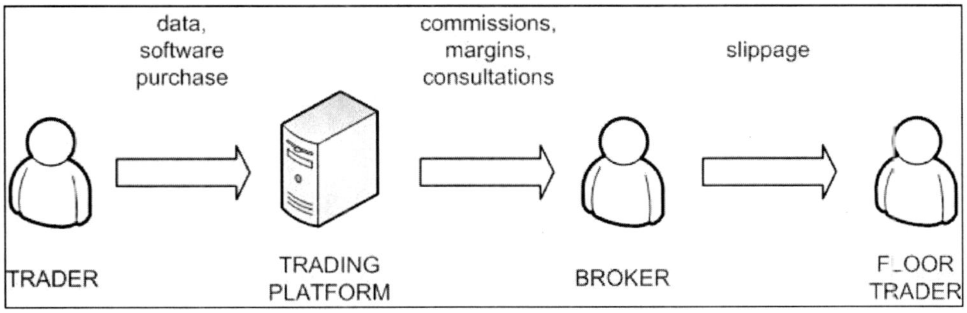

ecuted trade, there is a commission fee, which is deducted from the trading account. Margins are refundable deposits (see part *Futures contracts*) but they block part of portfolio. Consultations are voluntary expenses, but it is usually very useful service for inexperienced traders.

The third arrow between the broker and the floor trader is labeled "slippage". It is explained in (Elder, 1993, pp. 8-9) that the slippage is filling of orders at different price than that which existed when the order was placed. It is common and legal phenomena. Big markets with high levels of liquidity have narrow spreads while on the less frequently traded markets (with lower liquidity) are spreads much wider.

These payments together strongly influence the way of trading. Every trader has to get over the limit represented by the sum of these fees in order to make profit. Therefore, only very good business opportunities have to be accepted. This fact is closely related to the notion of so-called RRR – Risk Reward Ratio. Every trade has certain levels of investment and expected profit. If the expected profit is high enough then it may be profitable to use the opportunity, even if the probability is relatively low. E.g. when the risk/reward ratio is 1:10 and probability of success 25% we succeed in every fourth attempt but it bring us profit of ten times of the invested sum. Because of all the payments involved (represented on the Figure 3), the RRR is more important than probability of success.

Automatic Trading System Principles

Since the rudimentary background information about the futures markets was provided in the second chapter, we may now focus on the ATS principles. We will discuss the issues regarding autonomy of the ATS system, testing data, money management problems and environment selection in this chapter. The purpose of this part is to provide the overview of the ATS functioning. The (Kaufman, 2005) is an excellent source of information on this topic, providing more detailed discussion of all aspects of ATS.

ATS Autonomy Level

One of the most important decisions we have to make is set the level of autonomy for the ATS. There are many software solutions on the market. According to (Elder, 1993, pp. 115-118), these systems may be divided into three categories according to amount of information they provide to trader:

(a) Black Boxes – this solution provides no information to trader. This solution cannot be recommended because the lack of control. This kind of system is usually fully automated and user cannot change or adjust its parameters (or only to a limited extend). Although this solution may work for some time, due to the continuously changing environments of markets these systems are failing in long term use.

(b) Toolboxes – it is the opposite of black box solution. This kind of software provides tools for technical (and sometimes even fundamental) analysis. The description of algorithms is public and all the parameters may be changed by user. This is the choice of professional traders.

(c) Gray Boxes – these systems usually have its main algorithm public and allow the user to adjust some of its parameters. Gray boxes are in the middle between the black box and toolbox solutions. However, part of the process remains hidden from the user and this is the reason why to do not use them.

The most important issue is usually lack of control and information. In order to make the ATS used by traders it has to be fully transparent. This can be in contradiction to the need of trade secret protection. The trader must have confidence in his tools. The confidence cannot be obtained if a part of the process remains hidden from trader. Therefore, only fully open solution may be accepted. Possibility of adjustment and optimization is also required.

Backtesting Data

Before the system is put into use, thorough testing is required. This is a necessary step in the ATS development process. (Kaufman, 2005, pp. 847-934) or (Tinghino, 2008, pp. 215-221) are presenting system testing in more detail.

In the case of futures trading, process of testing is usually called backtesting. The outcome of the backtesting is the backtesting report (also may be called performance report). Example of such report is shown at the Figure 4.

In general, there are two basic sources of training data:

(a) Historical data – these are price graphs of commodities, often going back several decades into past.

(b) Real-time data feed from the stock market.

Both types of data have its advantages and disadvantages.

The historical data is used for testing solutions of special trading situations, or simply for testing the use of ATS in the horizon of months and years. It is more useful to use more recent data because the market is evolving continuously and more recent information is more relevant to the actual situation. The results of performance testing can be obtained in the form showed on the Figure 4.

The real-time data are obtained directly from the stock market. The backtesting on real-time data is very useful because it is extremely close to the real (and actual) situation. There is also a disadvantage in expenses. High quality data feed can be quite expensive (tens of USD dollars per month for each stock market). More detailed time frame of the data means higher cost. But required data time frame depends on the intended way of trading.

Many software platforms also allow incorporation of such features as margins, fees, etc. This makes the simulation very realistic and the results can be very accurate. Every ATS should be tested before practical use.

Money Management Problem

It is well-said in (Elder, 1993, p. 258) that money management should ensure survival. This is the purpose of the money management. Sometimes, it is also called risk management.

The common mistake of beginner traders is investing of a large portion of their money into single trade. Rational money management system allows use of maximum 5% of investment funds. Experts and authors (e.g. Williams, Elder) differ in opinion on how much can be spent, but 2-4%

Figure 4. Example of the performance report. All information about the tested strategy can be found in several tables

Performance Summary			
Total Net Profit	$2,480.00	Profit Factor	1.71
Gross Profit	$5,950.00	Gross Loss	($3,470.00)
Total Number of Trades	99	Percent Profitable	45.45%
Winning Trades	45	Losing Trades	51
Even Trades	3		
Avg. Trade Net Profit	$	Ratio Avg. Win: Avg. Loss	1.94
Avg. Winning Trade	$	Avg. Losing Trade	($68.04)
Largest Winning Trade	$	Largest Losing Trade	($240.00)
Max. Consecutive Winning Trades	6	Max Consecutive Losing Trades	6
Avg. Bars in Winning Trades	5.69	Avg. Bars in Losing Trades	4.29
Avg. Bars in Total Trades	4.93		
Max. Shares/Contracts Held	1	Account Size Required	$570.00
Return on Initial Capital	2.48%	Annual Rate of Return	44.58%
Return Retracement Ratio	5.03	RINA Index	177.80
Trading Period	20 Dys, 9 Hrs, 20 mins	Percent of Time in the Market	35.10%
Max. Equity Run-up	$2,960.00		
Max. Drawdown (Intra-day Peak to Valley)		**Max. Drawdown (Trade Close to Trade Close)**	
Value	($660.00)	Value	($570.00)
Net Profit as % of Drawdown	375.76%	Net Profit as % of Drawdown	435.09%
Max Trade Drawdown	($240.00)		

is most common recommendation. The specific range depends on the type of market. The more volatile markets needs strict money management and even a lower maximum of 1-3% is sometimes recommended; less volatile environment can be traded with maximum of 3-5%. The main idea is to ensure continuation in the case of failure. E.g. when a 4% rule is in effect, it would take sequence of 25 failures to be forced to finish with trading.

Another well-known argument for the sake of good money management is elimination of the critical loss scenario. Generally, any trade may end in one of the following five situations:

- Great profit
- Small profit
- No profit
- Small loss
- Great loss

It is obvious that any kind of loss is something we would like to avoid. Although the loss in general cannot be avoided completely - for we are dealing with uncertainty all the time - it can be minimized to a bearable level. The great loss option may, therefore, be avoided by application of an appropriate money management system.

The stop-loss condition should be implemented as an integral part of any money management system. The stop-loss is special trading order which is automatically triggered when specified price level is reached and it will stop the trade. When buying (resp. selling) futures contract, at the beginning of the trade is the stop-loss order placed near the initial price against direction of anticipated movement of the price. In case of bad prediction, the stop-loss will terminate unsuccessful trade before it reaches the great loss phase. The stop-loss is a powerful tool. It may be moved when the price is moving in desirable direction, securing the profit. Using of stop-loss orders is one of the most accented advices. Trading without the stop-loss is more like gambling and even best trading system may be beaten by a short series of great losses. In order to ensure the profitability of trading system, the stop-loss orders should always be used.

Environment Selection

The selection of an appropriate market (commodity) is very important. The ATS is usually designed to indicate special type of business opportunities and not all types of commodities are equivalently suitable for this kind of analysis. Therefore, a preliminary analysis should be done before the appropriate type of commodity is selected. When choosing a market to trade, be it a stock, a future or an option, it has to meet two criteria: liquidity and volatility. These two attributes are described at the end of this chapter and are the most important for the environment selection.

Type of Trading

One of the most important decisions we have to make in trading is to choose the way of trading we would like to conduct. There are basically two options:

- Position trading – it is focused on the long-term trading. Open positions are hold for more than 1 day. Position trader holds open position for days, weeks, even months or years (holding open positions for months or years is typical for standard stock trading). Position trader is primarily working with charts with timeframe of days, weeks and sometimes months.
- Intraday trading – trading is conducted primarily during the day. Futures contracts are hold for minutes, even hours, but almost never through the night. Typical intraday trader is beginning and finishing his trade when in the stock market's RTH (Regular Trading Hours). Typical timeframe of charts is 1, 2, 5, 15 or 30 minutes.

Intraday trading requires more experience, because decisions have to be made quickly. Trader has enough time for decision making in position trading and this form of trading is not so time-consuming. On the other hand, the intraday trading gives more frequent opportunities for trading, which may bring greater profits.

For the ATS, the intraday trading option may seem more suitable. At the end of the trading day it is easy to evaluate the performance of the system and sum up profits and losses, because trading positions are closed. Moreover, the intraday trading may be alleviated by the ATS use. Still, the ATS may be used for both position and intraday trading, the principles are the same.

There is also a possibility of night sessions trading. This type of trading is done in addition to RTH. Theoretically, it is possible to buy or sell contracts during the night, but it is not recommended. The volume of night session markets is very low; there is also very low liquidity and volatility. It is caused by lack of traders; there are only a few traders conducting business this way. For the mentioned reasons, it is best to avoid night sessions trading with ATS. Signals of ATS during the night session are not reliable. There may also be a problem with pairing of the trading orders.

Electronic or Floor Based Trading

It was mentioned in the introduction that the internet technologies made it possible to easily conduct the electronic trade. Today, most of the stock markets allow both types of trading (meant electronic and floor based) and they are equal. The arbitrages done by floor traders are equalizing prices and there are no differences between prices in electronic or floor based trading. The main difference is in the height of commissions. The commissions are significantly lower for electronic trading (about $10 USD for contract). Classical trading involves higher commissions (circa $40-50 USD). Electronic is also usually faster.

For the purposes of ATS functioning, the electronic trading is more suitable.

Stock Market Selection

Some important information about the futures markets may not be obvious from the charts. As an example of such information can be mentioned the rate of carrying out the trading orders (i.e. pairing, for more details see part *Futures markets*). E.g. the New York stock markets are, according to (Nesnídal & Podhajský, 2006), comparably slower than stock markets in Chicago. This is the reason why many traders prefer Chicago stock market before New York stock market. This may lead to problems with setting the stop-loss orders (see part *Money management problem*), for the time required for trading orders processing can be even several minutes and situation can drastically change during that time.

Volatility

Very important aspect of markets is volatility. The volatility refers to the average trading range. It is a fluctuation range of the price. The trading range is difference between the high and the low of the bar in the bar chart. According to volatility of the market, we may calculate approximate rate of price movements and decide whether we may or may not invest enough money to withstand them.

Liquidity

Liquidity refers to the average (usually daily) volume. The volume is amount of trades conducted during the selected time period. The higher the liquidity, the better, because more traders are present and market orders are filled faster. It is necessary to have a market with high level of liquidity in order to use an ATS.

ATS Lifecycle

The system development process does have several phases that are common for every type of system. This includes:

- Analysis of the problem
- Finding a solution
- Implementation of solution (algorithm)
- Testing
- Use

These steps are similar when designing any system for automatic trading. In this part of the chapter, we will provide more detailed description of each of these phases.

Designing ATS: Description of Process

The development of the ATS is iterative process. This means sometimes we have to return to previous steps and repeat them. Before we start the preparations, it is necessary to clarify:

- What type of trading are we focused on? (position/intraday)
- How much money do we have?
- Which stock market we would like to trade on? (NYBOT, CBOT, etc.)
- What is the cost of commissions for every trade? (depends on broker)

After all these questions are answered, we may proceed to the ATS development. The diagram representing individual steps of this process is shown at the Figure 5.

The first three steps cover fundamental analysis and preparation phase. The fundamental analysis may help to decide which commodity is suitable for our purposes.

(1) Commodity selection – in this step we have to decide which commodity we will be focused on. There are many differences, but among the most important is the margin cost. As we are describing commodity trading from the point of view of small speculator, we are always dealing with a limited account. According to rules described in the part *Money management problem*, we need to

Figure 5. The ATS lifecycle

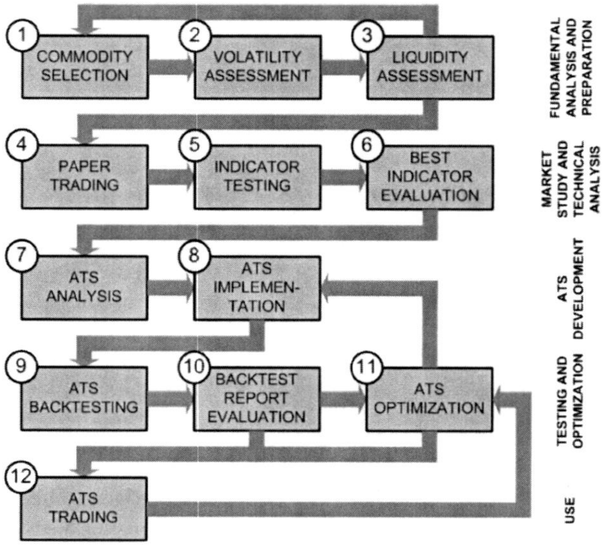

have at least a starting amount of money at our disposal in order to trade. The amount required is usually about $10.000 USD for trading futures (stock trading is financially less demanding). This is the minimum level of financial resources needed. Many broker companies have this as a condition before they start providing their services to trader. More detailed information can be found on web pages of broker companies.

(2) Volatility assessment – the notion of volatility is described in section *Volatility*. This step is important to assure we have the necessary capital. Highly volatile markets are in general more difficult for trading, because they are fast-evolving. E.g. oil markets are usually highly volatile while sugar markets are not. For beginner or inexperienced traders, slower markets are recommended.

(3) Liquidity assessment – the importance of this factor was explained in the part *Liquidity*. The high level of liquidity is necessary for the ATS use. The individual behavior cannot be predicted while the behavior of a large mass of people can be (to a limited extend). Therefore, we have to focus on markets where is price development cannot be influenced by individual traders.

The next sequence of steps is focused on market study and technical analysis:

(4) Paper trading – the notion of paper trading usually refers to trading training. However, in this case, it is necessary to try trading in selected market without risk and get to understand the environment. In order to create a functioning ATS of toolbox type (for details see part *ATS autonomy level*), it is necessary to fully understand the principles of both indicator and the commodity. Elder in (Elder, 2002, p. 145) mentions the "personality" of the market: every market is slightly different than the other and the price movements are specific for each of them. In other words, there may be some rules present, which are obvious only after thorough study. Some simplified performance reports should be generated in this step as well.

(5) Indicator testing – many indicators should be tried before the final set is chosen for implementation. The trader must have full

understanding of the indicator principle before he starts to use them, otherwise it would be a black box situation (which we would like to avoid at all costs). The selection of indicators should be also adjusted to software trading platform capabilities. Trading platforms usually do not support all existing indicators, but only a few of them.

(6) Best indicator evaluation – after the fifth step is finished, the most appropriate set of indicators should be selected. It is usually a beginner trader's mistake to apply a large number of indicators at once. Such approach is contra productive for different indicators give trading signals for different trading opportunities. Selection may be based on correspondence of signals to similar trading opportunities. It is usually recommended by experts (Nesnídal & Podhajský, 2006), (Elder, 1993), (Williams, 2007) to use only a limited number of indicators, the limit is 3 or 4 indicators at once. Simplicity is a key to success in this matter.

Following two steps are representing ATS development phase:

(7) ATS analysis – the output of previous steps gives the foundations for the ATS analysis. Before this phase begins, we know the following: commodity to be traded, market environment, indicators which will be used. We should also have first simplified performance reports for better orientation. This information is sufficient to make analysis of ATS and design its algorithm.

(8) ATS implementation – this step is similar to the standard implementation of small information system. Many trading platforms allow implementation of ATS, but not all of them. Sometimes, the trading platform uses its own programming language. Generally, the simplicity of the process is accented because of traders who are not IT specialists.

The fourth level is focused on testing and optimization:

(9) ATS backtesting – the backtesting is described in section *Backtesting data*. There are two approaches to backtesting: using historical or real data.

(10) Backtest report evaluation – the most important is the long-term profitability of ATS use. We have a specific, clearly defined goal in futures trading and this is the advantage. Profitability may be ensured by two aspects of the trading system – high probability of successful prediction and the RRR. The latter is described in section *Commissions and slippage barrier*. Prediction can always be reliable only to a limited extend. However, more important is the RRR. The system may have only low probability of success, but high RRR will make it more profitable. When commissions and slippage costs are taken into account, it is better to have less highly profitable opportunities than many trades with low-profit.

(11) ATS optimization – optimization is only a natural continuation of testing phase. Although there are no universal rules to follow in this matter, the optimization should not make simple system complicated. The robust, universal systems have usually simple trading idea and simple algorithm, using only a few indicators together. Often, the indicators known for several decades (which may today seem very primitive) are very popular due to their simplicity and understandability. On the other hand, complicated indicators or trading systems make trading signals incomprehensible. It may be necessary to return to the implementation

step (8) in order to implement changes for optimization.

The final step is describing the use of ATS:

(12) ATS trading – in this moment, the ATS is ready for use. However, due to the continuously changing nature of markets, the system functioning today may be useless after some time. Therefore, there should to be a possibility of adaptation or further optimization. This is the known weak spot of black box solutions. These systems cannot adapt to changes of the environment in the long-term use.

These twelve steps describe the lifecycle of ATS development.

Use of ATS

There are reasons to prefer use of the ATS instead of hand trading:

- There is no need to physically trade the system.
- Use of several different strategies simultaneously by using several ATS.
- No time limitations of trading. ATS can trade anytime of the day or night, 24 hours a day.
- Trading is less affected by human psychology, even if the ATS is used as decision-support tool.
- Application for business environments (markets) that are difficult for a human to trade because of a large amount of business opportunities or simply because of frequent occurrence of important signals. It is virtually impossible for a human to maintain concentration for long periods of time – ATS can help solve this problem.
- It is easy to monitor the performance.

On the other hand, there are drawbacks related to the use of ATS:

- Continuous change of environment. Even good adaptation or machine learning algorithms may not provide certainty that system will be able to adapt infinitely. In fact, lifespan of ATS may be short. Also, in time of crisis, market is acting unpredictably, making it impossible for any machine learning method to adapt.
- High return value obtained in training on historical data does not guarantee profit in real-life situation.
- Risk of prolonged loss. In case of high level of autonomy of the ATS, the mistake in calibration (or failure of adaptation mechanism) may result in long series of losses. The system, although autonomous, should be monitored to avoid such situations.
- Complexity of the system may render the user unaware of reasons which lead the ATS to identification of business opportunities. In complex system, it is necessary to rely on the system, which can be unacceptable for a trader. The very complex ATS`s are tend to appear as a black box solution (see part *ATS autonomy level for more details*).

The mentioned aspects of the ATS represents important reasons why to use or do not use the ATS. Strong arguments are especially against very complex or very autonomous systems.

The ATS Information Sources and Further Discussion of the Topic

There is a lot of information sources available which are connected to the design of an ATS. We will provide a discussion regarding this subject in this part of the text.

Overview of trading principles and market mechanisms can be found in (Carter, 2006). Carter also provides a description of psychological aspects of trading (Carter, 2006, pp. 355-390). As a source of overview information, also (Elder, 1993) and (Elder, 2002) can be mentioned.

The fundamental analysis is a topic which is usually only shortly discussed in trading related books. Description of fundamental aspects of trading of different types of commodities (energy, grains and oilseeds, livestock, industrial materials and softs) is provided by Dunsby (2008). This book does not cover the topic of financial derivatives, but presents fundamental analysis on real market situations.

The short and comprehensible introduction of technical analysis presents Pesavento & Jouflas (2007). Their book is mainly related to pattern recognition, but covers also discussion of essential elements of trading (Pesavento & Joulfas, 2007, pp. 149-190).

The mentioned books are covering basics and gives overview of the market topic. More specialized books are aimed at the topic of technical analysis. It is usually presumed that the reader has knowledge of basic mechanisms of markets.

The excellent technical analysis book is (Murphy, 1999). It covers all sub-topics related to technical analysis in general. It is not strictly specialized on stock market indicators only, but also explains the technical analysis indicators for futures trading.

The (Kirkpatrick & Dahlquist, 2007) is presenting topic of technical analysis for the financial markets. The book gives reader an important overview of trend analysis (Kirkpatrick & Dahlquist, 2007, pp. 189-298, 409-452) and system testing and optimization (Kirkpatrick & Dahlquist, 2007, pp. 537-590).

Very specialized book is (Aronson, 2007). It is focused on technical analysis only, and provides more technical explanation of technical analysis terms, together with case study on S&P index 500 (Aronson, 2007, pp. 387-473).

The (Tinghino, 2008) is dealing with the topic of creating a trading system. The book is divided in two parts. First part is discussing technical analysis tools in general. The second part (Tinghino, 2008, pp. 179-232) is focused on creation of functional trading system.

Specialized and very informative book covering the topic of trading systems is (Kaufman, 2005). This is an excellent source of information about trading systems in general.

FUTURE TRENDS

Recent research and scientific effort are both aimed at the commercial applications. There is a distinguishable trend in using artificial intelligence (AI) techniques in ATS implementation. Most of commercial trading systems which claim to be high-end solutions rely on AI.

Selected techniques used in ATS based on AI:

- Neural networks. The neural network is able to recognize patterns in graphs very efficiently in order to determine best times to buy or sell. As a set of training data, the historical data may be used. Neural network can be successfully used because of the complexity of patterns they can identify. For human it may be difficult to recognize patterns quickly and it requires a lot of training and experience.
- Genetic algorithms. Can be used together with neural network to adapt setting of neural connections more precisely, using historical data.
- Multiagent systems. Agents are artificial entities able to perceive its environment and act in it with certain level of autonomy in order to complete given goal. Agents may form social structures called multi-agent systems. The optimal strategy of trading may be indentified through interaction of agents with market environment.

These are only examples of AI applications. The list is not complete because there is a large amount of possible different approaches in the area of AI. For further details on this topic, we may refer to (Russell & Norvig, 2003). The overview of multi-agent approach is described in (Ferber, 1995).

The risks of accepting such solutions usually lay in incomprehensible complexity and high level of autonomy. See above for more information about these issues.

In our opinion, a certain level of human control should be maintained in every ATS. It strengthens the confidence of the user in the system. Also, simplicity should be preferred wherever it is possible. Keeping the system open to the user is prerequisite of a successful product. The list of steps covering ATS design lifecycle describes the method of creation of such open system.

CONCLUSION

A short introduction of automated futures trading was presented in the previous text. The environment of futures markets was described in the second chapter. The automatic trading system principle was described in the third part. Information presented in these two chapters was used to describe steps forming the ATS lifecycle.

This chapter was focused on providing the overview of the ATS problem area. To sum up the facts presented in previous chapters, the ATS should have following properties:

- Transparency – there are no algorithms or parts of the system hidden from the user. Black box solution must be avoided at all costs.
- Simplicity – system should not be complicated, its signals must have intelligible meaning.
- Understandability – the user must know how the system operates, know the principles of indicators.
- Functionality – the system must be profitable in the long-term perspective.
- Money management – system should follow the rules of money management described in part *Money management problem.*
- Adaptability – even after the system is put into use, is should still be adjustable.

The user must have confidence in his ATS to use it and must fully understand its principles as well. The ATS is usually used for decision support – it alerts trader whenever interesting business opportunity occurs. This is the most frequent use of these systems. The development of the ATS is continuous and in this aspect similar to the development of information system, because the process is not finished when the system is ready to use.

ACKNOWLEDGMENT

The work and contribution were supported by the project of Czech Science Foundation “Decision-making processes in autonomous systems” no. 402/09/0662.

REFERENCES

Aronson, D. (2007). *Evidence-based Technical Analysis*. NJ: John Wiley & Sons.

Carter, J. F. (2006). *Mastering the Trade*. McGraw-Hill.

Dunsby, A., Eckstein, J., Gaspar, J., & Mulholland, S. (2008). *Commodity Investing – Maximizing Returns Through Fundamental Analysis*. NJ: John Wiley & Sons.

Elder, A. (1993). *Trading for a Living*. John Wiley & Sons.

Elder, A. (2002). *Come Into My Trading Room – A Complete Guide to Trading*. John Wiley & Sons.

Ferber, J. (1995). *Multi-Agent Systems – An Introduction to Distributed Artificial Intelligence*. New York: Addison Wesley Longman.

Kaufman, P. J. (2005). *New Trading Systems and Methods* (4th Ed,). New Jersey: John Wiley & Sons.

Kirkpatrick, C. D., & Dahlquist, J. R. (2007). *Technical Analysis – The Complete Resource for Financial Market Technicians*. NJ: Pearson Education (Prentice Hall).

Murphy, J. J. (1999). *Technical Analysis of the Financial Markets – A Comprehensive Guide to Trading Methods and Applications*. New York: New York Institute of Finance.

Nesnídal, T., & Podhajský, P. (2006). *Průvodce spekulanta* (2nd ed.). Prague: Grada.

Pesavento, L., & Jouflas, L. (2007). *Trade What You See – How to Profit From Pattern Recognition*. New Jersey: John Wiley & Sons.

Russell, S., & Norvig, P. (2003). *Artificial Intelligence – A Modern Approach* (2nd Ed.). New Jersey: Pearson Education (Prentice Hall).

Stevens, L. (2002). *Essential Technical Analysis – Tools and Techniques to Spot Market Trends*. NJ: John Wiley & Sons.

Tinghino, M. (2008). *Technical Analysis Tools – Creating a Profitable Trading System*. New York: Bloomberg Press.

Williams, L. R. (1979). *How I Made One Million Dollars... Last Year... Trading Commodities*. Windsor Brooks.

ADDITIONAL READING

Aronson, D. (2007). *Evidence-based Technical Analysis*. New Jersey: John Wiley & Sons.

Bollinger, J. A. (2001). *Bollinger on Bollinger Bands*. New York: McGraw-Hill.

Brown, C. (1999). *Technical Analysis for the Trading Professional*. New York: McGraw-Hill.

Carter, J. F. (2006). *Mastering the Trade*. New York: McGraw-Hill.

Douglas, M. (2001). Trading in the Zone. New Jersey: Prentice Hall.

Dunsby, A., Eckstein, J., Gaspar, J., & Mulholland, S. (2008). Commodity Investing – Maximizing Returns Through Fundamental Analysis. New Jersey: John Wiley & Sons.

Elder, A. (1993). Trading for a Living. New Jersey: John Wiley & Sons.

Elder, A. (2002). *Come Into My Trading Room – A Complete Guide to Trading*. New Jersey, United States of America: John Wiley & Sons.

Kaufman, P. J. (2005). *New Trading Systems and Methods* (4th Ed.). New Jersey: John Wiley & Sons.

Kirkpatrick, C. D., & Dahlquist, J. R. (2007). *Technical Analysis – The Complete Resource for Financial Market Technicians*. New Jersey: Pearson Education (Prentice Hall).

Morris, G. L. (1995). *Candlestick Charting Explained*. New York: McGraw-Hill.

Murphy, J. J. (1991). *Intermarket Technical Analysis*. New Jersey: John Wiley & Sons.

Murphy, J. J. (1999). *Technical Analysis of the Financial Markets – A Comprehensive Guide to Trading Methods and Applications*. New York: New York Institute of Finance.

Nison, S. (1991). *Japanese Candlestick Charting Techniques*. New York: New York Institute of Finance.

Pesavento, L., & Jouflas, L. (2007). *Trade What You See – How to Profit From Pattern Recognition*. New Jersey: John Wiley & Sons.

Pring, M. J. (1995). Investment Psychology Explained – Classic Strategies to Beat the Market. New Jersey: John Wiley & Sons.

Pring, M. J. (2002). *Technical Analysis Explained*. New York: McGraw-Hill.

Stevens, L. (2002). *Essential Technical Analysis – Tools and Techniques to Spot Market Trends*. New Jersey: John Wiley & Sons.

Tinghino, M. (2008). *Technical Analysis Tools – Creating a Profitable Trading System*. New York: Bloomberg Press.

Williams, L. R. (1979). *How I Made One Million Dollars... Last Year... Trading Commodities*. Windsor Brooks.

KEY TERMS AND DEFINITIONS

Automatic Trading System: system used for mechanical processing of the trading procedures. The extend of work which is processed by the ATS may differ depending on user`s preferences. Most common use of the ATS is trading data analysis with implementation of technical analysis indicators.

Backtesting: process of verification of selected trading strategy using historical or real-time data. As a result of backtesting process, the backtesting report is generated. Report contains statistical information about the given strategy, its rate of success and profitability. Backtesting is necessary step of the ATS design.

Fundamental Analysis: the analysis technique which is focused on data related to aspects of market behavior different than price. The fundamental analysis may involve analysis of financial statements, competitors, financial health of economy, market, etc.

Futures Contract: is a standardized contract to buy or sell a certain underlying instrument at a certain date in the future at a specified price.

Technical Analysis: the process in which a set of mathematical tools is used to analyze (stock, futures, etc.) market data to indentify moments with certain level of business importance. The aim of technical analysis is to forecast future direction of prices through the study of market data. The analyzed set of data is usually related to market price.

Trading: continuous process including steps of analysis of trading (stock market) data, identification of business opportunities and issuing business orders (instructions). Tools of fundamental or technical analysis are usually used in trading. These tools can be implemented into coherent system - automatic trading system – which can make trading more effective.

Chapter 13
Pervasive Computing, Firm Characteristics, and Environmental Factors Conducive to the Adoption of Activity-Based Costing:
Evidence from Bahrain

Sayel Ramadhan
Ahlia University, Kingdom of Bahrain

ABSTRACT

The main purpose of this study is to provide evidence on the contextual featutres of firms adopting Activity-Based Costing (ABC) compared to those not adopting ABC. The study examines certain organisational and business environment variables which appear to have influenced the adoption of ABC. Based on a review of the relevant literature, it is hypothesised that firm size, the amount of overhead costs, the level of product variety, production complexity, the degree of competition, and the degree of computer usage are factors which encourage firms to adopt ABC. A list of manufacturing companies operating in Bahrain (332 firms) was obtained from the Ministry of Industry. Firms with (50) workers or more were selected for the study. The reason for limiting the study to firms with this number of workers is that small firms are less likely to be able to afford the cost of adopting and implementing an ABC system and its required changes. Total of (111) firms met this size criterion and a questionnaire was developed and distributed to the entire sample. Fifty seven questionnaires were returned completed; a response rate of (51.4%). The results of the study show that a small percentage of Bahraini manufacturing companies are adopting or planning to adopt ABC systems (26.3%). There were significant relationships between the adoption of ABC and the variables selected for the study except production complexity and the degree of computer usage. The results are consistent with previous research. However, further research using a case study approach with semi-structured interviews could be conducted in those firms which claim to have adopted ABC. This approach might be fruitful and would provide more insight in identifying the characteristics of ABC companies in the Bahraini context.

DOI: 10.4018/978-1-60566-996-0.ch013

INTRODUCTION

Activity based costing (ABC) has been regarded as a management accounting innovation that has rapidly spread across many organizations, industries, and nations exhibiting different diffusion processes (Colwyn and Dugdale, 2002; Malmi, 1999; Bjornenak, 1997; Cooper 1987, 1988a; 1988b; 1989 and Cooper and Kaplan 1987 and 19881988). A major benefit of ABC is that it is a tool for more accurate, relevant and reliable cost information than traditional costing systems. Moreover, it is a tool for improved cost management practices. As a result of having more accurate cost information, managers have greater confidence in the accuracy of the costs of products and services reported by ABC. This gives a more solid basis for strategic decisions such as, pricing, product retention, product mix and cost management (see for example: Innes and Mitchell, 1990, Cooper and Kaplan 1992, Garrison and Noreen, 1994 and Horngren et al. 2009). An important problem mentioned in the literature on ABC implementation is the complexity of the ABC system and the substantial costs involved in maintaining it. It requires an extensive process of training, identifying activities and cost drivers for each activity, and it may be necessary to maintain an ABC system separate from the accounting system used for external reporting purposes (Estrin et al., 1994).

Although the implementation of ABC involves certain limitations, some firms are implementing it. The characteristics of firms conducive to the adoption of ABC have received some attention in the management accounting literature. Researchers have investigated studies addressing the relationships between ABC adoption and several contextual factors such as organizational structure, product diversity and production complexity (Cooper, 1988a and 1989; Cooper1989 and Kaplan, 1987; Baker, 1994; and Nguyen and Brooks, 1997; Bjornenak, 1997; Gosselin, 1997; Malmi, 1999 and Bjornenak and Mitchell, 2000). Moreover, Lukka and Granlund (1999) indicate that the need for ABC systems has putatively arisen from increasingly complex production and marketing environments and from a changing cost structure which includes more indirect costs.

An increasing number of companies around the world is using ABC systems. To name a few, American Airline, Hewlett-Packard (HP), Daimler Benz, Norwegian State Railway's passenger transport, Scottish National Blood Transfusion Service, and United States Postal Service, use or have used it. A major computer company HP, realized that continuous improvement and innovation require the use of ABC. For example, more than half of net revenues are derived from products launched less than 2 years ago. The research and development (R & D) budget represented about 10% of net revenues at beginning of 1990s. Because the computer section is very competitive, HP must also reduce its costs to keep its margins up. In the past, competition was based on technological innovation, the quality of the products, and the efficiency of the resellers. Now, it is important to control costs and for this purpose to improve the traditional costing system. Managers of HP realized that competition had increased and prices were greatly reduced. Complexity became more and more important: the number of services delivered and the number of products supported increased. This created a need to improve cost measurement and to identify the most profitable products. The new management accounting system ABC would provide information to help in the conceptualization of new products (target costing), to produce at low costs and make decisions about localization of factories (Lacombe and Bescos, 2000). The strategy of HP was to advise all subsidiaries and business units to adopt ABC.

The present study seeks to focus specifically on the association between ABC adoption and certain organizational and environmental factors. Five variables are selected for the study: the size of the firm, the amount of overhead costs, the degree of product variety and production complexity, the degree of competition faced by the firm, and the degree of computer usage. The purpose is to provide empirical evidence on the existence of these variables in firms which adopt ABC compared to those which do not adopt ABC.

The motivation for the study stems from the prior accounting literature which conceptually suggests the existence of relationships between firm characteristics and environmental variables and ABC adoption. However, there is little research documenting the stability of relationships between these variables and ABC adoption (see for example, Nguyen and Brooks, 1997; Alcouffe, 2002 and Drury and Al-Omiri, 2002). Furthermore, it is fair to point out that most of these factors have been addressed in earlier research except for the fact that this paper applies to Bahraini companies on which the readers have limited prior insight.

The paper is organized as follows. In the next section, the results of previous studies relating to linkages between organizational variables and ABC adoption are reviewed. This section also develops the hypotheses that are tested in the light of previous research. Section three focuses on the research method including the questionnaire instrument used and the data collection process. Section four provides a description of the analysis performed to test the hypotheses and a discussion of the results. The last section concludes the study, highlights its limitations, and suggests directions for future research.

Literature Review

Activity-based costing is a useful tool but not necessarily one that is appropriate for all companies. The literature has shed some light on the characteristics of firms which might be suitable to ABC adoption (see Cooper and Kaplan 1988 and Baker 1994). Scholarly research on activity based costing has been carried out on the influence of cost structure and organizational size (Armitage and Nicholson, 1993, Gosselin, 1997, Innes et al., 2000, Alcouffe, 2002, Drury and Al-Omiri, 2002), level of automation (Drury and Tayles, 1994), complexity of production processes and product diversity (Bjornenak, 1997) and the amount of overhead costs as a percentage of total costs and ABC adoption (Nguyen and Brooks, 1997). Consideration of the following factors helps provide a measure to judge whether ABC will be advantageous for a particular business and when it is appropriate to use it.

The Size of the Firm

The cost-benefit approach in accounting specifies that the primary criterion for choosing accounting systems is how well they help achieve organisational objectives in relation to the costs of these systems. Thus, when the installation of an ABC system is considered to replace the traditional costing system, it should be borne in mind that such a system is complex, costly and time consuming (Estrin et al., 1994). An ABC system tends to be more complex and have more cost pools and cost drivers than volume-based traditional systems. In addition, consultants are needed and the costs of educating managers and training other personnel on implementing ABC systems can be quite high. Friedman and Lyne (1999) surveyed 1000 UK companies and found that ABC was viewed by respondents as a complex and costly system. In this regard, Cobb et al. (1992) show that small companies do not adopt ABC because it is costly. Parker and Lettes (1991) point out that the economy of scale factor may limit the use of a complex accounting system in small firms. They suggest that larger firms may have greater access to expertise to design and implement an appropriate costing system. Furthermore, Johnson and Kaplan (1987) argue that the distortion of cost information is possibly greater in large firms because of the greater subservience of the costing system to external reporting. This suggests that large firms can afford to support a more complex costing system than smaller firms.

The Amount of Overhead Costs

ABC started as a model of cost allocation and its objective is to provide more accurate cost information. If an ABC system is implemented effectively, it is likely that it will give rise to information concerning costs which is more reflective of resource consumption and therefore of providing cost information that is perceptively regarded as more accurate than the conventional system being replaced. Influences on user perceptions of ABC are based on the usefulness and reliability of the information. Norris (1994) found that most respondents have greater confidence in decisions based on ABC information. According to Krumwiede (1998), the higher the potential for cost distortions, the more motivated an organisation to adopt ABC. The reason is that misallocations of the indirect costs, under the traditional costing system, will result in significantly distorted costs of products or services. This can lead to distorted prices and wrong managerial decisions. Krumwiede also reported that adopting firms had higher percentage of overhead costs to total production costs. Thus, firms which have a greater proportion of overheads in total manufacturing costs are more likely to adopt ABC than firms with smaller proportion of overheads. Firms with a small amount of overhead may feel that they would not need to adopt ABC because the distortions created by a traditional costing system would be insignificant (see Baker, 1994; Jenkinson and Hui, 1994 and Nguyen and Brooks, 1997).

Product Variety and Production Complexity

The increased diversity and complexity in today's manufacturing implies increased product ranges, an increase in the number of process operations and greater complexity in product design. Product **variety** refers to the number and diversity of different types of products produced. As product diversity increases, the amount of resources required for handling and support activities also increases. This increases the distortions of reported product costs by traditional costing systems. Therefore, companies with a wide variety of products should review their costing systems because traditional costing systems may cause distortions in product cost information. In this regard, Baker (1994) and Jenkins and Hui (1994) argue that companies with many products may require sophisticated costing systems to capture the variation in resource consumption by different products and, as a result, should consider ABC system because it has the most impact on firms that have numerous products.

Production **complexity** refers to the number of components in a product or the number of processes or operations through which a product flows. Processes are complex when they create difficulties for the people attempting to perform production operations or the people using manufacturing machinery (Raiborn et al., 1996). Cooper and Kaplan (1988) found that the more complex the product lines of firms, the larger the number of support departments needed to perform the operations. Cooper (1988a) argued that the distortion of product cost information may arise because of diversity in production volume, batch size, complexity, number of parts and components of raw material, number of processes, and setup of production equipment. A good illustration is to consider the manufacturing plant of the Cooper Pen Company used by Atkinson et al. (2001) and the ice cream example of Maher et al. (1997). Analysis of these studies indicates that firms with higher degrees of production complexity are more likely to have distortions in individual product costs. Therefore, they are expected to benefit from the implementation of an ABC system.

Degree of Competition

Increased competition may occur if other companies may have recognized the profit potential of a particular product or service. In highly competitive markets where price is the primary competitive factor, it is more difficult for a firm to sustain a high price because of inaccurate product or service costs. A change in the competitive environment in which a company operates, may require better and more accurate cost information. In order to keep abreast of competition, companies must continuously improve their manufacturing system. As a result of high competitive pressures, the best estimate of product cost must be available to management so that profit margins and prices can be reasonably set. Cooper (1988b) suggested that a company should consider ABC if the existing cost system was designed when "competition was weak". This occurs particularly with a rapid pace of technological change that shortens product life cycle time. Therefore, if a costing error is discovered, companies do not have enough time to make price or cost adjustments, and, as a result of inaccurate product costs, they may not be able to compete in the market with a consequent decline in market share. Competition increases the costs of errors because there is greater chance that a competitor will take advantage of any error made (Cooper, 1988, pp.43-48). This indicates that increased competition requires more sophisticated costing systems. Therefore, ABC system is implemented because stronger competition increases the cost of erroneous pricing (Nair, 2000).

The above analysis indicates that firms which operate in a highly competitive environment have higher demands for accurate cost information. On the other hand, firms that operate in markets with a low degree of competition may prefer to stay with the traditional costing system because the costs of making errors in product costs would be less than the costs to adopt and implement a complex costing system.

The Degree of Computer Usage

Maciariello and Kirby (1994) state that the rapid increase in the use of information technology is one of the main factors contributing to the rise of ABC. Horngren et al. (2009) suggest that improved computer technology is likely to create refinements in cost accounting systems and ABC is one of the means to refine a costing system. The use of ABC requires analysis of activities and identifying cost drivers. Computer technology has reduced the costs of developing and operating costing systems that track many activities. They enable an increasing percentage of costs to be classified as direct. Introduction of computers, and other advanced technology means that significantly more information can be readily and cost-effectively supplied. Therefore, we can expect a wider use of overhead allocation bases other than direct labor. We can also expect the use of ABC.

Research Hypotheses

Based upon the aforementioned review of the literature, the following research hypotheses are developed.

H_1: Larger firms are more likely to adopt activity-based costing than smaller firms.

H_2: Firms with a higher percentage of overhead costs in total costs are more likely to adopt activity-based costing than firms with a lower percentage of overhead costs.

H_3: Firms with more product variety and production complexity are more likely to adopt activity-based costing than firms with less product variety and production complexity.

H_4: Firms which operate in highly competitive industries are more likely to adopt ABC than firms which operate in less competitive industries.

H_5: Firms with higher levels of computer usage are more likely to adopt ABC than firms with lower levels of computer usage.

RESEARCH METHODOLOGY

a. Sample, Questionnaire and Procedure

A list of all manufacturing companies operating in Bahrain during the year 2007 was obtained from the Ministry of Industry; a total of (332) firms. The number of employees in the firm was used as a basis to select sample companies. Companies with (50) employees or more were selected for the study. The reason for limiting the study to companies with this number of employees is that firms with small number of employees are unlikely to have cost accounting systems and, if they do have, they are less likely to be able to afford the cost of implementing an ABC system and its required changes. Number of employees, as a measure of size, was used only to select the sample of the study; total of (111) firms met the above size criterion.

To test the research hypotheses, a questionnaire survey was used. The instrument enabled the collection of information concerning ABC adoption as well as firm specific information. Since it is impossible to predict how questionnaire items will be interpreted by respondents, the questionnaire was pilot-tested on a small sample (three firms). The results and feedback of the pilot test were used to refine the questionnaire and a final draft was developed and administered to the entire sample. In order to avoid different interpretations of what is meant by an ABC system by respondents, a definition of ABC was included in the questionnaire.

Access to the firms was obtained through the authors with the help of a group of accounting students who were taking the cost accounting course during the first semester 2006/2007. A copy of the questionnaire was delivered to each of the (111) firms in the sample together with a cover letter directing the manager of the accounting department, chief accountant, controller, or someone who is responsible for cost accounting to fill in the questionnaire and return it to the address of the author. Total of (57) questionnaires were returned. This represents an overall response rate of (51.4%) of the sample selected.

b. The Variables of the Study

The following company characteristics and business environment variables are used in the study.

1. **The size of the firm.** Sales revenue is used as a proxy to measure the size of the firm. As was mentioned earlier, the absolute size of the companies covered, as measured by number of employees, was used only to select the sample of the study.
2. **The amount of overhead costs.** This is measured directly by asking the respondents to indicate the amount of overhead costs as a percentage of total costs. Both overhead related to manufacturing and non-manufacturing was considered. Consideration is given to the size of the firm, product variety, production complexity, and the level of automation in the manufacturing process because they are assumed to affect the amount of overhead costs.
3. **Product variety**. This variable refers to the number of different types of products manufactured by the firm. Respondents were notified that products of different colors, tastes, shapes, sizes or simply packaging a product differently, is counted as introducing another different product.
4. **Production complexity**. Eight variables, derived from the relevant literature, were used to measure production complexity. Respondents were asked to indicate, on a five-point scale, the extent to which products manufactured by their companies, differ with respect to each of the following variables.
    - Variation in production volume between products.

- ◦ Number of processes through which a product flows.
- ◦ Hours of specialized machine processing.
- ◦ Hours of specialized labor processing.
- ◦ Time and effort spent on quality inspection.
- ◦ Number of parts, components, raw materials included in a product.
- ◦ Number of production equipment setups.
- ◦ Batch size.

5. **Degree of competition in industry.** Competition was measured in a direct manner by asking the respondents to indicate, on a five-point Likert-type scale, the level of competition in the industry in which their firms operate. This approach is consistent with Swenson (1995) and Nguyen and Brooks (1997).
6. **Degree of computer usage.** This variable was measured in a direct manner by asking the respondents to indicate, on a five-point scale, the extent of computer usage in their firms (1=very low; 2=low; 3=moderate; 4=high and 5=very high degree of usage).

Respondents were classified in two distinct groups. The first group (a total of fifteen companies which forms a homogeneous group) consists of those companies which could be described by one of the following statements (see Table 3).

a. ABC system is currently implemented and it is operating as a replacement to the traditional costing system.
b. ABC system is currently implemented and it is operating as a supplementary to the traditional costing system. It should be pointed out here that three companies stated that they considered ABC and a decision have been made to introduce and implement it in the next 12 months. These companies were excluded from the first group (the adopters). This elimination is based on the assumption that such companies may not adopt ABC in the future. The empirical evidence from the ABC literature shows that some companies plan to implement ABC but in fact never do so. Moreover, if we include such companies in the first group, some might cast doubts that companies considering ABC may not have similar characteristics to those companies actually using ABC.

The second group consists of those companies which have not yet considered ABC and those which have no plans to consider it in the coming 12 months (a total of 42 companies). Taking only companies which have not yet considered ABC and those which have no plans to consider it in the following twelve months might be a better basis of comparison with the fifteen ABC companies. This approach is consistent with that of Bjornenak (1997).

Given the sample sizes are small and of different size, and given that some variables (e.g., firm size and the amount of overhead costs) are designed in the form of open-end answer, Mann-Whitney U test was used to test the hypotheses. The Mann-Whitney test for two independent samples is employed with ordinal (rank-order) data. In conducting this test, the two sample means are employed to estimate the values of the means of the population from which the samples are derived. If the Z value for two independent samples is significant, it indicates there is a significant difference between the two sample means, and as a result the researcher can conclude there is a high likelihood that the samples represent populations with different mean values (Sheskin, 1997). Finally, a conventional level of significance of >.10 was used in testing the hypotheses.

Table 1. Line of business-population and sample

No.	Type of firm	Population N	Sample*		Responses*	
			N	%	N	%
1.	Manufacturing of food, beverages and tobacco	50	12	10.8	7	12.3
2.	Textile, wearing apparel, and leather industries	22	21	18.9	8	14.0
3.	Manufacturing of wood and wood products	10	3	2.7	3	5.3
4.	Manufacturing of paper products, printing and publishing	16	7	6.3	3	5.3
5.	Chemicals, petroleum, coal, rubber, and plastic products	46	19	17.2	8	14.0
6.	Non-metallic mineral products except products of petroleum and coal	58	15	13.5	4	7.0
7.	Basic metal industries	7	6	5.4	2	3.5
8.	Fabricated metal products, machinery, and equipment	116	26	23.4	22	38.6
9.	Other manufacturing industries	7	2	1.8	0	0
	Totals	**332**	**111**	**100**	**57**	**100**

*** The percentages in the sample and responses columns, are based on the total**
Sample of 111 companies and total responses of 57 (see totals row).

ANALYSIS OF RESULTS

a. Characteristics of Respondents

The manufacturing companies selected for the study, represent different sectors of the economy. The nature of their activities varied from food, beverages and tobacco to fabricated metal products, machinery and equipment. Table 1 shows the population, sample of the study, and the responses according to the line of business.

It is interesting to report that all respondents are indigenous Bahraini companies. None of them is a division of a multi-national corporation operating in Bahrain. Furthemore, sales revenue was more than BD5 million in 56% of the respondents (BD=$2.65). This may be considered as an indicator that companies of different sizes are included in the study. Respondents were asked to indicate the proportion of overhead costs as a percentage of total indirect costs and as a percentage of direct labor cost.The amount of overhead costs ranges between less than 10% and 70% of total costs. The majority of respondents (70%) indicated that the amount of overhead costs is about 50% of direct labor cost; only four companies indicated that it is over 100% of direct labor cost. Thus, manufacturing overheads do not represent a significant portion of total costs.

The somewhat low level of overhead costs may be due to the low level of automation in the manufacturing process. Increased level of automation in the manufacturing process is likely to reduce direct labor cost and increase the amount of overhead costs. Therefore, respondents were asked to indicate the level of automation in the manufacturing process in their companies. In about 50% of the respondents less than 75% of the manufacturing process was automated. The remaining percentage had more than 75% automated.

The variation in product volume or units produced was high. About 46% of the respondents indicated that they produce more than 16 products.In about 10% the number of products is between 5 and 8 products; 12% between 9 and 16. The remaining 32% have between one and four products. Respondents were also asked about eight variables used as proxies for the level of production complexity. Most respondents indicated that products manufactured differ with respect to the raw materials and component parts used, specialized machine hours, and specialized

*Table 2. Means by which respondents became aware of ABC**

Means	Means of awareness	N	%
A	By reading professional magazines and journals	11	26.8
b.	By talking to friends, colleagues, or management.	5	12.2
c.	By attending a workshop, conference, or training course	7	17.1
d.	Through college education	16	39.0
e.	Others	2	4.9
	Totals	**41**	**100.0**

*Only 41 firms answered this question

labor hours required for processing. The number of specialized machine hours and hours of specialised labor received high scores. This may be a common characteristic of firms operating in the new manufacturing environment.Finally, the results show that about 75% of the respondents face moderate to exremely high degrees of competition in the industry. Only 12% indicated that they face a low degree of competition. This is consistent with the view that firms are currently facing fierce competition.

b. Degree of ABC Awareness

Respondents were asked to indicate whether or not they are aware of ABC. About 72% (41 companies) indicated that they were aware of ABC (Table 2). One respondent added that **"we know ABC but we do not implement it"**. However, some respondents were not familiar with ABC, so they did not answer this question. The means by which respondents came to know about ABC are: by reading professional magazines and journals; by talking to friends or colleagues; by attending a workshop; conference; or a training course; and through college education. In this regard, Nielsen et al. (2004) found that education, journals and consultants have a great influence on knowledge and utilization of ABC in Danish firms.

c. The Extent of ABC Adoption

An issue which is left somewhat unanswered in other articles on ABC is exactly what an ABC system is. The decision was not left to the respondents to categorise the system. Therefore, respondents were informed, in the questionnaire, of what is meant by ABC. Table 3 shows that a reasonable percentage of Bahraini manufacturing companies are currently adopting or planning to adopt ABC. Fifteen (26.3%) of the (57) respondents are using ABC system as a replacement or as a supplementary to the traditional costing system. Of these firms, four have a full ABC system and two partially implement ABC. The ipetus to introduce it came from top management, typically the finance manager or the accountant. This implies that firms in Bahrain that have adopted ABC have not been influenced or motivated by consultancy firms advocating ABC. In this context, Al-Omiri (2004) found that the least important motives to use ABC relate to external pressure groups such as, external auditors, consultants, government/ regulatory pressures and fad or imitation. The results also show that some of the companies using ABC are listed in the stock exchang. However, the stock exchange listing agreement does not require firms to adopt ABC.

The majority of the firms in the sample (73.6%) indicated that they have not considered ABC and they have no plans to consider it in the coming twelve months. None of these companies indicated

Table 3. Extent of ABC sdoption

	Extent of ABC Adoption	N	%
a.	ABC system is currently implemented and it is operating as a ***replacement*** to the traditional costing system.	4	7.0
b.	ABC system is currently implemented and it is operating as a ***supplementary*** to the traditional costing system.	11	19.3
c.	ABC system was considered and a plan has been made to introduce/implement it in the next 12 months.	3	5.2
d.	ABC system was considered and a decision has been made not to introduce/implement it in the next 12 months.	4	7.0
e.	ABC system was considered and a decision has been made not to introduce/ implement it.	2	3.6
f.	ABC system was not yet considered and we have no plans to consider it in the coming 12 months.	33	57.9
	Totals	**57**	**100**

that they used ABC before and then abandoned it. This could be because of complexity of ABC system and substantial costs involved in implementing ABC or management resistance to change. In this regard, the financial controller in one of the responding companies indicated that "**management need be convinced of the advantages of using ABC. I believe this is a difficult task**". This is a useful quote from a practitioner. Another reason may be because all respondents were Bahraini companies rather than divisions of multinational companies. None of the respondents indicated that they use ABC as a pilot study only.

Respondents indicated that the main objectives of ABC adoption are product costing, performance management and profitability assessment. The finance manager in one company adopting ABC indicated that:

ABC system provides more accurate cost information relating to products which in turn helps to price scientifically and have better bottom line. This also provides competitive edge over the competitors. Therefore, it has been seriously considered and implemented in our company.

They also indicated that the problems management face in ABC adoption are lack of experience and high costs, because consultants are needed and there is a need to educate managers and other operating personnel on how to implement ABC.

The somewhat low adoption rate of ABC systems by Bahraini manufacturing companies is not surprising. ABC is a technique that is still not widely adopted even in some developed countries such as the UK, Canada and Finland. Several surveys have been conducted in different countries to assess the degree to which ABC has been adopted (see for example, Innes and Mitchell, 1991; Cobb et al., 1992; Drury and Tayles, 1994; Innes and Mitchell, 1999; Bjornenak, 1997; Gosselin, 1997; Innes et al., 2000; Gierusz et al., 2004; Cohen and Kaimenaki, 2004). Innes and Mitchell (1991) found that among the 187 UK Company respondents, only 6% had begun to implement an ABC system while 52% had not considered implementing ABC. Also, Innes and Mitchell (1994) reported adoption rates around 20%. Moreover, Drury et al. (1993) found that 13% of 303 manufacturing companies in the UK had implemented or intended to implement ABC.

During the same period, Bright et al. (1992) surveyed manufacturing firms again in the UK. The percentage of ABC adopters 32% was much larger than in Innes and Mitchell (1990). Another survey conducted in the UK by Nicholls (1992) showed that 10% of the respondents had implemented ABC (see also Armitage and Nicholson, 1993 and Lukka and Grenlund, 1996). Innes et al. (2000) compared the adoption rate in two surveys. They reported that in 1994, UK companies revealed a 19.5% rate of ABC adoption with 27.1% of firms actively considering ABC. By 1999, the respective figures were 17.5% and 20.3%. Al-Omiri (2004) and Drury and Tayles (2000) in studies of ABC, in UK enterprises, develop similar arguments. In Canada, Armitage and Nicholson (1993) surveyed the 740 largest corporations. The results showed that 14% of the respondents had implemented ABC, 15% were reflecting on implementing ABC and 67% had not considered implementing an ABC system. Studies of ABC implementations in US firms by Green and Amenkhienan (1992) and Shim and Stagliano (1997) report similar results. Finally, Eden (2002) surveyed approximately 200 companies in high tech area in Canada. The results suggest a low level of ABC adoption. The reasons cited the lack of ABC adoption principally included that ABC is not well understood and that the accuracy of information obtained from ABC implementation was not encouraging.

d. Hypotheses Test

Hypothesis 1

It is assumed that large firms have the volume and resources to support the costs of an ABC system. ABC systems tend to be more complex and have more cost pools and cost drivers than volume-based traditional systems; hence, they are more expensive. Based on this, it was hypothesised that larger firms are more likely to adopt ABC than smaller firms. The size of the sample companies was measured using annual turnover. The question regarding the firm size variable is designed in the form of open-end answer and it might cast doubts on how we could base on such an unclassified number to get the group mean for the two sample groups as listed in Table 4. This variable was divided into small and large firms. Small firms are those with sales of BD2 million or less and large firms of more than BD2 million. The results of Mann-Whitney U test (Table 4) indicate that the relationship between annual turnover and the adoption of ABC is significant at the 0.1 level. The difference between the turnover of ABC adopters and non-adopters was found to be significant. This result indicates that large companies have the tendency to adopt ABC. Therefore, the null hypothesis can be rejected. The result is consistent with a study undertaken in the UK by Hussein and Rickwood (1993). Further, Davies and Sweeting (1993) and Malmi (1996) found that company size affect ABC adoption. A survey conducted by Nguyen and Brooks (1977) indicated that a relatively small number of respondents had fully implemented ABC and amongst these were larger businesses.

Similarly, Alcouffe (2002) examined the relationship between several organizational variables and the adoption or non-adoption of ABC systems among French firms. The results show significant differences between adopters and non-adopters only for firm size. Finally, Bubbio et al. (1999) found quite a large diffusion in the largest firms. They found that a considerable number of them are currently evaluating the possibility of introducing ABC and about 50% of the respondents had rejected or had not considered ABC.

Hypothesis 2

It was hypothesised that firms with higher amounts of overhead costs are more likely to adopt ABC than firms with smaller amounts of overheads. The Mann-Whitney U test results indicate that the mean values of the amount of overhead costs, as a percentage of total costs between the two groups, are significantly different (Table 4). Therefore, the null hypothesis that there is no difference in the amount of overhead costs between the two groups can be rejected.

The result is inconsistent with that of Nguyen and Brooks (1997) who did not find a significant relationship between the adoption of ABC and the amount of overhead costs. Bjornenak (1997) found significance only at 10% level. The hypothesis was based on previous research which indicates that firms apply ABC for more accurate product cost information (Al-Bastaki and Ramadhan, 1997). However, as ABC has become increasingly popular, product costing may not be the major objective for ABC adoption. One possible explanation for Nguyen and Brooks result is that managers' day-to-day focus is on managing activities not costs. Activity-Based Management (ABM) requires an analysis of what the organisation does. Because ABC systems also focus on activities, they are very useful in cost management. ABM is used to identify and eliminate nonvalue-added activities, waste and their related costs. Therefore, some firms may adopt ABC systems to improve their operations and obtain useful activity-information, rather than to improve product cost information (Nguyen and Brooks, 1997 and Horngren et al., 2009).

Hypothesis 3

It was hypothesized that firms with varied and complex products or services whose consumption of resources is not closely related to volume are likely to adopt ABC. Respondents were informed in the questionnaire that products of different colors, tastes, shapes, sizes, or packaging differently should be counted as different products. This variable was divided into two groups: firms with twelve products or less and firms with more than twelve products. The results of the Mann-Whitney U test (Table 4) indicate, for the first part of the hypothesis (product variety), that there were significant differences between the two groups. In other words, the mean ranks between the two groups were significantly different at the .10 level. Therefore, the null hypothesis that firms which adopt ABC have no significant differences, in terms of product variety, compared with firms that have not adopted ABC, can be rejected.

The result is inconsistent with that of Nguyen and Brooks (1997). However, it is consistent with some previous empirical studies. For example, Banker and Johnson (1993) examined the links between the cost of complexity and diversity and certain organizational transactions in US airline industry. They found that production process complexity is an important secondary cost driver. Additionally, Hussain and Rickwood (1993) examined the contextual features of firms adopting ABC in the UK. They found a strong correlation between product variety and diversity and ABC adoption. Product variety was significantly high in organizations which had adopted or planned to adopt ABC. There was a high correlation between the number of products and the variation in volume between products (.82) which may give support for this explanation (see also Baker, 1994; Jenkinson and Hui, 1994).

To test for the second part of hypothesis 3, respondents were asked about eight variables as proxies for production complexity (Table 4). The results for all variables indicate that the mean ranks between the two groups were not significantly different. Thus, firms which adopt ABC are no more likely to have higher levels of production complexity than firms which do not adopt ABC. Therefore, the null hypothesis cannot be rejected. Based on this result, it is possible to suggest that production complexity may not be an important factor in the decision to adopt ABC.

Hypothesis 4

Highly competitive markets, where the price is the primary competitive factor, require accurate cost of product or service. Thus, it can be concluded that competition is a contributor to firm's adoption of ABC. It was hypothesised that firms which face high degrees of competition in the market, are more likely to adopt ABC. The Mann-Whitney U test result (Table 4) shows that the mean ranks of the two groups are significantly different, indicating that companies which are exposed to a more competitive environment are more likely to adopt ABC and the null hypothesis can be rejected. This result is consistent with that of Nguyen and

Brooks (1997). It should be pointed out that one respondent using ABC indicated that

ABC is the ideal costing technique for manufacturing companies where competition is high and the company looks for costing edge.

Hypothesis 5

It was hypothesised that companies with higher levels of computer usage are more likely to adopt ABC than companies with lower levels of computer usage. The results of the Mann-Whitney U test indicate that there are no significant differences between the two groups, in the extent of computer usage and the null hypothesis cannot be rejected (see Table 4). This could be because almost all firms nowadays use computers and it is inevitable that firms use computers in their accounting systems. The evidence regarding the use of computers and ABC adoption is not consistent with views expressed in the prevailing management accounting literature on this variable. Nevertheless, this result is consistent with some previous empirical studies. For example, Hussain and Rickwood (1993) found that the evidence regarding technological change and ABC adopting was not consistent with views expressed in the prevailing management accounting literature on this variable. Moreover, Cobb et al. (1993) examined the problems of ABC. A survey of British management accountants revealed that the most common problems perceived by 20 interviewees who had been assessing ABC for at least one year were the amount of work, lack of staff, lack of staff time and scarce computer resources. During the first year of implementing ABC, the major problems experienced by organisations were the amount of time spent on ABC by both accountants and computer staff. This indicates that there is a strong relationship between the use of ABC and use of computers.

CONCLUSION

The main purpose of this study was to examine company characteristics and business environment variables conducive to the adoption of ABC. The results show that a low percentage of manufacturing firms in Bahrain has started implementing ABC systems. Additionally, the variables selected seem to affect the decision to implement ABC. The hypothesis test results suggest statistically significant relationships between these variables and the ABC adoption decision. However, there were no significant relationships between ABC adoption and production complexity and degree of computer usage.

The results of previous research indicate that ABC is not a passing fad. A majority of companies still use traditional costing methods, but the use of ABC appears to be increasing. The question which can be raised here is: why do few companies adopt ABC? This may indicate that firms use ABC for their demonstrated benefits, mainly more accurate product or service cost information. Furthermore, Friedman and Lyne (1999) argue that ABC may be used because of a compelling business need, not just because ABC techniques being good in principle. If ABC has demonstrated benefits, why are more firms not actually adopting the technique?

One should think of an explanation of the diffusion process in the use of ABC. That is, further explanation for this paradox is required. In this regard, Gosselin (1999) examined theories of bandwagons to provide such an explanation. According to Gosselin, Bandwagons are diffusion processes by which organisations adopt or reject an innovation, not because of competitive and institutional pressures, caused by the sheer number of organisations that already adopted or rejected this innovation but by joining others in applying ABC because it seems to be fashionable or likely to be successful. His research provided additional insight on the diffusion process for the use of ABC.

Table 4. Mann-Whitney U test results

1. The size of the firm - Sales						
Group	No. of respondents	Mean rank	Sum of ranks	Mann Whitney U	Z value	Two-tail sig.
1	15	26.87	403	283	-2.745	.095
2	42	29.10	1193			
2. The amount of overhead costs						
1	15	25.60	384	264	-1.932	.087
2	37	26.86	994			
3. Product variety – number of products						
1	15	30.20	453	252	-1.716	.103
2	39	26.46	1032			
4. Production complexity: **a. Variation in production volume between products**						
1	14	21.71	304	199	-.913	.361
2	34	25.65	872			
b. Hours of specialized machine processing						
1	14	24.39	341.5	225.5	-.132	.895
2	33	23.83	786.5			
c. Hours of specialized labor processing						
1	14	28.29	396	171	-.1.432	.152
2	33	22.18	732			
d. Number of parts or components or materials						
1	14	17.11	239.5	134.5	-2.431	.015
2	34	27.54	936.5			
e. Time and effort spent on quality inspection						
1	14	23.00	322	217	-.336	.737
2	33	24.42	806			
f. Number of processes through which a product flows						
1	13	22.77	296	205	-.401	.689
2	34	24.47	832			
g. Number of production equipment setups						
1	14	21.50	301	196	-.854	.393
2	35	25.06	827			
h. Batch size						
1	14	18.75	302	197	-.814	.416
2	33	26.23	826			
5. Degree of competition						
1	14	27.50	385	224	-1.876	.081
2	36	24.72	890			
6. Degree of computer usage						
1	14	24.39	341.5	225.5	-.132	.895
2	33	23.83	786.5			

LIMITATIONS

The findings of the study should be considered in light of the following limitations.

1. The number of ABC adopters is small (15 companies adopt ABC as a replacement or supplement to the existing costing system). This could probably not be representative and may affect the validity of the statistical analysis and inference, particularly when testing the hypotheses. It may be difficult to highlight a clear relationship between the factors selected and the adoption of ABC. Nevertheless, the results of the study provide a strong foundation for future studies on ABC.
2. There is a difficulty in finding appropriate measures for the potential explanatory variables. For some of the variables (e.g. production complexity, competition and extent of computer usage) objective measures are not available and proxy measures have to be used.
3. Non-Bahraini firms operating in Bahrain where excluded. The issue was to focus on Bahraini companies only.

FUTURE RESEARCH

Friedman and Lyne (1999) suggest that observation of the implementation of ABC should continue over a substantial period of time. In this respect, a way to take the material forward might be to use the findings as a background on which to build. For example, the results section contains a useful quote from a practitioner. Perhaps, this company could be used to illustrate some of the factors applied pointing out the benefits achieved through the use of ABC. As Norris (1994) suggests, a case study on companies claiming to have adopted ABC might provide some insight concerning the characteristics of firms using ABC. Even better would be to conduct several case studies, using various sources such as interviews, documents, and observations. Other issues which could be investigated include: the requirements to successfully implement ABC; the problems companies face in implementation; why adopters support ABC and what are the influences on their perceptions; and the interaction between management accountants and operational managers when ABC techniques are used. Finally, further research could investigate the impact of culture, environment and stage of economic development of Bahraini firms' adoption of ABC.

REFERENCES

Al-Bastaki, H., & Ramadhan, S. (1998). A Survey of Activity-Based Costing Practices in Bahraini Manufacturing Firms. *Journal of King Abdul Aziz University*, *11*, 17–29.

Al-Omiri, M. (2004). *The Diffusion of Management Accounting Innovations: The Motives behind ABC Systems Adoption in the UK Companies*. Paper presented at the 27th Annual Congress of the European Accounting Association, Prague-Czech Republic, 1-3 April.

Alcouffe, S. (2002). *Organisational determinants of Activity-Based Costing systems adoption: an empirical study among French firms*. Paper presented at the 25th Annual Congress of the European Accounting Association.

Armitage, H.M., & Nicholson, R.(1993). *Activity Based Costing: A survey of Canadian Practice*. Issue Paper No.3, Society of Management Accountants of Canada, Issue Paper Series, September.

Atkinson, A., Banker, R., Kaplan, R., & Young, M. (2001). Management Accounting (3rd ed., pp. 160-161). NJ: Prentice-Hall.

Baker, W., (1994). Understanding Activity-Based Costing. *IM*, March / April, 28-30.

Banker, R., & Johnson, H. (1993). An empirical study of cost drivers in the US airline industry. *Accounting Review, 68*(3), 576–588.

Bjornenak, T. (1997). Diffusion and Accounting: the Case of ABC in Norway. *Management Accounting Research, 8*, 3–17. doi:10.1006/mare.1996.0031

Bjornenak, T., & Mitchell, F. (2000). *A study of the development of the ABC journal literature 1987-1998*. Paper presented at the LSE Seminar on Management Accounting Change, (April)

Bright, J., Davies, R. E., Downes, C. A., & Sweeting, R. C. (1992). The deployment of Costing Techniques and Practices: a UK Study. *Management Accounting Research, 3*, 201–211. doi:10.1016/S1044-5005(92)70011-0

Bubbio, A., Alberti, F., & Toscano, G. (1999). *A Survey of ABC/ABT in the Italian Medium and Large companies*. Paper presented at the 22nd Annual Congress of the European Accounting Association, Bordeaux-France, 5-7 May.

Cobb, I., Innes, J., & Falconer, M. (1993). *ABC problems: The British Experience*. Paper presented at the 16th Annual Congress of the European Accounting Association, Turku-Finland, April 28-30.

Cobb, J., Innes, J., & Mitchell, F. (1992). *Activity-Based Costing: Problems in Practice*. London: The Chartered Institute of Management Accountants.

Cohen, S., & Kaimenaki, E. (2004). *ABC in Greece: Adopters, Supporters, Deniers and Ignorers*. Paper presented at the Annual Congress of the European Accounting Association, Prague, 1-3 April.

Colwyn, J. T., & Dugdale, D. (2002). The ABC Bandwagon and the Juggernaut of Modernity. *Accounting, Organizations and Society, 27*(1/2), 121–164.

Cooper, R. (1987). The Two-stage Procedure in Cost Accounting. *Journal of Cost Management* (summer), 43-51.

Cooper, R. (1988a). The Rise of Activity-Based Costing – Part One: What is an Activity-Based Cost System? *Journal of Cost Management* (summer), 45-54.

Cooper, R. (1988b). The Rise of Activity-Based Costing – Part Two: When do I need an Activity-Based Cost System? *Journal of Cost Management* (fall), 45-54.

Cooper, R. (1989). The Rise of Activity-Based Costing – Part Three: How Many Cost Drivers Do You Need and How Do You Select Them? *Journal of Cost Management*, Summer, 45-54.

Cooper, R., & Kaplan, R.S. (1987). How cost accounting systematically distorts product costs. *Management Accounting*, April, 20-27.

Cooper, R., & Kaplan, R. S. (1988). Measure Cost Right: Make the Right Decision. *Harvard Business Review*, (Sept-Oct): 96–103.

Davies, R. E., & Sweeting, R. (1993). *Accounting Innovations and Development of Manufacturing Cost Management Systems*. The 16th Annual Congress of the European Accounting Association, Finland, 28-30 May.

Drury, C., & Al-Omiri, M. (2002). *The diffusion of management accounting innovations: A study of the factors influencing the adoption, implementation levels and success of ABC in UK*. Paper presented at the 22nd Annual Congress of the European Accounting Association.

Drury, C., Braund, S., Osborne, P., & Tayles, M. (1993). *A Survey of Management Accounting Practices in UK Manufacturing Companies*. London: ACCA.

Drury, C., & Tayles, M. (1994). Product Costing in UK Manufacturing Organizations. *European Accounting Review*, *3*, 443–469. doi:10.1080/09638189400000031

Eden, R. (2002). *Activity-based costing in high tech companies in Canada*. Paper presented at the 22nd Annual Congress of the European Accounting Association.

Estrin, T., Kantor, J., & Albers, D. (1994). Is ABC Suitable for your Company? *Management Accounting*, April, 40-45.

Friedman, A., & Lyne, S. (1999). *Success and Failure of Activity-Based Costing Techniques*. CIMA, London.

Gierusz, J., Januszewski, A., & Kujawski, J. (2004). *The Needs and Possibilities of the Introduction of the Activity-Based Costing in Polish Enterprises-Research Results*. Paper presented at the Annual Congress of the European Accounting Association, Prague, 1-3 April.

Gosselin, M. (1997). The Effect of strategy and Organizational structure on the Adoption and Implementation of Activity-based Costing. *Accounting, Organizations and Society*, *22*(2), 105–122. doi:10.1016/S0361-3682(96)00031-1

Gosselin, M. (1999). *The ABC Paradox: Bandwagon Theories and Competitive Pressures*. Paper presented at the 22nd Annual Congress of the European Accounting Association, Bordeaux-France, 5-7 May.

Green, F. B., & Amenkhienan, F. (1992). Accounting Innovations: A Cross Sectional Survey of Manufacturing Firm. *Journal of Cost Management*, *6*, 58–64.

Horngren, C., Foster, G., Rajan, M., & Ittner, C. (2009). *Cost Accounting: A Managarial Emphasis* (11th ed.). Englewood Cliffs, NJ: Prentice-Hall.

Hussain, A., & Rickwood, C. (1993). *A Pilot Study into the Contextual Features of ABC Adopting Organisations*. Paper presented at the 16th Annual Congress of the European Accounting Association, Turku-Finland, 28-30 April.

Innes, J., & Mitchell, F. (1990). *Activity Based Costing: A Review with Case Studies*. The Chartered Institute of Management Accountants.

Innes, J., & Mitchell, F. (1991). ABC: A Survey of CIMA members. [UK]. *Management Accounting*, *69*(9), 34–35.

Innes, J., & Mitchell, F. (1999). A Survey of Activity-Based Costing in the UKs Largest Companies. *Management Accounting Research*, *10*, 137–153. doi:10.1006/mare.1998.0097

Innes, J., Mitchell, F., & Sinclair, D. (2000). A Tale of Two Surveys, CIMA Research Update (spring), 4.

Jenkinson, H., & Hui, J. (1994). Activity Based Costing. *Accounting Communique*, *56*, 1–4.

Johnson, H. T., & Kaplan, R. S. (1987). *Relevance Lost: The Rise and fall of Management Accounting*. Boston, MA: Harvard Business School Press.

Krumwiede, K. R. (1998). ABC: Why It's Tried and How it Succeeds. *Strategic Finance*, April, 32-38.

Lacombe, I., & Bescos, P.-L. (2000). ABC-ABM at Hewlett-Packard Europe for customer support. In T. Groot & K. Lukka (Eds.), *Cases in Management Accounting: Current Practices in European Companies*. Prentice Hall.

Lukka, K., & Granlund, M. (1996). Cost Accounting in Finland: Current Practice and Trends of Development. *European Accounting Review*, *5*, 1–28. doi:10.1080/09638189600000001

Lukka, K., & Grenlund, M. (1999). *The Asymmetric Communication Structure within the Accounting Academia: The Case of Activity-based Costing Research Genres*. Paper presented at the 22nd Annual Congress of the European Accounting Association, Bordeaux-France, 5-7 May.

Maher, M., Stickeny, C., & Weil, R. (1997). Managerial Accounting: An Introduction to concepts, methods and uses (6th ed.). New York: The Dryden press.

Malmi, T. (1999). Activity-based costing diffusion across organizations: an exploratory empirical analysis of Finnish firms. *Accounting, Organizations and Society*, *20*, 137–150.

Nair, M. (2000). Activity-Based Costing: Who is using it and Why? *Management Accounting Quarterly*, Spring, 29-33.

Nguyen, H. V., & Brooks, A. (1997). An Empirical Investigation of Adoption Issues Relating to Activity-Based Costing. *Asian Review of Accounting*, *5*(1), 1–18. doi:10.1108/eb060679

Nicholls, B. (1992). ABC in the UK - A Status Report. *Management Accounting* (UK), May, 22-23.

Nielsen, S., Melander, P., & Jakobsen, M. (2004). *Implementation and Utilization of ABC: A Danish perspective*. Paper presented at the 27th Annual Congress of the European Accounting Association, Prague-Czech Republic, 1-3 April.

Norris, G. (1994). User Perception of an Application of Activity-Based Costing. *Advances in Management Accounting*, *3*, 139–177.

Parker, T., & Lettes, T. (1991). Is Accounting Standing in the Way of Flexible Computer-Integrated Manufactuting? *Management Accounting* (USA), February.

Raiborn, G., Barfield, J., & Kinney, M. (1996). *Managerial Accounting* (2nd ed.). New York: West Publishing Company.

Sheskin, D. J. (1997). *Handbook of Parametric and Nonparametric Statistical Procedures*.New York: CRC Press Inc.

Shim, E., & Stagliano, A. (1997). A Survey of US Manufacturers' Implementation of ABC. *Journal of Cost Management* (March/April), 39-41.

Swenson, D. (1995). The Benefits of Activity Based Cost Management to the Manufacturing Industry, *Journal of Management Accounting Research*, Fall, 167-180.

ADDITIONAL READING

Anderson, S. W. (1995). A framework for assessing cost management system changes: The case of ABC implementation at General Motors. *Journal of Management Accounting Research, 7*, fall, 1-51.

Baily, J. (1991). Implementation of ABC systems by UK companies. *Management Accounting* (UK), February, 30-32.

Berliner, C., & Brimson, J. A. (1988). *Cost Management for today's advanced manufacturing: The CAM-I Conceptual design*. Boston, Harvard Business School Press.

Bhimani, A., & Pigott, D. (1992). Implementing ABC: A case study of organizational and behavioral consequences. *Management Accounting Research*, *3*, 119–132. doi:10.1016/S1044-5005(92)70007-9

Brimson, J. (1997). *Activity accounting: An activity-based costing approach*. New York: John Wiley and Sons.

Burns, J., Ezzame, M., & Scapens, R. (2003). *Challenge of management accounting change*. London, UK: Chartered Institute of Management Accountants.

Cooper, R., & Kaplan, R. (1999). *The design of cost management systems*. Upper Saddle River, NJ: Prentice-Hall.

Cooper, R., Kaplan, R. S., Maisel, L. S., Morrissey, E., & Oehm, R. (1992). *Implementing Activity-Based Cost Management: Moving from analysis to action*. Montvale, NJ: Institute of Management Accountants.

Cummings, G. (1991).Practical implications of implementing ABC. *Journal of the Institute of Industrial Engineers*, June, 20-23.

Eiler, R. G., & Campi, J. P. (1990). Implementing ABC at a process company. *Journal of Cost Management*, Spring, 43-50.

Hendricks, J.A. (1988). Applying cost accounting to factory automation. *Management Accounting*, December, 24-30.

Innes, J., & Norris, G. (1997). *The use of Activity-Based information-A Managerial Perspective*. London: Chartered Institute of Mnagement Accountants.

Jeans, M., & Morrow, M. (1989). The practicalities of using ABC. *Management Accounting*, UK, November, 42-44.

Kaplan, R., & Anderson, S. (2007). *Time driven Activity-Based Costing: A simpler and more powerful path to higher profits*. Boston, MA: Harvard Business School Press.

Kaplan, R., & Norton, D. (2006). *Alignment: Using the balanced scorecard to create corporate synergies*. Boston, MA: Harvard Business School Press.

King, A. M. (1991). The current status of ABC: An interview with Robin Cooper and Robert S. Kaplan. *Management Accounting*, September, 22-26. Malmi, T. (197). Towards explaining ABC failure, Accounting and control in a decentralized organization . *Management Accounting Research*, *8*, 459–480.

Monden, Y. (2003). Cost reduction systems: Target costing and Kaisen costing. Portland, OR: Productivity Press.

Oliver, L. (1995). Designing strategic cost systems. New York, John Wiley and Sons.

Young, M. (Ed.). (2003). Reading's ion Management Accounting (4th ed.). Upper Saddle River, NJ: Prentice-Hall.

KEY TERMS AND DEFINITIONS

ABC Adopters: This consists of those companies which currently implement ABC and it is operating as a replacement or as a supplementary to the traditional costing system.

Activity Driver: A measure of the demands placed on activities and, thus, the resources consumed by products and services.

Activity: Any event, action, task, or work that causes a cost to be incurred in producing a product or providing a service.

Activity-Based Costing (ABC): an approach to cost assignment that categorises all indirect costs by activities, traces indirect costs to those activities and then assigns costs of activities to products and services based on each product or service use of activities.

Environment Variables: these are variables related to the environment in which the firm operates (e.g., degree of competition).

Firm Characteristics: contextual or organizational variables which are conducive to ABC adoption (e.g. size of the firm, amount of overhead costs, product variety, and production complexity).

Indirect Costs: these are all overhead costs, manufacturing and non-manufacturing.

Non-Adopters of ABC: This group consists of those companies which have not yet considered ABC and those which have no plans to consider it in the coming 12 months.

Pervasive Computing: The widespread use of information technology by the firms selected for the study. The degree of computer usage was used as a proxy measure for this variable.

Product Variety: the number and diversity of different types of products produced or services rendered by the firm. Products of different colors, tastes, shapes, sizes, or packaging products differently are counted as different products.

Production Complexity: the number of components in a product or the number of processes or operations through which a product flows.

Chapter 14
The Effects of Innovative Instruments to Market Participants and the Financial System:
The Particular Role of Information Technologies

Demetres N. Subeniotis
University of Macedonia, Greece

Ioannis A. Tampakoudis
University of Macedonia, Greece

ABSTRACT

Financial innovation triggered new ways in which financial institutions and corporates cope with credit risk since the advent of credit derivatives. A variety of new developed financial instruments, often complex products, offers significant advantages to market participants and its key players and in particular financial institutions. As statistics indicate, advanced computerization is by large the most important factor for the wide use of credit derivatives. More efficient loans portfolio management, further business expansion and confidentiality are the main benefits for banks. In addition, various non financial firms benefit from these tailor-made products. More importantly, credit derivatives are key elements of the financial systems' stability, through increased liquidity, risk reallocation and credit risk pricing. Nevertheless, these innovative products are accompanied by significant considerations on behalf of users and policy makers. Out of which documentation, pricing, regulation and concentration are the central concerns. Market participants and regulators should face the challenges of credit derivatives market so as to boost the trouble-free intensive growth of these instruments.

DOI: 10.4018/978-1-60566-996-0.ch014

INTRODUCTORY OBSERVATIONS

One of the fundamental issues that concern financial institutions and corporates is risk management. A vital component of business risk, among others, is credit risk, since the risk of borrower default can impair the lender's capital structure and trigger similar effects upon the entire organization. Until recently, conventional techniques available to lenders, mainly banks, were loan monitoring and portfolio diversification. However, the expansion of credit and the greater focus on risk management from a number of market participants induced the development of more effective risk transfer markets and instruments, such as syndication, securitization, asset back securities and loan sales.

In overall, the available risk transfer techniques could not meet the needs of the market and, indeed, during the last few years credit risk management experienced a revolution, which primarily generated by the emergence of credit derivatives. The advent of credit derivatives formulated the grounds for increased market efficiency, better risk management and the development of sophisticated financial products. However, these new innovative instruments have raised some concerns due to the robust empirical and theoretical considerations regarding the effectiveness of credit derivatives. Indeed, the market turmoil caused by the collapse of subprime mortgage loans in the USA revived the interest around credit derivatives, since many corporations have been involved in the market through complex products[1].

Although credit derivatives are newly developed financial products, the corresponding market shows an impressive growth in depth, sophistication and diversification and has overtaken previous predictions. Similarly, the increased effectiveness of credit derivatives is confirmed by the number and kind of institutions participating in the market, where the key players are financial institutions like universal and investment banks, securities dealers, insurance companies and investment funds. Nevertheless, the market of credit derivatives has not yet fully matured and it comprises a relative small share of the entire derivatives market, representing a small fraction of the underlying principal value of the global volume of over-the-counter derivatives.

The present paper's overarching objective is to discuss the benefits and effectiveness of credit derivatives from the perspective of financial and non financial institutions. Equally, the effective contribution of credit derivatives to the entire financial system is analyzed. However, the concerns and limitations accompanying the use of these instruments possibly affecting their scope of use are also discussed. Regarding the limitations of credit derivatives, the analysis follows the viewpoint of users and policy makers. More specifically, the paper is structured as follows: the second section presents data for the credit derivatives market and the third section describes the main instruments. In the fourth section the contribution of information technology to the expansion of credit derivatives and more efficient risk management is analyzed. In the fifth section the potential advantages that derive from the application of credit derivatives are examined. In the sixth section, the most important considerations associated with these products are presented. Finally, the section of conclusions highlights the main key points of the paper, while concrete further suggestions are proposed in order to improve the framework of credit derivatives market and increase the efficiency of credit risk transfer techniques.

MARKET STATISTICS

The rapid growth of credit derivatives is confirmed by market statistics, although no single data source provides precise information for the entire market. Credit derivatives are considered over-the-counter products thus the accurate determination of their values outstanding is complicated. Two main sources publish credit derivatives statistics twice a

Table 1. Statistics of credit derivatives (in $US trillion)

Date of publication (Mid-Year) (Year-End)	ISDA			BIS		
	Notional amounts	*Semi-annual change*	*Annual change*	*Notional amounts*	*Semi-annual change*	*Annual change*
2008MY	54.6	-12%	20%	57.3	-1%	35%
2007YE	62.2	37%	81%	57.9	36%	102%
2007MY	45.5	32%	75%	42.6	49%	109%
2006YE	34.4	32%	101%	28.7	41%	106%
2006MY	26.0	52%	109%	20.4	46%	100%
2005YE	17.1	38%	105%	13.9	36%	118%
2005MY	12.4	48%	128%	10.2	60%	128%
2004YE	8.4	55%	123%	6.4	43%	
2004MY	5.4	44%	100%	4.5		
2003YE	3.8	41%	76%			
2003MY	2.7	25%	69%			
2002YE	2.2	40%	144%			
2002MY	1.6	70%	154%			
2001YE	0.9	45%				
2001MY	0.6			0.7		

Source: http://www.isda.org, http://www.bis.org. Authors' calculations

year, i.e. the International Swaps and Derivatives Association (ISDA) and the Bank of International Settlements (BIS)[2], collecting data from dealers[3]. In both sources a considerable increase either in notional amounts[4] or gross market values[5] is identified, despite the minor differences of the statistical data surveys. Table 1 and Figure 1 present the notional amounts of credit derivatives as depicted in both the organisations from the outset of semi-annual surveys publishing. Additionally, for each notional amount the semi-annual and annual percentage differences have been calculated.

The notional amounts of credit derivatives market show a substantial increase both on a semi-annual and annual level. More specifically, the semi-annual percentage growth of notional amounts varies from 25% to 70%, with an average growth rate roughly 44%. Importantly, the annual percentage increase for the majority of notional amounts exceeds 100% and the subsequent average growth indicates that the outstanding value of credit derivatives almost doubles every twelve months. However a unique exception concerns the slight semi-annual decrease in the 2008 mid-year statistics from both the ISDA and the BIS surveys, although the annual percentage change remains positive. As a fact, from the first survey performed in June 2001 until the previous one in June 2008, the notional amounts outstanding soared from approximately $700 billion to more than $54 trillion. Undoubtedly, the market statistics represent the greatest evidence regarding the significant implications of these innovative instruments to the market of credit risk.

Definition of Main Instruments

Credit derivatives can be defined as a specific class of financial instruments, the value of which is derived from an underlying market value driven by the credit risk of private or government entities, other than the counterparties to the credit deriva-

Figure 1. Notional amounts growth of credit derivatives (in $US trillion)

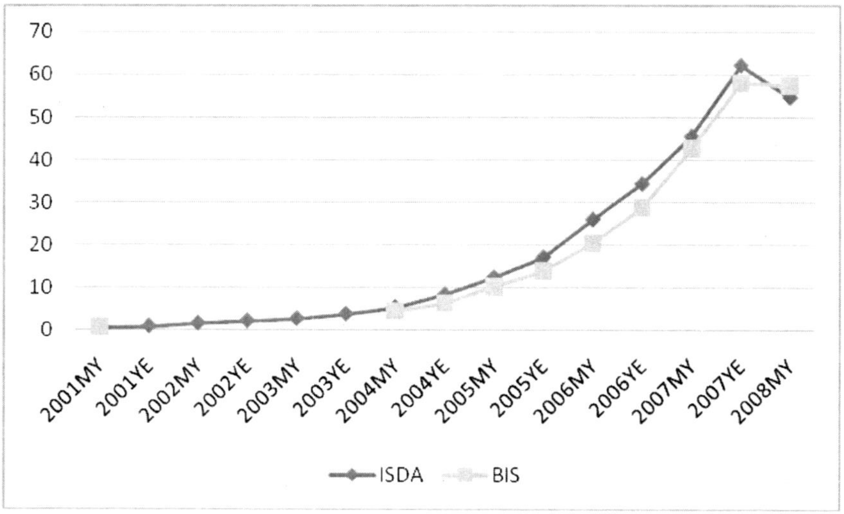

tive transaction itself. The last component of the definition is critical, due to the fact that it captures the role of credit derivatives in trading the credit risk of the reference entity by two parties who may have no commercial or financial relationship with the entity whose credit risk is being traded. The reference entity may be a corporate, a sovereign or any legal unit competent to issue debt. Generally, credit derivatives are bilateral financial contracts that isolate specific aspects of credit risk from an underlying product. As in the case of any contract, there is a buyer and a seller where the risk of the reference entity (or the underlying product) is transferred from the former to the latter.

The most important and widely used credit derivatives are the following: credit default swap, total return swap, credit intermediation swap, credit-linked notes, credit default option and credit spread option. The next paragraphs shortly describe these products.

The credit default swap (CDS) is the indispensable credit derivative, since it represents a big fraction of the credit derivatives market. A CDS is a transaction in which an investor, who has acquired an asset of doubtful quality, seeks to purchase protection against a credit event. The event may take many forms such as bankruptcy, payment moratorium in the case of a sovereign borrower, failure to meet a debt payment, a major and adverse change in the borrower's debt structure, the acceleration of other obligations, or simply a downgrade in the borrower's credit rating. The protection seller agrees to accept a contingent responsibility, receiving a periodic fee from the protection buyer, typically expressed in annual basis points paid on the notional amount. The definitions of a credit event, the contingent obligations and the settlement mechanism are flexible and determined by negotiation between the counterparties. In case at which a relevant credit event does occur, the protection buyer receives a contingent compensation payment. It should be noted that the protection buyer does not need to suffer a loss, since it is sufficient to provide available information for the event at the same time.

The total return swap (TRS) was essentially developed from the credit swap. The key difference is that, while the credit swap is triggered only if a defined credit event takes place, the total return swap contains any change in the market value of the underlying asset. The total return swap provides protection against the loss of value irrespective of cause. The protection seeker contracts to transfer to the protection seller the entire cash flows associated with the specified asset in return for an agreed payment, usually a floating rate payment set at a spread above LIBOR.

The credit intermediation swap differs from the above two instruments in that three rather than two parties are involved. In particular, a high rated corporate or financial institution acts as an intermediary between two relatively small corporates, probably not rated, wishing to enter into a fixed\ floating swap transaction even if they are not of sufficient quality which is normally required in a swap transaction. Each of the initial counterparties is free from the credit risk associated with the other party, and hence the intermediary can be thought of performing a role similar to that of a clearinghouse.

The credit-linked note (CLN) is a device by which the coupon payments on a note issue are linked to the performance of some other reference entity or index, such as corporate loans, entire portfolios, sovereign debt instruments and indexes like the Emerging Market Bond Index. If the reference asset performs consistently, the notes will be paid as to the agreed coupon and eventually repaid at par. In contrast, any shortfall in the payments on the reference asset will result in a reduction or elimination of the coupon payments on the notes, and possibly repayment below par on the maturity. Several different types of credit linked notes (CLNs) have been structured and placed in the past few years.

Credit options are in essence conventional options used as a hedge against a deterioration in the rating or market value of a specified asset. Indeed, they are puts or calls on some predetermined reference asset, which may be a note, loan or bond, but is regularly a floating rate instrument. The buyer has the right, but not the obligation, to sell or buy the specified floating rate instrument at a specified strike price. They are settled either in cash or by delivering the instrument itself. Concerning the time where they can be exercised, they may be either American or European style options. As with other options, the credit option premium is sensitive to the volatility of the underlying market price and the extent to which the strike spread is in or out of the money.

A further development of the simple credit options is the credit spread options, which are options based upon interest rate spreads. One side of the spread is typically the rate on US Treasury bonds, while the other side, the risk asset, may be a corporate bond or a sovereign issue of a foreign government. A spread, probably the market spread at the time of writing, is set as the strike price. In fact, an increase in the spread means that the required yield on the risk asset has increased relative to the Treasury yield, leading to the exercise of the option. Credit spread options are usually embedded in other products, such as floating-rate loans, asset swaps and credit default swaps.

The Contribution of Computing to Credit Risk Management

The precise estimation of credit risk exposures and a pricing mechanism for the various credit derivative products are decisive factors for the effective use of them by financial and non-financial institutions. Credit risk measurement is quite a complex process, since qualitative characteristics should be modeled. In this line, financial economists have developed various econometric models used by firms to determine the level of their credit exposure. Likewise, credit derivatives are tradable products and thus they should have a fairly determined value. Considering that the existing models of derivatives pricing could not be applied, new and complex pricing procedures have emerged. Indeed, to a great extent, the initial separation of risk management into market and credit risk and the further expansion of the latter occurred due to the conceptualization and development of sophisticated financial econometrics in the frame of advanced computerization. It could be argued that the significant role credit derivatives play in the financial system can be attributed to the rapid growth of statistical computing tools. A presentation of the conceptual framework of credit risk modeling follows to illustrate the significant contribution of information technology to risk management.

Credit Risk Estimation

The primary step in credit risk management is the estimation of a firm's expected loss, defined as the product of the borrower default probability and the loss given default. The former is estimated taking into account either bond prices, historical data or equity prices[6], while the latter is the expected loss in case of borrower's default. According to the adopted approach, the analysts apply the corresponding procedures and calculate the particular statistical measures. For instance, financial institutions have to estimate generic zero-coupon yields, expected default losses, hazard rates, default probability densities, recovery rates, historical default probabilities, non linear equations and models such as Merton's and formulas like Black-Scholes. Apart from the applied methodology, a significant amount of market or historical data is equally required as an input to the statistical models. Highly specialized statistical software could exclusively calculate the above mentioned parameters and make the utilization of data efficient. In fact, every financial institution applies its own models in order to estimate default probabilities, while many information technology companies provide quantitative credit analysis solutions and offer a wide range of statistical tools. Financial and non-financial institutions have indeed a variety of options at their disposal to deal with credit risk, varying from developing internal procedures and models to outsourcing credit risk analysis, an advantage thanks to information technology.

In parallel to default probabilities modeling, the credit value-at-risk (VaR) measure has been developed in order to provide a definite and unified information basis to senior management, shareholders and regulators. The specific parameter determines the largest possible credit loss that in a specific time period would not be exceeded at a certain confidence level. The time horizon is typically one year, while historical data is used in order to calculate default probabilities. The credit VaR focuses on either counterparties default or both credit rating changes and defaults, taking into account the probability distribution of losses. Financial institutions have developed outstanding analytical methodological approaches to calculate credit VaR, although the theoretical framework remains the same[7]. All the available models have been developed based on the functions available at highly developed information technologies, since measures such as Monte Carlo simulation, Gaussian copula model and complicated probability distributions can be calculated solely through computer software.

Credit Derivatives Pricing

Credit derivatives are in essence traded products therefore they need to be priced. However, the special characteristics of these over-the-counter financial instruments render their pricing difficult. The valuation of the credit derivative instruments, mainly credit default swaps, is performed through the application of complex equations, while the borrowers default probabilities are input parameters. Moreover, the Monte Carlo simulation applies for valuing synthesized products, like basket credit default swaps. The basic pricing formula for options, namely the Black-Scholes, adjusted of default probability, is used in order to price credit spread options. In addition, the price of a derivative product should incorporate the default probability of the counterparty.

The pricing procedures of credit derivatives obviate that the entire calculations range should be performed through computing techniques and in these terms, specialized computer software allows for large input data, numerous trials and statistical testing, which in turn attribute more accurate pricing. In overall, the use of advanced technology permits the rapid calculation of several complex models in order to estimate a fair and cost-effective value of credit derivative products.

Applications of Credit Derivatives

To a large extent, banks in business or geographic terms focus on specific areas according to their branch network or sectors with particular expertise. Consequently, loan portfolios issued by banks tend to be concentrated, a fact which, in turn, limits their ability to diversify credit risks across borrowers. The implication of various credit derivatives instruments provides banks with an effective tool in order to diversify their loan portfolios and hedge their credit exposure. These products offer a means for more active and, potentially, more successful portfolio management of banks' credit exposure, by adding hedging instruments for particular counterparty risk and by considerably extending the possibilities of geographical and sectorial diversification. Credit risk management could become further centralised and more market priced oriented, accelerating the integration of credit risk and market risk. In fact, there is a significant increase in the use of credit derivatives for hedging purposes, since banks transfer their credit exposure that derives from loans to small and medium-sized corporates, loans to emerging markets and the counterparties[8].

In addition to hedging, commercial and investment banks active in the credit derivatives market so as to enhance their profitability through the development of new products, proprietary trading and market-making. As previously indicated, the notional amounts of credit derivatives have substantially augmented and this in turn stands as an indication of risk-free income for many market participants. Investment banks in particular, are more enabled to act as underwriters since they can transfer the risk of specific credit assets until these assets are sold bundled into the market[9].

As previously mentioned, a credit derivative contract is a private financial agreement between two parties only which does not publicize available information. The reference entity, whose credit risk is traded, does not appear on the contract, since the transfer of credit exposure does not require its approval or knowledge. Consequently, credit derivatives allow banks to manage their credit exposure, without affecting or damaging the underlying customer relationships. Likewise, they can expand their business through the existing customer network, providing their borrowers with new credit facilities. Banks do not need to seek new lending relationships in new markets or beyond their geographic network. Thus, confidentiality is a unique characteristic and a key advantage of credit derivatives, which contributes to the separation of credit exposure from the lending relationship. In order to underline the significance of that characteristic, we note that alternative and well known risk management techniques, such as loan sales, syndication or securitisation cannot be implemented concealedly from the borrower.

Apart from confidentiality, another distinct characteristic of credit derivatives is the fact that they are over-the-counter products, which renders each of the contract terms negotiable. Market participants can satisfy their specific needs to a great extent, since they can choose the particular counterparty and sign the corresponding contract. The two parties modify the duration, the contingent payments, the value and the credit coverage of the derivative contract to accommodate their specific needs, without taking into consideration characteristics of the underlying product.

Even though financial institutions dominate the market of credit derivatives, other corporations exploit these instruments as a means to hedge credit risk on receivables and cross-border credit risk. Compared to alternatives traditionally utilized by firms – such as reducing the level of business, factoring or insurances – derivatives can offer more cost-effective solutions, with some trade-offs on the level of protection. Credit derivatives also allow for confidential hedging (as opposed to factoring), which most corporates would be sensitive to.

Taking into account the significant benefits of credit derivatives to financial and non financial institutions, it could be argued that these products, eventually, contribute to the stability and efficiency of the entire financial system. Indeed, credit derivatives are likely to enhance the overall liquidity and effectiveness of markets for risky products, by allowing market participants to separate and transparently price and trade credit risk, in order to optimise their credit exposure. Likewise, the further expansion of the market leads to the development of exceptionally sophisticated products, which in turn increase the available choices for institutional and private investors. More importantly, the growth of new credit products suggests a potential key role of corporates in this market, currently dominated by banks and other financial institutions.

Credit derivatives enable the reallocation of credit risk among corporates, industries and nations, thus eliminating credit concentration. When credit risk is transferred outside the banking system, there is a possibility to increase the overall level of credit available and when credit risk is spread across countries, it may reduce banks' vulnerability to domestic business cycles. Thus, the existence of numerous and various participants worldwide enhances market monitoring, transparency and supervision. In addition, these instruments improve the price-discovery process for credit risk by facilitating the trading of such risks for which cash markets are illiquid or distorted by various technical factors. Increased transaction frequency and the availability of more objective pricing will probably lead to increased liquidity and the presence of additional market players.

Considerations of Credit Derivatives

Inferring from the above, the introduction of credit derivatives provides significant benefits to market participants. Nevertheless, important considerations have been raised in parallel, as addressed in the following paragraphs.

Critical Concerns for Market Participants

An emerging key issue is the method which should be used in order to estimate a fair price for a credit derivative. The assessment of credit risk is more complicated than market risk, due to the nature of the credit exposure. In the case of credit derivatives, apart from the market risk, the counterparty risk should be estimated as well. Regarding the former, it is quite straightforward to estimate default probabilities taking into account the volatility of a reference asset. On the contrary, the calculation of the latter meets crucial methodological difficulties, since the individual default history does not affect its likelihood of defaulting in the future[10]. Moreover, changes in counterparties' credit worthiness are generally not directly observable, unlike changes in most market prices. Currently, the area of credit default swaps has met significant progress towards standardised pricing models. Additionally, a number of institutions make markets on these products and consequently valuation may be directly derived from dealer bids, offers or mid market prices.

Further, financial institutions and corporates cope with legal risks associated with credit derivatives. The documentation underlying the transactions can be complex, while the interpretation of credit events clauses can be ambiguous. Transfer of credit exposure by credit derivatives could be problematic, since a derivative contract may be deemed illegal or incompatible. Additionally, each counterparty may contribute to the occurrence of a transferred credit event and consequently requires the bilateral payments, which consists of a source of moral hazard. Numerous well known examples in the past illustrate this point, such as payment delays noticed by the City of Moscow, the debt restructurings of Conseco and Xerox, the Railtrack case and the loss of J.P. Morgan which missed hedge against the credit risk of Enron. In the specific last case, the bank had to add a potential $1.1 billion to its unsecured exposure to Enron, since eleven insurance companies refused to pay on surety bonds arguing that the derivatives contracts were misleading and there was suspicion of fraudulent inducement[11]. The JP took legal actions against insurers and other banks, leading to the assumption that other investors could equally pursue legal actions in the case of ambiguity, unless transfers of risk are explicit.

Taking into consideration the practical inefficiencies of credit derivatives, as from 1999 the ISDA introduced strict and rigorous documentation clauses so as to minimize disputes arising from interpretation. Thus, financial institutions have to adhere to the standardised documentation regarding the interpretation of the credit event. The standardised definition decreases the possibility of opportunistic behaviour between the parties, clarifies rights and obligations and boosts market liquidity. However, although there have been efforts for new and updated documentation, the distinctive nature of credit risk, contrary to the other forms of risk, renders unfeasible the precise documentation of all the credit clauses.

Moreover, credit derivatives markets are currently over-the-counter, relatively illiquid and not transparent. Indeed, it appears that there are no associated active secondary markets to allow market participations to take long or short positions. Thus, firms should first consider the uncertainty associated with their selling potential or offsetting an existing position. Still, the recent launches of two internet trading platforms for credit derivatives, Credit Trade and Creditex[12], could generate the needed transparency to the market. Another important development, that should facilitate the growth and the liquidity of the market, regards the European Credit Swap Index[13], launched in March 2000 by J.P. Morgan, and a series of US credit-spread indexes, launched by Standard and Poors in April 2000. Nevertheless, liquidity risk for corporates using credit derivatives only for hedging purposes is not to be mentioned.

A further issue is that a potential group of credit derivatives market players is quite limited with small and medium sized financial and non financial firms, highly concentrated in geographic areas or business sectors. These corporates could be involved in transactions with tailor-made and complex derivative products, which are directly comprehensible. Apart from hedging purposes, many companies trade sophisticated instruments in order to speculate, without properly comprehending the potential risks. Equally, investment funds, such as pension or mutual funds, may invest in synthesized products of unwanted risk and volatility. As a result, unexpected or unfavourable market movements can lead to serious financial damages affecting large and prestigious financial institutions (such as American Express) who have recently admitted they had trouble understanding the complex products[14].

Regulatory Issues

The spreading usage of credit derivatives by banks and other financial institutions for trading credit exposures poses relevant concerns to regulatory authorities. The rapid growth and global presence of credit derivatives generated the need for generally accepted regulations from an international authority, such as the Bank of International Settlements, instead of regional guidelines from national regulators. Nevertheless, there is not a unique regulatory framework for the credit derivatives market and for certain issues national authorities provide different interpretations and guidance. The situation furthers complicates with the rapid development of new structured and highly sophisticated products, such as credit linked notes and "basket" structures. Besides, there are distinctive features associated with credit derivatives, which in turn complicate their regulatory treatment. In particular, asset, maturity and currency mismatches pose additional difficulties for regulatory bodies, which deal with these issues independently from each other.

An important concern regarding the regulatory treatment of credit derivatives is associated with their disclosure. The trading of credit derivatives affects the riskiness of the counterparties, an essential issue for the shareholders and other stakeholders. Credit derivatives are tailored, over the counter, products, for which the financial institutions are not obliged to provide public information or to clearly record their transactions at the balance sheet or the financial statement. Indeed, adequate disclosure and transparency of credit derivatives markets is a challenging issue, which conditionally enhances the efficiency and the further development of the financial system.

Concerning the obligations of the two counterparties, for a protection seller the credit exposure is identical to that of a lender to or bondholder of the same reference entity and consequently the exposure that should be registered on the banking book is according to the capital requirements of the 1998 Basel Accord[15]. The distinct characteristics of credit derivatives renders their positioning in the traditional regulatory framework difficult, providing the grounds for regulatory arbitrage between the banking and the trading book[16], since more sophisticated banks might try to shift part of their credit business to the latter with lower capital requirements,. On the other hand, the capital requirements for the protection buyer depend on the terms of the credit derivative. If the credit risk is entirely undertaken by the seller, the former has no further obligations. In case of specific and limited protection for the credit derivative, the buyer is required to hold capital relative to the risk of the protection seller. Taking into account all the above limitations associated with the accounting and regulatory treatment of credit derivatives, the accurate and unified documentation and interpretation of the credit derivatives instruments becomes a necessity for regulators and authorities, for the clarification needs of the market conditions and the participants' obligations.

The Risks of Credit Derivatives to the Financial System

A significant argument against credit derivatives is that they are mainly used to trade risks already traded in existing markets, since the underlying products are corporate bonds, large leveraged bank loans and pools of homogeneous small loans. In essence, credit derivatives are used in order to repackage the existing risks in other forms. In this perspective, the implications of credit derivatives for risk management would be positive in case of usage for trading other exposures particularly small and medium sized loans. In addition, even though the new instruments should make the credit markets more efficient and complete, the overall risk allocation might deteriorate instead of ameliorating, since financial innovation could result in the breakdown of other markets, such as loan sales, syndicated loans or securitization. In a more general perspective, the introduction of a new market in an economy with asymmetric information will typically alter the equilibriums in existing markets by changing the economy's' information structure. Notwithstanding these facts, the entire financial system could derive benefits from the complementary function of existing markets for sharing the credit risk.

Two critical issues emerge relative to the increased development of credit derivatives: adverse selection and moral hazard (Duffe and Zhou, 1999; Gorton and Pennacchi, 1995). Both implications are due to asymmetric information among market participants, since banks are better informed on the quality of their loans' portfolio. Adverse selection occurs when a bank either decides to lend money to riskier borrowers or buy protection for certain time periods during the life of a loan. In any case, banks implement their strategy by using credit derivatives and consequently the overall risk of the system increases. Similarly, moral hazard occurs when the banks' incentive to efficiently and rigorously assess the creditworthiness of a borrower is reduced, since the bank has the ability to hedge any credit position. Likewise, the use of credit derivatives can reduce the loan monitoring incentives. If a bank is not able to transfer the credit risk to another party, then it becomes more concerned and increases its monitoring efforts for the timely and final repayment of the loan. Moral hazard and adverse selection are the main sources of inefficient risk migration, initiating increased systemic risk.

An additional issue contingent to credit derivatives is the high degree of concentration in the market. In particular, a number of major investment banks and securities dealers dominate the market, trading the vast majority of credit derivatives contracts. According to BIS statistics the more concentrated markets are those in Latin America, in contrast with USA and Europe where the applied indices[17] are relatively low. This fact could be attributed to the expertise and the market share of certain financial institutions, although there are disguised risks for the corresponding institutions and the entire financial system. Furthermore, due to globalization and the multinational presence of many financial institutions, the threat of contagion effect is a central issue. Taking into account the disclosure issue of credit derivatives and the increased concentration and consolidation in the financial industry, the regulatory authorities should develop the adequate legislation with the intention of ensuring market credibility and stability.

CONCLUDING REMARKS AND FURTHER CHALLENGES

The advent of credit derivatives has provided the market participants of the financial system with efficient tools for conducting risk management. Although these products initially originated for hedging purposes, they now offer increased benefits to the users. Apart from the financial institutions which are the key players in the market of credit derivatives, various corporates intend to exploit the efficiency of these innovative instruments. Primarily, credit derivatives improved credit risk management, provided the opportunity of simultaneously expanding business and enhancing financial stability of the banks, satisfied the specific needs of financial or non financial institutions and eventually eliminated several threats to the financial system, while reinforcing its credibility. A variety of recently used hedging and investment instruments is structured with the inclusion of credit derivatives, providing the market with sophisticated products, which in turn increased the available options for financial institutions, institutional and private investors.

The rapid development of credit derivatives is by large attributed to advanced information technology. Financial institutions and specialized computing firms provide highly sophisticated consulting and software in the domain of credit risk management which can be conducted through various mathematical models. The existence of a wide array of options for financial and non-financial firms to effectively and economically manage their credit exposures is closely intertwined with the development of computerization. Likewise, the high level of computer software enables the development and further sophistication of statistical models. Information technology can benefit and optimize credit risk management but the risks do not eliminate in themselves. In this aspect, the recent credit crunch and the collapse of well-known financial institutions can certainly alarm market players.

Notwithstanding the positive contribution of credit derivatives to the entire financial system and its participants, these instruments are associated with significant considerations regarding the users and the competent authorities. Users are primarily concerned with the pricing, documentation and limited liquidity whilst regulators and authorities are faced with the lack of a unique and general accepted framework, which in turn creates market inefficiencies and user misconduct. Furthermore, there are hidden threats for the financial system, which both the market participants and the regulators should effectively confront, although significant steps have been made towards the reduction or elimination of the above inconveniences.

The current rapid pace in the credit derivatives market is expected to continue holding in mind the all inclusive benefits in credit risk management and the further elaboration of tailored products. At the same time, market participants and regulators should focus on the associated limitations of credit derivatives so as to improve the overall market efficiency. In this line, the introduction of precise and comprehensive legislative rules and the collaboration of national authorities, international organizations and financial institutions would be required. Last but not least, market participants bear the responsibility for proper and cost-effective use of credit instruments. Financial and non financial firms should get familiar with their risk tolerance, understand the risks underlying any transaction, avoid concentrating risks, and demonstrate caution with complex and sophisticated instruments, as well as identify the risk profile of their counterparties, realize the value their off-balance-sheet investments and assess the liquidity risk of their credit derivative products. The nature of the financial system and significantly the inherent contagion threat cannot afford to bear individual initiatives but instead joint action is required.

ACKNOWLEDGMENT

The authors would like to thank Efraxia Dalakiouridou, D.E.S.S, University of Macedonia for her useful comments.

REFERENCES

Altman, E., & Saunders, A. (1998). Credit risk measurement: Developments over the last 20 years. *Journal of Banking & Finance*, *21*, 1721–1742. doi:10.1016/S0378-4266(97)00036-8

Bank for International Settlements. (2008). *OTC derivatives market activity in the first half of 2008* (Regular OTC Derivatives Market Statistics). Retrieved February 25, 2009, from http://www.bis.org/publ/otc_hy0811.htm

Basel Committee on Banking Supervision. (2005). *Credit risk transfer* (Report submitted by a Working Group established by the Committee on the Global Financial System). Retrieved February 25, 2009, from http://www.bis.org/publ/cgfs20.pdf

Beattie, J. (2000). *Contagion in Latin America: An Analysis of Credit Derivatives* (Working Paper). Duke University, Durham.

Berger, N., & Udell, G. (1995). Relationship lending and lines of credit in small firm finance. *The Journal of Business*, *68*, 351–381. doi:10.1086/296668

Boot, A., & Thakor, A. (1997). Financial System Architecture. *Review of Financial Studies*, *10*, 693–733. doi:10.1093/rfs/10.3.693

Carlstrom, C., & Samolyk, K. (1995). Loan sales as a response to market-based capital constraints. *Journal of Banking & Finance*, *19*, 627–646. doi:10.1016/0378-4266(94)00144-R

Das, S. (1998). *Credit derivatives: Trading and management of credit and default risk*. Singapore: John Wiley & Sons.

Das, S. (2000). *Credit Derivatives and Credit Linked Notes*. New York: John Wiley & Sons.

Diamond, D., & Rajan, G. (2000). A theory of bank capital. *The Journal of Finance*, *55*, 2431–2465. doi:10.1111/0022-1082.00296

Dufey, G., & Rehm, F. (2000) An Introduction to Credit Derivatives (Working Paper). University of Michigan Business School.

Duffee, G., & Zhou, C. (2001). Credit Derivatives in Banking: Useful Tools for Managing Risk. *Journal of Monetary Economics*, *48*, 25–54. doi:10.1016/S0304-3932(01)00063-0

Duffie, D., & Garleanu, N. (2001). Risk and valuation of collateralised debt obligations. *Financial Analysts Journal*, 41–59. doi:10.2469/faj.v57.n1.2418

Fama, E. (1985). What's different about banks? *Journal of Monetary Economics*, *15*, 29–40. doi:10.1016/0304-3932(85)90051-0

Froot, K., & Stein, J. (1998). Risk Management, Capital Budgeting, and Capital Structure for Financial Institutions: An Integrated Approach. *Journal of Financial Economics*, *47*, 55–82. doi:10.1016/S0304-405X(97)00037-8

Gibson, M. (2007). *Credit Derivatives and Risk Management. Finance and Economics Discussion Series* (Federal Reserve Board). Washington, D.C.

Goodhart, C. (1998). *The Evolution of Central Banks*, Cambridge: The MIT Press.

Goodman, L. (2002). Synthetic CDOs: an introduction. *Journal of Derivatives*, 60–72. doi:10.3905/jod.2002.319180

Gorton, G., & Pennacchi, G. (1995). Banking and loan sales: marketing nonmarketable assets. *Journal of Monetary Economics*, *35*, 389–411. doi:10.1016/0304-3932(95)01199-X

Henke, S., Burghof, H., & Rudolph, B. (1998). Credit Securitization and Credit Derivatives: Financial Instruments and the Credit Risk Management of Middle Market Commercial Loan Portfolios (Working Paper). Munchen University.

http://www.bis.org/statistics/derstats.htm, Retrieved February 25, 2009.

http://www.isda.org/statistics/recent.html, Retrieved February 25, 2009.

Instefjord, N. (2005). Risk and hedging: Do credit derivatives increase bank risk? *Journal of Banking & Finance*, *29*, 333–345. doi:10.1016/j.jbankfin.2004.05.008

Kiff, J., Michaud, F., & Mitchell, J. (2002). *Instruments of Credit Risk Transfer: Effects on Financial Contracting and Financial Stability* (Working Paper).

Kiff, J., & Morrow, R. (2000). *Credit Derivatives*. Bank of Canada Review.

Longstaff, A., & Scwartz, E. (1995). Valuing Credit Derivatives. *Journal of Fixed Income*, 6–12. doi:10.3905/jfi.1995.408138

Minton, B., Stulz, R., & Williamson, R. (2009). How much do Banks Use Credit Derivatives to Reduce Risk. *Journal of Financial Services Research*, *35*, 1–31. doi:10.1007/s10693-008-0046-3

Morrison, A. (2005). Credit Derivatives, Disintermediation, and Investment Decisions. *The Journal of Business*, *78*, 621–647. doi:10.1086/427641

Neal, S. (1996). *Credit Derivatives: New Financial Instruments for Controlling Credit Risk*, (Economic Review). Federal Reserve Bank of Kansas City.

Schonbucher, P. (2000). *Credit Risk Modelling and Credit Derivatives*. Unpublished doctoral dissertation, Bonn University.

Stulz, R. (2003). *Risk Management and Derivatives*, Cincinnati, Ohio: South-Western Publishing.

Tavakoli, M. (1998). *Credit derivatives. A guide to instruments and applications.* New York: John Wiley & Sons.

ADDITIONAL READING

Acharya, V., & Johnson, T. (2007). Insider trading in credit derivatives. *Journal of Financial Economics*, *84*, 110–141. doi:10.1016/j.jfineco.2006.05.003

Allen, F., & Carletti, E. (2006). Credit risk transfer and contagion. *Journal of Monetary Economics*, *53*, 89–111. doi:10.1016/j.jmoneco.2005.10.004

Basel Committee on Banking Supervision. (2005). *Credit risk transfer* (Report submitted by a Working Group established by the Committee on the Global Financial System). Retrieved February 25, 2009, from http://www.bis.org/publ/cgfs20.pdf

Chance, D. (1998). *An Introduction to Derivatives* (4th ed.). Orlando, Florida: The Dryden Press.

Das, S. (2000). *Credit Derivatives and Credit Linked Notes.* New York: John Wiley & Sons.

Errais, E., Giesecke, K., & Goldberg, L. (2007). Pricing Credit from the Top Down with Affine Point Processes. In J. Miller, D. Edelman, J. Appleby (Eds.), *Numerical Methods for Finance* (pp. 195-201). Chapman & Hall/CRC Financial Mathematics Series.

Hirtle, B. (2009). Credit Derivatives and Bank Credit Supply. *Journal of Financial Intermediation*, *18*, 125–150. doi:10.1016/j.jfi.2008.08.001

Hull, J. (2003). *Options, Futures and Other Derivatives* (5th ed.). Upper Saddle River, New Jersey: Prentice Hall.

Jackson, M., & Staunton, M. (2001). *Advanced modelling in finance using Excel and VBA*. Chichester, West Sussex: John Wiley & Sons.

Levy, G. (2004). *Computational Finance. Numerical Methods for Pricing Financial Instruments*. Jordan Hill, Oxford: Elsevier.

London, J. (2007). *Modeling Derivatives Applications in MATLAB, C_{++}, and Excel.* Upper Saddle River, New Jersey: FT Press.

Lucas, D., Goodman, L., & Fabozzi, F. (2007). *Collateralized Debt Obligations and Credit Risk Transfer* (Working Paper). Yale ICF.

Morrison, A. (2005). Credit Derivatives, Disintermediation, and Investment Decisions. *The Journal of Business*, *78*, 621–647. doi:10.1086/427641

Nicolò, A., & Pelizzon, L. (2008). Credit derivatives, capital requirements and opaque OTC markets. *Journal of Financial Intermediation*, *17*, 444–463. doi:10.1016/j.jfi.2008.03.001

Norden, L., & Wagner, W. (2008). Credit derivatives and loan pricing. *Journal of Banking & Finance*, *32*, 2560–2569. doi:10.1016/j.jbankfin.2008.05.006

Saunders, A., & Allen, L. (2002). *Credit Risk measurement. New Approaches to Value at Risk and Other Paradigms* (2nd ed.). John Wiley & Sons. Retrieved February 25, 2009, from http://books.google.com/books

Schonbucher, P. (2003). *Credit derivatives pricing models: model, pricing and implementation*. New York: John Wiley & Sons.

Sinkey, J. (2002). *Commercial Bank Financial Management. In the Financial-Services Industry* (6th ed.). Upper Saddle River, New Jersey: Prentice Hall.

Skeel, D., & Partnoy, F. (2006). The Promise and Perils of Credit Derivatives. *University of Cincinnati Law Review*, *75*, 1019–1051.

Wagner, N. (Ed.). (2008). *Credit Risk: Models, Derivatives, and Management.* Chapman & Hall/CRC Financial Mathematics Series.

KEY TERMS AND DEFINITIONS

Adverse Selection: The problem created be asymmetric information before a transaction occurs: the people who are the most undesirable from the other party's point of view are the ones who are most likely to want to engage in the financial transaction.

Asymmetric Information: The inequality of knowledge that each party to a transaction has about the other.

Black-Scholes Model: A model for pricing European option on stocks, developed by Fischer Black, Myron Scholes and Robert Merton.

Bond: A debt security that promises to make payments periodically for a specified period of time.

Bond Rating: Grades assigned to debt securities denoting their underlying credit quality.

Bootstrap Method: A procedure for calculating the zero-coupon yield curve from market data.

Clearinghouse: A corporation that guarantees the performance of the parties in an exchange-traded derivatives transaction.

Collateralized Debt Obligation: A way of packaging credit risk. Several classes of securities are created from a portfolio of bonds and there are rules for determining how defaults are allocated to classes.

Commercial Bank: Narrowly defined legally as a banking institution that both accepts demand deposits and makes commercial loans.

Copula: A way of defining the correlation between variables with known distribution.

Counterparty: The opposite side in a financial transaction.

Credit (Intermediation) Swap: Protection against non-payment through a fee paid to a third party who compensates the bank in the event of a default.

Credit Default Swap: An instrument that gives the holder of credit asset the right to receive compensation in the case of a credit event by the issuer.

Credit Derivative: A derivative whose payoff depends on the creditworthiness of one or more entities.

Credit Event: Default, change in solvency status, late payment, or some other indication of a change in a borrower's financial status.

Credit Migration: The movement of a borrower's credit rating or score to another category, either an upgrade or a downgrade.

Credit Rating: A measure of a borrower's creditworthiness by a ratings agency such as Moody's or S&P's, AAA vs. "junk".

Credit Risk: The risk arising from the possibility that the borrower will default.

Credit Spread Option: Option whose payoff depends on the spread between the yields earned on two assets.

Credit Value at Risk: The credit loss that will not be exceeded at some specified confidence level, during a certain time period.

Default: A situation in which the party issuing a debt instrument is unable to make interest payments or pay off the amount owed when the instrument matures.

Default Probability Density: Measures the unconditional probability of default in a future short period of time.

Default Risk Premium: The spread between the interest rate on bonds with default risk and the interest rate on default-free bonds, or the spread between one risky bond and another.

Default Risk: The risk that a loan customer may fail to repay a loan as promised.

Derivatives: Off-balance-sheet activities that can be used for hedging or speculating and that derive their value from previously issued securities, such as interest rates, exchange rates, equity prices, or commodity prices.

Econometric Model: A model whose equations are estimated using statistical procedures.

Embedded Option: An option that is an inseparable part of another instrument.

Hazard Rate: Measures probability of default in a short period of time conditional on no earlier default.

Historical Simulation: A simulation based on historical data.

Investment Banks: A financial services organization specializing in the raising of capital through the issuance of new securities in the primary market and in linking buyers with sellers of existing securities in the secondary market.

Monte Carlo Simulation: A procedure for randomly sampling changes in market variables in order to value a derivative.

Moral Hazard: The risk that one party to a transaction will engage in behaviour that is undesirable from the other party's point of view.

Off-Balance-Sheet Products: Financial products that affect banks' profits but are not visible on their balance sheet.

Over-the-Counter Market: A secondary market in which dealers at different locations who have an inventory of securities stand ready to buy and sell securities to anyone who comes to them and is willing to accept their prices.

Recovery Rate: Amount recovered in the event of a default as a percent of the claim.

Securitization: The process of transforming illiquid financial assets into marketable capital market instruments. Each participant attempts to market the security and shares in losses.

Syndicate: A group of investment banks that come together for the purpose of issuing a security. The syndicate spreads the risk of the issue among the members.

Value at Risk: A comprehensive measure of risk that incorporates all the major risks a bank faces. Measured as the potential loss in a bank's portfolio associated with price movements of a given probability over a specified time horizon.

Yield: A return provided by an instrument.

Zero-Coupon Yield Curve: A plot of the zero-coupon interest rate against time to maturity.

ENDNOTES

1. The main products were asset backed securities, such as collateralised debt obligations, which focused on US subprime residential mortgage backed securities.
2. The statistics of BIS public surveys cover the notional amounts and gross market values outstanding of major banks and dealers in the G10 countries.
3. The surveys are based on data collected by the major global dealers. In fact, not all dealers participate, while some others do not respond.
4. Nominal or notional amounts outstanding are defined as the gross nominal or notional value of all deals concluded and not yet settled on the reporting date. Actually, this measure is widely used since it is relatively easy to be collected.
5. Gross market values are defined as the sums of the absolute values of all open contracts with either positive or negative replacement values evaluated at market prices.
6. The first two approached are based on the company's credit rating, as it is determined by independent rating agencies, such as Moody's Investor Services and Standard & Poor's (S&P).
7. Regarding the estimation of the portfolio credit risk there are three well-known models, which are CreditMetrics, Credit Risk Plus and Credit Portfolio View.
8. The BIS statistics indicate double digits hedging of their total credit exposure after 2005, while previously it was below 10%.
9. For instance, banks can hedge the credit risk of particular credit assets until they collect a significant amount of homogeneous assets and launch a securitization.
10. The shape of many credit events is not as smooth as market price changes; market risk distributions are more symmetric. Asymmetry results in a distribution of returns, due to

credit risk, that is skewed to the left. Although this feature can become less pronounced in a large and highly diversified loan portfolio, it will not disappear altogether.

11 For an analysis of the J.P. Morgan's problem, see The Economist, 26th January 2002, p.78.

12 Both CreditTrade and Creditex are backed by major market participants, such as The Chase Manhattan Bank, J.P. Morgan, Deutsche Bank.

13 This index tracks default-swap premiums on about 100 European corporations.

14 See Financial Times, 31 January 2002, p.20.

15 The capital requirements of the 1998 Basel Accord are 100% for corporates, 20% for OECD banks and 0% for OECD sovereigns.

16 At the present, both the Fed and the Bank of England, indicate their willingness to make most credit default products and total return swaps eligible for the trading book, taking into account the characteristics of single transactions(case-by-case approach). However, the Bank also pointed out that this eligibility mainly refers to products referenced to listed securities (trading book items), not to those where the underlying asset is a loan (banking book items).

17 The measure that is used by the BIS in order to estimate market concentration is the Herfindahl index.

Chapter 15
Bivariate Causality between FDI Inflows and Economic Growth in India Since 1990

Behrooz Shahmoradi
University of Mysore, India

Enayatallah Najibzadehr
University of Mysore, India

ABSTRACT

Nowadays, most of the countries in the world mostly concentrate on the flow of FDI, because it has direct relationship with economic development. The present study attempts to make a contribution in this context, by analyzing the existence and nature of causalities, if any, between FDI and economic growth in India since 1990, where growth of economic activities and FDI has been one of the most pronounced. The results indicate that there is a strong correlation between FDI inflows and GDP in India. And also there is unidirectional causal relation between FDI and GDP. Finally as co-integration shows there is no long run relationship between FDI and economic growth in India.

INTRODUCTION

The name Foreign Direct Investment (FDI) usually brings to mind a significant contribution of FDI to domestic investment. However, there has been a lot of skepticism concerning the contribution of inward FDI to domestic investment. It is considered as the most powerful driver of the economic development. Nowadays, most of the countries in the world mostly concentrate on the flow of FDI, because it has direct relationship with economic development.

DOI: 10.4018/978-1-60566-996-0.ch015

Over the past two decades, many countries around the world have experienced substantial growth in their economies, with even faster growth in international transactions, especially in the form of FDI. The share of net FDI in world GDP has grown five-fold through the eighties and the nineties, making the causes and consequences of FDI and economic growth a subject of ever growing interest. This study attempts to make a contribution in this context, by analyzing the existence and nature of causalities, if any between FDI and economic growth, where growth of economic activities and FDI has been one of the most pronounced.

Figure 1.

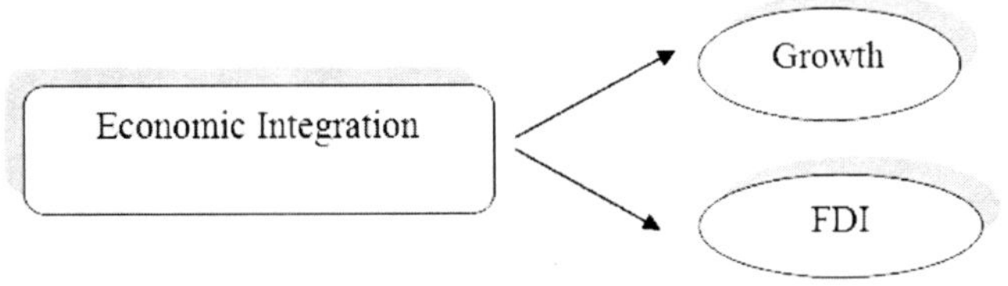

FDI has a major role to play in the economic development of the host country. Over the year it has helped the economies of the host countries to obtain a launching pad from where they can make further improvements. This trend has manifested itself in the last twenty years. Any form of FDI pumps in a lot of capital knowledge and technological resources into the economy of a country.

This is where the foreign direct investment can come in handy. It can also assist in helping economically under developed countries build their own researches and development bases that can contribute to the technological development of the country. This is a very crucial contribution as most of these countries are not able to perform these functions on their own. These assistances come in handy, especially in the context of the manufacturing and services sector of the particular country, that are able to enhance their productivity and ultimately advance from an economic point of view.

Today attracting FDI has become an integral part of the economic strategies for developing countries like India. FDI ensures a huge amount of domestic capital, production level and employment opportunities in the developing countries, which is a major step towards the economic growth of the countries. FDI has been a booming factor that has bolstered the economic life.

By contrast, according to the bulk of the literature on FDI and growth, causation would run from FDI to growth. Economic integration could then also be accommodated in either of two ways, as shown in Figure 1.

There is a general theoretical consequences ensure among development economists that FDI inflow is likely to play a crucial role in explaining growth of recipient countries. FDI inflows in fact represent additional resources a country needs to improve its economic performance and provides both physical capital and employment possibilities that may not be available in the host market while many studies observe positive impacts of FDI on economic growth.

FDI has been proved in the literature to be an important promoter of growth in its own right. In fact, FDI is argued to increase the level of domestic capital formation. This also implies producing on large scale which in turn results in benefits of economies of scale and specialization and also increasing export and employment opportunities. These are likely to result in positive economic impacts.

In general, economists agree that FDI inflows lead to an increased rate of economic growth. A major growth enhancing characteristic of FDI is the advanced technology that often accompanies foreign capital investment. In addition, domestic investors can also adopt this advanced technology. In other words, FDI generates positive externalities through technology spill over. At the same time, increased foreign capital can help to narrow the savings gap i.e. the gap between the domestic savings ratio and the desired level of investment ratio. In short, FDI should exert positive effects on economic growth. Particularly in developing countries which suffer from low productivity and capital stock delicacies.

Therefore this present study attempts to make a contribution in this context, by analyzing the existence and nature of causalities, if any, between FDI and economic growth, where growth of economic activities and FDI has been one of the most pronounced.

BACKGROUND

Concept of Growth

There is a positive relationship between global FDI inflows and the level and growth of world GDP. FDI acts as a "catalyst of Economic growth" in other words it acts as an "Engine of Growth".

Let us first explore what economic growth means. According to G.M. Mier (2002) – "A Process whereby the RPCI of a country increases over a long period of time". Here "Process" refers to dynamic changes that bring about an increase in the national income. "RPCI" refers to average income of the country which can be used to measure economic development. It also refers to purchasing power of people and thus in a way indicates price stability. "Long" refers that growth should be in long run.

Growth is the outcome result of the development. Between all the contributed tools for development pervasive computing as intermediate goods plays a crucial role.

REVIEW OF LITERATURE

Empirical evidence that FDI has made a positive contribution to the economic growth of developing countries has accumulated fast. Some recent examples are Marwah and Klein (1998) for India; Li, Liu and Rebelo (1998), Sun (1998) and Liu (2002) for China; Ramirez (2000) for Mexico; Lim and McAleer (2002) for Singapore; Marwah and Tavakoli (2004) for Indonesia, Malaysia, the Philippines and Thailand and Makki and Somwaru (2004) are also among the cross- country studies which find positive impacts of FDI on economic growth in developing countries.

In general, most governments believe inward FDI can contribute to the growth of the host country's economy. Not surprisingly, since the 1980s, attracting FDI has been one of the most important policy goals of developing countries. These economies have not only liberalized restrictions on the inflows of FDI but also provided incentives to attract foreign investors. However, despite a higher return on investment, Asiedu (2002) finds that Africa is different and policies successful in other developing countries may not be as successful in attracting investors to the Sub-Saharan Africa.

So far many factors like infrastructure, human capital, low wages, natural resources, political stability are mentioned in the literature as determinants of FDI, but we should also consider changes in the global economy, especially the new information and communication technology (ICT) that has been reshaping the global system. There is a large literature on FDI, some of it dating 40 years or more. But the global economy has undergone massive change over the last 20 years, and what was relevant to attracting FDI in the 1970s may no longer be the case today (Addison and Heshmati 2004).

Many studies, both theoretical and empirical indicate that FDI may have a strong positive effect on growth rates in developing countries like India. Some of these literatures are as follows:

Roghieh. G, et al (2005) investigated the simultaneous casual relationship between investments in information and communication technology (ICT) and flows of FDI, with reference to its implications on economic growth. Using data for 23 major countries with heterogeneous economic development for the period 1976-99 they found that there is causal relationship from ICT to FDI in developed countries but there is no significant causality from ICT to FDI in developing countries. Instead, there is partial evidence of opposite causality relationship. The inflow of FDI causes further increase in ICT investment and production capacity.

Dharmendra, D. et al., (2005) analyzed the existence and nature of causal relationships between FDI and Economic Growth. In their analysis they focused on South and Southeast Asia. Using Granger causality tests, they found substantial variation in the FDI-growth relationship across countries. Further analyses, based on regression techniques, reveal that FDI-to-growth causality is strengthened by the presence of greater trade openness, more limited rule of law, lower receipts of aid, and lower income level of the host country. Growth-to-FDI causality, on the other hand, is reinforced by greater political rights and more limited rule of law.

Puja Guha and Chandan Mukherjee (2005) in their work, they argued that inflow of FDI is not develops human capital. Rather than, the developed human capital leads to the inflow of FDI and in the process human capital gets enhanced. This article highlights this fact in the light of the experience of different countries and also they found that FDI induced development of human capital acts as a deterrent to the economic development of the country.

Sreenivasulu A, (2007) points out the fact that FDI is seen as a means to supplement domestic investment for achieving a higher level of economic growth and development and FDI benefits domestic industry as well as the Indian consumers by providing opportunities for technological up gradation, access to global managerial skills and practices, optimal utilization of human resources making Indian industry internationally competitive opening up exports markets providing backward and forward linkages and access to internationally quality goods and services.

Dharmendra Dhakal, Saif Rahman (2008) by using Granger causality tests, they identified FDI and economic growth generally points a positive relationships between each other. This paper finds substantial variation in the FDI, growth relationship across countries. Further analyze based, on regression techniques. Reveal that FDI to growth causality is strengthened by the presence of greater trade openness, more limited rule of law, lower receipts of aid, and lower income level of the host countries. Growth to FDI causality, on the other hand, is reining forced by greater political rights and more limited rule of law.

IMPORTANCE OF THE STUDY

There has been very little discussion on FDI in Indian context. There is a need to document and analyze the concepts, problem, policies, and effectiveness of the FDI relating to economic growth.

As we know the new economic policy has produced strong impact on technology, licensing, FDI, competitive, etc. It is true that reforms may create some modification in the FDI issues. Therefore in this context a detailed research study is warranted and the present study is an attempt in this direction.

In view of the growing importance of Globalization and Liberalization a study of this kind may prove to be useful and also timely. After the Liberalization of new economic policy in 1991, globalizations are drawing the attention of all. On these grounds a study of this kind would be very essential in order to examine the relationship between FDI inflows and economic growth.

RESEARCH GAP

A large number of studies have focused on the relation between FDI inflows and growth, factor effecting on FDI inflows, some studies also attempted impact on exports, and enhancement of human capability. It is clear that FDI inflows and economic growth at regional level is scanty. By and large all the studies have invariably touched upon the various FDI issues. Precisely we can say that there is no unanimous among researchers related to the relationship between FDI inflows and economic growth. Even in the empirical literature the relationship is not unanimous. Thus the measurement of the relationship is an empirical question .So this study tries to measure that relationship in India during post reform period.

THEORETICAL BACKGROUND

Theories play an important role in shaping legal attitude both nationally and internationally, FDI theories play an important role in providing the theoretical base and case in favor of FDI. To understand the link between FDI flows and economic growth, it is necessary to review the existing theories of growth.

Theories of FDI

Some major theoretical backgrounds which provide a case for FDI are summed up below:

(a) *Neo Classical Economic Theory of FDI.* The central message of this theory is that, FDI contributes positively to the economic development and increases the level of social well being, because foreign investors are bringing capital into the host country, thereby influencing the quality and quantity of capital formation.

(b) *Dependency Theory of FDI.* According to this theory foreign investment is harmful to the long term economic growth of developing nations. The theory asserts that First world nations became wealthy by extracting labor and other resources from the Third world nations. Developing countries are inadequately compensated for their natural resources. Global division of labor causes distortions; hinder growth and increases income inequality. Hence, third world nations must develop independently without depending on foreign capital and goods.

(c) *Industrialization Theory on FDI.* FDI represents not simply a transfer of Capital, but the transfer of a "package" in which capital, management, and new technology and combined termed as industrialization theory of FDI (Stephen Hymer, 1976). FDI entails a cross border transfer of resources including process and product technology, managerial skills, marketing and distribution know how and human capital.

(d) *International Product Life Cycle Theory.* A generalization and extension of the technological gap model is the product cycle model which was fully developed by Vernon in 1966. According to this theory the production of product shifts to different stages called a product life cycle. Thus it can explain both trade and FDI. It can thus explain a firms shifting from exporting to FDI. Initially a firm produces the product at home and enjoys monopolistic advantage in ex market. Once the product becomes standardized in its growth product phase, the firm may tend to invest abroad and export from there itself to retain its monopoly power. This may be accompanied by FDIs from the innovating nations to nations with cheaper labor.

(e) *Theory of Capital Movement.* The earliest theoreticians who assumed in the classical tradition the existence of a perfectly competitive market considered FDI as a form of factor movement to take advantage of differential profit.

(f) *Market Imperfections Theory.* One of the important market imperfections approach to the explanation of foreign investment is the monopolistic advantage theory propounded by Stephen in 1966. Hymer suggested that the decision of firm to invest on foreign markets was based on certain advantages the firm possessed over the local firms (In

Foreign country) such as economies of scale, superior technology, skills, production, marketing and finance.

(g) *Internationalization Theory.* This theory which is an extension of previous theory states that foreign investment results from the decision of a firm to internalize a superior knowledge.

(h) *Appropriability Theory.* According to appropriability theory, a firm should be able to appropriate the benefits resulting from a technology it has generated. If not, the firm would not be able to bear the cost of technology generation and would have no incentive for Research and Development. It is clear that, this theory is similar to internalization theory in terms of creating an internal market for exploiting the firm's specific advantages.

(i) *Eclectic Theory.* This was propounded by Dunning in 1988. It is a holistic analytic approach for FDI and organizational issues of MNCs relating to foreign production. According to him FDI by MNC's results from 3 competitive advantages as follows:

   (1) **Firm Specific Advantages:** This results from the tangible and intangible resources held exclusively at least temporarily by firm and which provide and the firm a comparative advantage over other firms.

   (2) **Internalization Advantages:** The firm specific advantages would not result in foreign investments unless the firm internalizes these advantages.

   (3) **Location Specific Theory:** Even when firm internalizes its exclusive resources it may be able to serve foreign market.

(j) *Oligopoly Theory of Advantage.* Vertical FDI is explained by oligopoly theory. The oligopolistic big firms tend to dominate in global market on according to entry barriers. Thus this theory by Knickerbocker says that when one firm especially the harder in an oligopolistic industry entered a market, other firms followed as a defensive strategy. It explains the defensive investment behavior to retain monopoly firm.

(k) *Monopoly Theory of Advantage.* The theory states that investing firm possesses relative monopolistic advantage abroad against the competitive local firms.

The firm enjoys monopolistic advantages on 2 counts:

1. Superior Knowledge
2. Economies of Scale

Thus it explains first course of investment of a business firm in a foreign country. Empirically it suggested horizontal FDI of US firm's knowledge technology intensive industries.

METHODOLOGY

In the processing of data suitable statistical techniques are used. A review of relevant literature available in the form of books, reports, articles, journals, editorials etc were analyzed to understanding the flows and pattern and relation between FDI inflows and economic growth. The sources of secondary data here the Government publications, world investment reports-UNCTAD, central statistical organization, Economic Political Weekly, Hand book of statistics on the Indian economy, RBI bulletin. Data was also collected from internet.

The quantitative and statistical techniques employed in the present study are as follows:

1. Correlation method is used to analyze the strength of linear relationship between FDI inflows and other factors considered in the study.

Figure 2. Estimated correlation between FDI and GDP. Correlation is significant at the 0.01 level (2 – tailed).

Pearson Correlation	FDI	GDP
FDI Sig (2-tailed)	1.000	.865**
N	-	.000
	17	17
Pearson Correlation	.865**	1.000
GDP Sig (2-tailed)	.000	-
N	17	17

2. Granger causality test will be used to examine the direction of causality between FDI and economic growth.

AN ECONOMIC ANALYSIS OF FDI INFLOWS AND ECONOMIC GROWTH

Despite plausible theoretical grounds for presuming a positive relationship between foreign direct investment inflows and economic growth, existing empirical evidence on this nexus is inconclusive. In an effort to add to the empirical literature, this study estimates the relationship between FDI and the rate of growth of GDP using correlation and granger causality test and employing time series data over the period 1991 to 2006-07.

Correlation

In Economics we widely use correlation techniques to measure the strength of linear relationship between variables. The present study has employed correlation technique to study the degree of association between selected variables based on present research study.

Figure 2 shows the correlation between FDI and GDP. The correlation coefficient between FDI and GDP is significant at 1% level with a value of 0.86 .On the other hand the correlation between GDP and FDI is significant at 1% level with a value of 0.86 It indicates strong correlation between FDI inflows and GDP.

Granger Causality Test

The present study has employed the Granger Causality test procedure, an innovative and more efficient econometric method to test the direction of causality between the FDI inflows and GDP growth rate. Before proceeding to Granger causality test the non stationary problem in time series data (as annual data on GDP and FDI) was taken into consideration. Unit root tests were conducted on the levels of both GDP and FDI series. Figure 3 gives the result of unit root test conducted.

The present study tested the non stationary of the selected time series data by using Augmented Dickey Fuller (AFD) test and the task is to verify the rejection /acceptance of null hypothesis of non stationary. The result of unit root test is reported in Figure 3. It indicates that there is presence of unit root in both FDI and GDP data in both the models with and without trend. The null hypothesis of non stationary (i.e. unit root) cannot be rejected because the calculated T- statistics is substantially lower than its critical value.

On the other hand both FDI and GDP turn out to be stationary at the first difference level in both the model. The null hypothesis of unit root has

Figure 3. Test results of unit roots ('Δ' indicates the first difference of the variables). Regressions were run both with intercept and trend and with intercept but no trend.

Variables	ADF Test - Statistics		Variables	ADF Test Statistics	
	With intercept but without trend	with intercept and trend		With interrupt but without trend	with intercept and trend
GDP	2.1171	1.2555	ΔGDP	3.5062	-3.8288
FDI	-0.3425	-3.2184	ΔFDI	-7.5629	-7.3524
5% Critical Values	-3.1003	-3.7921	5% Critical Values	-3.1222	-3.4617

been rejected because the calculated T – Statistics is substantially higher than its critical value.

Granger – Causality Test

Figure 4 shows the result of Granger – Causality Test.

Granger Causality Test
Pair wise Granger Causality Tests
Sample: 1991- 2007
Lags: 2

The first null hypothesis can be accepted, which means GDP does not Granger cause FDI. Because F statistic is 32.2357, the probability value is greater than our assumed level of α that is 5%. On the other hand the second null hypothesis is rejected because the F statistics is 7.3325 with a probability of 0.0421 which is less than the assumed level of α that is 0.05, this shows FDI granger causes GDP. This results reveals causal relation between FDI and GDP is unidirectional.

Co-Integration

Co-integration is an efficient statistical technique, which is used to know the long run equilibrium relationship between two time series variable. The technique properly handles the non-stationary problems that frequently exist in most of the time series variables. So our next step is to examine the FDI inflows of India whether is co-integrated with:

Economic growth or none
Sample (adjusted): 1994- 2006
Included observations: 13 after adjusting endpoints
Trend assumption: Linear deterministic trend
Series: GDP FDI
Lags interval (in first differences): 1 to 2
Unrestricted Co-integration Rank Test

Figure 5 revealed that the null hypothesis of co-integration cannot be rejected because the calculated Trace Statistic is substantially lower than

Figure 4. Results of granger causality test

Null Hypothesis	Obs	F. Statistic	Probability
GDP Does not Granger Cause FDI	14	32.2357	0.3271
FDI Does not Granger Cause GDP	14	7.3325	0.0421

Figure 5. Results of co-integration

Table D: Results of Co-integration

Hypothesized No. of CE(s)	Eigen value	Trace Statistic	5 Percent Critical Value	1 Percent Critical Value
None	0.331126	8.274419	15.41	20.04
At most 1	0.208902	3.046339	3.76	6.65

*(**) denotes rejection of the hypothesis at the 5%(1%) level

Trace test indicates no co integration at both 5% and 1% levels

Hypothesized No. of CE(s)	Eigen value	Max-Eigen Statistic	5 Percent Critical Value	1 Percent Critical Value
None	0.331126	5.228080	14.07	18.63
At most 1	0.208902	3.046339	3.76	6.65

Max-Eigen value test indicates no co integration at both 5% and 1% levels

its critical value. On the other hand Max-Eigen statistic value also lowers than its critical value. This conformed that null hypotheses of non-co integration have been rejected for India. It means that there is no long run relationship between FDI and economic growth in India. So we need not to go for further steps.

FURTHER TRENDS

The above analysis, thus establishes that FDI plays a significant role in the process of economic development of India. It is seen as a means to supplement domestic investment for achieving a higher level of economic growth and development. By recognizing the importance of FDI towards GDP, therefore, it's essential to find out the attractiveness of FDI by host country. Nowadays we notice the shift in the inflows of FDI to pervasive computing area in India. Therefore by paying more attention to this new phenomenon we can attract more FDI and also increase the GDP. The development of ICTs increases the potential to attract further FDI, which will in turn spur economic development. Consequently FDI offers significant potential for development by providing access to both capital and technology. Therefore there is a link between these three phenomena. For further research one can have a causality test between these three variables and investigate how they are interacting in the Indian Economy (Figure 6).

CONCLUSION

Using the Granger Causality test procedure to test the direction of causality between the FDI

Figure 6.

inflows and GDP growth results show causal relation between FDI and GDP is unidirectional, means that FDI Granger causes GDP where as GDI does not granger cause FDI. Furthermore, this study has seen that FDI means to supplement domestic investment for achieving a higher level of economic growth and development. FDI benefits domestic industry as well as the Indian consumers by providing opportunity for technological up gradations, access to global managerial skills and practices making Indian industry internationally competitive, opening up exports markets, providing backward and forward linkages and access to internationally quality goods and services and better pervasive computing. Most importantly, FDI is central for India's integration into global production chain, which involves production by Multinational Corporation spread across all over the world.

This study has been yet one more attempt at shedding light on the relationship between FDI inflows and economic growth. Finally this study concludes that FDI can enhance domestic capability, our export competitiveness, and therefore our economy would be better placed in the long term. There by on all grounds FDI essential for developing countries. Significant FDI inflows are required by the Indian economy. A stable political environment with good administration is crucial. Consider some good policies by government regarding to the new wave of computing technologies can led to increase the amount of FDI and GDP as well.

REFERENCES

Addison, T., & Heshmati, A. (2004). The New Global Determinants of FDI Flows to Developing Countries: The Importance of ICT and Democratization. *Research in Banking and Finance*, *4*, 151–186.

Asiedu, E. (2002). On the Determinants of Foreign Direct Investment to Developing Countries: Is Africa Different? *World Development*, *30*(1), 107–119. doi:10.1016/S0305-750X(01)00100-0

Dhakal, D., & Rahman, U. (2008). FDI and economic growth in Asia. *Indian Journal of Economics and Business*, *6*, 15.

Dharmendra, D. et al., (2005). Foreign Direct Investment and Economic Growth in Asia. *Journal of Economic Literature,* F21,O17,O19

Dunning, J. H. (1988). *Multinationals, Technology and Competitiveness.* London: Unwin Hyman.

Gerald, M. M., & James, E. R. (2002). *Leading issues in economic development* (7th ed., pp. 209-211). Oxford University Press.

Godley, A. C. (1999). Pioneering Foreign Direct Investment in British Manufacturing. *Business History Review*, *73*, 394–429. doi:10.2307/3116182

Hymer, S. H. (1968). The Large Multinational Corporation. In M. Casson (1990) (ed), *Multinational Corporation* (pp. 6-31). Hants: Edward Elgar.

Hymer, S. H. (1976). *The International Operations f National Firms: A study of Foreign Direct Investment*. Cambridge, MA: MIT Press.

Knickerbocker, F. (1973). *Oligopolistic Reaction and Multinational Enterprise*. Cambridge, MA: Harvard University Press.

Li, H., Liu, Z., & Rebelo, I. (1998). Testing the Neoclassical Theory of Economic Growth: Evidence from Chinese Provinces. *Economics of Planning*, *31*(2/3), 117–132. doi:10.1023/A:1003571107706

Lim, L. K., & McAleer, M. (2002). Economic Growth and Technological Catching Up by Singapore to the USA. *Mathematics and Computers in Simulation*, *59*(1-3), 133–141. doi:10.1016/S0378-4754(01)00401-3

Liu, Z. (2002). Foreign Direct Investment and Technology Spillover: Evidence from China. *Journal of Comparative Economics*, *30*(3), 579–602. doi:10.1006/jcec.2002.1789

Makki, S. S., & Somwaru, A. (2004). Impact of Foreign Direct Investment and Trade on Economic Growth: Evidence From Developing Countries. *American Journal of Agricultural Economics*, (August): 795–801. doi:10.1111/j.0002-9092.2004.00627.x

Marwah, K., & Klein, L. R. (1998). Economic Growth and Productivity Gains from Capital Inflow: Some Evidence for India. *Journal of Quantitative Economics*, *14*(1), 81–108.

Marwah, K., & Tavakoli, A. (2004). The Effect of Foreign Capital and Imports on Economic Growth: Further Evidence from Four Asian Countries (1970–1998). *Journal of Asian Economics*, *15*(2), 399–413. doi:10.1016/j.asieco.2004.02.008

Melina, D. (2004). A Causal Relationship between Trade, Foreign Direct Investment. *American Journal of Applied Sciences*, *1*(3), 230–235. doi:10.3844/ajassp.2004.230.235

Puja, G., & Chandan, M. (2005). FDI-Its role in building human capital. *Treasury Management International*, *5*, 53.

Ramirez, M. D. (2000). Foreign Direct Investment in Mexico: A Cointegration Analysis. *The Journal of Development Studies*, *37*(1), 138–162. doi:10.1080/713600062

Sham, K. B., & Durai, R. (2007). Long run causal nexus between FDI and foreign trade in India. *The ICFAI . Journal of Applied Econometrics*, *6*(5), 7.

Sreenivasulu, A. (2007). Issues in FDI –a bird eye view. *Southern Economist*, *8*, 17.

Sun, H. (1998). Macroeconomic Impact of Direct Foreign Investment in China: 1979-96. *World Economy*, *21*(5), 675–694. doi:10.1111/1467-9701.00156

Vernon, R. (1966). International investment and international trade in the product cycle. *The Quarterly Journal of Economics*, *80*(May), 190–207. doi:10.2307/1880689

ADDITIONAL READING

Bosworth, B., & Collins, S. (1999). Capital Flows to Developing Economies: Implications for Saving and Investment. *Brookings Papers on Economic Activity: 1, Brookings Institution*, (pp.143-69).

Carkovic, M., & Levine, R. (2002*). Does Foreign Direct Investment Accelerate Economic Growth.* National bureau of Economic Research Working Paper 8028. Cambridge, MA.

Caves, R. E. (1982). *Multinational Enterprise and Economic Analysis*. Cambridge University Press.

Coase, R. H. (1937). The Nature of the Firm. *Economical*, *4*, 386–405. doi:10.1111/j.1468-0335.1937.tb00002.x

De Mello, L. R. (1999). Foreign Direct Investment-led Growth: Evidence from Time Series and Panel Data. *Oxford Economic Papers*, *51*, 133–151. doi:10.1093/oep/51.1.133

Dunning, J. H. (1977). Trade, Location of Economic Activity and the MNE: A Search for an Eclectic Approach. In B. Ohlin, P. O. Hesselborn, & P. M. Wijkman (Eds.). *The International Allocation of Economic Activity*. London, UK: Macmillan.

Dunning, J. H. (1979). Explaining Changing Patterns of International Production: In Defence of the Eclectic Theory. *Oxford Bulletin of Economics and Statistics*, *41*, 269–295.

Dunning, J. H. (1988). The Eclectic Paradigm of International Production: A Restatement and Some Possible Extensions. *Journal of International Business Studies*, *19*, 1–31. doi:10.1057/palgrave.jibs.8490372

Horst, T. (1972). The Industrial Composition of U.S. Exports and Subsidiary Sales to the Canadian Market. *The American Economic Review*, *62*, 37–45.

Hymer, S. H. (1976[1960 as a thesis]). *The International Operations of National Firms: A Study of Direct Foreign Investment*. Cambridge, MA: MIT Press.

Kinckerbocker, F. T. (1973). *Oligopolistic Reaction and Multinational Enterprise*. Boston, MA: Division of Research, Harvard University Graduate School of Business Administration.

Kindleberger, C. P. (1969). *American Business Abroad: Six Lectures on Direct Investment*. New Haven, CT: Yale University Press.

Kokko, A., Zejan, M., & Tansini, R. (2001). Trade Regimes and Spillover Effects of FDI: Evidence from Uruguay. *Weltwirtschaftliches Archiv*, *137*(1), 124–149. doi:10.1007/BF02707603

Lizondo, J. S. (1991). Foreign Direct Investment, in International Monetary Fund, Determinants and Systematic Consequences of International Capita Flows. *IMF Occasional Papers* No. 77 (Washington DC), 68-82.

Markowitz, H. M. (1959). *Portfolio Selection: Efficient Diversification of Investments*. John Wiley, New York.

Martin, S. (1991). Direct Foreign Investment in the United States. *Journal of Economic Behavior & Organization*, *16*, 283–293. doi:10.1016/0167-2681(91)90015-P

Vernon, R. (1966). International Investment and International Trade in the Product Cycle. *The Quarterly Journal of Economics*, *80*, 190–207. doi:10.2307/1880689

Vernon, R. (1971). *Sovereignty at Bay: The Multinational Spread of U.S. Enterprises*. London: Pelican.

Zhang, K. H. (2001). Does Foreign Direct Investment Promote Economic Growth from East Asia and Latin America. *Contemporary Economic Policy*, *19*(2), 175–185. doi:10.1111/j.1465-7287.2001.tb00059.x

KEY TERMS AND DEFINITIONS

Economic Development: Is the development of economic wealth of countries or regions for the well-being of their inhabitants. From a policy perspective, economic development can be defined as efforts that seek to improve the economic well-being and quality of life for a community by creating and/or retaining jobs and supporting or growing incomes and the tax base.

FDI: Is a category of investment that reflects the objective of establishing a lasting interest by a resident enterprise in one economy (direct investor) in an enterprise (direct investment enterprise) that is resident in an economy other than that of the direct investor.

GDP (Gross Domestic Product): One of the main measures of economic activity. 'Gross' indicates that it is calculated without subtracting any allowance for capital consumption; 'domestic' that it measures activities located in the country regardless of their ownership. It thus includes activities carried on in the country by foreign-owned companies, and excludes activities of firms owned by residents but carried on abroad. 'Product' indicates that it measures real output produced rather than output absorbed by residents. GDP is reported at both current and constant price.

Growth: An increase in an economic variable, normally persisting over successive periods.

Inflow: Refers to direct investment in the reporting economy.

Multinational Corporation: Is a corporation or enterprise that manages production or delivers services in more than one country.

Outflow: Refers to direct investment abroad.

Pervasive Computing: Is a rapidly developing area of Information and Communications Technology (ICT). The term refers to the increasing integration of ICT into people's lives and environments, made possible by the growing availability of microprocessors with inbuilt communications facilities.

Chapter 16
Regional and Sectoral Disparities in Inflow of FDI in India:
An Empirical Analysis

Behrooz Shahmoradi
University of Mysore, India

ABSTRACT

During the last two decades, Foreign Direct Investment (FDI) has become increasingly important in the developing world, with a growing number of developing countries seeking in attracting substantial and rising amounts of inward FDI. Furthermore, FDI has become the most important source of finance that can contribute to economic development. Recognizing this, all the governments want to attract it. India as a developing country is not an exception in this regard therefore study the different aspects of FDI can be helpful for policy makers in macro as well as micro level. Since 1990, FDI has been considered as the most powerful driver of economic development. While India has seen a steady increase in FDI inflows in the post-reform period, therefore, this study tries to analyze the regional and sectoral disparities in Inflow of FDI in India since 1990. The analysis showed that there is a disparity between states in India and it also indicates a shift from primary and secondary sectors to tertiary sectors and pervasive computing areas.

INTRODUCTION

FDI has been instrumental in the economic growth of the developing countries. To what extent it is to be invited depends upon the type of economy. If it is an open economy flow of FDI is high. Since the under developed countries are having lack of capital, certainly the foreign capital will make a dent in the process of economic development of that country. Besides most important driver of the FDI and internationalization of production net work owes to the increasing globalization of firms consequent on the liberalization moves of most of the countries. So for as, Indian economy is concerned the welcoming of the FDI is limited. But after liberalization of the economy the inflow of FDI into India is very high.

DOI: 10.4018/978-1-60566-996-0.ch016

It is a misleading opinion that India is new to foreign capital. Foreign capital had a substantial presence in Indian industry prior to 1947, and was mostly concentrated in the primary sectors and services. Foreign firms mostly British dominated India's mining, plantations, trade and much of the fledging manufacturing base.

- In the early post independence years as India turned abroad for both technology and capital.
- By late 1950's, Indian government invited foreign capital in many sectors like drugs, aluminum etc.
- During 1960's also FDI was concentrated in manufacturing.
- By end of the 1960's around 60% of FDI was concentrated in manufacturing industries.
- But after math of 2 famines and the devaluation of rupee in 1960's there was a hardening of policy foreign oil, majors were nationalized in early 1970's.

Thus the Foreign Exchange Regulation Act (FERA 1973) was its outcome. By mid 1980's growing concern about stagnation and technological obsolescence in Indian industry led to push for economic reform and regulation.

The 1990's began a major crisis. In the wake of gulf war, the consequent expulsion of Indian expatriate laborers from Middle East, foreign exchange remittances fell. As the balance of payment position has deteriorated. Thus after the serious crisis we opened up our economy in 90's and thus our FDI increased.

To fully realize the country's immense economic potential the government of India launched the economic reforms programmed in July 1991. These reforms have ascertained the potential growth of the economy and stimulated international trade, out sourcing and FDI, in a way that according to the world investment report, for the year 2005, India has attracted FDI of US$ 5.33 billion in 2004 from US$ 4.27 billion in 2003; in 2005-06 the FDI inflows touched 8 billion. The target rate of FDI inflows in the eleventh plan will be 16 billion. (WIR 2006)

India's share in world FDI is minor, notably when considering its size as the entire world is watching the miracle growth of India and china. China opened up to FDI a decade before India did. Indeed, the opening of the India is relatively new and the history of its FDI on a large scale is very short, India has to go a long way for enhancing the existing volume of FDI inflows to meet its financing development needs.

Since 1990, FDI has been considered as the most powerful driver of economic development. And also India has seen a steady increase in FDI inflows in the post reform period. Therefore objectives of this study are as follows:

- To analyze the cause and consequences of regional disparities in Inflow of FDI in India since 1990.
- To trace the reasons for the sectoral disparities in Inflow of FDI in India since 1990.
- To discuss the recent emerging trends in FDI in India
- To highlight the major investing countries in India and reasons behind that

BACKGROUND

Importance of the Study

There has been very little discussion on FDI in Indian context. There is a need to document and analyze the concepts, problem, policies, and effectiveness of the FDI relating to economic growth. As we know the new economic policy has produced strong impact on technology, licensing, FDI, competitive law etc. It is true that reforms may create some modification in the FDI issues.

Therefore in this context a detailed research study is warranted and the present study is an attempt in this direction.

In view of the growing importance of Globalization and Liberalization a study of this kind may prove to be useful and also timely. After the Liberalization of new economic policy in 1991, globalizations are drawing the attention of all. On these grounds a study of this kind would be very essential in order to examine the relationship between FDI inflows and economic growth.

REVIEW OF LITERATURE:

Various review of literature available have been thrown light on the particulars issue or topic helps identifying the trends of FDI and even focus on various dimensions of the related subjects to FDI. Some of these studies are as follow:

Sebastian Morries (1994) discussed the trends and patterns of foreign direct investment and of the policy and structural changes in India for FDI in the 90's. It is argued that while the FDI inflow into India is likely to increase in the 90's, it would never be anywhere near the $4 billion or so per year that is anticipated by the government and hoped for by business. By contrast, international subcontracting by foreign firms could play a major role in manufactured export growth. This is an aspect which, while vitally important for Indian manufacturing has attracted little attention in terms of policy.

Pradhan, J. P. (2005) provides an overview of the changing patterns of outflow of FDI from India over 1975-2001. It shows that the increasing number of Indian TNCs during 1990s has been accompanied by a number of changes in the character of such investment. These, notably include overwhelming tendency of Indian outward investors to have full or majority ownership, expansion into new industries and service sector, and the emergence of developed country as the most important host region for trans-border activity.

Chennappa (2005) highlighted the Indian telecom service sector is becoming one of the fastest growing factors in the world. The Government of India recently increased the limit on FDI in telecom providers from 49 percent to 74 percent. The higher FDI has led to the increase of urban tele-density and also it observed that continuous increase in the actual inflow of foreign direct investment in telecom sector from 1993 to 2004.

Sahana Joshi (2006) examined the trends of FDI inflows in the five major service sector in India and empirically estimates the impact of openness on the FDI inflows in service sector. The empirical work is conducted using time series data from 1991 to 2005. It is found that FDI in service sector responds well to increased openness. Further liberalization of service involves potential advantages for Indian economy other than openness growth of service sector, incentives offered by government to foreign investors, availability of infrastructure and others needs to the taken into account in future flows.

KameshGakhar (2007) in his book is devoted to a descriptive and analytical study of FDI trends and policies in India during the post-Independence period. He investigated that though India has one of the most transparent and liberal FDI regimes among the developing countries with strong macro-economic fundamentals, it share in FDI inflows is dismally low. According to him India still suffers from weaknesses and constraints, in terms of policy and regulatory framework, which restricts the inflow of FDI.

Dutta, M.K. and Sarma, G.K (2008) in their study found that traditional industrial sectors like food processing industries, textiles, etc. which were once important sectors attracting larger FDI, have given way to modern industrial sectors like electronics and electrical equipments, etc. furthermore, they noticed negative growth rate in inflow of FDI during the period 1998-2000 primarily due to falling share of major investor countries.

SCOPE OF THE STUDY

Since 1990, FDI has been considered as the most powerful driver of economic development. It traces the role of FDI in economic growth and it also tries to analyze the trends and patterns of FDI in India in the post reform period.

LIMITATION OF THE STUDY

More often than not, research in social science is confronted with limitations that extend far beyond the control of researchers. This study at the outset may look quite satisfactory, but there are certain drawbacks,

1. This study has concentrated only on one part of foreign investment (FDI). It has thus relegated FDI to the core which is also an important component of investment.
2. It does not deal with the analysis of FDI outflows.
3. This study has taken the flow of FDI relating to only India and not all countries.

METHODOLOGY

A descriptive design is proposed to be employed for the present study. A review of relevant literature available in the form of books, reports, articles, journals, editorials etc were analyzed to understanding the flows and pattern of FDI in India. The facts and figures are obtained from secondary sources. The sources of secondary data are the Government publications, world investment reports-UNCTAD, central statistical organization, Economic Political Weekly, Hand book of statistics on the Indian economy, RBI bulletin. Data was also collected from internet.

GLOBAL TRENDS IN FDI INFLOWS

FDI flows increased in all the major country groups both developed and developing countries but at varying rates. The sustained growth of FDI and related international production primarily reflect the strong economic performance and increasing profits of many countries in the world. Further liberalization of their policies and other specific factors such as currency movement's stock exchange, and increases in cross border mergers and acquisitions (M&As) fuelled substantially by private equity funds, also added to FDI growth.

Figure 1 clearly indicates that Global regional flows of FDI inflows has increased during the period from 1991 to 1998, representing a more than quadruple increase from a level of US$ 158.94 billion in 1991 to US$ 690.91 billion in 1998. It also shows that the growth momentum of global FDI flows continued till 2000 touching a high level of US$ 1388 billion and thereafter it registered a slow down to US$817 billion in 2001 and further to US $560 billion in 2003, in 2004 it is US $742.1 and $945.7 in 2005, further it is go on increasing. A major share of FDI flows, nearly 62 percent during the 1991 to 1998 was flown to developed countries leaving about 34 percent to developing countries. Developing countries share showed a steady improvement during 1991 to 1998 which increased from about 26 percent in 1991 to a high of 41 percent in 1994 and 28 percent in 1998. During the period from 1999 to 2006,share of FDI flows in developing countries steadily increasing 21.3 percent in 1999 to 29 percent in 2006.

The declining developed countries share of FDI flows during the period from 1991 to 1998 could be attributable to locations shift of the business activities of transnational corporations (TNCs) to developing countries, FDI flows to Asian countries remained dominant throughout which rose from a mare US$23 billion in 1991 to US$102 billion in 1998 representing an annual average growth of 26 percent and a percentage share of around

Figure 1. Trends in global regional inflows of FDI from 1991 to 2006 (in Billion US$). Source: World Investment Report, 2007, UNCTAD.

Region/Year	1991	1992	1993	1994	1995	1996	1997	1998	1999	2000	2001	2002	2003	2004	2005	2006
Word inflows	158.94	175.84	219.42	255.99	331.07	384.91	477.92	690.91	1086.8	1388	817.6	678.8	559.6	742.1	945.7	1305.8
developed countries	114.79	120.29	133.85	145.14	203.46	219.69	271.38	472.55	828.4	1108	571.5	489.9	366.6	418.8	590.3	857.4
% Share in Total	72.23	68.41	61	56.7	61.46	57.08.	56.78	68.4	76.22	79.83	69.9	72.18	65.51	56.43	62.41	65.66
developing countries	41.7	51.11	78.81	104.92	113.34	152.49	187.35	194.06	231.9	252.5	219.7	157.6	172	283	314.3	379
% Share in Total	26.23	29.06	35.92	40.09	34.23	39.62	39.2	28.09	21.3	18.2	26.9	23.2	30.7	38.13	33.23	29.02
Asia	23.13	29.65	54.84	68.61	75.29	94.35	107.21	102.21	112.6	146.1	111.9	94.4	107.1	169.9	208.7	259.4
% Share in Developing countries	55.47	58.02	69.58	65.39	66.43	61.87	57.22	52.67	48.55	57.86	50.91	59.88	62.27	60.06	66.41	68.43
India % share in developing countries	0.42	0.46	0.73	0.93	1.89	1.7	1.93	1.36	0.93	0. 93	1.55	2.19	2.48	2.03	2.12	4.45

60 percent in developing countries percentage share of India in developing countries showed a steady improvement during the above period, which increased from 0.42 in 1991 to a high of 1.93 in 1997 and 1.36 percent in 1998. The share of Asian countries maintained the maximum percentage share in developing countries total inflows, though it increasing to 48.55 percent in 1999 to 68 percent in 2006.Percetage share of India in developing countries showed a increasing tendency during the above period, which increased from 0.93 in 1999 to 2.48 percent in 2004 and in 2006 it was 4.45.

TRENDS OF FDI IN INDIA

FDI inflows into India are increasing trend after the post perform period. Figures 2 and 3 which show FDI flows in India from 1991-06 reveal the trends in FDI flows.

These figures show the trend of FDI in India along with annual growth rate. Since 1991 the figure points out clearly that FDI inflows as well as annual growth rate have continuously been showing upward trend from 1991 to 1997 .FDI inflows, which were merely Rs. 174 crore in 1991, reached Rs. 13.220 crore in 1997-98.But during 1998, 1999, 2002 and 2003 the FDI inflows declined considerably. Besides the Asian crisis and sanctions imposed on India as a consequences of nuclear explosion test froze FDI flows to India to a considerable extent. But the FDI flows again showed increasing trend from 2004 to 2006. It is evident from the data given above table, that the FDI inflow into India was increased from Rs. 174 crore in 1990-91 to Rs. 88.446 crore in 2006-07.

COUNTRY WISE TRENDS IN THE FLOWS OF FDI IN INDIA

India as a capital starved country has now access heavy inflows of capital from 10 major countries of the world.

Figures 4 and 5 reveal that Mauritius is the major source of FDI in India during 1991-2003-04. Mauritius alone contributed nearly 7.98 billion, followed by USA and UK around 3.867, 1.660 billion respectively. According to data relating to the period 2007-08 Mauritius is the biggest source of foreign direct investment, it contributed around 46.99 percent of total inward FDI. Apart

Figure 2. FDI inflows in India from 1991 to 2006 (Rs in crores). Source: Statistical Handbook.

Year	Inflows	Annual Growth Rate
1990-91	174	_
1991-92	316	81.609
1992-93	965	205.37
1993-94	1838	90.466
1994-95	4126	124.48
1995-96	7172	73.824
1996-97	10015	39.640
1997-98	13220	32.001
1998-99	10358	-21.649
1999-2000	9338	-9.84
2000-01	18406	97.108
2001-02	29235	58.83
2002-03	24367	-16.651
2003-04	19860	-18.496
2004-05	27188	36.898
2005-06	34188	25.746
2006-07	88446	158.70

Figure 3.

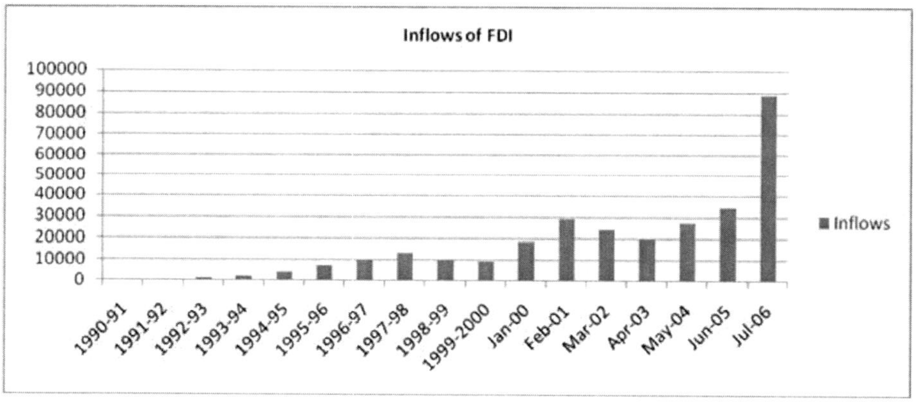

from Mauritius, Singapore is the major investor in India, it contributed about 8.2 percent of total inward FDI in 2007-08.Far behind United Kingdom (5.54), United States (5.07), Japan (3.77), are significant investors in 2007-08.

STATE WISE OF FDI INFLOWS IN INDIA

The State wise-flow of FDI in India shows the concentration of investment in some regions (states). All the states give top priority to attract FDI on a large scale for developmental purposes. The trend (overall) from 1991-2003 have revealed that in India, Maharashtra has topped the list, while Delhi is second, Karnataka is third, the fourth place goes to Tamil Nadu. Nearly First eight States account for about 64% most of the states expecting MadyaPradesh have an industrialized background.

Figures 6 and 7 clearly indicate that few state of India such as Maharashtra, Delhi, Karnataka, Tamil Nadu are having more FDI. However, the

Figure 4. Country wise trends in the flows of FDI in India from 1991-2007 ($billion). Source: RBI bulletin and FDI data cell Ministry of Commerce.

Country	1991-2003-04	2004-05	2005-06	2006-07	2007-08	%with total inflow
Mauritius	7.987	1.129	2.570	6.363	9.463	46.99
USA	3.867	0.669	0.502	0.856	1.021	5.07
UK	1.66	0.101	0.266	1.878	1.117	5.54
Singapore	0.59	0.184	0.275	0.578	1.664	8.26
Netherlands	1.651	0.267	0.076	0.644	0.601	2.98
Japan	1.78	0.126	0.208	0.085	0.761	3.77
Germany	1.133	0.145	0.303	0.120	0.440	2.18
South Korea	0.657	0.003	0.070	0.058	0.73	3.62
France	0.642	0.117	0.018	0.117	0.120	0.59
Switzerland	0.463	0.077	0.096	0.056	0.0247	0.12
total inflows FDI	29.776	3.754	5.546	15.726	20.136	-

Figure 5. Country wise trends in the flows of FDI in 2007-08 ($billion)

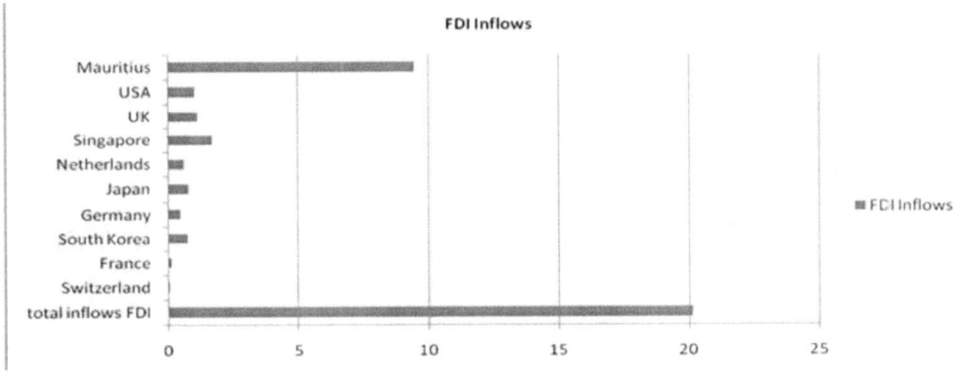

distribution of FDI is heavily skewed among the states as seen from the above figure. Among the states, Maharashtra bagged 17.4 percent of FDI flows during 1991-2003 followed by Delhi (11.9 Percent), Karnataka (8.3) Tamilnadu (8.3) could attract a sizeable percentage of FDI. Kerala is able to absorb a mere 0.5 percent of the total FDI investment during 1991-2003.

The data in Figures 8 and 9 (2000-2008) reveals that the state of Maharashtra attracts the highest share of FDI bagged 29.51 percentage of FDI flows during 2000-08 followed by Delhi (20.27 percent), Karnataka, (7.15 Percent). TamilNadu (5.80 Percent). Utter Pradesh is able to absorb mere 0.03 percent of the total FDI investment during 2000-2008.

The reason why these states are ahead of others in receiving FDI is because of favorable government responses, quick bureaucracy, good infrastructure facilities and lastly rich heritage of entrepreneurship. By looking at these states we can find that these states possessing high level of pervasive computing which can directly and indirectly lead to attract FDI. Therefore we can consider pervasive computing is one of the main reasons in order to answer why top four-five states in this figure are having most part of the FDI. Another interesting feature of higher inflow of FDI is generally concentrated in south and northern regions since these states fall in the coastal line due to which the transportation changes are why low. The states like Punjab have locational dis-

Figure 6. State wise inflows of FDI from 1991-2003 (Rs in crores). Source: Ministry of Commerce and SIA New Letter 2003 (April).

Ranks	States	Amount	Percentage
1	Maharastra	49587	17.4
2	Delhi	34087	11.9
3	Tamil Nadu	23689	8.3
4	Karnataka	23657	8.3
5	Gujrath	18679	6.5
6	Andhra Pradesh	13218	4.6
7	West Bengal	9014	3.2
8	Madya Pradesh	9271	3.2
9	Orrissa	8229	2.9
10	Uttar Pradesh	4815	1.7
	Other	93192	32
	Total	287438	100

Figure 7.

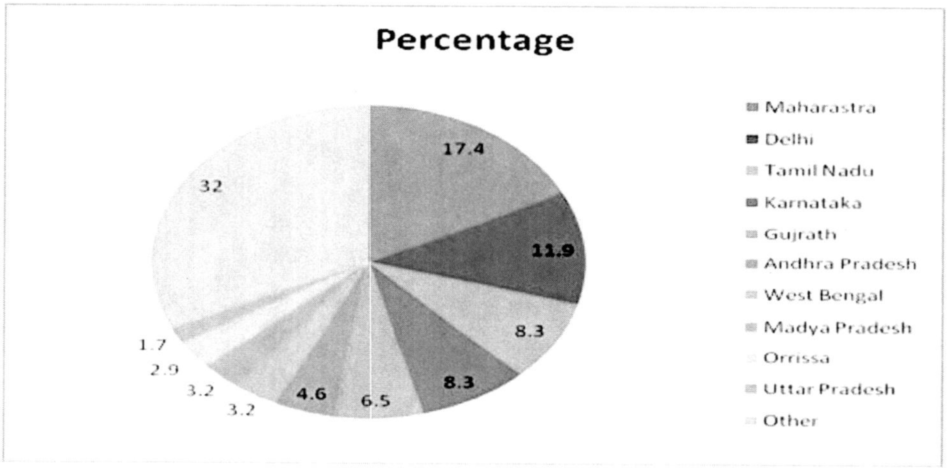

advantages as far as FDI is uncovered similarly due to poor infrastructure in big stated like Bihar also failed to attract any FDI.

SECTOR WISE FDI INFLOWS IN INDIA (INCREASE IN THE PERVASIVE COMPUTING AREA)

Figure 10 reveals that the inflows of FDI was more pronounced in some sectors during the year 1991 to 2000.

The sector wise breaks up of FDI provide a wide list of items in which India is welcoming FDI as a part of its reform policies. The top 10 sectors transportation, electricity included telecommunication, chemical, fuels, food processing etc. from 1991 – 2000. The trend shows that after the economic reforms were carried out FDI was heavily concentrated in manufacturing activities, which was due to the import substitution principle. The share of service sector was around 5% during 1991-2000 .Now the trend has changed towards an increase in foreign investment in tertiary sector

Figure 8. State wise FDI inflows from 2000 to Feb 2008 (Rs in crores). Source: RBI bulletin and FDI data cell Ministry of Commerce 2008.

Ranks	States	Amount	Percentage (Rs in crores)
1	Maharastra	67316.73	29.51
2	Delhi	46250.39	20.27
3	Karnataka	16312.83	7.15
4	Tamil Nadu	13243.47	5.8
5	Andhra Pradesh	9692.8	4.25
6	Gujarat	8629.99	3.78
7	West Bengal	3310.22	1.45
8	Chandigarh	1754.72	0.77
9	Goa	994.17	0.44
10	Kerala	520.97	0.23
	Others	60121.82	26.35
	Total	228148.11	100

Figure 9. State wise FDI inflows from 2000 to Feb 2008 (%)

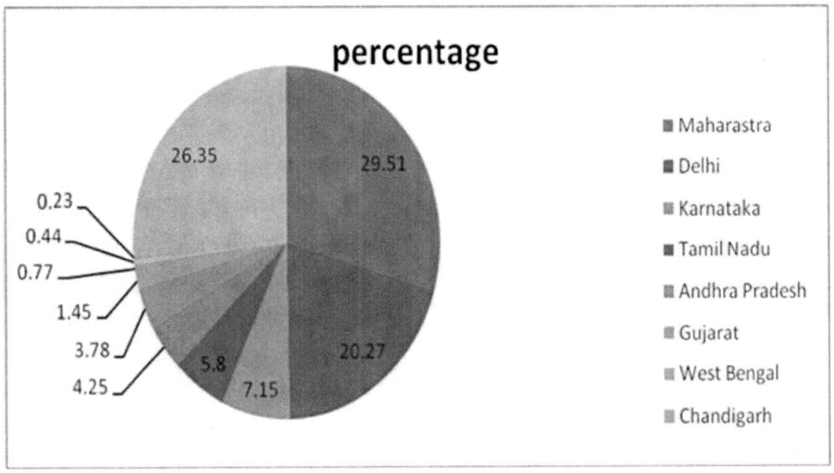

mainly that encompasses service activities; they include ICT or pervasive computing area, power, hotel tourism etc.

Figure 11 again highlights that the inflows of FDI was more pronounced in some sectors. The most important sector to attract FDI during 2000 to Feb 2008 is service sector (22.42 Percent), computer software and Hardware (14.03 Percent), Telecommunications (7.23 Percent), construction activities (5.49 Percent). These four sectors account roughly to 50 percent of the total FDI inflows into the country. This showed a tendency that a relatively low share of consumer goods sectors.

RESULTS AND FINDINGS

The analyses reveal that after post reform period India has seen a steady increase in FDI inflows. Study shows that in the case of country wise trends in the flows of FDI in India, Mauritius is the major source of FDI in India and it followed by USA and UK. And from the state wise view, Maharashtra, Delhi, Karnataka and Tamil Nadu are having more FDI. It is mainly because of the favorable government responses, quick bureaucracy, good infrastructure facilities, rich heritage of entrepreneurship and lastly high pervasive

Figure 10. Sector wise FDI inflows from 1991 to Dec 2000. Source: Ministry of Commerce and SIA New Letter 2004.

S. No.	Sector	Amount of FDI inflows (million crores)	% of total FDI inflows
1	Transportation Industry	63,780.45	7.12
2	Electrical Equipments	58,436.99	6.5
3	Telecommunications	47,232.24	5.27
4	Chemicals	45.241.94	5.05
5	Fuels	41,359.94	4.61
6	Food Processing	25.901.37	2.89
7	Paper and Pulp	11.258.88	1.25
8	Drugs & Pharmaceuticals	10301.63	1.15
9	Miscellaneous Mechanical and Engineering	9.609.70	1.07
10	Textiles	8,374.48	0.93
11	Others	5.73,960.48	64.09
	Total	8,95,458.10	100

computing area. And in the sector wise the trend has changed towards an increase in foreign investment in pervasive computing sectors.

The reasons behind of these transitions are mostly cause of government policies. As part of the reform agenda, the Indian Government has taken major steps to promote ICT including the creation in 1988 of a World Market Policy, with a focus on software development for export; telecommunications policy reform; privatization of the national long-distance and mobile phone markets; and development of a more comprehensive approach to ICT.

FURTHER TRENDS

In view of the growing importance of Globalization and Liberalization a study of this kind may prove to be useful and also timely. After the Liberalization of new economic policy in 1991, globalizations are drawing the attention of all. On these grounds a study of this kind would be very essential in order to realize the advantages and disadvantages of FDI and also to know how FDI is going to shape our economy so that we can use appropriate policies towards getting the highest benefit.

Changing the patterns of FDI is not only relevant to India but it's a global phenomena. According to UNCTAD (2004) since the 1990, however, other services have seen more dynamic FDI growth. Notable among them are electricity, telecommunications, water supply and business services – the last of these a diverse group, ranging from real state to professional services to IT – enabled corporate sectors. Therefore the role of new emerging trends look like pervasive computing is very crucial to attract more FDI.

CONCLUSION

India is likely to increase in state wise and sector wise. Significant FDI inflows are required by the Indian economy. A stable political environment with good administration is crucial. Some good policies are essential but a clean uncorrupt administration and better infrastructure facilities would go a long way in shaping India's destiny in order to attract more FDI.

India's focus on self-reliant industrialization in the 1970s and 1980s has been replaced with reforms aimed at positioning India in the world economy: the foreign direct investment process has

Figure 11. Sector wise FDI inflows from 2000 to 2008 Feb. Source: RBI Bulletin and FDI data cell Ministry of Commerce 2008.

S.No	Sector	Amount of FDI inflows (Rs in crores)	% to total
1	Service sector	511,618.62	22.42
2	Computer Software and Hardware	320,195.21	14.03
3	Telecommunications	164,910.23	7.23
4	Construction activities	125,148.95	5.49
5	Housing and real Estate	95,978.61	4.21
6	Automobile industry	93,627.36	4.10
7	Power	77,547.88	3.40
8	Metallurgical industry	65,187.28	2.86
9	Chemicals	60,910.02	2.67
10	Drugs and Pharmaceuticals	56,067.78	2.46
11	Others	710287.94	22.1
	Total	2,281,474.90	100

been streamlined, new sectors have been opened up to foreign direct investment and ownership, and the government has exempted the ICT industry from corporate income tax for five years. These reforms have helped India to become increasingly integrated into the global economy through growth in the export of software and skill-intensive software services, such as call-centers.

The developing countries including India can't stay away from FDI flows after being liberalized. It is clear that after liberalized policy towards foreign direct investment, there has been considerable increase in the flow of FDI to India. The policy reforms have enabled the country to widen the sectoral as well as source composition of FDI inflows. Therefore we must need a clear cut strategy to enhance FDI.

REFERENCES

Agarwal, (2004). *Indian Economy* (29th ed., p. 639). New Delhi: Vishwa Prakashan.

Channappa, D. (2007, December 1). Role of FDI in Indian Telecom Industry. *Southern Economist*, p 15.

Dutta, M. K., & Sarma, G. K. (2008). Foreign Direct Investment in India Since 1991: Trends, Challenges [New Delhi: Wisdom Publications.]. *Prospects*, 18–32.

Gakhar, K. (2007). *Foreign Direct Investment in India 1947 to 2007: Policies, Trends and Outlook* (p. 124). New Delhi: New Century Publications.

Indu, B. (2003). *Foreign Resources and Economic Development* (pp. 82-115). New Delhi: Deep and Deep Publications PVT, LTD.

Mishra, S. K., & Puri, V. K. (2007). *Indian Economy* (pp 627-648). Mumbai: Himalayan Publication House.

Pradhan, J. P. (2005). *Outward Foreign Direct Investment from India: Recent Trends and Patterns.* Unpublished doctoral dissertation, ISID, New Delhi.

Sahana, J. (2005, December 17). Liberalization and FDI flows in Service Sector; The Indian Experience. *EPW*, pp.53-88.

Sebastian, M. (1994, May 7). Prospects for FDI and Multinational Activity in the 90's. *EPW*, pp 11-41.

Uma, K. (2003). *Understanding the Problems of Indian Economy* (4th ed., pp. 332-345). New Delhi: Academic Foundation.

UNCTAD. (2006). *World Investment Report: FDI from Developing and Transition Economies: Implications for Development*. Geneva: UNCTAD.

World Bank. (1991). *World Development Report*. Washington, D.C.: World Bank Publications.

ADDITIONAL READINGS

Agarwal, J. P. (1980). Determinants of Foreign Direct Investment: A Survey. *Weltwirtschaftliches Archiv*, *116*, 739–773. doi:10.1007/BF02696547

Balasubramanayam, V. N. (1999). Foreign Direct Investment in EP and IS Countries. *The Economic Journal*, *106*, 92–105. doi:10.2307/2234933

Bengoa, M., & Scanchez-Robles, B. (2003). Foreign Direct Investment, Economic Freedom and Growth: New Evidence from Latin America. *European Journal of Political Economy*, *19*, 529–545. doi:10.1016/S0176-2680(03)00011-9

Bhagwati, J. N. (1973). *The Theory of Immiserizing Growth: Further Applications.* In M.B. Connoly & A.K. Swoboda (Eds.), *International Trade and Money* (pp. 45-54). University of Toronto Press.

Carkovic, M., & Levine, R. (2002). *Does Foreign Direct Investment Accelerate Economic Growth* (National bureau of Economic Research Working Paper 8028). Cambridge, MA.

Caves, R. E. (1974, May). Multinational Firms, Competition, and Productivity in Host-country markets. *Economica*, 1.

Caves, R. E. (1982). *Multinational Enterprise and Economic Analysis*. Cambridge University Press.

Choe, J. I. (2003). Do Foreign Direct Investment and Gross Domestic Investment Promote Economic Growth? *Review of Development Economics*, 7(1), 44–57. doi:10.1111/1467-9361.00174

Coase, R. H. (1937). The Nature of the Firm' . *Economical*, *4*, 386–405. doi:10.1111/j.1468-0335.1937.tb00002.x

De Mello, L. R. (1999). Foreign Direct Investment-led Growth: Evidence from Time Series and Panel Data. *Oxford Economic Papers*, *51*, 133–151. doi:10.1093/oep/51.1.133

Dunning, J. H. (1977). *Trade, Location of Economic Activity and the MNE: A Search for an Eclectic Approach.* In B. Ohlin, P. O. Hesselborn, & P. M. Wijkman (Eds), The International Allocation of Economic Activity (London: Macmillan).

Horst, T. (1972). The Industrial Composition of U.S. Exports and Subsidiary Sales to the Canadian Market. *The American Economic Review*, *62*, 37–45.

Hymer, S. H. (1976[1960 as a thesis]). *The International Operations of National Firms: A Study of Direct Foreign Investment*. Cambridge, MA: MIT Press.

Kinckerbocker, F. T. (1973). *Oligopolistic Reaction and Multinational Enterprise*. Boston, MA: Division of Research, Harvard University Graduate School of Business Administration.

Kindleberger, C. P. (1969). *American Business Abroad: Six Lectures on Direct Investment*. New Haven, CT: Yale University Press.

Lizondo, J. S. (1991). Foreign Direct Investment, in International Monetary Fund, Determinants and Systematic Consequences of International Capita Flows. *IMF Occasional Papers* No. 77 (Washington DC): pp.68-82.

Markowitz, H. M. (1959). *Portfolio Selection: Efficient Diversification of Investments*. John Wiley, New York.

Tobin, J. (1958). Liquidity Preference as Behavior towards Risk. *The Review of Economic Studies*, *25*, 65–86. doi:10.2307/2296205

Vernon, R. (1966). International Investment and International Trade in the Product Cycle. *The Quarterly Journal of Economics*, *80*, 190–207. doi:10.2307/1880689

KEY TERMS AND DEFINITIONS

Disparity: Refers to inequality in the distribution of economic assets and income.

Entrepreneurship: The practice of starting new organizations or revitalizing mature organizations, particularly new businesses generally in response to identified opportunities.

FDI: A category of investment that reflects the objective of establishing a lasting interest by a resident enterprise in one economy (direct investor) in an enterprise (direct investment enterprise) that is resident in an economy other than that of the direct investor.

Inflow: Refers to direct investment in the reporting economy.

Multinational Corporation: A corporation or enterprise that manages production or delivers services in more than one country.

Outflow: Refers to direct investment abroad.

Pervasive Computing: A rapidly developing area of Information and Communications Technology (ICT). The term refers to the increasing integration of ICT into people's lives and environments, made possible by the growing availability of microprocessors with inbuilt communications facilities.

Tertiary Sector: Provision of services to businesses as well as final consumers.

Compilation of References

Aaker, D. A., Batra, R., & Myers, J. G. (1992). *Advertising management*. Englewood Cliffs, NJ: Prentice Hall.

Abbasi, Ahmed & Chen, Hsinchun. (2008). Cybergate: A Design framework and System For Text Analysis of Computer-Mediated Communication. *MIS Quarterly, 32*(4), 811–837.

Abdi, M. R., & Labib, A. W. (2003). A design strategy for reconfigurable manufacturing systems (RMS) using Analytical hierarchical process (AHP): A Case Study. *International Journal of Production Research, 41*(10), 2273–2299. doi:10.1080/0020754031000077266

Acharya, V., & Johnson, T. (2007). Insider trading in credit derivatives. *Journal of Financial Economics, 84*, 110–141. doi:10.1016/j.jfineco.2006.05.003

Addison, T., & Heshmati, A. (2004). The New Global Determinants of FDI Flows to Developing Countries: The Importance of ICT and Democratization. *Research in Banking and Finance, 4*, 151–186.

Adell, J., Bonafonte, A., & Escudero, D. (2005). *Analysis of prosodic features: towards modeling of emotional and pragmatic attributes of speech.*

Adelman, S., Moss, L., & Barbusinski, L. (2002). I found several definitions of BI. *DM Review*.

Advances in Consumer Research. (2008). The Value of Human Warmth: Social Presence Cues and Computer-Mediated Communications. *North American Conference Proceedings* (Vol. 35, pp. 793-794).

Agarwal, (2004). *Indian Economy* (29th ed., p. 639). New Delhi: Vishwa Prakashan.

Agarwal, J. P. (1980). Determinants of Foreign Direct Investment: A Survey. *Weltwirtschaftliches Archiv, 116*, 739–773. doi:10.1007/BF02696547

Ahire, S., & Golhar, D. (1996). Quality management in large versus small firms. *Journal of Small Business Management, 34*(1), 1–13.

Aktouf, O. (1992). Management and theories of organizations in the 1990s: Towards a critical radical humanism? *Academy of Management Review, 17*, 407–431. doi:10.2307/258717

Aladwani, A., & Palvia, P. (2002). Developing and validating an instrument for measuring user-perceived Web quality. *Information & Management, 39*(6), 467–476. doi:10.1016/S0378-7206(01)00113-6

Alba, J. W., Hutchinson, J. W., & Lynch, J. G. (1991). Memory and decision making. In T. Robertson & H. Kassarjian (Eds.), *Handbook of consumer behavior* (pp. 1-50). Engelwood Cliffs, NJ: Prentice-Hall.

Al-Bastaki, H., & Ramadhan, S. (1998). A Survey of Activity-Based Costing Practices in Bahraini Manufacturing Firms. *Journal of King Abdul Aziz University, 11*, 17–29.

Alcouffe, S. (2002). *Organisational determinants of Activity-Based Costing systems adoption: an empirical study among French firms.* Paper presented at the 25th Annual Congress of the European Accounting Association.

Allen, F., & Carletti, E. (2006). Credit risk transfer and contagion. *Journal of Monetary Economics, 53*, 89–111. doi:10.1016/j.jmoneco.2005.10.004

Al-Omiri, M. (2004). *The Diffusion of Management Accounting Innovations: The Motives behind ABC Systems Adoption in the UK Companies*. Paper presented at the 27th Annual Congress of the European Accounting Association, Prague-Czech Republic, 1-3 April.

Alshuwaikhat, H. M., & Abubakar, I. (2008, November). An integrated approach to achieving campus sustainability: Assessment of the current campus environmental management practices. *Journal of Cleaner Production*, *16*(16), 1777–1785. doi:10.1016/j.jclepro.2007.12.002

Altman, E., & Saunders, A. (1998). Credit risk measurement: Developments over the last 20 years. *Journal of Banking & Finance*, *21*, 1721–1742. doi:10.1016/S0378-4266(97)00036-8

Amburgey, T. L., Kelly, D., & Barnett, W. P. (1993). Reseting the clock. The dynamics of organizational change and failure. *Administrative Science Quarterly*, *38*, 51–73. doi:10.2307/2393254

American Institute of Certified Public Accountants (2002). *Consideration of Fraud in a Financial Statement Audit*, Statement on Auditing Standards No (99). New York: AICPA.

Amin, S. H., & Razmi, J. (2009, May). An integrated fuzzy model for supplier management: A case study of ISP selection and evaluation. *Expert Systems with Applications*, *36*(4), 8639–8648. doi:10.1016/j.eswa.2008.10.012

Anderson, S. W. (1995). A framework for assessing cost management system changes: The case of ABC implementation at General Motors. *Journal of Management Accounting Research, 7*, fall, 1-51.

Ankorion, I. (2005, January). Change Data Capture Efficient ETL for Real-Time BI. *DM Review*. Chapter, D. P. M. (n.d.). Data Warehouse Glossary. Retrieved November 19, 2008, from www.dama-pdx.org/Glossary28.doc.

Armitage, H.M., & Nicholson, R.(1993). *Activity Based Costing: A survey of Canadian Practice*. Issue Paper No.3, Society of Management Accountants of Canada, Issue Paper Series, September.

Armstrong, M. (2001). *A Handbook of Human Resource Management Practice* (8th ed.). London: Kogan Page.

Armstrong, M., & Baron, A. (2004). Strategic HRM: *The key to improved business performance. Encyclopedia of Human Resource Development* (Vol. 5). Mumbai: Jaico Publication.

Arnold, V., Sutton, S., Stephen, C., Hayne, S., & Smith, C. (2000). Group decision making: The impact of opportunity-cost time pressure and group support systems. *Behavioral Research in Accounting*, *12*, 69–96.

Aronson, D. (2007). *Evidence-based Technical Analysis*. NJ: John Wiley & Sons.

Asiedu, E. (2002). On the Determinants of Foreign Direct Investment to Developing Countries: Is Africa Different? *World Development*, *30*(1), 107–119. doi:10.1016/S0305-750X(01)00100-0

Atkinson, A., Banker, R., Kaplan, R., & Young, M. (2001). Management Accounting (3rd ed., pp. 160-161). NJ: Prentice-Hall.

Atkinson, W. (2007). Communicating with your risk managers. *Risk Management*, *54*(11), 28–32.

Atwood, C. (2007). Implementing your succession Plan. *Training & Development*, *61*(11), 54–55.

Babbage, C. (1832). *On the Economy of Machinery and Manufacturers*. London: Charles Night.

Back, T. (2002). Adaptive Business Intelligence Based on Evolution Strategies: Some Application Examples of Self-adaptive Software. *Information Sciences*, *148*, 113–121. doi:10.1016/S0020-0255(02)00283-9

Badri, M. A., Abdulla, M., & Al-Madini, A. (2005). Information technology center service quality assessment and application of SERVQUAL. *International Journal of Quality & Reliability Management*, *22*(8), 819–848. doi:10.1108/02656710510617247

Baily, J. (1991). Implementation of ABC systems by UK companies. *Management Accounting* (UK), February, 30-32.

Baïna, S., Panetto, H., & Morel, G. (2009, April). New paradigms for a product oriented modelling: Case study for traceability. *Computers in Industry*, *60*(3), 172–183. doi:10.1016/j.compind.2008.12.004

Baird, L., & Meshoulam, I. (1988). Managing two fits of strategic human resource management. *Academy of Management Review, 13*(1), 116–128. doi:10.2307/258359

Baker, W., (1994). Understanding Activity-Based Costing. *IM*, March / April, 28-30.

Balasubramanayam, V. N. (1999). Foreign Direct Investment in EP and IS Countries. *The Economic Journal, 106*, 92–105. doi:10.2307/2234933

Bamber, E. M., Watson, R. T. & Hill, M.C. (1996). The effects of group support system technology on audit group decision making. *Auditing: A Journal of Practice & Theory, 15*(1), 122-134.

Bandopadhyay, A. (2002) *Some Important Aspects of Bengali Speech Synthesis System*, Retrieved June 24-25, 2002, from IEMCT, Pane.

Bandyopadhyay, S., & Natarajan, V. (2008). Service quality of educational Websites: an empirical study. *Journal of Business & Economics Research, 6*, 49–54.

Bank for International Settlements. (2008). *OTC derivatives market activity in the first half of 2008* (Regular OTC Derivatives Market Statistics). Retrieved February 25, 2009, from http://www.bis.org/publ/otc_hy0811.htm

Banker, R., & Johnson, H. (1993). An empirical study of cost drivers in the US airline industry. *Accounting Review, 68*(3), 576–588.

Barbosa, P. A., & Bailly, G. (1994). Characterization of rhythmic patterns for text-to-speech synthesis. *Speech Communication, 15*, 127–137. doi:10.1016/0167-6393(94)90047-7

Barnard, C. (1938). The Functions of the Executive. *Harvard University Press.*

Barnard, C. I. (1938). *The Functions of the Executive*. Cambridge, MA: Harvard University Press.

Barnett, W. P., & Carroll, G. R. (1995). Modeling internal organizational change. *Annual Review of Sociology, 21*, 217–236. doi:10.1146/annurev.so.21.080195.001245

Barney, J. (1986). Types of competition and the theory of strategy: Toward an integrative framework. *Academy of Management Review, 11*(3), 791–800. doi:10.2307/258397

Barney, J. (1991). Firm resources and sustained competitive advantage. *Journal of Management, 17*(1), 99–120. doi:10.1177/014920639101700108

Barney, J. (1995). Looking inside for competitive advantage. *The Academy of Management Executive, 9*(4), 49–61.

Barney, J. (1996). The resource-based theory of the firm. *Organization Science, 7*, 469. doi:10.1287/orsc.7.5.469

Barney, J. (2001). Is the resource-based view a useful perspective for strategic management research? Yes. *Academy of Management Review, 26*, 41–56. doi:10.2307/259393

Barras, C., Geoffrois, E., Wu, Z., & Liberman, M. (2001). Transcriber: development and use of a tool for assisting speech corpora production. *Speech Communication, 33*(1), 5–22. doi:10.1016/S0167-6393(00)00067-4

Baruch, Y. (1997). Evaluating quality and reputation of human resource management . *Personnel Review, 26*(5), 377–394. doi:10.1108/00483489710176057

Basel Committee on Banking Supervision. (2005). *Credit risk transfer* (Report submitted by a Working Group established by the Committee on the Global Financial System). Retrieved February 25, 2009, from http://www.bis.org/publ/cgfs20.pdf

Batia, D. (1997). Reconfigurable computing technology. *Journal of Design & Manufacturing, 2*(4), 312–315.

Baum, J. A. C. (1996). Organizational Ecology. In S. R. Clegg, C. Hardy, & W. R. Nord (Eds.), *Handbook of organization studies* (pp. 77-114). London: Sage Publications.

Bayles, M. E. (2002). *Designing online banner advertisements: Should we animate?* Paper presented at the CHI 2002 Conference, Minneapolis, Minnesota, USA.

Beattie, J. (2000). *Contagion in Latin America: An Analysis of Credit Derivatives* (Working Paper). Duke University, Durham.

Beattie, K. R., & Sohal, A. S. (1999). Implementing ISO 9000: a study of its benefits among Australian organisations. *Total Quality Management*, *10*(1), 95–106. doi:10.1080/0954412998090

Beaumont, P. B., Hunter, L. C., & Phayre, R. M. (1994). Human Resources and Total Quality Management Some Case Study Evidence. *Training for Quality*, *2*(1), 7–13. doi:10.1108/09684879410056166

Becht, M., & Röell, A. (1999). Blockholdings in Europe: An International Comparison. *European Economic Review*, *43*, 1049–1056. doi:10.1016/S0014-2921(98)00113-5

Beck, N., Bruderl, J., & Woywode, M. (2008). Momentum or deceleration? Theoretical and methodological reflections on the analysis of organizational change. *Academy of Management Journal*, *51*(3), 413–435.

Becker, B. E., & Gerhart, B. (1996). The impact of human resource management on organizational performance: Progress and prospects. *Academy of Management Journal*, *39*, 779–802. doi:10.2307/256712

Becker, B. E., & Huselid, M. A. (1998). High performance work systems and firm performance: A synthesis of research and managerial implications. *Research in Personnel and Human Resources Management*, *16*, 53–101.

Becker, B. E., & Huselid, M. A. (2006). Strategic human resources management: Where do we go from here? *Journal of Management*, *32*(6), 898–925. doi:10.1177/0149206306293668

Beckford, J. (2002). *Quality* (2nd ed.). New York: Routledge.

Beer, M., Spector, B., Lawrence, P. R., Quinn Mills, D., & Walton, R. E. (1984). *Managing Human Assets*. New York: The Free Press.

Bei, W., Wang, S., & Hu, J. (2006, October). An analysis of supplier selection in manufacturing supply chain management. *International Conference on Service Systems and Service Management, 2,* 1439-1444.

Bengoa, M., & Scanchez-Robles, B. (2003). Foreign Direct Investment, Economic Freedom and Growth: New Evidence from Latin America. *European Journal of Political Economy*, *19*, 529–545. doi:10.1016/S0176-2680(03)00011-9

Benway, J. P., & Lane, D. M. (1998) Banner Blindness: Web Searches Often Miss "Obvious" Links.

Berger, A.J., & Gattorna, J.L. (2001). *Supply Chain Cybermastry: Building High Performance Supply Chains of the future*. London: Gower Publishing Limited.

Berger, N., & Udell, G. (1995). Relationship lending and lines of credit in small firm finance. *The Journal of Business*, *68*, 351–381. doi:10.1086/296668

Berle, A. A., & Means, G. C. (1932). *The Modern Corporation and Private Property*. New York: Macmillian.

Berliner, C., & Brimson, J. A. (1988). *Cost Management for today's advanced manufacturing: The CAM-I Conceptual design*. Boston, Harvard Business School Press.

Berlyne, D. (1970). Novelty, complexity and hedonic value. *Perception & Psychophysics*, *8*, 279–286.

Bernard, M. L. (2001). *Developing schemas for the location of common web objects.* Paper presented at the Human Factors and Ergonomics Society 45th Annual Meeting, Minneapolis, Minnesota.

Berry, G. (2006). Can Computer-Mediated, Asynchronous Communication Improve, Team Processes and Decision Making? *Journal of Business Communication*, *43*(4), 344–366. doi:10.1177/0021943606292352

Bertacco, M. (2007). Social Norms and Behavioral Regulation in Asynchronous Communication: The Shift of Attention During Speed Communication. *Human-Computer Interaction*, *22*(3), 299–324.

Bevilacqua, M., Ciarapica, F. E., & Giacchetta, G. (2009, July). Business process reengineering of a supply chain and a traceability system: A case study. *Journal of Food Engineering*, *93*(1), 13–22. doi:10.1016/j.jfoodeng.2008.12.020

Bhagwati, J. N. (1973). *The Theory of Immiserizing Growth: Further Applications.* In M.B. Connoly & A.K. Swoboda (Eds.), *International Trade and Money* (pp. 45-54). University of Toronto Press.

Bharatti, P., & Berg, D. (2003). Managing information systems for service quality: a study from the other side. *Information Technology & People*, *16*, 183–201. doi:10.1108/09593840310478685

Bhattacharya, M., & Wright, P. M. (2005). Managing human assets in an uncertain world: Applying real options theory to HRM. *International Journal of Human Resource Management*, *16*(6), 929–948.

Bhimani, A., & Pigott, D. (1992). Implementing ABC: A case study of organizational and behavioral consequences. *Management Accounting Research*, *3*, 119–132. doi:10.1016/S1044-5005(92)70007-9

Bhote, K. R. (1996). Beyond Customer Satisfaction to Customer Loyalty. In *Proceedings of the American Management Association*. New York, NY.

Biocca, F., Owen, C., Tang, A., & Bohil, C. (2007). Attention issues in spatial information systems: Directing mobile user's visual attention using augmented reality. *Journal of Management Information Systems*, *23*(4), 163–184. doi:10.2753/MIS0742-1222230408

Bititci, U. S., & Carrie, A. S. (1998). *Strategic Management of Manufacturing Value Chain*. Boston: Kluwer Academic Publishers.

Bjornenak, T. (1997). Diffusion and Accounting: the Case of ABC in Norway. *Management Accounting Research*, *8*, 3–17. doi:10.1006/mare.1996.0031

Bjornenak, T., & Mitchell, F. (2000). *A study of the development of the ABC journal literature 1987-1998*. Paper presented at the LSE Seminar on Management Accounting Change, (April)

Blackburn, R., & Rosen, B. (1993). Total Quality and Human Resources Management: Lessons learned from Baldrige award-winning companies. *The Academy of Management Executive*, *17*(3), 49–66.

Bohn, J., Coroama, V., Langheinrich, M., Mattern, F., & Rohs, M. (2004). Living in a World of Smart Everyday Objects—Social, Economic, and Ethical Implications. *Human and Ecological Risk Assessment*, *10*(5), 763–785. doi:10.1080/10807030490513793

Bohoris, G. (1995). A comparative assessment of some major quality awards . *International Journal of Quality & Reliability Management*, *12*(9), 30–43. doi:10.1108/02656719510101178

Bollinger, J. A. (2001). *Bollinger on Bollinger Bands*. New York: McGraw-Hill.

Bonne, L., & Kurtz, D. (1992). *Management*. New York: McGraw-Hill.

Boot, A., & Thakor, A. (1997). Financial System Architecture. *Review of Financial Studies*, *10*, 693–733. doi:10.1093/rfs/10.3.693

Bordia, P. (1997). Face-to-Face versus Computer-Mediated Communication: A synthesis of the experimental literature. *The Journal of Business Communication*, *34*(1), 99–120. doi:10.1177/002194369703400106

Boselie, P., & van der Wiele, T. (2002). Employee perceptions of HRM and TQM, and the effects on satisfaction and intention to leave . *Managing Service Quality*, *12*(3), 165–172. doi:10.1108/09604520210429231

Bosworth, B., & Collins, S. (1999). Capital Flows to Developing Economies: Implications for Saving and Investment. *Brookings Papers on Economic Activity: 1, Brookings Institution*, (pp.143-69).

Bottazzi, D., Montanari, R., & Rossi, G. (2008, August). A self-organizing group management middleware for mobile ad-hoc networks. *Computer Communications*, *31*(13), 3040–3048. doi:10.1016/j.comcom.2008.02.027

Bowersox, D. J., Closs, D. J., & Cooper, M. B. (2002). *Supply chain logistics management*. New York: McGraw-Hill.

Boxall, P. (1998). Achieving competitive advantage through human resource strategy: Towards a theory of industry dynamics. *Human Resource Management Review*, *8*(3), 265–288. doi:10.1016/S1053-4822(98)90005-5

Braddick, C., Pfefferle, M., & Gandossy, R. (1993). How Malcolm Baldrige winners reward employee performance. *Journal of Compensation and Benefits*, *9*, 47–52.

Braun, Robert. L., & Davis, Harold. E. (2003). Computer-assisted audit tools and techniques: analysis and perspectives. *Managerial Auditing Journal*, *18*(9), 725–731. doi:10.1108/02686900310500488

Brewer, J., & Dourish, P. (2008, December). Storied spaces: Cultural accounts of mobility, technology, and environmental knowing. *International Journal of Human-Computer Studies*, *66*(12), 963–976. doi:10.1016/j.ijhcs.2008.03.003

Brewster, C., & Larsen, H. H. (1992). Human resource management in Europe: evidence from ten countries. *International Journal of Human Resource Management*, *3*(3), 409–434.

Bridgefield Group, Inc. (n.d.). Bridgefield Group ERP/Supply chain Glossary. Retrieved November 19, 2008, from http://www.bridgefieldgroup.com/bridgefieldgroup/glos1.htm.

Bright, J., Davies, R. E., Downes, C. A., & Sweeting, R. C. (1992). The deployment of Costing Techniques and Practices: a UK Study. *Management Accounting Research*, *3*, 201–211. doi:10.1016/S1044-5005(92)70011-0

Brimson, J. (1997). *Activity accounting: An activity-based costing approach*. New York: John Wiley and Sons.

Brown, C. (1999). *Technical Analysis for the Trading Professional*. New York: McGraw-Hill.

Brown, J. L. (2004). How does Face-to-Face communication differ from online communication? *OMBA 600*, Assignment 2. Retrieved from http://www.mtholyoke.edu

Brown, K. L., & Inman, A. R. (1993). Small business and JIT: A managerial overview. *International Journal of Operations & Production Management*, *13*(3), 57–66. doi:10.1108/01443579310026032

Brugnara, F., Falavigna, D., & Omologo, M. (1993). Automatic Segmentation and Labeling of Speech based on Hidden Markov Models. *Speech Communication*, *12*(4), 357–370. doi:10.1016/0167-6393(93)90083-W

Bubbio, A., Alberti, F., & Toscano, G. (1999). *A Survey of ABC/ABT in the Italian Medium and Large companies*. Paper presented at the 22nd Annual Congress of the European Accounting Association, Bordeaux-France, 5-7 May.

Burke, M., Hornof, A., Nilsen, E., & Gorman, N. (2005). High-cost banner blindness: Ads increase perceived workload, hinder visual search, and are forgotten. *Transactions on Computer-Human Interaction*, *12*(4), 423–445. doi:10.1145/1121112.1121116

Burke, W. W. (2002). *Organization Change: Theory and Practice*. Thousand Oaks, CA: Sage Publications.

Burns, J., Ezzame, M., & Scapens, R. (2003). *Challenge of management accounting change*. London, UK: Chartered Institute of Management Accountants.

Burns, K. S., & Lutz, R. J. (2006). The function of format consumer responses to six on-line advertising formats. *Journal of Advertising*, *35*(1), 53–63. doi:10.2753/JOA0091-3367350104

Burns, P., & Dewhurst, J. (1996). *Small Business and Entrepreneurship*. London: McMillan Business.

Burstein, F. and C. W. Holsapple (2008). New horizons at the core of information systems: decision support system advances. *Information Systems and eBusiness Management*, *6*(2), 109.

Butschi, G., & Steyn, B. (2006). Theory on Strategic Communication Management is the key to Unlocking the Board Room. *Journal of Communication Management*, *10*, 106–109. doi:10.1108/13632540610646436

Buttle, F. (1996). SERVQUAL: review, critique, research agenda. *European Journal of Marketing*, *30*, 8–32. doi:10.1108/03090569610105762

Byron, K., & Baldridge, D. C. (2007). E-Mail Recipients' Impressions of Senders' Likability. *Journal of Business Communication*, *44*(2), 137–160. doi:10.1177/0021943606297902

Cacioppo, J. T., & Petty, R. E. (1979). Effects of message repetition and position on cognitive responses, recall, and persuasion. *Journal of Personality and Social Psychology*, *37*, 97–109. doi:10.1037/0022-3514.37.1.97

Campbell, M. C., & Keller, K. L. (2003). Brand familiarity and advertising repetition effects. *The Journal of Consumer Research, 30*, 292–304. doi:10.1086/376800

Cao, M., Qingyu, Z., & Seydel, J. (2005). B2C e-commerce Web site quality: an emprical examination. *Industrial Management & Data Systems, 105*(5), 645–661. doi:10.1108/02635570510600000

Carbonara, J. (2008). It's time for Technology. *Foodservice Equipment & Supplies, 61*(7), 28–36.

Carkovic, M., & Levine, R. (2002). *Does Foreign Direct Investment Accelerate Economic Growth.* National bureau of Economic Research Working Paper 8028. Cambridge, MA.

Carlstrom, C., & Samolyk, K. (1995). Loan sales as a response to market-based capital constraints. *Journal of Banking & Finance, 19*, 627–646. doi:10.1016/0378-4266(94)00144-R

Carman, J. M. (1990). Consumer perception of service quality: an assessment of the servqual dimensions. *Journal of Retailing, 66*(1), 33–55.

Carter, J. F. (2006). *Mastering the Trade*. New York: McGraw-Hill.

Casabona, P. A., & Grego, M. J. (2003). Consideration of fraud in a financial statement audit. *Review of Business, Jamaica, 24*(2), 16–21.

Casadesús, M., & Karapetrovic, S. (2005). The erosion of ISO 9000 benefits: a temporal study. *International Journal of Quality & Reliability Management, 22*(2), 120–136. doi:10.1108/02656710510577198

Castelli, G., Mamei, M., Rosi, A., & Zambonelli, F. (2009). Extracting High-Level Information from Location Data: The W4 Diary Example. *Mobile Networks and Applications, 14*(1), 107–119. doi:10.1007/s11036-008-0104-y

Caves, R. E. (1974, May). Multinational Firms, Competition, and Productivity in Host-country markets. *Economica*, 1.

Caves, R. E. (1982). *Multinational Enterprise and Economic Analysis.* Cambridge University Press.

Cecelja, F. (2002). *Manufacturing Information and Data System: Analysis, Design and Practice*. London: Penton Press.

Celik, M. (2009). Establishing an Integrated Process Management System (IPMS) in ship management companies. *Expert Systems with Applications, 36*(4), 8152–8171. doi:10.1016/j.eswa.2008.10.022

Chance, D. (1998). *An Introduction to Derivatives* (4th ed.). Orlando, Florida: The Dryden Press.

Chang. S. & Mayers. D. (1995). *Who Benefits in a Negotiated Block Trade?* (Working Paper, University of California at Riverside).

Channappa, D. (2007, December 1). Role of FDI in Indian Telecom Industry. *Southern Economist*, p 15.

Chatfield, D. C., Harrison, T. P., & Hayya, J. C. (2009, July). SCML: An information framework to support supply chain modeling. *European Journal of Operational Research, 196*(2), 651–660. doi:10.1016/j.ejor.2008.03.027

Chatterjee, P. (2004, October). *Changing Banner Ad Executions on the Web: Impact on Clickthroughs and Communication Outcomes*. Paper presented at Association for Consumer

Chatterjee, S., Chakraborty, S., Sarker, S., Sarker, S., & Lau, F. Y. (2009, February). Examining the success factors for mobile work in healthcare: A deductive study. *Decision Support Systems, 46*(3), 620–633. doi:10.1016/j.dss.2008.11.003

Chen, W. H. (1997). The human side of TQM in Taiwan: leadership and human resources management. *International Journal of Quality & Reliability Management, 14*(1), 24–45. doi:10.1108/02656719710156761

Cheng, S. P., & Tummala, R. (1998). An employee involvement strategy for ISO 9000 registration and maintenance: a case study for Hong Kong and China companies. *International Journal of Quality & Reliability Management, 15*(8/9), 860–891. doi:10.1108/02656719810198980

Cherng-Jyh, Y., & Chih-Hsiung, T. (2008). Online Social Presence: A Study of Score Validity of the Computer-

Mediated Communication Questionnaire. *Quarterly Review of Distance Education*, *9*(3), 297–310.

Cheung, C., Lee, M., & Rabjohn, N. (2008). The Impact of Electronic Word-of-Mouth: The Adoption of Online Opinions in Online Customer Communities. *Internet Research*, *18*(3), 229–247. doi:10.1108/10662240810883290

Chick, J., Hooman, & Roosmalenl, O.V. (2000). Modular Control for Machine Tools: Cross- Coupling control with friction compensation. *International Journal of Machine Control*, *2*(21), 455–462.

Chidambaram, L., & Jones, B. (1993). Impact of communication medium and computer support on group perceptions and performance: A comparison of face-to-face and dispersed meetings. *MIS Quarterly*, *17*(4), 465–491. doi:10.2307/249588

Cho, C.-H., & Cheon, J. H. (2004). Why do people avoid advertising on the internet? *Journal of Advertising*, *33*(4), 89–97.

Choe, J. I. (2003). Do Foreign Direct Investment and Gross Domestic Investment Promote Economic Growth? *Review of Development Economics*, *7*(1), 44–57. doi:10.1111/1467-9361.00174

Chow, W. M. (1998). Assembly lines Design Methodology and Applications. *Journal of Manufacturing Technology*, *1*(2), 61–65.

Christensen, J., & Hughes, B. (2007). Voice-enabled IT transformation: The new Voice technologies. *IBM Systems Journal*, *46*(4), 763–775.

CIPD. (2001). *The change agenda: People management and business performance*. London, Charted Institute of Personnel and Development.

Claessens, S., & Djankov, S. (1999). Ownership Concentration and Corporate Performance in the Czech Republic. *Journal of Comparative Economics*, *27*(3), 498–513. doi:10.1006/jcec.1999.1598

Coase, R. (1937). The Nature of the Firm. *Economica, New Series, IV*

Coase, R. H. (1937). The Nature of the Firm. *Economical*, *4*, 386–405. doi:10.1111/j.1468-0335.1937.tb00002.x

Cobb, I., Innes, J., & Falconer, M. (1993). *ABC problems: The British Experience*. Paper presented at the 16th Annual Congress of the European Accounting Association, Turku-Finland, April 28-30.

Cobb, J., Innes, J., & Mitchell, F. (1992). *Activity-Based Costing: Problems in Practice*. London: The Chartered Institute of Management Accountants.

Coffee, C. (1999). The Future as History: The Prospects for Global Convergence in Corporate Governance and its Implications . *Northwestern University Law Review*, 93.

Cohen, S., & Kaimenaki, E. (2004). *ABC in Greece: Adopters, Supporters, Deniers and Ignorers*. Paper presented at the Annual Congress of the European Accounting Association, Prague, 1-3 April.

Coleman, S., & Douglas, A. (2003). Where next for ISO 9000 companies? *The TQM Magazine*, *15*(2), 88–92. doi:10.1108/09544780310461099

Collier, J. E., & Bienstock, Carol C. (2006). Measuring service quality in e-retailing. *Journal of Service Research*, *8*, 260–275. doi:10.1177/1094670505278867

Colwyn, J. T., & Dugdale, D. (2002). The ABC Bandwagon and the Juggernaut of Modernity. *Accounting, Organizations and Society*, *27*(1/2), 121–164.

Connolly, R., & Bannister, F. (2008). eTax filing & service quality: the case of the revenue online service. Proceedings of World Academy of Science. *Engineering and Technology*, *28*, 313–317.

Conti, T. (2002). Human and social implications of excellence models: are they really accepted by the business community? *Managing Service Quality*, *12*(3), 151–158. doi:10.1108/09604520210429213

Cooper, R. (1987). The Two-stage Procedure in Cost Accounting. *Journal of Cost Management* (summer), 43-51.

Cooper, R. (1988). The Rise of Activity-Based Costing – Part One: What is an Activity-Based Cost System? *Journal of Cost Management* (summer), 45-54.

Cooper, R. (1988). The Rise of Activity-Based Costing – Part Two: When do I need an Activity-Based Cost System? *Journal of Cost Management* (fall), 45-54.

Cooper, R. (1989). The Rise of Activity-Based Costing – Part Three: How Many Cost Drivers Do You Need and How Do You Select Them? *Journal of Cost Management*, Summer, 45-54.

Cooper, R., & Kaplan, R. (1999). *The design of cost management systems*. Upper Saddle River, NJ: Prentice-Hall.

Cooper, R., & Kaplan, R. S. (1988). Measure Cost Right: Make the Right Decision. *Harvard Business Review*, (Sept-Oct): 96–103.

Cooper, R., & Kaplan, R.S. (1987). How cost accounting systematically distorts product costs. *Management Accounting*, April, 20-27.

Cooper, R., Kaplan, R. S., Maisel, L. S., Morrissey, E., & Oehm, R. (1992). *Implementing Activity-Based Cost Management: Moving from analysis to action*. Montvale, NJ: Institute of Management Accountants.

Cortellessa, V., Marinelli, F., & Potena, P. (2008, October). An optimization framework for "build-or-buy" decisions in software architecture. *Computers & Operations Research*, *35*(10), 3090–3106. doi:10.1016/j.cor.2007.01.011

Costa, M., & Martinez-Lorente, A. R. (2003). ISO 9000: The past, The Present and The Future. A case study in the Spanish Industry. In *Proceedings of the 8th International Conference on ISO 9000 and TQM, Montreal, Part II.*

Coulthard, L. J. M. (2004). Measuring service quality a review and critique of research using servqual. *The Market Research Society*, *46*, 479–497.

Cox, J., & Dale, B. G. (2001). Service Quality and e-commerce: an exploratory analysis. *Managing Service Quality*, *11*(2), 121–131. doi:10.1108/09604520110387257

Cristiano, J. J., Liker, J. K., & White, C. C. III. (2000). Customer-driven product development through quality function deployment in the U.S. and Japan. *Journal of Product Innovation Management*, *17*, 286–308. doi:10.1016/S0737-6782(00)00047-3

Cristoal, E., Flavian, C., & Guinaliu, M. (2007). Perceived eservice quality: Measurement validity and effects on consumer satisfaction and Web site loyalty. *Managing Service Quality*, *17*(3), 317–340. doi:10.1108/09604520710744326

Cronin, J. J. (2003). Looking back to see forward in services marketing: some ideas to consider. *Managing Service Quality*, *13*(5), 332–337. doi:10.1108/09604520310495813

Crosby, P. B. (1979). *Quality is free*. New York: McGraw-Hill.

Crosby, P. B. (1989). *Let's talk quality*. New York: McGraw-Hill.

Cruz, U. S. (n.d.). Data Warehouse Glossary. Retrieved November 19, 2008, from http://planning.ucsc.edu/irps/dwh/DWHGLOSS.HTM.

Cuff, D. (2003). Immanent Domain Pervasive Computing and the Public Realm. *Journal of Architectural Education*, 43-49.

Cuff, D., Hansen, M., & Kang, J. (2008). Urban Sensing: Out of the Woods. *Association for Computing Machinery. Communications of the ACM*, *51*(3), 24. doi:10.1145/1325555.1325562

Cummings, G. (1991).Practical implications of implementing ABC. *Journal of the Institute of Industrial Engineers*, June, 20-23.

Cutugno, F., D'Anna, L., Petrillo, M., & Zovato, E. (2002). *APA: towards an Automatic Tool for Prosodic Analysis*. Speech Prosody 2002, Aix-en-Provence, pp.231-234.

CXOToday.com. (n.d.). Tech Terms. Retrieved November 19, 2008, from http://www.cxotoday.com/cxo/jsp/home.jsp?cat=1003.

Dabbish, L., Hsieh, G., Kraut, R., & Hudson, S. (2007). Prioritization in Computer-Mediated Communication: Influences of Urgency, Notification, and Identity. *Academy of Management Proceedings* (pp.1-6).

Dabholkar, P. (1996). Consumer evaluations of new technology based self-service options: An investigation of alternative modes of service quality. *International Journal of Research in Marketing, 13*(1), 29–51. doi:10.1016/0167-8116(95)00027-5

Dale, B. G., Zairi, M., Van der Wiele, A., & Williams, A. R. T. (2000). Quality is dead in Europe - long live excellence - true or false? *Measuring Business Excellence, 4*(3), 4–10. doi:10.1108/13683040010377737

Das, S. (1998). *Credit derivatives: Trading and management of credit and default risk.* Singapore: John Wiley & Sons.

Das, S. (2000). *Credit Derivatives and Credit Linked Notes.* New York: John Wiley & Sons.

Dass, R., & Mahanti, A. (2005). *An Efficient Brute-Force Technique for Frequent Pattern Mining in Real-Time Business Applications.* Paper presented at the Hawaii International Conference on System Sciences.

Davies, R. E., & Sweeting, R. (1993). *Accounting Innovations and Development of Manufacturing Cost Management Systems.* The 16th Annual Congress of the European Accounting Association, Finland, 28-30 May.

De Mello, L. R. (1999). Foreign Direct Investment-led Growth: Evidence from Time Series and Panel Data. *Oxford Economic Papers, 51,* 133–151. doi:10.1093/oep/51.1.133

De Ruyter, K., Bloemer, J., & Peeters, P. (1997). Merging service quality and service satisfaction: an emprical test of an integrative model. *Journal of Economic Psychology, 18,* 387–406. doi:10.1016/S0167-4870(97)00014-7

Decenzo, D. A., & Robbins, S. P. (2005). *Fundamentals of Human Resource Management* (8th ed.). New Delhi: Wiley India.

Delery, J. E. (1998). Issues of fit in strategic human resource management: Implications for research. *Human Resource Management Review, 8*(3), 289–310. doi:10.1016/S1053-4822(98)90006-7

Delery, J. E., & Doty, D. H. (1996). Modes of theorizing in strategic human resource management: Tests of universalistic, contingency, and configurational performance predictions. *Academy of Management Journal, 39,* 802–835. doi:10.2307/256713

Deming, W. E. (1982). *Quality, productivity, and competitive position.* Cambridge, MA: Center for Advanced Engineering Study, Massachusetts Institute of Technology.

Demirag, I. S., & Serter, M. (2003). Ownership Patterns and Control in Turkish Listed Companies. *Corporate Governance, 11,* 40–51. doi:10.1111/1467-8683.00300

Demsetz, H., & Lehn, K. (1958). The Structure of Corporate Ownership. *The Journal of Political Economy, 93,* 1155–1177. doi:10.1086/261354

Dennis, A. R. (1996). Information exchange and use in group decision making: You can lead a group to information, but you can't make it think. *MIS Quarterly, 20*(4), 433–457. doi:10.2307/249563

Dennis, A. R., Wixom, B. H., & Vandenberg, R. J. (2001). Understanding fit and appropriation effects in group support systems via Meta analysis. *MIS Quarterly, 25*(2), 167–193. doi:10.2307/3250928

Desilva, Moon. D. B., Stewart, R. A., Volpe, & Khosla, P.K. (2000). Design of dynamically re-configurable real-time software using port-based objects. *Journal of Automation & Control, 1*(23), 759–775.

Dessler, G. (2008). *Human Resource Management* (10th ed.). New Delhi: Dorling Kindersley.

Devanna, M. A., Fombrun, C., & Tichy, N. M. (1981). Human resource management: A strategic perspective. *Organizational Dynamics, 9*(3), 51–68. doi:10.1016/0090-2616(81)90038-3

Dhakal, D., & Rahman, U. (2008). FDI and economic growth in Asia. *Indian Journal of Economics and Business, 6,* 15.

Dharmendra, D. et al., (2005). Foreign Direct Investment and Economic Growth in Asia. *Journal of Economic Literature,* F21,O17,O19

Diamond, D., & Rajan, G. (2000). A theory of bank capital. *The Journal of Finance, 55,* 2431–2465. doi:10.1111/0022-1082.00296

Diaper, D., & Waeland, P. (2000). World wide web working whilst ignoring graphics: Good new for web page designer. *Interacting with Computers, 13,* 163–181. doi:10.1016/S0953-5438(00)00036-9

Dick, G. P. M. (2000). ISO 9000 certification benefits, reality or myth? *The TQM Magazine, 12*(6), 365–371. doi:10.1108/09544780010351517

Diesbach, P., & Midgley, D. (2008). Embodied Agents on Commercial Websites: Modeling Their Effects through an Affective Persuasion Route. In H. Oinas-Kukkonen, P. Hasle, M. Harjumaa, K. Segerståhl & P. Øhstrøm (Eds.), *Proceedings of Third International Conference on Persuasive Technology,* June 2008, Oulu, Finland (pp. 283-286), Berlin, Springer-Verlag.

Ding, Y., Ceglarek, D., & Shi, J. (2002). Fault diagnosis of multistage manufacturing processes by using state space approach. *Journal of Manufacturing Science, 1*(24), 313–322. doi:10.1115/1.1445155

Dobrev, S. D., Kim, T. Y., & Hannan, M. T. (2001). Dynamics of niche width and resource partitioning. *American Journal of Sociology, 106,* 1299–1337. doi:10.1086/320821

Douglas, A., Coleman, S., & Oddy, R. (2003). The case for ISO 9000. *The TQM Magazine, 15*(5), 316–324. doi:10.1108/09544780310487712

Douglas, M. (2001). Trading in the Zone. New Jersey: Prentice Hall.

Dowling, C., Leech, S. A., & Moroney, R. (2008). Audit Support System Design and the Declarative Knowledge of Long-Term Users. *Journal of Emerging Technologies in Accounting, 5,* 99–108. doi:10.2308/jeta.2008.5.1.99

Dréze, X., & Hussherr, F.-X. (2003). Internet advertising: Is anybody watching? *Journal of Interactive Marketing, 17*(4), 8–23. doi:10.1002/dir.10063

Drogosz, J. D. (2002). Applying Lean Above the Factory Floor. *Journal of Ship Production, 18*(3), 159–166.

Drury, C., & Al-Omiri, M. (2002). *The diffusion of management accounting innovations: A study of the factors influencing the adoption, implementation levels and success of ABC in UK.* Paper presented at the 22nd Annual Congress of the European Accounting Association.

Drury, C., & Tayles, M. (1994). Product Costing in UK Manufacturing Organizations. *European Accounting Review, 3,* 443–469. doi:10.1080/09638189400000031

Drury, C., Braund, S., Osborne, P., & Tayles, M. (1993). *A Survey of Management Accounting Practices in UK Manufacturing Companies.* London: ACCA.

Duchowski, A. T. (2007) *Eye Tracking Methodology: Theory and Practise,* London: Springer Verlag

Dufey, G., & Rehm, F. (2000) An Introduction to Credit Derivatives (Working Paper). University of Michigan Business School.

Duffee, G., & Zhou, C. (2001). Credit Derivatives in Banking: Useful Tools for Managing Risk. *Journal of Monetary Economics, 48,* 25–54. doi:10.1016/S0304-3932(01)00063-0

Duffie, D., & Garleanu, N. (2001). Risk and valuation of collateralised debt obligations. *Financial Analysts Journal,* 41–59. doi:10.2469/faj.v57.n1.2418

Dunning, J. H. (1977). Trade, Location of Economic Activity and the MNE: A Search for an Eclectic Approach. In B. Ohlin, P. O. Hesselborn, & P. M. Wijkman (Eds.). *The International Allocation of Economic Activity.* London, UK: Macmillan.

Dunning, J. H. (1979). Explaining Changing Patterns of International Production: In Defence of the Eclectic Theory. *Oxford Bulletin of Economics and Statistics, 41,* 269–295.

Dunning, J. H. (1988). *Multinationals, Technology and Competitiveness.* London: Unwin Hyman.

Dunning, J. H. (1988). The Eclectic Paradigm of International Production: A Restatement and Some Possible

Extensions. *Journal of International Business Studies, 19*, 1–31. doi:10.1057/palgrave.jibs.8490372

Dunsby, A., Eckstein, J., Gaspar, J., & Mulholland, S. (2008). *Commodity Investing – Maximizing Returns Through Fundamental Analysis*. NJ: John Wiley & Sons.

Durvasula, S., Lysonski, S., & Mehta, S. C. (1999). Testing the SERVQUAL scale in the business-to-business sector: The case of ocean freight shipping service. *Journal of Services Marketing, 13*(2), 132–150. doi:10.1108/08876049910266040

Dutta, M. K., & Sarma, G. K. (2008). Foreign Direct Investment in India Since 1991: Trends, Challenges [New Delhi: Wisdom Publications.]. *Prospects*, 18–32.

Dyer, J. H. (2000). *Collaborative Advantage: Winning Through Extended Enterprise Supplier Network*. New York: Oxford University Press.

Earle, J., S., Kucsera, C. & Telegdy, Á. (2005). Ownership Concentration and Corporate Performance in the Budapest Stock Exchange: do too many cooks spoil the goulash? *Corporate Governance, 13*, 254–264. doi:10.1111/j.1467-8683.2005.00420.x

Ebrahimpour, M., & Cullen, J. B. (1993). Quality Management in Japanese and American Firms operating in the United States: A comparative study of styles and motivational beliefs. *Management International Review, 33*(1), 23–38.

Eckerson, W. (2004, August). The "Soft Side" of Real-Time BI. *DM Review*.

Eden, R. (2002). *Activity-based costing in high tech companies in Canada*. Paper presented at the 22nd Annual Congress of the European Accounting Association.

Edwards, J., & Nibler, M. (2000). Corporate Governance in Germany: the Role of Banks and Ownership Concentration. *Economic Policy, 15*(31). doi:10.1111/1468-0327.00062

Eide, E., Bakis, R., Hamza, W., & Pitrelli, J. (2003). Multilayered Extensions to the Speech Synthesis Markup Language for Describing Expressiveness. In *Proc. of EuroSpeech'03* (pp. 1645-1648), September. 2003.

Eiler, R. G., & Campi, J. P. (1990). Implementing ABC at a process company. *Journal of Cost Management*, Spring, 43-50.

Elder, A. (1993). *Trading for a Living*. John Wiley & Sons.

Elder, A. (2002). *Come Into My Trading Room – A Complete Guide to Trading*. John Wiley & Sons.

Epoch Synchronous Non-Overlapping Add (ESNOLA) Approach Concatenative Text to Speech Synthesis - A Technical Report. (2005, January). Retrieved 2005, from http://tdil.mit.gov.in/Jan_issue%202005/10-EPOCH.pdf

Errais, E., Giesecke, K., & Goldberg, L. (2007). Pricing Credit from the Top Down with Affine Point Processes. In J. Miller, D. Edelman, J. Appleby (Eds.), *Numerical Methods for Finance* (pp. 195-201). Chapman & Hall/CRC Financial Mathematics Series.

Escudero-Mancebo, D., Gonzalez-Farreras, C., & Cardeñoso, V. (2002). *Quantitative evaluation of relevant prosodic factors for text-to-speech synthesis*. In the Proceedings of ICSLP.

Estrin, T., Kantor, J., & Albers, D. (1994). Is ABC Suitable for your Company? *Management Accounting*, April, 40-45.

Evers, L., & Havinga, P. (2007, October). Supply chain management automation using wireless sensor networks. *IEEE International Conference on Mobile Adhoc and Sensor Systems*, 1-3.

Eversheim, W., Klocke, F., Pfeifer, T., & Weck, M. (1997). *Manufacturing Excellence in Global Markets*. London: Chapman and Hall.

Fama, E. (1985). What's different about banks? *Journal of Monetary Economics, 15*, 29–40. doi:10.1016/0304-3932(85)90051-0

Fang, X., Singh, S., & Ahluwalia, R. (2007). An examination of different explanations for the mere exposure effect. *The Journal of Consumer Research*, *34*(1), 97–103. doi:10.1086/513050

Ferber, J. (1995). *Multi-Agent Systems – An Introduction to Distributed Artificial Intelligence*. New York: Addison Wesley Longman.

Ferris, G. R., Hochwarter, W. A., Buckley, M. R., Harrell-Cook, G., & Frink, D. D. (1999). Human resource management: Some new directions. *Journal of Management*, *25*(3), 385–415. doi:10.1177/014920639902500306

Field, J. M., Heim, G. R., & Sinha, K. K. (2004). Managing quality in the eservice system: Development and application of a process model. *Production and Operations Management*, *13*(4), 291–306.

Fisher, J. G. (2001). *E-Business for Small Businesses*. London: Kogan Page.

Fleisch, E. (2004). *Business Impact of Pervasive Technologies: Opportunities and Risks*.

Francas, D., & Minner, S. (2009, August). Manufacturing network configuration in supply chains with product recovery. *Omega*, *37*(4), 757–769. doi:10.1016/j.omega.2008.07.007

Frank, K. A., Gupta, S. K. S., Richard, G. G., & Schwiebert, L. (2005). *Fundamentals of Mobile and Pervasive Computing*. New York: McGraw Hill.

Franks, J., & Mayer, C. (1994). *Corporate Control: A Comparison of Insider and Outsider Systems* (Working Paper, London Business School).

Franks, J., & Mayer, C. (2001). Ownership and Control of German Corporations. *Review of Financial Studies*, *14*, 943–977. doi:10.1093/rfs/14.4.943

Friedman, A., & Lyne, S. (1999). *Success and Failure of Activity-Based Costing Techniques*. CIMA, London.

Froot, K., & Stein, J. (1998). Risk Management, Capital Budgeting, and Capital Structure for Financial Institutions: An Integrated Approach. *Journal of Financial Economics*, *47*, 55–82. doi:10.1016/S0304-405X(97)00037-8

Fujisaki, H., Ohno, S., & Narusawa, S. (2000). Physiological mechanisms and biomechanical modeling of fundamental frequency control for the common Japanese and the standard Chinese. In *the Proceedings of the 5th Seminar on Speech Production* (pp 145-148). Bavaria, Germany.

Gakhar, K. (2007). *Foreign Direct Investment in India 1947 to 2007: Policies, Trends and Outlook* (p. 124). New Delhi: New Century Publications.

Gangadharan, G. R., & Swamy, S. N. (2004). *Business intelligence systems: design and implementation strategies*. Paper presented at the 26th International Conference on Information Technology Interfaces, Cavtat, Croatia.

Gerald, M. M., & James, E. R. (2002). *Leading issues in economic development* (7th ed., pp. 209-211). Oxford University Press.

Ghobadian, A., & Gallear, D. N. (1996). Total quality management in SME. *Omega*, *24*(1), 83–106. doi:10.1016/0305-0483(95)00055-0

Gibson, M. (2007). *Credit Derivatives and Risk Management. Finance and Economics Discussion Series* (Federal Reserve Board). Washington, D.C.

Gierusz, J., Januszewski, A., & Kujawski, J. (2004). *The Needs and Possibilities of the Introduction of the Activity-Based Costing in Polish Enterprises-Research Results*. Paper presented at the Annual Congress of the European Accounting Association, Prague, 1-3 April.

Gilberg, L., Sangwan, S., & Ian, M. (2005). Beyond usability: the OoBE dynamics of mobile data services markets. *Personal and Ubiquitous Computing*, *9*, 198–208. doi:10.1007/s00779-004-0321-8

Girelli, M., & Luck, S. J. (1997). Are the same attentional mechanisms used to detect visual search targets defined by colour, orientation and motion? *Cognitive Neuroscience*, *9*(2), 238–253. doi:10.1162/jocn.1997.9.2.238

Godara, V. (2009). Pervasive Computing: A Conceptual Framework. In V. Godara (Ed.), *Risk Assessment and Management in Pervasive Computing* (pp. 1-19). Hershey, PA: Idea Group Inc.

Godley, A. C. (1999). Pioneering Foreign Direct Investment in British Manufacturing. *Business History Review*, *73*, 394–429. doi:10.2307/3116182

Goldsmith, W., & Clutterbuck, D. (1998). *The Winning Streak Mark II*. London: Orion Business Books.

Gonzales, M. L. (2004). Unearth BI in Real-time. *Teradata*.

Goodhart, C. (1998). *The Evolution of Central Banks*, Cambridge: The MIT Press.

Goodhue, D. L. (1995). Understanding user evaluations of information systems. *Management Science*, *41*(12), 1827–1844. doi:10.1287/mnsc.41.12.1827

Goodhue, D. L., & Thompson, R. T. (1995). Task-Technology Fit and individual performance. [Retrieved from http://www.misq.org - http://www.highbeam.com/library]. *MIS Quarterly*, *19*(2), 213–236. doi:10.2307/249689

Goodman, L. (2002). Synthetic CDOs: an introduction. *Journal of Derivatives*, 60–72. doi:10.3905/jod.2002.319180

Gorton, G., & Pennacchi, G. (1995). Banking and loan sales: marketing nonmarketable assets. *Journal of Monetary Economics*, *35*, 389–411. doi:10.1016/0304-3932(95)01199-X

Gorton, G., & Schmid, F. A. (2000). Universal Banking and the Performance of German Firms. *Journal of Financial Economics*, *58*, 29–80. doi:10.1016/S0304-405X(00)00066-0

Gosselin, M. (1997). The Effect of strategy and Organizational structure on the Adoption and Implementation of Activity-based Costing. *Accounting, Organizations and Society*, *22*(2), 105–122. doi:10.1016/S0361-3682(96)00031-1

Gosselin, M. (1999). *The ABC Paradox: Bandwagon Theories and Competitive Pressures*. Paper presented at the 22nd Annual Congress of the European Accounting Association, Bordeaux-France, 5-7 May.

Goswami, D., Kallimani, J. S., & Ananthashayana, V. K. (2008). An Efficient Concatenated Speech Generator for Bengali Language. In *Proceedings of International Congress on Pervasive Computing and Management (ICPCM-2008)*.

Grant, M. R., Shani, R., & Krishnan, R. (1994). TQM's Challenge to Management Theory and Practice. *Sloan Management Review*, (Winter): 25–35.

Green, F. B., & Amenkhienan, F. (1992). Accounting Innovations: A Cross Sectional Survey of Manufacturing Firm *Journal of Cost Management*, *6*, 58–64.

Grimshaw, D., Cooke, F. L., Grugulis, I., & Vincent, S. (2002). New Technology and Changing Organizational forms: Implications for managerial Control and skills. *New Technology, Work and Employment*, *17*, 86–203. doi:10.1111/1468-005X.00104

Guan, S., Dong, X., Mei, Y., Zhu, Z., & Wu, W. (2008). Trust force-based service selection in pervasive computing environments. *Journal of Communication and Computer*, *5*(6), 27–31.

Guest, D., Michie, I., Sheehan, M., & Conway, N. (200b). *Employee relations, HRM & Business Performance: An analysis of the1998Workplace Employee Relations Survey*. London: Institute of Personnel & Development.

Gunasekaran, A. (2000). World class manufacturing in small and medium enterprises. *International Journal of Manufacturing Technology and Management*, *2*(1-7), 777-789.

Gunasekaran, A., & Ngai, E. (2009, June). Modeling and analysis of build-to-order supply chains. *European Journal of Operational Research*, *195*(2), 319–334. doi:10.1016/j.ejor.2008.03.026

Haas, E., Schwarz, R. C., & Papazian, J. M. (2002). Design and test of a reconfigurable forming die. *Journal of Manufacturing Process*, *1*(4), 77–86. doi:10.1016/S1526-6125(02)70134-5

Hackman, J. R., & Wageman, R. (1995, June). Total Quality Management: Empirical, Conceptual, and Practical Issues. *Administrative Science Quarterly*, *40*, 309–342. doi:10.2307/2393640

Hall, K. W. *(2005).* Identifying non-value added practices in manufacturing: An instructional design. *Doctoral dissertation, Illinois State University.*

Hamzah, A., & Zairi, M. (1996). People management: where is the evidence of best practice? Part III. *Training for Quality*, *4*(4), 37–44. doi:10.1108/09684879610149026

Hancock, J. T., Curry, L. E., Goorha, S., & Woodworth, M. (2008). On Lying and Being Lied To: A Linguistic Analysis of Deception in Computer Mediated Communication. *Discourse Processes*, *45*(1), 1–23. doi:10.1080/01638530701739181

Hannan, M. T., & Freema, J. (1984). Structural inertia and organizational change. *American Sociological Review*, *49*, 149–164. doi:10.2307/2095567

Hart, A. J., Slocum, A., & Willoughby, P. (2004). Kinematic coupling interchangeability . *Journal of Manufacturing Engineering*, *1*(28), 1–15.

Hart, C., & Schlesinger, L. (1991). Total Quality Management and the HR professional: Applying the Baldrige Framework to human resources. *Human Resource Management*, *30*(4), 433–454. doi:10.1002/hrm.3930300402

Heath, R., & Nairn, A. (2008). How Creativity of Advertising Influences Consumer Behaviour. In Proceedings of the Conference on Neuroeconomics, Copenhagen Business School., May 15 -16, Denmark.

Henderson, J. M., & Hollingworth, A. (1999). High-level scene perception. *Annual Review of Psychology*, *50*, 243–271. doi:10.1146/annurev.psych.50.1.243

Hendricks, C. F., & Triplett, A. (1989). TQM: Strategy for 90's management. *The Personnel Administrator*, *34*(12), 42–48.

Hendricks, J.A. (1988). Applying cost accounting to factory automation. *Management Accounting*, December, 24-30.

Hendry, C., & Pettigrew, A. (1986). The practice of strategic human resource management. *Personnel Review*, *15*, 2–8. doi:10.1108/eb055547

Henke, S., Burghof, H., & Rudolph, B. (1998). Credit Securitization and Credit Derivatives: Financial Instruments and the Credit Risk Management of Middle Market Commercial Loan Portfolios (Working Paper). Munchen University.

Henning-Thurau, T., Gwinner, K. P., Walsh, G., & Gremler, D. D. (2004). Electronic Word-of-Mouth via Consumer-opinion platforms: What motivates consumers to articulate themselves on the Internet? *Journal of Interactive Marketing*, *18*(1), 38–52. doi:10.1002/dir.10073

Hill, S. (1991). How do you manage the flexible firm? The Total Quality Model. *Work, Employment and Society*, *5*(3), 397–416. doi:10.1177/0950017091005003005

Hill, S., & Wilkinson, A. (1995). In search of TQM. *Employee Relations*, *17*(3), 8–25. doi:10.1108/01425459510147002

Hilty, L., Som, C., & Köhler, A. (2004). Assessing the Human, Social, and Environmental Risks of Pervasive Computing. *Human and Ecological Risk Assessment*, *10*(5), 853–874. doi:10.1080/10807030490513874

Hirtle, B. (2009). Credit Derivatives and Bank Credit Supply. *Journal of Financial Intermediation*, *18*, 125–150. doi:10.1016/j.jfi.2008.08.001

Ho, C. I., & Lee, Y. L. (2007). The development of an e-travel service quality scale. *Tourism Management*, *28*(6), 1434–1449. doi:10.1016/j.tourman.2006.12.002

Hoffman, K. D., & Bateson, J. E. G. (Eds.). (1997). *Essentials of services marketing.* Fort Worth, TX: Dryden Press.

Holderness, C. G., & Sheehan, D. P. (1988). The role of majority shareholders in publicly held corporations: An exploratory analysis. *Journal of Financial Economics*, 20.

Hong, W., Thong, J. Y. L., & Tam, K. Y. (2004). Does animation attract online users' attention? The effects of flash on information search performance and perceptions. *Information Systems Research*, *15*(1), 60–86. doi:10.1287/isre.1040.0017

Horngren, C., Foster, G., Rajan, M., & Ittner, C. (2009). *Cost Accounting: A Managarial Emphasis* (11th ed.). Englewood Cliffs, NJ: Prentice-Hall.

Horrey, W. J., Wickens, C. D., & Consalus, K. P. (2006). Modeling Driver's Visual Attention Allocation while Interacting with In-Vechile technologies. *Journal of Experimental Psychology. Applied*, *12*(2), 67–78. doi:10.1037/1076-898X.12.2.67

Horst, T. (1972). The Industrial Composition of U.S. Exports and Subsidiary Sales to the Canadian Market. *The American Economic Review*, *62*, 37–45.

Hovey, M., Lee, L., & Naughton, A. (2003). The Relationship Between Valuation and Ownership of Listed Firms in China. *Corporate Governance: An International Review*, *11*, 112–122. doi:10.1111/1467-8683.00012

Howard, S., Kjeldskov, J., & Skov, M. B. (2007). Pervasive computing in the domestic space. *Personal and Ubiquitous Computing*, 329–333. doi:10.1007/s00779-006-0081-8

Hsu, S-F., & Chiang, C-H. (2007, August). Wireless Technology: A challenge toward supply chain management. *Portland International Center for Management of Engineering and Technology* (pp. 2361-2364).

Huang, A. H. (2002). E-mail communication and supervisor-subordinate exchange quality: an empirical study. *Human Systems Management*, *21*, 193–204.

Huang, T. (1998). The Strategic level of human resource management and organizational performance: An empirical investigation. *Asia Pacific Journal of Human Resources*, *36*(2), 59–72. doi:10.1177/103841119803600206

Hull, J. (2003). *Options, Futures and Other Derivatives* (5th ed.). Upper Saddle River, New Jersey: Prentice Hall.

Hunt, V. D. (1993). *Managing Quality: Integrating quality and business strategy*. Homewood, IL, Irwin

Huselid, M. A. (1995). The impact of human resource management practices on turnover, productivity, and corporate financial performance. *Academy of Management Journal*, *38*(3), 635–672. doi:10.2307/256741

Huselid, M. A., Jackson, S. E., & Schuler, R. S. (1997). Technical and strategic human resource management effectiveness as determinants of firm performance. *Academy of Management Journal*, *40*(1), 171–188. doi:10.2307/257025

Hussain, A., & Rickwood, C. (1993). *A Pilot Study into the Contextual Features of ABC Adopting Organisations*. Paper presented at the 16th Annual Congress of the European Accounting Association, Turku-Finland, 28-30 April.

Hwang, Y., & Kim, D. J. (2007). Customer self-service systems: The effects of perceived Web quality with service contents on enjoyment, anxiety, and e-trust. *Decision Support Systems*, *43*, 746–760. doi:10.1016/j.dss.2006.12.008

Hymer, S. H. (1968). The Large Multinational Corporation. In M. Casson (1990) (ed), *Multinational Corporation* (pp. 6-31). Hants: Edward Elgar.

Hymer, S. H. (1976[1960 as a thesis]). *The International Operations of National Firms: A Study of Direct Foreign Investment*. Cambridge, MA: MIT Press.

Hyönä, J., Munoz, D., Heide, W., & Radach, R. (Eds.). (2002) *The brain's eye: Neurobiological and clinical aspects of oculomotor research.* Amsterdam: Elsevier Science

Iida, A., Campbell, N., Iga, S., Higuchi, F., & Yasumura, M. (2000). A Speech Synthesis System for Assisting Communication. *ISCA Workshop on Speech & Emotion, Northern Ireland 2000* (pp.167-172).

Ilic, A., Andersen, T., & Michanelles, F. (2009). Increasing supply-chain visibility with rule-based RFID data analysis. *IEEE Internet Computing*, *13*(1), 31–38. doi:10.1109/MIC.2009.10

Ilic, A., Staake, T., & Fleisch, E. (2009). Using sensor information to reduce the carbon footprint of perishable goods. *IEEE Pervasive Computing / IEEE Computer Society [and] IEEE Communications Society*, *8*(1), 22–29. doi:10.1109/MPRV.2009.20

Indu, B. (2003). *Foreign Resources and Economic Development* (pp. 82-115). New Delhi: Deep and Deep Publications PVT, LTD.

Innes, J., & Mitchell, F. (1990). *Activity Based Costing: A Review with Case Studies*. The Chartered Institute of Management Accountants.

Innes, J., & Mitchell, F. (1991). ABC: A Survey of CIMA members. [UK]. *Management Accounting, 69*(9), 34–35.

Innes, J., & Mitchell, F. (1999). A Survey of Activity-Based Costing in the UKs Largest Companies. *Management Accounting Research, 10*, 137–153. doi:10.1006/mare.1998.0097

Innes, J., & Norris, G. (1997). *The use of Activity-Based information-A Managerial Perspective*. London: Chartered Institute of Mnagement Accountants.

Innes, J., Mitchell, F., & Sinclair, D. (2000). A Tale of Two Surveys, CIMA Research Update (spring), 4.

Instefjord, N. (2005). Risk and hedging: Do credit derivatives increase bank risk? *Journal of Banking & Finance, 29*, 333–345. doi:10.1016/j.jbankfin.2004.05.008

Internetworking (December1998: 1.3), ITG Newsletter. Retrieved March 27, 2009 from http://www.intertg.org/newsletter/dec98/banner blindness.html

IPM. (1993). *Quality: People Matters*. London: IPM.

Iriondo, I., Guaus, R., Rodríguez, A., Lázaro, P., Montoya, N., Blanco, J. M., et al. (2000). Validation of an Acoustical Modelling of Emotional Expression in Spanish using Speech Synthesis Techniques. *ISCA Workshop on Speech & Emotion, Northern Ireland 2000* (pp.161-166).

Iwaarden, J. V., & Wiele, T. V. D. (2003). New research applying servqual to Web sites: an exploratory study. *International Journal of Quality & Reliability Management, 20*, 919–935. doi:10.1108/02656710310493634

Jackson, M., & Staunton, M. (2001). *Advanced modelling in finance using Excel and VBA*. Chichester, West Sussex: John Wiley & Sons.

Jackson, S. E., & Schuler, R. S. (1995). Understanding human resource management in the context of organizations and their environments. In J. T. Spence, J. M. Darley & D. J. Foss (Eds.), *Annual review of psychology, 46* (pp. 237–264). Palo Alto, CA: Annual Reviews, Inc.

Jagadish, S. Kallimani., & Ananthashayana V K. (2006). Text-to-speech engine for Kannada language. In *Proceedings of national conference on convergence of linguistics, e-governance & IT for making kannada – A tech-savvy language* (pp.78-84).

Janiszewski, C., Hayden, N., & Sawyer, A. G. (2003). Meta-analysis of the Spacing Effect in Verbal Learning: Implications for Research on Advertising Repetition and Consumer Memory. *The Journal of Consumer Research, 30*, 138–149. doi:10.1086/374692

Jeans, M., & Morrow, M. (1989). The practicalities of using ABC. *Management Accounting*, UK, November, 42-44.

Jenkinson, H., & Hui, J. (1994). Activity Based Costing. *Accounting Communique, 56*, 1–4.

Jensen, C., Michael, M., & Kevin, J. (1990). CEO incentives – it's not how much you pay, but how. *Harvard Business Review, 86*(3).

Jensen, M. C., & Meckling, H. W. (1976). Theory of firm. Managerial Behaviour, Agency Costs and Ownership Structure. *Journal of Financial Economics, 3*(4), 305–360. doi:10.1016/0304-405X(76)90026-X

Jensen, M., & Murphy, J. (1990). Performance Pay and Top management Incentives. *The Journal of Political Economy*, 98.

Jessup, L. M., Connolly, T., & Tansik, D. A. (2004). *Toward a theory of automated group work: The deindividuating effects of anonymity, 1990.* In D. S. Kerr & U. S. Murthy (Eds.), *Divergent and convergent idea generation in teams: A comparison of Computer-Mediated and Face-to-Face Communication, Group Decision and Negotiation* (Vol. 13, pp. 381-399).

Jiang, D.-N., Zhang, W., Shen, L.-Q., & Cai, L.-H. (2005). Prosody analysis and modeling for emotional speech synthesis. In *Proceedings of ICASSP 2005.*

Jiang, J. J., Klein, G., & Carr, C. L. (2002). Measuring information system service quality: SERVQUAL from the other side. *MIS Quarterly, 26*(2), 145–166. doi:10.2307/4132324

Johnson, H. T., & Kaplan, R. S. (1987*). Relevance Lost: The Rise and fall of Management Accounting.* Boston, MA: Harvard Business School Press.

Johnson, S., Boone, P., Breach, A., & Friedman, E. (2000). Corporate Governance in the Asian Financial Crisis. *Journal of Financial Economics, 58*(1/2), 141–186. doi:10.1016/S0304-405X(00)00069-6

Jones, G. J. (2004). *Organizational Theory, Design, and Change, Text and Cases* (4th ed.). New Jersey: Pearsons Education.

Joo, J., & Lee, S. M. (2009, April). Adoption of the semantic web for overcoming technical limitations of knowledge management systems. *Expert Systems with Applications, 36*(3), 7318–7327. doi:10.1016/j.eswa.2008.09.005

Junglas, I., Abraham, C., & Ives, B. (2009, February). Mobile technology at the frontlines of patient care: Understanding fit and human drives in utilization decisions and performance. *Decision Support Systems, 46*(3), 634–647. doi:10.1016/j.dss.2008.11.012

Juran, J. M., & Gryna, F. M., Jr. (1993). *Quality planning and analysis: From product development through use* (3rd ed.). New York: McGraw-Hill.

Juran, J.M. (1986). The quality trilogy. *Quality Progress*, August, 19-24.

Jyothi, P., & Venkatesh, D. N. (2006). *Human Resource Management.* New Delhi: Oxford University Press.

Kamimura, A., Murata, S., Yoshida, S., Kurakawa, H., Tomita, K., & Kokaji, S. (2001). Self reconfigurable modular robot-experiments on reconfiguration and locomotion's. *International Journal of Intelligent Robots and Systems*, 606-612

Kanellopoulos, C. (1990). *Personnel Management and Personnel Managers in Greece.* Greek Productivity Centre, Athens

Kaplan, R., & Anderson, S. (2007). *Time driven Activity-Based Costing: A simpler and more powerful path to higher profits.* Boston, MA: Harvard Business School Press.

Kaplan, R., & Norton, D. (2006). *Alignment: Using the balanced scorecard to create corporate synergies.* Boston, MA: Harvard Business School Press.

Kara, D. (2000). Pervasive Computing Era - Get ready to integrate intelligent devices into the enterprise. *Softwaremag.commentary*, 18-22.

Karau, S. J., & Kelly, J. R. (1992). The effects of time scarcity and time abundance on group performance quality and interaction process. *Journal of Experimental Social Psychology, 28*(6), 542–571. doi:10.1016/0022-1031(92)90045-L

Kartha, C.P. (2002). ISO 9000:2000 quality management systems standards: TQM focus in the new revision. *The Journal of American Academy of Business, September*, 1-6.

Karthik, V. N. (2006, June). An integrated supplier selection methodology for designing robust supply chains. *IEEE International Conference on Management of Innovation and Technology*, 2, 906-910.

Katz, R. H., Long, D., Satyanarayanan, M., & Tripathi, S. (1996, October). *Workspaces in the Information Age.* In report of the NSF Workshop on Workspaces in the Information Age. Leesberg,VA.

Kaufman, P. J. (2005). *New Trading Systems and Methods* (4th Ed,). New Jersey: John Wiley & Sons.

Kazmi, A., & Ahmad, F. (2001). Differing approaches to strategic human resource management. *Journal of Management Research, 1*(3), 133–140.

Kelly, D., & Amburgey, T. L. (1991). Organizational inertia and momentum. A dynamic model of strategic change. *Academy of Management Journal, 34*, 591–612. doi:10.2307/256407

Kerr, D. S., & Murthy, U. S. (1994). Group decision support systems and cooperative learning in auditing:

An experimental investigation. *Journal of Information Systems*, *8*(2), 85–96.

Kerr, D. S., & Murthy, U. S. (2004). Divergent and convergent idea generation in teams: A comparison of Computer-Mediated and Face-to-Face Communication. *Group Decision and Negotiation*, *13*, 381–399. doi:10.1023/B:GRUP.0000042960.38411.52

Kerr, D. S., & Murthy, U. S. (2009). The effectiveness of Synchronous Computer-Mediated Communication for solving hidden-profile problems: Further empirical evidence. *Information and Management*. Available at http://www.elsevier.com/locate/im

Khanka, S. S. (2003). *Human Resource Management* (1st ed.). New Delhi: S.Chand & Co.

Khilji, S. E., & Wang, X. (2006). Intended and implemented HRM: The missing linchpin in strategic human resource management research. *International Journal of Human Resource Management*, *17*(7), 1171–1189. doi:10.1080/09585190600756384

Kiff, J., & Morrow, R. (2000). *Credit Derivatives*. Bank of Canada Review.

Kiff, J., Michaud, F., & Mitchell, J. (2002). *Instruments ofCredit Risk Transfer: Effects on Financial Contracting and Financial Stability* (Working Paper).

Kinckerbocker, F. T. (1973). *Oligopolistic Reaction and Multinational Enterprise*. Boston, MA: Division of Research, Harvard University Graduate School of Business Administration.

Kindleberger, C. P. (1969). *American Business Abroad: Six Lectures on Direct Investment*. New Haven, CT: Yale University Press.

King, A. M. (1991). The current status of ABC: An interview with Robin Cooper and Robert S. Kaplan. *Management Accounting*, September, 22-26. Malmi, T. (197). Towards explaining ABC failure, Accounting and control in a decentralized organization . *Management Accounting Research*, *8*, 459–480.

Kirkpatrick, C. D., & Dahlquist, J. R. (2007). *Technical Analysis – The Complete Resource for Financial Market Technicians*. NJ: Pearson Education (Prentice Hall).

Kočenda, E. (2002). Ownership structures and corporate performance: Czech firms vaucher sheme. *An Enterprise Odyssey: Economics and Business in the New Millennium 2002, International Conference, University of Zagreb, Graduate School of Economics and Business, Zagreb.*

Kohavi, R., & Provost, F. (2001). Applications of Data Mining to Electronic Commerce. *Journal of Data Mining and Knowledge Discovery*, *5*, 5–10. doi:10.1023/A:1009840925866

Kohler, A., & Erdmann, L. (2004). Expected Environmental Impacts of Pervasive Computing. *Human and Ecological Risk Assessment*, *10*(5), 831–852. doi:10.1080/10807030490513856

Kokko, A., Zejan, M., & Tansini, R. (2001). Trade Regimes and Spillover Effects of FDI: Evidence from Uruguay. *Weltwirtschaftliches Archiv*, *137*(1), 124–149. doi:10.1007/BF02707603

Kondalapati, K., & Prasanna, V. K. (2002). Reconfigurable Computing System. *Journal of Manufacturing Process*, *90*, 1201–1217.

Koren, Y., Pasek, Z., Ulsoy, A., & Benchetrit, U. (1996). Real time Open Control Architectures and System Performance. *Journal of Manufacturing Process*, *1*(45), 377–380.

Korgaonker, M. G. (1992). *Just In Time Manufacturing*. New Delhi: Macmillan India Limited.

Kovač, J. (2000). Dimensions of organizational change. *Management*, *5*(1), 73–81.

Kristensen, K., & Juhl, H. J. (1999). Five years with quality awards in Denmark. *The TQM Magazine*, *11*(2), 80–83. doi:10.1108/09544789910257019

Krugman, E. P. (2008). *Consumer Behavior and Advertising Involvement: Selected Works of Herbert Krugman*. New York: Routledge, Taylor & Francis Group.

Krugman, H. E. (1972). Why three exposures may be enough. *Journal of Advertising Research*, *12*(6), 11–14.

Krumwiede, K. R. (1998). ABC: Why It's Tried and How it Succeeds. *Strategic Finance*, April, 32-38.

Kufidu, S., & Vouzas, F. (1998). Human Resources aspects of quality management: evidence from MNEs operating in Greece. *International Journal of Human Resource Management, 9*(5), 818–830. doi:10.1080/095851998340810

Kung, H.-Y., Hsub, C.-Y., & Lin, M.-H. (2007). Sensor-based Pervasive Healthcare System: Design and implementation. *Journal of High Speed Networks*, 35-49.

Kuo, T., Lu, I., Huang, C., & Wu, G. (2005). Measuring users' perceived portal service quality: an emprical study. *Total Quality Management, 16*(3), 309–320.

Kuo, Y. (2003). A study on service quality of virtual community Website. *Total Quality Management, 14*(4), 461–473.

La Porta, R., Lopez-de-Silanes, F., & Shleifer, A. (1999). Corporate Ownership around the World. *The Journal of Finance, 54*(2), 737–778.

Lacombe, I., & Bescos, P.-L. (2000). ABC-ABM at Hewlett-Packard Europe for customer support. In T. Groot & K. Lukka (Eds.), *Cases in Management Accounting: Current Practices in European Companies*. Prentice Hall.

Lado, A. A., & Wilson, M. C. (1994). Human resource systems and sustained competitive advantage: A competency-based perspective. *Academy of Management Review, 19*(4), 699–727. doi:10.2307/258742

Lado, A. A., Boyd, N. G., & Wright, P. (1992). A competency-based model of sustainable competitive advantage: Toward a conceptual integration. *Journal of Management, 18*(1), 77–91. doi:10.1177/014920639201800106

Lai, Y., & Burchell, B. (2008). Distributed work: communication in an officeless firm. *New Technology, Work and Employment, 23*(1-2), 61–76. doi:10.1111/j.1468-005X.2008.00203.x

Landers, R., & Ulsoy, A. (1998). Supervisory Machining Control: Design approach and experiments. *Journal of Manufacturing Technology, 1*(47), 301–306.

LaPorta, R., Lopez-de-Silanes, F., Schleifer, A., & Vishny, R. (1998). Law and Finance. *The Journal of Political Economy*, 106.

Laszo, G. P. (1996). Quality awards - recognition or model? *The TQM Magazine, 8*(5), 14–18. doi:10.1108/09544789610145999

Laszo, G. P. (2000). ISO 9000-2000 version: implications for applicants and examiners. *The TQM Magazine, 12*(5), 336–339. doi:10.1108/09544780010341941

Lavinson, W. A. (2002). Lean Manufacturing: Made in USA. *Quality Digest, 22*(2), 64.

Lawler, E. E. (1994). Total Quality Management and Employee Involvement: Are they compatible. *The Academy of Management Executive, 8*(1), 68–76.

Lawrence, R., & Almasi, G. (2001). Personalization of Supermarket Product Recommendations. *Journal of Data Mining and Knowledge Discovery, 5*, 11–32. doi:10.1023/A:1009835726774

Lee, A., Kang, H.-Y., Hsu, C.-F., & Hung, H.-C. (2009, May). A green supplier selection model for high-tech industry. *Expert Systems with Applications, 36*(4), 7917–7927. doi:10.1016/j.eswa.2008.11.052

Lee, C. H., & Rhee, B.-D. (2008, September). Optimal guaranteed profit margins for both vendors and retailers in the fashion apparel industry. *Journal of Retailing, 84*(3), 325–333. doi:10.1016/j.jretai.2008.07.002

Lee, D.-E., Lim, T.-K., & Arditi, D. (2009, May). Automated stochastic quality function deployment system for measuring the quality performance of design/build contractors. *Automation in Construction, 18*(3), 348–356. doi:10.1016/j.autcon.2008.10.002

Lee, G., & Lin, H. (2005). Customer perceptions of e-service quality in online shopping. *International Journal of Retail & Distribution Management, 33*(2), 161–176. doi:10.1108/09590550510581485

Lee, J., & Wang, B. (1999). *Computer Aided Maintenance: Methodology and Practices*. Dordrecht: Kluwer Academic Publishers.

Lee, S. Y., & Sundar, S. S. (2002). *Psychological effects of frequency and clutter in web advertising*. Paper presented at the 52nd annual conference of the International Communication Association (ICA), Seoul, South Korea.

Lee, Y., & Kozar, K. (2006). Investigating the effect of Website quality on e-business success: an analytic hierarchy process (AHP) approach. *Decision Support Systems, 42*, 1383–1401. doi:10.1016/j.dss.2005.11.005

Lee, Y.-W., Leung, K.-S., & Satyanarayanan, M. (2002). Operation shipping for mobile file systems. *IEEE Transactions on Computers, 51*(12), 1410–1422. doi:10.1109/TC.2002.1146707

Leech, D. (1987). Ownership Concentration and the Theory of the Firm: a Simple Game Theoretic Approach. *The Journal of Industrial Economics, 35*(3), 225–240. doi:10.2307/2098631

Leech, D., & Leahy, J. (1991). Ownership Structure, Control Type Classifications and the Performance of Large British Companies. *The Economic Journal, 101*, 1418–1437. doi:10.2307/2234893

Legge, K. (1995), *Human Resource Management: Rhetorics and Realities.* Chippenham: Macmillan Business.

Legner, C., & Thiesse, F. (2006). RFID-based maintenance at Frankfurt airport. *IEEE Pervasive Computing / IEEE Computer Society [and] IEEE Communications Society, 5*(1), 34–39. doi:10.1109/MPRV.2006.14

Lengnick-Hall, C. A., & Lengnick-Hall, M. L. (1998). Strategic human resource management: A review of the literature and a proposed typology. *Academy of Management Review, 13*(3), 454–470. doi:10.2307/258092

Levy, G. (2004). *Computational Finance. Numerical Methods for Pricing Financial Instruments*. Jordan Hill, Oxford: Elsevier.

Lewis, P. S., Goodman, S. H., & Fandt, P. M. (1998). *Management, Challenges in the 21st Century.* Ohio: South-Western College Publishing.

Li, H., Liu, Z., & Rebelo, I. (1998). Testing the Neoclassical Theory of Economic Growth: Evidence from Chinese Provinces. *Economics of Planning, 31*(2/3), 117–132. doi:10.1023/A:1003571107706

Li, Y. N., Tan, K. C., & Xie, M. (2002). Measuring Web-based service quality. *Total Quality Management, 13*(5), 685–700. doi:10.1080/0954412022000002072

Li, Y. N., Tan, K. C., & Xie, M. (2003). A service quality framework for Web-based information systems. *Total Quality Management, 15*(3), 164–172.

Liker, J. K. (2004). *The Toyota Way: 14 Management Principals from World's Greatest Manufacturer.* New York: McGraw Hill Publications.

Lim, L. K., & McAleer, M. (2002). Economic Growth and Technological Catching Up by Singapore to the USA. *Mathematics and Computers in Simulation, 59*(1-3), 133–141. doi:10.1016/S0378-4754(01)00401-3

Lipovatz, D. (1998). Leadership performance in Greek enterprises using the EQA framework . *The TQM Magazine, 10*(3), 194–203. doi:10.1108/09544789810214792

Little, D., & McKinna, A. (2005). *A lean manufacturing assessment tool for use in manufacturing.* Paper presented at Seventh SMESME International Conference: Stimulating Manufacturing Excellence in Small & Medium Enterprise, University of Strathclyde, Glasgow.

Liu, C., & Arnett, K. P. (2000). Exploring the factors associated with Web site success in the context of electronic commerce. *Information & Management, 38*(1), 23–33. doi:10.1016/S0378-7206(00)00049-5

Liu, C., Du, T., & Tsai, H. (2009). A study of the service quality of general portals. *Information & Management, 46*, 52–56. doi:10.1016/j.im.2008.11.003

Liu, Z. (2002). Foreign Direct Investment and Technology Spillover: Evidence from China. *Journal of Comparative Economics, 30*(3), 579–602. doi:10.1006/jcec.2002.1789

Lizondo, J. S. (1991). Foreign Direct Investment, in International Monetary Fund, Determinants and Systematic Consequences of International Capita Flows. *IMF Occasional Papers* No. 77 (Washington DC): pp.68-82.

Llosa, S., Chandan, J., & Orsingher, C. (1998). An emprical study of SERVQUAL's dimensionality. *The Service Industries Journal, 18*(2), 16–44. doi:10.1080/02642069800000017

Lo, S.-K. (2008). The Nonverbal Communication Functions of Emoticons in Computer-Mediated communication. *Cyberpsychology & Behavior, 11*(5), 595–597. doi:10.1089/cpb.2007.0132

Lohse, G. L. (1997). Consumer eye movement patterns on yellow pages advertising. *Journal of Advertising, 26*(1), 61–73.

London, J. (2007). *Modeling Derivatives Applications in MATLAB, C_{++}, and Excel*. Upper Saddle River, New Jersey: FT Press.

Longstaff, A., & Scwartz, E. (1995). Valuing Credit Derivatives. *Journal of Fixed Income*, 6–12. doi:10.3905/jfi.1995.408138

Lucas, D., Goodman, L., & Fabozzi, F. (2007). *Collateralized Debt Obligations and Credit Risk Transfer* (Working Paper). Yale ICF.

Lukka, K., & Granlund, M. (1996). Cost Accounting in Finland: Current Practice and Trends of Development. *European Accounting Review, 5*, 1–28. doi:10.1080/09638189600000001

Lukka, K., & Grenlund, M. (1999). *The Asymmetric Communication Structure within the Accounting Academia: The Case of Activity-based Costing Research Genres*. Paper presented at the 22nd Annual Congress of the European Accounting Association, Bordeaux-France, 5-7 May.

Lumsden, G., & Lumsden, D. (2000). *Communicating in Groups and Teams* (3rd ed.). Wadsworth Thomson Learning.

Lundvall, B., Johnson, B., Andersen, E. S., & Dalum, B. (2002). National systems of production innovation and competence building. *Research Policy, 31*, 213–231. doi:10.1016/S0048-7333(01)00137-8

Lyytinen, K., & Yoo, Y. (2002). Issues and challenges in Ubiquitous computing. *Communications of the ACM, 45*(12), 62–65. doi:10.1145/585597.585616

Ma, X. J., Zhang, W., Zhu, W. B., et al. (2004). Probability based Prosody Model for Unit Selection. In *Proc. of ICASSP'04, Montreal, Canada* (pp. 649-652), May 2004.

MacDuffie, J. P. (1995). Human resource bundles and manufacturing performance: Organizational logic and flexible production systems in the world auto industry. *Industrial & Labor Relations Review, 48*(2), 197–221. doi:10.2307/2524483

Madu, C. N., & Madu, A. A. (2002). Dimensions of e-quality. *International Journal of Quality & Reliability Management, 19*(3), 246–258. doi:10.1108/02656710210415668

Magd, H., & Curry, A. (2003). ISO 9000 and TQM: are they complementary or contradictory to each other? *The TQM Magazine, 15*(4), 244–256. doi:10.1108/09544780310486155

Maher, M., Stickeny, C., & Weil, R. (1997). Managerial Accounting: An Introduction to concepts, methods and uses (6th ed.). New York: The Dryden press.

Maier-Speredelozzi, V., & Husoy, J. S. (2002). Selecting manufacturing system configuration based on performance using AHP. *Journal of Robotic and Automation, 1*(1), 23–28.

Makki, S. S., & Somwaru, A. (2004). Impact of Foreign Direct Investment and Trade on Economic Growth: Evidence From Developing Countries. *American Journal of Agricultural Economics*, (August): 795–801. doi:10.1111/j.0002-9092.2004.00627.x

Malaviya, P. (2007). The moderating influence of advertising context on ad repetition effects: The role of amount and type of elaboration. *The Journal of Consumer Research, 34*(1), 32–40. doi:10.1086/513044

Malhotra, Y. (2000). Information management to knowledge management: beyond 'hi-tech hidebound' systems. *Knowledge Management for the Information Professional*. Markintell.com. (n.d.). Market Intelligence & Marketing Glossary. Retrieved November 19, 2008, from http://www.markintell.com/market-intelligence-glossary-a.

Malmi, T. (1999). Activity-based costing diffusion across organizations: an exploratory empirical analysis of Finnish firms. *Accounting, Organizations and Society, 20*, 137–150.

Mandal, S. K. D., & Pal, B. (2002). *Bengali Text to Speech Synthesis System: A Novel Approach for Crossing Literacy Barrier*. CSI-YITP A (E).

Mann, R., & Kehoe, D. (1995). Factors affecting the implementation and success of TQM. *International Journal of Quality & Reliability Management, 12*(1), 11–23. doi:10.1108/02656719510076212

Mark, W. (1999). Turning Pervasive into Mediated Spaces. *IBM Systems Journal, 38*(4), 677–692.

Markowitz, H. M. (1959). *Portfolio Selection: Efficient Diversification of Investments*. John Wiley, New York.

Martell, K., Gupta, A., & Carroll, S. J. (1996). Human resource management practices, business strategies, and firm performance: A test of strategy implementation theory. *Irish Business and Administrative Research, 17*(1), 18–35.

Martin, R. L., & Milway, J. B. (2007). *Enhancing the productivity of Small and Medium Enterprises through Greater Adoption of Information and Communication Technology*. Ottawa, Canada: Information and Communication Technology Council (ICTC).

Martin, S. (1991). Direct Foreign Investment in the United States. *Journal of Economic Behavior & Organization, 16*, 283–293. doi:10.1016/0167-2681(91)90015-P

Martínez-Lorente, A. R., & Martínez-Costa, M. (2004). ISO 9000 and TQM: substitutes or complementaries? An empirical study in industrial companies. *International Journal of Quality & Reliability Management, 2*(3), 260–276. doi:10.1108/02656710410522711

Marumoto, T., & Campbell, N. Control of speaking types for emotion in a speech re-sequencing system [in Japanese]. In *Proc. of the Acoustic Society of Japan, Spring meeting2000* (pp. 213-214).

Marwah, K., & Klein, L. R. (1998). Economic Growth and Productivity Gains from Capital Inflow: Some Evidence for India. *Journal of Quantitative Economics, 14*(1), 81–108.

Marwah, K., & Tavakoli, A. (2004). The Effect of Foreign Capital and Imports on Economic Growth: Further Evidence from Four Asian Countries (1970–1998). *Journal of Asian Economics, 15*(2), 399–413. doi:10.1016/j.asieco.2004.02.008

Mascha, M. F., Bellovary, J., & Matczynski, M. (2004). The Benefits and Risks of Data Communication Methods. *American Accounting Association Conference, Aug. 7* (pp. 23-26).

Mather, G. (2009). *Foundations of Sensation and Perception*. New York: Taylor & Francis Group

Mathis, R. L., & Jackson, J. H. (2003). *Human Resource Management* (10th ed.). Bangalore: South Western.

McAdam, R., & Jackson, N. (2002). A sectoral study of ISO 9000 and TQM transitions: the UK and Irish brewing sector. *Integrated Manufacturing Systems, 13*(4), 255–263. doi:10.1108/09576060210426958

McAdam, R., & O'Neill, E. (1999). Taking a critical perspective to the European Business Excellence Model using a balanced scorecard approach: a case study in the service sector. *Managing Service Quality, 9*, 191–197. doi:10.1108/09604529910267091

McConnell, J., & Servaes, H. (1990). Additional Evidence on Equity Ownership and Corporate Value. *Journal of Financial Economics, 27*, 595–612. doi:10.1016/0304-405X(90)90069-C

McCoy, S., Everard, A., Polak, P., & Galletta, D. F. (2007). The effects of online advertising. *Communications of the ACM, 50*(3), 84–88. doi:10.1145/1226736.1226740

McDonald, I., & Zairi, M., Mohd Ashari Idris. (2002). Sustaining and transferring excellence A framework of best practice of TQM transformation based on winners of Baldrige and European Quality Awards. *Measuring Business Excellence, 6*(3), 20–30. doi:10.1108/13683040210441959

McDougall, S., & Tyrer, V. (2006). Searching for Signs, Symbols and Icons: Effects of Time of Day, Visual Complexity, and Grouping. *Journal of Experimental Psychology. Applied, 12*(2), 118–128. doi:10.1037/1076-898X.12.2.118

McGee, D. (1999). From Craftsmanship to Drafmanship: Naval Architecture and the Three Traditions of Early Modern Design. *Journal of Technology and Culture*, *1*(40), 209–236.

Medland, A. J., & Burnett, P. (1986). *CADCAM in Practice: A Manager's Guide to Understanding and using CADCAM*. London: Kogan Page.

Mehrabi, M. G., Ulsoy, A. G., & Koren, Y. (2000). Reconfigurable manufacturing systems and their enabling technologies. *International Journal of Manufacturing Technology*, *1*(1), 113–130.

Meixell, M. J., & Gargeya, V. B. (2005). Global supply chain design: A literature review and critique. *Transportation Research Part E, Logistics and Transportation Review*, 531–550. doi:10.1016/j.tre.2005.06.003

Melina, D. (2004). A Causal Relationship between Trade, Foreign Direct Investment. *American Journal of Applied Sciences*, *1*(3), 230–235. doi:10.3844/ajassp.2004.230.235

Mendenhall, W., Reinmuth, J. E., & Beaver, R. J. (1993). *Statistics for management and economics* (7th ed.). Belmont, CA: Duxbury.

Michnik, J., & Lo, M.-C. (2009). The assessment of the information quality with the aid of multiple criteria analysis. *European Journal of Operational Research*, *195*(3), 850–856. doi:10.1016/j.ejor.2007.11.017

MicroStrategy. (2008). Application of Industrial-Strength Business Intelligence. Retrieved October 11, 2008 from http://www.microstrategy.com/Solutions/AppsBook.asp

Miles, R. E., & Snow, C. C. (1984). Designing strategic human resource management systems. *Organizational Dynamics*, *28*(3), 62–74.

Milner, D. A., & Vasiliou, V. C. (1986). *Computer Aided Engineering for Manufacturing*. London: Kogan Page.

Minton, B., Stulz, R., & Williamson, R. (2009). How much do Banks Use Credit Derivatives to Reduce Risk. *Journal of Financial Services Research*, *35*, 1–31. doi:10.1007/s10693-008-0046-3

Mishra, S. K., & Puri, V. K. (2007). *Indian Economy* (pp 627-648). Mumbai: Himalayan Publication House.

Mitchell, R., Agle, B., & Wood, D. (1997). Toward a theory of stakeholder identification and salience: defining the principle of who and what really counts. *Academy of Management Review*, 4.

Mitra, A. (2008). *Fundamentals of quality control and improvement* (3rd ed.). Hoboken, NJ: Wiley.

Monden, Y. (2003). Cost reduction systems: Target costing and Kaisen costing. Portland, OR: Productivity Press.

Montgomery, D. B., & Weinberg, C. E. (1981). Toward Strategic Intelligence Systems. *The McKinsey Quarterly*, Spring, 82-102.

Montgomery, D. C. (2004). *Statistical quality control* (5th ed.). Hoboken, NJ: Wiley.

Moody, P. D., & Morley, R. E. (1999). *The Technology Machine: How Manufacturing Will Work in Year 2020*. New York: The Free Press.

Moon, S. K., Moon, Y., Kota, S., & Landers, R. (2001). Screw theory based methodology for design and error compensation of machine tools. *Journal of Computer Aided Manufacturing*, *1*(1), 45–49.

Morck, R., Shleifer, A., & Vishny, W. R. (1988). Management Ownership and Market Valuation: An Empirical Analysis. *Journal of Financial Economics*, *20*, 293–315. doi:10.1016/0304-405X(88)90048-7

Morris, G. L. (1995). *Candlestick Charting Explained*. New York: McGraw-Hill.

Morrison, A. (2005). Credit Derivatives, Disintermediation, and Investment Decisions. *The Journal of Business*, *78*, 621–647. doi:10.1086/427641

Morrison, A. (2005). Credit Derivatives, Disintermediation, and Investment Decisions. *The Journal of Business*, *78*, 621–647. doi:10.1086/427641

Mraovic, B. (2003). Social audit and accountability in IT management. *Managerial Auditing Journal*, *18*(3), 166–179. doi:10.1108/02686900310469943

Mukhopadhya, A., Chakraborty, S., Chowdhury, M., Lahiri, A., Dey, S., & Basu, A. (2005) Shruti: an embedded text to Speech system for Indian Languages. *Software Engineering, Special Issue on Microsoft Research.*

Mulholland, A., & Gibbs, J. (2004). *A Point of View on Business Intelligence and Service Architecture.*

Mullins, L. J. (2005). *Management and Organizational Behaviour* (7th ed.). Harlow: Prentice Hall.

Munzer, S., & Borg, A. (2008). Computer-mediated communication: synchronicity and compensatory effort. *Applied Cognitive Psychology, 22*(5), 663–683. doi:10.1002/acp.1387

Murphy, J. J. (1991). *Intermarket Technical Analysis.* New Jersey: John Wiley & Sons.

Murphy, J. J. (1999). *Technical Analysis of the Financial Markets – A Comprehensive Guide to Trading Methods and Applications.* New York: New York Institute of Finance.

Murray, I. R., & Arnott, J. L. (1993). Towards the simulation of emotion in synthetic speech: A review of the literature on human vocal emotion. *The Journal of the Acoustical Society of America, 93*(2). doi:10.1121/1.405558

Murray, I. R., Edgington, M. D., Campion, D., et al. (2000). Rule-Based Emotion Synthesis Using Concatenated Speech. In *Proc. of ISCA Workshop on Speech and Emotion, Belfast, North Ireland* (pp. 173-177).

Murthy, U. S. & Kerr, D. (2004). Comparing audit team effectiveness via alternative modes of Computer-Mediated Communication. *Auditing: A Journal of Practice & Theory, 23*(1), 141-151.

Nair, M. (2000). Activity-Based Costing: Who is using it and Why? *Management Accounting Quarterly,* Spring, 29-33.

Najmi, M., & Kehoe, D. F. (2000). An integrated framework for post-ISO 9000 quality development . *International Journal of Quality & Reliability Management, 17*(3), 226–258. doi:10.1108/02656710010300117

Narayan, S., Obregon, R., Uppal, C., & Sundar, S. S. (1998). Does web advertising work? Memory for print vs. Online media. *Journalism & Mass Communication Quarterly, 75*(4), 822–835.

Neal, S. (1996). *Credit Derivatives: New Financial Instruments for Controlling Credit Risk,* (Economic Review). Federal Reserve Bank of Kansas City.

Nesnídal, T., & Podhajský, P. (2006). *Průvodce spekulanta* (2nd ed.). Prague: Grada.

Netreturn.com.au. (n.d.). Netsuite Glossary. November 19, 2008, from http://www.netreturn.com.au/about-us/Faq-s/netsuite-glossary.html.

Nguyen, H. V., & Brooks, A. (1997). An Empirical Investigation of Adoption Issues Relating to Activity-Based Costing. *Asian Review of Accounting, 5*(1), 1–18. doi:10.1108/eb060679

Nicholls, B. (1992). ABC in the UK - A Status Report. *Management Accounting* (UK), May, 22-23.

Nicolò, A., & Pelizzon, L. (2008). Credit derivatives, capital requirements and opaque OTC markets. *Journal of Financial Intermediation, 17,* 444–463. doi:10.1016/j.jfi.2008.03.001

Nielsen, J. (2000). *Designing Web Usability.* New Riders Publishing

Nielsen, S., Melander, P., & Jakobsen, M. (2004). *Implementation and Utilization of ABC: A Danish perspective.* Paper presented at the 27th Annual Congress of the European Accounting Association, Prague-Czech Republic, 1-3 April.

Nigrini, M. J., & Johnson, A. J. (2008). Using Key Performance Indicators and Risk Measures in Continuous Monitoring. *Journal of Emerging Technologies in Accounting, 5,* 65–80. doi:10.2308/jeta.2008.5.1.65

Nison, S. (1991). *Japanese Candlestick Charting Techniques.* New York: New York Institute of Finance.

Norden, L., & Wagner, W. (2008). Credit derivatives and loan pricing. *Journal of Banking & Finance, 32,* 2560–2569. doi:10.1016/j.jbankfin.2008.05.006

Norris, G. (1994). User Perception of an Application of Activity-Based Costing. *Advances in Management Accounting, 3*, 139–177.

O'Kane, P., Palmer, M., & Hargie, O. (2007). Workplace Interactions and the Polymorphic Role of e-mail. *Leadership and Organization Development Journal, 28*(4), 308–324. doi:10.1108/01437730710752193

Okunoye, A. (2004, June). *Increase in Computing Capability and its Influence on Service Provision.* Paper presented at the meeting of the Proceedings of the 37th Hawaii International Conference on System Sciences Technologies, Processes, and Institutions, Bled, Slovenia.

Olaniran, B. A., Savage, G. T., & Sorenson, R. L. (1996). Experimental and experiential approaches to teaching Face-to-Face and Computer-Mediated Group Discussion. *Communication Education, 45*(3), 244–260. doi:10.1080/03634529609379053

Oliver, L. (1995). Designing strategic cost systems. New York, John Wiley and Sons.

Orlando, S., Palmerini, P., et al. (2002). Adaptive and Resource-Aware Mining of Frequent Sets. In V. Kumar, S. Tsumoto, P. S. Yu, & N. Zhong (Eds.), *Proceedings of the 2002 IEEE International Conference on Data Mining* (pp. 338-345). IEEE Computer Society.

Owen, R. A. (1825). *A New View of Society.* New York: E.Blis & White.

Pagendarm, M., & Schaumburg, H. (2001). Why are users banner-blind? The impact of navigation style on perception of web banners. *Journal of Digital Information, 2*(1). Retrieved March 30, 2009 from http//jodi.tamu.edu/Articles/v02/01/Pagendarm/

Pajuste, A., & Olsson, M. (2001). *Ownership concentration: the case of the Baltic States.* Conference Corporate Governance and Disclosure in the Accession Process. Portorož: CEPR/University of Ljubljana.

Papalexandris, N. (1993). Human resource management in Greece. In C. Brewster & A. Hegewisch (Eds.), *European Developments in HRM* (pp. 163-180). London: Kogan Page.

Papalexandris, N., & Chalikias, J. (2002). Changes in training, performance management and communication issues among Greek firms in the 1990s: intercountry and intracountry comparisons. *Journal of European Industrial Training, 26*(7), 342–352. doi:10.1108/03090590210432697

Parasuraman, A., & Grewel, D. (2000). The impact of technology on quality-value-loyalty chain: a research agenda. *Journal of the Academy of Marketing Science, 28*(1), 168–174. doi:10.1177/0092070300281015

Parasuraman, A., Zeithaml, A. V., & Berry, L. L. (1985). A conceptual model of service quality and its implications for future research. *Journal of Marketing, 49*, 41–50. doi:10.2307/1251430

Parasuraman, A., Zeithaml, A. V., & Berry, L. L. (1988). SERVQUAL: a multiple-item scale for measuring consumer perception of service quality. *Journal of Retailing, 64*(1), 12–40.

Parasuraman, A., Zeithaml, V. A., & Malhotra, A. (2005). ESQUAL: a multipleitem scale for assessing electronic service quality. *Journal of Service Research, 7*(3), 213–234. doi:10.1177/1094670504271156

Parker, T., & Lettes, T. (1991). Is Accounting Standing in the Way of Flexible Computer-Integrated Manufactuting? *Management Accounting* (USA), February.

Pashler, H. (Ed., 2004). *Attention.* Hove, East Sussex, UK: Psychology Press

Patel, A. (1993). Total Quality Management: Paving the way for future training. *Industrial and Commercial Training, 25*(2), 23–32. doi:10.1108/00197859310036161

Patten, K., & Passerini, K. (2007). *Next Generation Small and Medium Enterprises Mobility Strategy Roadmap.* Paper presented at Sixth Annual ISOnE world Conference, Las Vegas, Nevada.

Pesavento, L., & Jouflas, L. (2007). *Trade What You See – How to Profit From Pattern Recognition.* New Jersey: John Wiley & Sons.

Pfeffer, J. (1994) *Competitive advantage through people.* Boston, MA: Harvard Business School Press.

Pfeffer, J. (1998). *The Human Equation: Building Profits by Putting People First.* Boston: Harvard Business School Press.

Pfeffer, J. (2005). Producing sustainable competitive advantage through the effective management of people. *The Academy of Management Executive, 19*(4), 95–106.

Pfeffer, J., & Salancik, G. (1978). *The external control of organizations: A resource dependence perspective.* New York: Harper & Row.

Pieters, F. G. M., & Wedel, M. (2004). Attention capture and transfer by elements of advertisements. *Journal of Marketing, 68*(2), 36–50. doi:10.1509/jmkg.68.2.36.27794

Pieters, R., & Wedel, M. (2008). Informativeness of Eye Movements for Visual Marketing: Six Cornerstones. In M. Wedel, & R. Pieters (Eds.), *Visual Marketing. From Attention to Action* (pp. 43-73). New York: Lawrence Erlbaum Associates, Taylor & Francis Group.

Pinkerton, A. (2006). Pervasive Computing. *postnote, 263*(May 2006).

Ployhart, R. E. (2006). Staffing in the 21st Century: New Challenges and Strategic Opportunities. *Journal of Management, 32*(6), 868–898. doi:10.1177/0149206306293625

Pomeranz, F. (2004). The US General Accounting office: Is freedom of audit access imperiled? *Managerial Auditing Journal, 19*(3), 394–399. doi:10.1108/02686900410524391

Porras, J. I., & Robertson, P. J. (1992). Organizational development: Theory, practice and research. In M. D. Dunnette & L. M. Hough (Eds.), *Handbook of industrial and organizational psychology* (2nd ed., pp. 719-822). Palo Alto: Consulting Psychologists Press.

Porras, J. I., & Silvers, R. C. (1991). Organization Development and Transformation. *Annual Review of Psychology, 42*, 51–78. doi:10.1146/annurev.ps.42.020191.000411

Pradhan, J. P. (2005). *Outward Foreign Direct Investment from India: Recent Trends and Patterns.* Unpublished doctoral dissertation, ISID, New Delhi.

Price, R. M. (1996). Technology and strategic advantage. *California Management Review, 38*(3), 38–56.

PriceWaterhouseCoopers. (2008). *Internet advertising revenues 2007.* Retrieved May 6, 2008 from http://www.workboxers.com/2008/02/27/record-internet-advertising-revenues-in-2007/

Pring, M. J. (1995). Investment Psychology Explained – Classic Strategies to Beat the Market. New Jersey: John Wiley & Sons.

Pring, M. J. (2002). *Technical Analysis Explained.* New York: McGraw-Hill.

Prowse, S. D. (1992). The Structure of Corporate Ownership in Japan. *The Journal of Finance, 47*, 1121–1140. doi:10.2307/2328979

Puja, G., & Chandan, M. (2005). FDI-Its role in building human capital. *Treasury Management International, 5*, 53.

Radach, R., Lemmer, S., Vorstius, C., Heller, D., & Radach, K. (2003). Eye movements in the processing of print advertisements. In J. Hyönä, R. Radach & H. Deubel (Eds.), *The mind's eye: Cognitive and applied aspects of eye movement research* (pp. 609-632). Amsterdam, The Netherlands: Elsevier.

Raiborn, G., Barfield, J., & Kinney, M. (1996). *Managerial Accounting* (2nd ed.). New York: West Publishing Company.

Raji, R. (1994). Smart Networks for Control. *Journal of Robotic and Automation, 6*(31), 49–55.

Raman, M., Stephenaus, R., Alam, N., & Kuppusamy, M. (2008). Information technology in Malaysia: e-service quality and uptake of internet banking. *Journal of Internet Banking and Commerce, 13*, 2–18.

Ramirez, M. D. (2000). Foreign Direct Investment in Mexico: A Cointegration Analysis. *The Journal of Development Studies, 37*(1), 138–162. doi:10.1080/713600062

Ranjan, J. (2008). Business justification with business intelligence. *VINE: The journal of information and knowledge management systems, 38*(4), 461-475.

Rapoza, J. (2001). Will Face-to-Face meetings be replaced? *Enterprise News & Reviews*.

Ravaja, N., Kallinen, K., Saari, T., & Keltikangas-Järvinen, L. (2004). Suboptimal exposure to facial expressions when viewing video messages from a small screen: Effects on emotion, attention and memory. *Journal of Experimental Psychology. Applied*, *10*(2), 120–131. doi:10.1037/1076-898X.10.2.120

Ray, C. D., Zuo, X., & Michael, J. H.(2006). *The Lean Index- Operational 'Lean' Metrices for Wood Product Industry.* Wood and Fibre Science- Society of Wood and Technology, 38*(2), 238-255.*

Rayner, K., Rotello, C. M., Stewart, A. J., Keir, J., & Duffy, S. A. (2001). Integrating text and pictorial information: Eye movements when looking at print advertisements. *Journal of Experimental Psychology. Applied*, *7*(3), 219–226. doi:10.1037/1076-898X.7.3.219

Resnick, P., & Varian, H. (1997). Recommender Systems. *Communications of the ACM*, *40*(3), 56–58. doi:10.1145/245108.245121

Richardson, R., & Thompson, M. (1999). *The Impact of People Management Practices on Business Performance: A literature review.* London: Institute of Personnel and Development.

Riggs, B. & P. McDougal (1999, October 18). Real-Time Analysis of Buying Habits. *Information week*, pp. 117.

Roe, M. (1992). Some Differences in Corporate Governence in Germany, Japan and America. *The Center for Law and Economic Studies, Columbia University School of Law.*

Rose-Andersen, C., Allen, P. M., Tsinopoulos, C., & McCarthy, I. (2005). Innovation in manufacturing as an evolutionary complex system. *Technovation*, *25*(10), 1093–1105. doi:10.1016/j.technovation.2004.03.006

Rosenthal, R., & Rosnow, R. (2008). *Essentials of Behavioural Research: Methods and Data Analysis.* New York: McGraw-Hill

Roth, W. F. (1989, November). Quality through people: A hit for HR. *Personnel*, 50–52.

Rothenberg, S., & Cost, F. *(2004).* Lean Manufacturing in Small and Medium Size Printers. *New York: A Research Monograph, Rochester Institute of Technology.*

Roussos, G., & Kostakos, V. (2009, February). RFID in pervasive computing: State of-the-art and outlook. *Pervasive and Mobile Computing*, *5*(1), 110–131. doi:10.1016/j.pmcj.2008.11.004

Russell, S., & Norvig, P. (2003). *Artificial Intelligence – A Modern Approach* (2nd Ed.). New Jersey: Pearson Education (Prentice Hall).

Rye, G., Lim, E. A. C., Tan, L. T. L., & Han, Y. J. (2006). Preattentive processing of banner advertisements: The role of modality, location and interference. *Electronic Commerce Research and Applications.* Elsevier

Saad, S. M. (2003). The Reconfiguration Manufacturing Systems. *Journal of Materials Processing Technology*, *34*(1), 3–20.

Saha, D., & Mukherjee, A. (2003). Pervasive computing: A paradigm for the 21st century. *Computer*, (March): 25–31. doi:10.1109/MC.2003.1185214

Saha, D., Mukherjee, A., & Bandyopadhyay, S. (2002). *Networking infrastructure for pervasive computing: Enabling technologies and systems.* Dordrecht, Kluwer Academic.

Sahana, J. (2005, December 17). Liberalization and FDI flows in Service Sector; The Indian Experience. *EPW*, pp.53-88.

Sanchez, D., Tentori, M., & Favela, J. (2008). Activity recognition for the smart hospital. *IEEE Intelligent Systems*, *23*(2), 50–57. doi:10.1109/MIS.2008.18

Sanchez-Franco, M. J., & Roldan, J. L. (2005). Web acceptance and usage model: A comparison between goal-directed and experiential web users. *Internet Research*, *15*(1), 21–48. doi:10.1108/10662240510577059

Santos, J. (2003). E-Service quality: a model of virtual service quality dimensions. *Managing Service Quality*, *13*(3), 233–246. doi:10.1108/09604520310476490

Saritas, T. (2008). The Construction of knowledge Through Social interaction via Computer-Mediated Communication. *Quarterly Review of Distance Education, 9*(1), 35–49.

Sarkar, T., Keri, V., Santosh, M., & Prahallad, K. (2005) *Building Bengali Voice Using Festvox.* ICLSI 2005, IIIT Hyderabad.

Sarkis, J., & Talluri, S. (2004). Evaluating and selecting e-commerce software and communications systems for a supply chain. *European Journal of Operational Research, 159*(2), 318–329. doi:10.1016/j.ejor.2003.08.018

Satyanarayanan, M. (2001). Pervasive computing: Vision and challenges. *IEEE Personal Communications, 8*(4), 10–17. doi:10.1109/98.943998

Satyanarayanan, M. (2002). Wearable computing: Is it just hype? *IEEE Pervasive Computing / IEEE Computer Society [and] IEEE Communications Society, 1*(2), 2–3. doi:10.1109/MPRV.2002.1012328

Saunders, A., & Allen, L. (2002). *Credit Risk measurement. New Approaches to Value at Risk and Other Paradigms* (2nd ed.). John Wiley & Sons. Retrieved February 25, 2009, from http://books.google.com/books

Schafer, J., Konstan, J., et al. (1999). Recommender Systems in e-Commerce. In *Proceedings of the ACM E-Commerce.*

Schick Huber, G., & McCarthy, O. (1997). Distributed Field bus and Control network system. *Journal of Computing & Control Engineering, 1*(8), 22–32.

Schiefer, J., List, B. et al. (2003). *Process Data Store: A Real-Time Data Store for Monitoring Business Processes* (LNCS 2736, pp. 760-770).

Schmidt, R. H. (2003). *Corporate Governance in Germany: An Economic Perspective, Center for Financial Studies.* Frankfurt am Main: Johann Wolfgang Goethe-Universität.

Schmitt, J., Hollick, M., Roos, C., & Steinmetz, R. (2008). Adapting the User Context in Realtime: Tailoring Online Machine Learning Algorithms to Ambient Computing. *Mobile Networks and Applications, 13*(6), 583. doi:10.1007/s11036-008-0095-8

Schonbucher, P. (2000). *Credit Risk Modelling and Credit Derivatives.* Unpublished doctoral dissertation, Bonn University.

Schonbucher, P. (2003). *Credit derivatives pricing models: model, pricing and implementation.* New York: John Wiley & Sons.

Schröder, M. (2001). Emotional Speech Synthesis: A Review. In *Proceedings of EUROSPEECH 2001, Scandinavia* (pp. 561-564).

Schröder, M., Cowie, R., Douglas-Cowie, E., Westedijk, M., & Gielen, S. (2001). Acoustic Correlates of Emotion Dimensions in View of Speech Synthesis. In *Proceedings of EUROSPEECH 2001, Scandinavia* (pp. 87-90).

Schuler, R. S., & Jackson, S. E. (1987). Linking competitive strategies with human resource management practices. *Academy of Management Executive, 1*(3), 207–219.

Schuler, R. S., & MacMillan, I. C. (1984). Gaining competitive advantage through human resource management practices. *Human Resource Management, 23*(3), 241–256. doi:10.1002/hrm.3930230304

Sebastian, M. (1994, May 7). Prospects for FDI and Multinational Activity in the 90's. *EPW,* pp 11-41.

Selim, H. M., Askin, R. G., & Vakharia, A. J. (1998). Cell formation in group Technology Review, Evaluation and Direction for Future Research. *Journal of Computers and Industrial Engineering, 34*(1), 3–20. doi:10.1016/S0360-8352(97)00147-2

Shah, R., & Ward, P. T. (2003). Lean Manufacturing: context, practice bundles and performance. *Journal of Operations Management, 21*(2), 129–149. doi:10.1016/S0272-6963(02)00108-0

Sham, K. B., & Durai, R. (2007). Long run causal nexus between FDI and foreign trade in India. *The ICFAI . Journal of Applied Econometrics, 6*(5), 7.

Shani, A. B., Mitki, Y., Krishnan, R., & Grant, R. (1994). Roadblocks in a quality management implementations: a cross-cultural investigation. *Total Quality Management*, *5*(6), 407–416.

Shein, E. H. (1987). *Process consultation: Vol. 2. Its role in organizational development*. 2nd ed. Reading: Addison-Wesley.

Shen, L., Callaghan, V., & Shen, R. (2008). Affective e-Learning in residential and pervasive computing environments. *Information Systems Frontiers*, *10*(4), 461. doi:10.1007/s10796-008-9104-5

Shenoy, P., Haritsa, J. R., et al. (2000). Turbo-Charging Vertical Mining of Large Databases. In W. Chen, J. F. Naughton & P. A. Bernstein (Eds.), *Proceedings of the 2000 ACM SIGMOD International Conference on Management of Data, 29*(2), 22-33.

Sheskin, D. J. (1997). *Handbook of Parametric and Nonparametric Statistical Procedures*.New York: CRC Press Inc.

Shim, E., & Stagliano, A. (1997). A Survey of US Manufacturers' Implementation of ABC. *Journal of Cost Management* (March/April), 39-41.

Shin, H., Benton, W. C., & Jun, M. (2009, August). Qualifying suppliers' product quality and delivery performance: A sourcing policy decision model. *Computers & Operations Research*, *36*(8), 2462–2471. doi:10.1016/j.cor.2008.10.005

Shleifer, A., & Vishny, R. (1986). Large Shareholders and Corporate Control. *The Journal of Political Economy*, 95.

Shleifer, A., & Vishny, R. W. (1986). Large Shareholders and Corporate Control. *The Journal of Political Economy*, *95*, 461–488. doi:10.1086/261385

Shleifer, A., & Vishny, R. W. (1997). A Survey of Corporate Governance. *The Journal of Finance*, *52*, 737–783. doi:10.2307/2329497

Shyamal, Kr., DasMandal, & Pal, B. (2002). *Bengali text-to-speech synthesis system, a novel approach for crossing literacy barrier*. CSI-YITP.

Siddarth, S. (2002). *Describing the dynamics of attention to TV commercials: A proportional hazards model of the time to zap and ad*. Los Angeles: CA: University of Southern California.

Simons, D. J., & Chabris, C. F. (1999). Gorillas in our midst: sustained inattentional blindness for dynamic events. *Perception*, *28*, 1059–1074. doi:10.1068/p2952

Singh, K. (2003). Strategic HR orientation and firm performance in India. *International Journal of Human Resource Management*, *14*(4), 530–543. doi:10.1080/0958519032000057574

Singh, S., Puradkar, S., & Lee, Y. (2006). Ubiquitous computing: connecting Pervasive computing through Semantic Web. *Information Systems & e-Business Management, 4*(4), 421-439.

Sinkey, J. (2002). *Commercial Bank Financial Management. In the Financial-Services Industry* (6th ed.). Upper Saddle River, New Jersey: Prentice Hall.

Skeel, D., & Partnoy, F. (2006). The Promise and Perils of Credit Derivatives. *University of Cincinnati Law Review*, *75*, 1019–1051.

Smith, A. (1776). *An Enquiry into the Nature and Causes of Wealth of Nations*. Oxford: Clarendon, 1976.

Smith, A. M. (1995). Measuring service quality: is SERVQUAL now redundant? *Journal of Marketing Management*, *11*, 257–276.

Sohal, A., & Marriot, F. (1993). Manufacturing Management in Australia: The Human Resource Management Implications. *International Journal of Manpower*, *14*(9), 13–20. doi:10.1108/01437729310048263

Soltani, E. (2003). Towards a TQM-driven HR performance evaluation: an empirical study, *Employee Relations . International Journal (Toronto, Ont.)*, *25*(4), 347–370.

Soltani, E., Gennard, J., van der Meer, R. B., & Williams, T. (2004). HR performance evaluation in the context of TQM A review of the literature. *International Journal of Quality & Reliability Management*, *21*(4), 377–396. doi:10.1108/02656710410530082

Song, M., Berends, H., Van der Bij, H., & Weggeman, M. (2007). The effect of IT and Co-location on Knowledge Dissemination. *Journal of Product Innovation Management, 24*(1), 52–68. doi:10.1111/j.1540-5885.2006.00232.x

Soroor, J., Tarokh, M. J., & Shemshadi, A. (2009, July). Initiating a state of the art system for real-time supply chain coordination. *European Journal of Operational Research, 196*(2), 635–650. doi:10.1016/j.ejor.2008.03.008

Sparrow, P. R., & Pettigrew, A. M. (1987). Britain's training problems: The search for a strategic human resource management approach. *Human Resource Management, 26*(1), 109–128. doi:10.1002/hrm.3930260107

Spencer, B. (1994). Models of organization and TQM: A comparison and a critical evaluation. *Academy of Management Review, 19*, 446–471. doi:10.2307/258935

Sreenivasulu, A. (2007). Issues in FDI –a bird eye view. *Southern Economist, 8*, 17.

Sridhar Krishna, N., Murthy, H. A., & Gonsalves, T. A. (2002). *Text-To-Speech (TTS) in Indian Languages*. International Conference on Natural Language Processing.

Stallo, J. (2000). *Simulating Emotional Speech for a Talking Head*, Honours Thesis, School of Computing, Curtin University of Technology, Australia, 2000. Retrieved from http://www.computing.edu.au/~stalloj/projects/honours

Stamm, C., & Golhar, D. (1990). *Can small manufacturing firms successfully implement JIT.* Paper presented at annual conference of Decision Science Institute, California.

Stapel, J. (1998). Recall and recognition: A very close relationship. *Journal of Advertising Research, 38*(4), 41–45.

Stavroulakis, D. (1997). Quality circle autonomy: evidence from a Japanese subsidiary and a Western subsidiary . *International Journal of Quality & Reliability Management, 14*(2), 146–159. doi:10.1108/02656719710165419

Stenfors, I., Morén, J., & Balkenius, C. (2003). Behavioural strategies in web interaction: A view from eye-movement research. In J. Hyönä, R. Radach & H. Deubel (Eds.), *The mind's eye: Cognitive and applied aspects of eye movement research* (pp. 633-644). Amsterdam, The Netherlands: Elsevier.

Stevens, J. (1998). *High Performance Working is for Every One*. London: Institute of Personnel and Development.

Stevens, L. (2002). *Essential Technical Analysis – Tools and Techniques to Spot Market Trends*. NJ: John Wiley & Sons.

Stevenson, T. H., & Barnes, F. C. (2001). Fourteen years of ISO 9000: impact, criticisms, costs and benefits. *Business Horizons, 44*(3), 45. doi:10.1016/S0007-6813(01)80034-3

Steventon, D. (1994). Quality Awards - a Means to an End or an End in Themselves? *The TQM Magazine, 6*(5), 7–8. doi:10.1108/09544789410067952

Stiefmeier, T., Roggen, D., Tröster, G., Ogris, G., & Lukowicz, P. (2008, July). Wearable activity tracking in car manufacturing. *IEEE Pervasive Computing / IEEE Computer Society [and] IEEE Communications Society, 7*(2), 42–50. doi:10.1109/MPRV.2008.40

Stiglitz, J. (1999). Quis custodiet ipsos custodes? Corporate governance failures in the transition. *Annual bank conference on development economics-Europe, Paris.*

Stokes, D. (2002). *Small Business Management*. New York: Continuum.

Straus, S. G. (1996). Getting a clue: The effect of communication media and information distribution on participation and performance in computer-mediated and face-to-face groups. *Small Group Research, 27*(1), 115–142. doi:10.1177/1046496496271006

Stulz, R. (2003). *Risk Management and Derivatives*, Cincinnati, Ohio: South-Western Publishing.

Sugimoto, F., Yazu, K., Marakami, M., & Yoneyama, M. (2004). *A method to classify emotional expressions of text and synthesize speech.* First International Symposium on Control, Communications and Signal Processing. (pp.611-614).

Sun, H. (1998). Macroeconomic Impact of Direct Foreign Investment in China: 1979-96. *World Economy, 21*(5), 675–694. doi:10.1111/1467-9701.00156

Sundar, S. S., & Kalyanaraman, S. (2004). Arousal, memory, and impression-formation effects of animation speed in web advertising. *Journal of Advertising, 33*(1), 7–17.

Swaid, S. I., & Wigand, R. T. (2007 June). *Key Dimensions of E-commerce Service Quality and Its Relationships to Satisfaction and Loyalty.* Paper presented at the meeting of 20th Bled eConference eMergence: Merging and Emerging Technologies, Processes, and Institutions, Bled, Slovenia.

Swenson, D. (1995). The Benefits of Activity Based Cost Management to the Manufacturing Industry, *Journal of Management Accounting Research*, Fall, 167-180.

Talluri, S., & Baker, R. C. (2002). A multi-phase mathematical programming approach for effective supply chain design. *European Journal of Operational Research, 141*(3), 544–558. doi:10.1016/S0377-2217(01)00277-6

Tan, K. C., Xie, M., & Li, Y. N. (2003). Service quality framework for measuring Web-based information systems. *The TQM Magazine, 15*(3), 164–172. doi:10.1108/09544780310469262

Tan, W., Li, S., & Yang, F. (2005, September). Zero-time enterprise modeling with component assembly and process model optimization techniques. *The Fifth International Conference on Computer and Information Technology* (pp. 1135-1139).

Tavakoli, M. (1998). *Credit derivatives. A guide to instruments and applications.* New York: John Wiley & Sons.

Tavassoli, N. T. (2008). The Effects of Selection and Ignoring on Liking. In Wedel, M., Pieters R. (Eds.), *Visual Marketing. From Attention to Action* (pp. 9-43). New York: Lawrence Erlbaum Associates, Taylor & Francis Group.

Taylor, F. W. (1911). *Principles of Scientific Management.* New York: Harper & Brothers.

Teas, K. R. (1993). Expectations, performance evaluation and consumers' perceptions of quality. *Journal of Marketing, 57*(4), 18–24. doi:10.2307/1252216

Tentori, M., & Favela, J. (2008). Activity-aware computing for healthcare. *IEEEE Pervasive Computing, 7*(2), 51–57. doi:10.1109/MPRV.2008.24

Tentori, M., Favela, J., & Rodriguez, M. D. (2006). Privacy-aware autonomous agents for pervasive healthcare. *IEEE Intelligent Systems, 21*(6), 55–62. doi:10.1109/MIS.2006.118

Thiesse, F., Fleisch, E., & Dierkes, M. (2006). LotTrack: RFID-based process control in the semiconductor industry. *IEEE Pervasive Computing / IEEE Computer Society [and] IEEE Communications Society, 5*(1), 47–53. doi:10.1109/MPRV.2006.9

Thomason, G. (1991). The management of personnel. *Personnel Review, 20*(2), 3–10. doi:10.1108/00483489110000390

Thyfault, M. E., & Stuart, J. J. (1998). The Service Imperative. *Information Week., 5*(October), 46.

Tilbury, D. M., & Kota, S. (1999). Integrated machine and control design for reconfigurable machine tools. *Journal of Advanced Intelligent Mechatronics, 1*(1), 629–634.

Till Johnson, J. (2008). The many modes of communication. *New World (New Orleans, La.), 25*(34), 24–24.

Tinghino, M. (2008). *Technical Analysis Tools – Creating a Profitable Trading System.* New York: Bloomberg Press.

Tobin, J. (1958). Liquidity Preference as Behavior towards Risk. *The Review of Economic Studies, 25*, 65–86. doi:10.2307/2296205

Torrington, D., & Hall, L. (1995). *Personnel Management: Human Resource Management in Action.* London: Prentice-Hall.

Truss, C., & Gratton, L. (1994). Strategic human resource management: A conceptual approach. *International Journal of Human Resource Management, 5*, 663–686.

Tsiotras, G., & Gotzamani, K. (1996). ISO 9000 as an entry key to TQM: the case Greek industry. *International Journal of Quality & Reliability Management, 13*(4), 64–77. doi:10.1108/02656719610114407

Turnbull, S. (2000). Corporate Governance: Theories, Challenges and Paradigms. *Social Science Research Network Electronic Paper Collection.*

Turner, T., Creighton, S., Nudurupati, S., & Bititci, U. (2004). Implementing a web enabled Performance measurement system. *Measuring Business Excellence, 8*(2), 40–54. doi:10.1108/13683040410539427

Tuttle, T. C. (1992). *Building HRM systems that support Total Quality.* Maryland Centre for Quality and Productivity

Tyson, S. (1985). Is this the very model of a modern personnel manager? *Personnel Management, 26*, 35–39.

Tyson, S. (2006). *Essentials of Human Resource Management* (5th ed.). New Delhi: Elsevier.

Ulrich, D. (1998). A new mandate for human resources. *Harvard Business Review, 76*(1), 124–135.

Ulrich, D., & Brockbank, W. (2005). *The HR Value Proposition.* Boston: Harvard Business School Press.

Uma, K. (2003). *Understanding the Problems of Indian Economy* (4th ed., pp. 332-345). New Delhi: Academic Foundation.

UNCTAD. (2006). *World Investment Report: FDI from Developing and Transition Economies: Implications for Development.* Geneva: UNCTAD.

Underwood, L. (1994). *Intelligent Manufacturing.* Wok Hingham, England: Addison-Wesley Publishing Company.

UzZaman, N., & Khan, M. (2005) A Double Metaphone Encoding for Bangla and its Application in Spelling Checker. In *Proceedings of IEEE International Conference on Natural Language Processing and Knowledge Engineering, IEEE NLP-KE '05* (pp.705-710).

Valacich, J. S., Dennis, A. R., & Connolly, T. (1994). Idea generation in computer-based groups: A new ending to an old story. *Organizational Behavior and Human Decision Processes, 57*(3), 448–467. doi:10.1006/obhd.1994.1024

Valacich, J. S., Paranka, D., George, J. F., & Nunamaker, J. F. Jr. (1993). Communication concurrency and the new media: A new dimension for media richness. *Communication Research, 20*(2), 249–276. doi:10.1177/009365093020002004

van den Hooff, B., & de Ridder, J. A. (2004). Knowledge sharing in context: the influence of organizational commitment, communication climate and CMC use on Knowledge sharing. *Journal of Knowledge Management, 8*(6), 117–130. doi:10.1108/13673270410567675

Van der Wiele, T., Dale, B., & Williams, R. (2000). Business improvement through quality management systems. *Management Decision, 38*(1), 19–23. doi:10.1108/00251740010311799

Van der Wiele, T., Dale, B., & Williams, R. (2000). ISO 9000 series and excellence models: fad to fashion to fit. *Journal of General Management, 25*(3), 50–66.

van Donk, P. D., & Sanders, G. (1993). Organizational culture as a missing link in quality management. *International Journal of Quality & Reliability Management, 10*(5), 5–15.

Van Riel, A. C. R., Liljander, V., & Jurriens, P. (2001). Exploring consumer evaluations of eservices: a portal site. *International Journal of Service Industry Management, 12*(4), 359–377. doi:10.1108/09564230110405280

Vernon, R. (1966). International Investment and International Trade in the Product Cycle. *The Quarterly Journal of Economics, 80*, 190–207. doi:10.2307/1880689

Vernon, R. (1966). International investment and international trade in the product cycle. *The Quarterly Journal of Economics, 80*(May), 190–207. doi:10.2307/1880689

Vernon, R. (1971). *Sovereignty at Bay: The Multinational Spread of U.S. Enterprises.* London: Pelican.

Vidnyánski, Z., & Sohn, W. (2004). Learning to suppress task-irrelevant visual stimuli with attention. *Vision Research, 45*, 677–685. doi:10.1016/j.visres.2004.10.009

Vloeberghs, D., & Bellens, J. (1996). Human resource aspects of ISO 9000 in Belgian organizations. *International Journal of Human Resource Management*, *7*(2), 413–435.

Vos, I., & Klein, P. D. (2002). *The Essential Guide to Mobile Business*. Englewood Cliffs, NJ: Prentice Hall.

Vouzas, F. (2004). HR Utilization and Quality Improvement: the Reality and the Rhetoric – the case of Greek Industry. *The TQM Magazine*, *16*(2), 125–135. doi:10.1108/09544780410523026

Vouzas, F., & Gotazamani, K. (2005). Best Practices of Selected Greek Organizations on Their Road to Business Excellence: The Contribution of the New ISO 9000:2000 Series of Standards. *The TQM Magazine*, *17*(3), 259–266. doi:10.1108/09544780510594225

Wadsworth, H. M., Jr., Stephens, K. S., & Godfrey, A. B. (2001). *Modern methods for quality control and improvement* (2nd ed.). New York: Wiley.

Wagner, N. (Ed.). (2008). *Credit Risk: Models, Derivatives, and Management*. Chapman & Hall/CRC Financial Mathematics Series.

Waite, K. (2006). Task scenario effects on bank Web site expectations. *Internet Research*, *16*(1), 7–22. doi:10.1108/10662240610642514

Walczyk, D., Lakshmikanthan, J., & Kirk, D. (1998). Development of a reconfigurable tools for forming aircraft body panels. *Journal of Manufacturing Systems*, *1*(17), 287–296. doi:10.1016/S0278-6125(98)80076-9

Walley, P., & Kowalski, E. (1992). The role of training in Total Quality Implementation. *Journal of European Industrial Training*, *16*(3), 25–31. doi:10.1108/03090599210008644

Walsh, J. P., & Bayma, T. (1996). Computer networks and scientific work. *Social Studies of Science*, *26*(3), 661–703. doi:10.1177/030631296026003006

Walton, R. E. (1985). From control to commitment in the workplace. *Harvard Business Review*, *63*, 76–84.

Wang, J., Xu, C., Chen, W., & Pan, Y. (2004). *Survey of the Study on Frequent Pattern Mining in Data Streams.* Paper presented at the International Conference on Systems, Man and Cybernetics.

Warshow, H. T. (1924). The Distribution of Corporate Ownership in the U.S. *The Quarterly Journal of Economics*, *39*, 15–38. doi:10.2307/1883952

Webb, H. W., & Webb, L. A. (2004). SiteQual: an integrated measure of Web site quality. *The Journal of Enterprise Information Management*, *17*(6), 430–440. doi:10.1108/17410390410566724

Wedel, M., & Pieters, F. G. M. (2000). Eye fixations on advertisements and memory for brands: A model and findings. *Marketing Science*, *19*(4), 297–312. doi:10.1287/mksc.19.4.297.11794

Wei, L. (2006). Strategic human resource management: Determinants of fit. *Research and Practice in Human Resource Management*, *14*(2), 49–60.

Wei, L., & Lau, C. M. (2005). Market orientation, HRM importance and HRM competency: Determinants of SHRM in Chinese firms. *International Journal of Human Resource Management*, *16*(10), 1901–1918. doi:10.1080/09585190500298586

Weick, K. E. (1999). Organizational change and development. *Annual Review of Psychology*, *50*, 361–386. doi:10.1146/annurev.psych.50.1.361

Weiser, M. (2003). The computer for the 21st century. *Scientific American*, 94–104.

Wei-Tsung, S., Yau-Hwang, K., & Po-Cheng, H. (2008). A QoS-driven approach for service-oriented device anycasting in ubiquitous environments. *Computer Networks*, *52*(18), 3342–3357. doi:10.1016/j.comnet.2008.09.001

White, C. (2008, October). Trends and research directions in supply chain & logistics engineering. *IEEE International Conference on Service Operations and Logistics, and Informatics*, 1, XII.

Wiele, V. T., Van, I. J., Dale, B. G., & Williams, R. (2006). A comparison of five modern improvement approaches. *International Journal of Productivity and Quality Management, 1*(4), 363–378. doi:10.1504/IJPQM.2006.009092

Wilkinson, A., Allen, P., & Snape, E. (1991). TQM and the Management of Labour. *Employee Relations, 13*(1), 24–31. doi:10.1108/01425459110002349

Williams, L. R. (1979). *How I Made One Million Dollars... Last Year... Trading Commodities*. Windsor Brooks.

Williamson, O. (1981). The Economics of Organization: The Transaction Cost Approach . *American Journal of Sociology*, 87.

Williamson, O. (1985). *The Economic Institutions of Capitalism: Firms, Markets, Relational Contracting*. The Free Press.

Williamson, O. (1991). Comparative Economic Organization: The Analysis of Discrete Structural Alternatives. *Administrative Science Quarterly*, 36.

Wilson, J. R., Cruz, M. D., Cobb, S., & Eastgate, R. (1996). *Virtual Reality for Industrial Applications: Opportunities and Limitations*. Nottingham, England: Nottingham University Press.

Wolfinbarger, M., & Gilly, M. C. (2003). eTailQ: Dimensionalizing, measuring and predicting retail quality. *Journal of Retailing, 79*(3), 183–198. doi:10.1016/S0022-4359(03)00034-4

Womack, J. P., & Jones, D. T. (1996). *Learn thinking – Banish waste and create wealth in your corporation*. New York: Simon & Schuster.

Womack, J. P., & Jones, D. T. (2005). *Lean Solutions: How Companies and Customers can Create Value and Wealth Together*. London: Simon and Schuster.

Womack, J. P., Jones, D. T., & Roos, D. (1990). *Machine that changed the world*. New York: Simon and Schuster.

Wood, S. (1996). High commitment management and organisation in the UK. *International Journal of Human Resource Management*, (February): 41–58.

Woodall, W. H., & Adams, B. M. (1993). The statistical design of cusum charts. *Quality Engineering, 5*(4), 559–570. doi:10.1080/08982119308918998

World Bank. (1991). *World Development Report*. Washington, D.C.: World Bank Publications.

Wright, P. M., & McMahan, G. C. (1992). Theoretical perspectives for strategic human resource management. *Journal of Management, 18*(2), 295–320. doi:10.1177/014920639201800205

Wright, P. M., & Snell, S. A. (1998). Toward a unifying framework for exploring fit and flexibility in strategic human resource management. *Academy of Management Review, 23*(4), 756–772. doi:10.2307/259061

Wruck, K. H. (1989). Equity ownership concentration and firm value: Evidence from private equity financings. *Journal of Financial Economics, 23*, 3–28. doi:10.1016/0304-405X(89)90003-2

Würtenberger, F., & Behrendt, S. (2004). Electromagnetic Field Exposure from Pervasive Computing. *Human and Ecological Risk Assessment, 10*(5), 801–815. doi:10.1080/10807030490513829

Wynne, R., & Lancaster, J. (1992). The importance of understanding the concept of TQM and the consequent training needs. *Total Quality Management, 2*(1), 19–29.

Xiao, L. (2009, May). An adaptive security model using agent-oriented MDA. *Information and Software Technology, 51*(5), 933–955. doi:10.1016/j.infsof.2008.05.005

Xie, J., & Wei, J. C. (2009, September). Coordinating advertising and pricing of a manufacturer-retailer channel. *European Journal of Operational Research, 197*(2), 785–791. doi:10.1016/j.ejor.2008.07.014

Xu, Q. (1994). *The making of TQM: History and Margins of the Hi(gh)-story*. Working paper presented at British Academy of Management Annual Conference at Lancaster, September, 1994

Yang, D. C., & Guan, L. (2004). The evolution of IT auditing and internal control standards in financial statement audits: The case of the United States. *Managerial Auditing Journal, 19*(4), 544–555. doi:10.1108/02686900410530547

Yang, Z., & Fang, X. (2004). Online service quality dimensions and their relationships with satisfaction: a content analysis of customer reviews of securities brokerage services. *International Journal of Service Industry Management, 15*(3), 302–326. doi:10.1108/09564230410540953

Yang, Z., & Jun, M. (2002). Consumer perception of eservice quality: from internet purchaser and nonpurchaser perspectives. *The Journal of Business Strategy, 19*(1), 19–41.

Yang, Z., Cai, S., Zhou, S., & Zhou, S. (2005). Development and validation of an instrument to measure user perceived service quality of information presenting Web portals. *Information & Management, 42*(4), 575–589. doi:10.1016/S0378-7206(04)00073-4

Yang, Z., Jun, M., & Peterson, R. T. (2004). Measuring customer perceived online service quality: scale development and managerial implications. *International Journal of Operations & Production Management, 24*(11), 1149–1174. doi:10.1108/01443570410563278

Yaveroglu, I., & Donthu, N. (2008). Advertising repetition and placement issues in on-line environments. *Journal of Advertising, 37*(2), 32–43. doi:10.2753/JOA0091-3367370203

Yearout, S. (1992). The international Quality study reveals which countries lead the race for total quality. *Journal of European Business, 3*(4), 27–30.

Yigit, A. S., & Ulsoy, A. G. (2002). Dynamic stiffness evaluation for reconfigurable machine tools including weakly non-linear joint characteristics. *Journal of Manufacturing Engineering, 1*(6), 87–101.

Ylikoski, T. (2005). A sequence analysis of consumers' online searches. *Internet Research, 15*(2), 181–194. doi:10.1108/10662240510590351

Yoo, B., & Donthu, N. (2001). Developing a scale to measure the perceived quality of an internet shopping site (Sitequal). *Quarterly Journal of Electronic Commerce, 2*(1), 31–46.

Yoo, C. Y., & Kim, K. (2006). Processing of animation in online banner advertising: The roles of cognitive and emotional responses. *Journal of Interactive Marketing, 19*(4), 18–34. doi:10.1002/dir.20047

Young, M. (Ed.). (2003). Reading's ion Management Accounting (4th ed.). Upper Saddle River, NJ: Prentice-Hall.

Yuan, Q., Xiaokang, Z., & Qiong, Z. (2008, August). Key technology and system design in mobile supply chain management. *International Symposium on Electronic Commerce and Security* (pp. 258-262).

Zajonc, R. B. (1968). Attitudinal affects on mere exposure. *Journal of Personality and Social Psychology Monograph, 9*(Supplement), 1–27. doi:10.1037/h0025848

Zarokostas, N., Dimitropoulos, P. D., & Soldatos, J. (2007, September). RFID middleware design for enhancing traceability in the supply chain management. *IEEE 18th International Symposium on Personal Indoor and Mobile Radio Communications* (pp. 1-5).

Zeithaml, V. A. (1987). *Defining and relating prices, perceived quality and perceived value*. Marketing Science Institute, Cambridge, MA.

Zeithaml, V. A., Parasuraman, A., & Malhotra, A. (2002). Service quality delivery through Web sites: a critical review of extant knowledge. *Journal of the Academy of Marketing Science, 30*(4), 362–375. doi:10.1177/009207002236911

Zhang, K. H. (2001). Does Foreign Direct Investment Promote Economic Growth from East Asia and Latin America. *Contemporary Economic Policy, 19*(2), 175–185. doi:10.1111/j.1465-7287.2001.tb00059.x

Zhang, X., & Prybutok, V. (2005). A consumer perspective of e-service quality. *IEEE Transactions on Engineering Management, 32*(4), 461–477. doi:10.1109/TEM.2005.856568

Zhang, X., Song, H., & Huang, G. Q. (2009). Tourism supply chain management: A new research agenda. *Tourism Management, 30*(3), 345–358. doi:10.1016/j.tourman.2008.12.010

Zhang, Z., & Tao, L. (2008, December). Multi-agent based supply chain management with dynamic reconfiguration capability. *IEEE/WIC/ACM International Conference on Web Intelligence and Intelligent Agent Technology*, 2, 92-95.

Zhao, F., He, Z., & Wu, D. (2008, September). Quality assurance of mass customization: A state-of-the-art review. *IEEE Symposium on Advanced Management of Information for Globalized Enterprise* (pp. 1-3).

Zhao, X., Zhao, H., & Hou, J. (2006, June). E-business and information integration in supply chain management. *IEEE International Conference on Service Operations and Logistics, and Informatics*, 919-924.

Zhu, F. X., Wymer, W., & Chen, I. (2002). IT- Based services and service quality in consumer banking. *International Journal of Service Industry Management, 13*(1), 69–90. doi:10.1108/09564230210421164

Zigurs, I., & Buckland, B. K. (1998). A theory of task-technology fit and group support systems effectiveness. *MIS Quarterly, 22*(3), 313–334. doi:10.2307/249668

Zovato, E., Sandri, S., Quazza, S., & Badino, L. (2004). *Prosodic analysis of a multi-style corpus in the perspective of emotional speech synthesis.* INTERSPEECH 2004 – ICSLP. Retrieved October 4-8, 2004. 8th International Conference on Spoken Language Processing, Korea.

About the Contributors

Varuna Godara is the CEO of Sydney College of Management, Australia and SAP Australia certified consultant. Dr. Godara is the chair of International Congress on Pervasive Computing and Management. Previously, she worked as Director of Marketing at SCBIT and was a permanent faculty in Department of Business Systems, School of Management in University of Western Sydney, Australia from July 2003 to September 2008. Dr. Godara received her Bachelor degree in Computer Science in 1997, MBA in 1999, Maters in Computer Applications, and PhD in 2003. Her research interests are mainly in ERP, Pervasive business, E-business management, e-governance and innovation in business. She has authored a book in 2008, has contributed chapters in refereed books, papers in many refereed journals and presented research work in reputed conferences. She has also published popular articles and poems in various books and magazines. She was awarded with Roll of Honour two times by Kurukshetra University, India and was awarded once by National Library of Poetry, US.

* * *

V.K. Ananthashayana received the B.E degree in Electronics & Communication Engineering from University of Mysore in 1979, M.Tech degree from Indian Institute of Technology, New Delhi in 1987, and PhD degree in Computer Science and Engineering from university of Mysore in 2000. Currently, he is working as Professor and Head, Department of Computer Science & Engineering, M.S.Ramaiah Institute of Technology, Bangalore. He was the recipient of **'Best Faculty Award'** from Wipro- Cisco university- from Wipro technologies, Bangalore during 2002. He has served as reviewer for IEEE transaction on Signal Processing, Internal journal of Electronics & Computer Science Elsevier publication book reviewer for IEEE circuits and systems magazine USA. He has chaired many national conferences and was a resource person for VTU short term courses. He has published more than 45 research papers in International & National journals & conferences. His research interests are in DSP, Image Processing, biometrics, Computer Networks & Neural Computing.

P.C. Bahuguna is Assistant Professor at College of Management and Economics Studies, at the University of Petroleum and Energy Studies, Dehradun, U.K., India. He is a post graduate in Business Management. He also holds a Master of Economics. His major teaching interests focus on general areas of human resource management, strategic human resource management, organizational behaviour and economics. He has presented/contributed research papers in national and international journal of repute. His research interests focus on talent management and strategic human resource management. He also has industry experience as administrator, consultant and a trainer to companies that include Consultancy Services, Hospitality and Printing industry.

Muhammet Mustafa Cerit was born on August 25, 1978 in Eskişehir, Turkey. He graduated from Hacettepe University Computer Science Engineering department in July 2000, received his master's degree from Hacettepe University Business Administration department in 2006. He has been working at Banking Regulation and Supervision Agency as a Banking Specialist since April 2001. His special working area is software development, database management and information technology audit.

Rajanish Dass is currently a faculty in the Computer & Information Systems Group at the Indian Institute of Management, Ahmedabad. He is also a member of the Centre for Retailing, Centre for Infrastructure Planning & Regulations and the Centre of e-Governance, at the Indian Institute of Management, Ahmedabad. He was the recipient of the Competitive Scholarship from the Marketing Management Association of the USA in 2003 and was one of the four invited members from India at the Copenhagen Consensus, 2004. He has worked extensively in real-life projects for clients like the County of Durham (North Carolina, USA) and was a member of the core team that had worked on Symantec's Norton Anti-virus.

Lovorka Galetić, PhD, was born in 1953 in Zagreb, Croatia. She graduated and received her PhD at the Faculty of Economics and Business, University of Zagreb. She is a professor and head of the Department of Organization and Management at the Faculty of Economics and Business in Zagreb. She is also the head of the Doctoral Study Programme and one of the heads of the Graduate Study Programme 'Strategy and Corporate Governance' at the same Faculty. She is the president of the programme board for the international conference 'An Enterprise Odyssey'. She is an author of more than a hundred scientific and expert papers in the areas of organization, strategic management and compensation management. Ms. Galetić is also an author and co-author of several books. She is a member of many prominent scientific and expert associations and programme or editorial boards of several scientific magazines.

Debjani Goswami has received her M.Tech degree in computer science and engineering, from MSRIT, Bangalore, India in 2008. Her research areas are: Artificial Intelligence and expert systems, Machine Learning and other related fields. She also has six years of experience in teaching and currently working for IBM, Bangalore, India. During her teaching career, some of the subjects she taught are: mobile communications, System software, data communications, compiler design, artificial intelligence and others.

Rasha Hamdy currently works as an accountant in the Principal Bank of Development and Agricultural Credit (PBDAC)'s Head Quarters in Cairo as an Accountant Since 2000. She is currently in the collection and client follow up department working as a first accountant. The researcher was admitted to the Faculty of Commerce at Cairo University where she finished her Undergraduate Higher Education studies in the Accounting Branch in 2000 and acquired a B.Sc. degree in Accounting with overall average merit of Excellent. Later on, the researcher completed and passed a 2-year preparatory period as part of the requirements of registering for a M.Sc. Degree in Accounting at Cairo University. The researcher was interested in the area of IT use in the companies operating in Egypt including communication techniques used by CPA firms. The researcher collected data from a number of different Auditing Firms working in Cairo - Egypt. Finally, the researcher obtained the M.Sc. degree in Auditing in June, 2008.

Chun Kwong Han is senior professor at the Faculty of Economics and Management of Universiti Putra Malaysia, and honorary professor at the Faculty of Accountancy and Management of Universiti Tunku Abdul Rahman. He obtained the PhD from the University of Cambridge. His research and consultancies are in the areas of management of knowledge-based and innovation-led economy and ICT in Malaysia. Prof Han was president of Association of Asian Pacific Operations Research Societies 2007-2008, founding president of ManagementSciences@Malaysia, and founding president of Customer Relationship Management and Contact Centre Association of Malaysia.

Mohamed Hegazy is a full time professor of Accounting and Auditing in the School of Business at the American University in Cairo. Dr Hegazy is a member of the Egyptian Association of Accountants and Auditors (EAAA) and the American Accounting Association (AAA). He is also an active member of the board of directors of a number of companies in the areas of insurance, medical and mortgage industries. In addition, Dr Hegazy is a member of the Audit Committees of the above companies. Professor Hegazy has got two Bachelor degrees from Cairo University: the first in Accounting and the second in Law. He holds two master degrees: one in Accounting from Birmingham University — U.K and the other in Knowledge Based Systems (i.e. Expert Systems) from Edinburgh University — U.K. Professor Hegazy has a PHD in Accounting and Finance from Birmingham University — U.K. Professor Hegazy has published in international and local journals as well as conferences more than twenty three articles in the areas of Financial Accounting and Auditing, in addition to eight books which are taught at the faculty of Commerce — Cairo University. Professor Hegazy prepared more than eight reports for government projects including valuation engagements, representation in the public companies general meeting and other related assignments. Professor Hegazy has taught undergraduate and postgraduate courses and has supervised students for the grant of the Master Degree in Accounting and seven students completed their Dissertations and were granted the Master degree and at the time being two students are expected to receive their degree by 2009. As a result of his wide knowledge, qualifications and experience, Dr Hegazy is also a specialist in providing Assurance Services as well as Management Advisory Services at a leading multinational CPA firm Horwath International"".He is an active partner in the firm and has over one hundred clients currently receiving assurance and other consultancy services.

Domagoj Hruška, M.Sc, was born in 1980 in Požega, Croatia. He graduated in 2002 from the Graduate School of Economics and Business at the University of Zagreb. He is currently enrolled in the EDAMBA doctoral study programme at the Faculty of Economics and Business Zagreb. He has received the Mijo Mirković award and published 20 scientific and expert papers in the area of business decision making, corporate strategy and corporate governance. He also participated in a series of scientific and expert projects.

Mei-Chih Hu is an Associate Professor at the Institute of Technology Management, National Tsing Hua University, Taiwan. She holds a PhD in Management from Macquarie Graduate School of Management, Australia. Her research interests are in the area of technology management, intellectual property rights management, and national innovation system for the developing or catching-up countries. Her papers have been published in a variety of journals including Research Policy, World Development, Technological Forecasting and Social Change and etc.

Jagadish S Kallimani was born in 1977. He received his BE degree from Basavesvara Engineering College, Bagalkot, Karnataka, in the year 1999. He joined as Lecturer in M S Ramaiah Institute of Technology (MSRIT), in 1999 and perused his post graduation there. Currently, he is working as Assistant Professor in the same institute. His research areas are Artificial Intelligence, Natural Language Processing, Machine Learning, speech synthesis, Algorithms, Data structures and others. He has published many papers in national and international conferences. He has been also considered as subject expert for UNIX and shell programming and Data structures with C for teaching in edusat classes which will be telecasted live to all engineering students under Visveswaraya Technological University (VTU), Karnataka, India.

Jarmo Kuisma, BSc(Econ.), MBA is PhD student at Helsinki School of Economics and managing director of Marketing Network Oy. He is specialized in eye tracking methodology in advertising research and has wide practical experience in marketing and advertising management. Currently he is working in the HSE research project on Consumer Behavior in Information Economy.

Ashok Kumar is working as Director in Y.M.C.A Institute of Engineering, Faridabad, India. He has 30 years of experience. He has 15 years of experience of teaching of P.G classes. His research papers are accepted / published in international journal.

Patiraj Kumari is Associate Professor in the Department of Management Studies, second Campus of Gurukul Kangri University, Hardwar, U.K. India. She earned her Ph.D. from Banaras Hindu University in Psychology. Besides attending National and International Conferences, she has contributed research papers, articles and chapters on various facets of Management and Psychology in leading journals/books of academic repute. She is a member of All India Management Association. Her teaching and research interests are Human resource Management, Strategic Human Resource Management, Organizational Behaviour, Human Resource Development, Industrial Psychology, Industrial Relations, Social Security and Labour Welfare, Corporate Governance and Ethical Aspects of Management, and Value based Management in Indian Ethos.

Chien-Hung Liu is currently working at United Ship Design and Development Center (Taiwan). He was a research assistant for Taiwan's National Telecommunications Project (funded by the National Science Council) when studied at the Graduate Institute of Management of Technology, Feng Chia University, Taiwan.

Vasdev Malhotra He is working as Lecturer in Mechanical Engineering Department in YMCA Institute of Engineering, Faridabad, India. He passed his B.E in Mechanical from NIT, Kurukshetra, India in 2000 with Honours, M.E. in Mechanical Engineering specialization (Production) from Guru Nanak Dev Engg. College Ludhiana , India in 2008 with distinction .His area of expertise is manufacturing technology. His research papers are accepted/published in Journal of Udyog pargati, International conferences, book published.

Amitava Mitra is Associate Dean in the College of Business and Professor in the Department of Management at Auburn University. His research interests are in the areas of quality assurance, quality management, warranty analysis, applied statistics, and multi-criteria modeling. He has published numerous articles, some of which have appeared in journals such as Management Science, Decision Sciences, Journal of the American Statistical Association, International Journal of Production Research, Journal of the Operational Research Society, European Journal of Operational Research, American Journal of Mathematical and Management Sciences, IEEE Transactions on Engineering Management, Computers and Operations Research, IEEE Transactions on Reliability, Quality Engineering, and International Journal of Quality and Reliability Management. He is also the author of the book titled, Fundamentals of Quality Control and Improvement, Third Edition, Wiley, 2008, which is used both nationally and internationally.

Enayatallah Najibzadeh is a PhD scholar in Economics, University of Mysore, India. He has done Masters in Arts (Economics) and Bachelors in Mathematics. He has publications in reputed journals and has presented papers in conferences.

Anssi Öörni, PhD (Econ.) is assistant professor of information systems at Helsinki School of Economics. His current research interests comprise consumer behaviour in electronic markets and diffusion of information systems.

Leyla Ozer is currently an Associate Professor in Department of Business Administration, Faculty of Economic and Administrative Sciences, Hacettepe University, Turkey. She received her BS, MA and PhD degrees from, Faculty of Economic and Administrative Sciences, Hacettepe University. She is specifically interested in Marketing Management, Service Management, and Consumer Behavior. Ozer has more than 10 articles published in national and international journals.

Sujoy Pal is currently working as a Researcher in Indian Institute of Management, Ahmedabad on various research projects related to Information Systems strategy and its applicability to different organizational scenarios. His latest work includes developing IT road map for an organization working in rural parts India. After obtaining a Masters in Computer Application, he has worked as a faculty in AES Institute of Computer Studies, Ahmedabad for more than five years.

Najla Podrug, MSc born in Split, Croatia. Graduated at the Faculty of Economics and Business, University of Zagreb in 2002. and finished the master thesis in 2005. (title „The influence of national culture on decision-making style"). Works as assistant at Department of organization and management (Faculty of Economics and Business, University of Zagreb). Started her PhD studies in 2005. Fields of interest are strategic and international management. Participated in several academic conferences.

Tilak Raj is working as Assistant Professor in Mechanical Engineering Department in YMCA Institute of Engineering, Faridabad, India. He passed his B.Sc (Engg.) in Mechanical from NIT, Kurukshetra, India in 1987 with **Honours,** M.E. in Production Engineering from Delhi College of Engineering, Delhi, India in 2004 with **distinction** and Ph.D. from Jamia Millia Islamia, New Delhi in 2009. He has been engaged with consultancy work also (in improving the manufacturing techniques in industries). His area of expertise is manufacturing technology. His research papers are accepted/published in International Journal of Flexible Manufacturing System, International Journal of Production Research, International Journal of Manufacturing Technology and Management, International Journal of Production Research and International Journal Logistics Systems and Management.

Sayel Ramadhan, Professor of Accounting at Ahlia University, Kingdom of Bahrain, B.Com 1970; CIMA 1981 and Ph.D. 1985, Glasgow University-UK. He joined Yarmouk University-Jordan in 1985 and served as Chairman of Accounting Department in both Yarmouk University and University of Bahrain. He is author of several articles on various accounting issues. He has had approximately (30) articles published in international and regional journals. His teaching and research interests include financial accounting, cost accounting, management accounting, governmental accounting and accounting education. He participated in about (15) international accounting conferences. He has received the award of excellence in research for the year 2001 at the College of Business Administration-University of Bahrain. Professor Ramadhan conducted many workshops and has been consultant to local firms in Jordan and Bahrain. He served as a member of the Council of Audit Profession in Jordan and as a member of the editorial board of the Journal of Performance Evaluation and Management. He was formerly Director of Costing and Pricing at the Ministry of Supply-Jordan and Head of internal audit section at Jordan Petroleum Refinery Company.

Behrooz Shahmoradi is a PhD scholar in Economics, University of Mysore, India. He has done Masters in Arts (Economics) and Bachelors in Economics. He has publications in reputed journals and has presented papers in conferences.

Jaana Simola, MA (Psychology) is PhD student at Helsinki University. She has strong experience in experimental research of visual and auditory perception and methodologies such as eye tracking, EEG and fMRI. Currently she is working in the project Consumer Behavior in Information Economy at the Helsinki School of Economics.

Ülkü Şişik is a full professor at the Department of Business Administration, the Faculty of Economic and Administrative Sciences, Hacettepe University in Ankara – Turkey, teaching Operations Management, Inventory Management, and Total Quality Management courses at graduate level, and Economics courses at undergraduate level since 1981. She received her BA degree at the Faculty of Political Sciences (Ankara University), her MA (1967) and Ph. D. Degrees (1972) at New York University (USA). She has some books, including e-books (for Ahmet Yesevi International University), and articles published in leading Turkish periodicals. She also had been a chair holder of the Department of Business Administration for six years.

Demetres N. Subeniotis is an Associate Professor in the department of Business Administration in the University of Macedonia, Greece. Studies include BA in Economics and Commercial Sciences (Greece), Master of Social Sciences in Economics and Doctorate in Economics from the University of Birmingham, UK. His membership is expanded to many professional bodies, such as the Economic Chamber, and the Institute of Management. He has participated in a number of Committees and Research Programs. He has also published books in the areas of Human Resources and Finance. Current research interests on Business Strategy, Finance, Information Technology and Employees Relationships. Research work has been published on domestic and international journals, participating in a number of conferences and seminars.

Ioannis A. Tampakoudis is a PhD Candidate in the department of Business Administration in the University of Macedonia, Greece. He holds a Bachelor Degree from the Department of Business Administration, University of Macedonia and a Master of Science in Banking and International Finance from City University Business School, London UK. Research areas are Mergers and Acquisitions, Derivatives, Portfolio Management and Financial Econometrics.

Deepak Tripathi is Ph. D and Post Graduate in Industrial Engineering from National Institute of Industrial Engineering (NITIE), Mumbai, India. He is presently working as Director (Quality Assurance) in Indian Railways. He has an industrial experience of 15 years in manufacturing, maintenance and quality management areas. He has been involved in implementation of quality systems and various manufacturing performance improvement projects. He has also contributed to the field of quality management through research papers and conferences at both international and national levels. He has published papers in prestigious journals like International Journal of Quality & Reliability Management (IJQRM), International Journal of Productivity and Performance Management (IJPPM) and Total Quality Management and Business Excellence (TQM &BE). One of his papers in IJQRM has received highly commended paper award for the year 2006.

Petr Tucnik has a Master Degree in Computer Science (2005) from Silesian University in Opava, based on thesis about multicriterial decision-making in multi-agent systems. He is presently doing PhD and teaching in Department of Information Technologies, University of Hradec Kralove. His research interests lies in Artificial Intelligence, Multi-agent Systems, Futures Trading, and Knowledge Management. He has many publications in reputed conferences, books and journals.

Fotis K. Vouzas is an Assistant Professor in the department of Business Administration in the University of Macedonia, Greece. Studies include BA in Management (Greece), MBA in Management and Organizational Behaviour, MSc in Technology Management (USA) and Doctorate from the University of Macedonia (Greece). Senior Researcher at Lancaster University (UK) in part of the European Union Research Project Human Capital and Mobility Programme. Participant in various European Union projects ADAPT, TEMPUS specialised in TQM related issues. Current research interests on TQM-HR relationship, Quality Assurance, Logistics, Business Excellence and Managerial Effectiveness. Referee in major TQM journals and research work published on domestic and international journals and in a collective book.

Ching-Yan Wu is currently a PhD candidate at Macquarie Graduate School of Management, Australia. He has a strong background in engineering and abundant experiences in new product development and project management across the automobile, house hardware and power tool industries. His research interests cover the fields of supply chain management, technology innovation and competition strategies. He is currently engaging in the research of the renewable energies and electric vehicle industry.

Index

D

E

Q

R

S

T

U

V

W

Y

Z